PRAISE FOR *STRATEGIC VALUE CREATION*

A fun book to read! It is informative and personal. There are so many insights covered to agree with. Concepts are distilled into pragmatic tools that make them easily applicable. The passion with which the book is written gives life to its theory and concepts. This embodies one of its ideas, that strategy is about passion which powers people to do great things.
Pär Åström, President Gardena Division and EVP Husqvarna Group

I enjoyed this book from beginning to end. It's a collection of valuable insights. It focuses on how to streamline board documents, so they are not only better but have significantly more impact in helping to steer businesses properly. Ultimately, the board is held accountable, and businesses are run by the board through the board meetings. Board meetings are a function of board documents, and we have all lived with poor board documentation and often equally poor meetings. I believe that Rupert and Jon's understanding and ideas to improve strategy and run businesses, in which board documentation is key, are invaluable. This book is infused with hard-won wisdom. I would recommend this read for anyone remotely interested in organizations, business or strategy at any level.
Ian Kantor, Co-Founder, Investec

An excellent book for anyone implementing or guiding strategic value creation. Rather than focusing on a specific aspect, it captures the full process from its thought-provoking introduction, methodical approach and tools for effective implementation. This isn't just a one-time read; it's a reference to revisit.
Martin Squier, Partner, Horizon Capital LLP

A timely reminder of some of what I had previously learned and a provoking challenge to my current thinking and behaviour, in an environment that only seems to become more challenging. Immensely approachable, *Strategic Value Creation* caused me to reflect, consider and then go back for more.
Jonathan Lawson, CEO, Liberation Group

A book that distils, clarifies and synthesizes the leading theories on strategy in a way that is invaluable to our business. I must have read 40 books on strategy. *Strategic Value Creation* is a masterful synthesis of what, until now, appeared to be competing ideas. An indispensable guide and reference book for every entrepreneur working on an audacious goal.
James Cartwright, Co-Founder, Grocery Post

For those feeling the strain of turning strategy into reality, this is a very good guide. *Strategic Value Creation* empowers you to craft a concrete, actionable plan using core principles of competitive strategy. It's a practical guide that managers from any industry can make a companion in their day-to-day decision-making.
Pinar Ozcan, Professor of Entrepreneurship and Innovation, Saïd Business School, University of Oxford

Laying out a clear, compelling and insightful framework for thinking about strategy and value creation, *Strategic Value Creation* is founded on a rich vein of research, whilst being packed with practical tools and approaches grounded in real-world application. It draws on Rupert and Jon's decades of experience to provide CEOs and boards with a route-map for strategy design and execution, with a particular emphasis on driving value creation in a private equity context.
Paul Reading, Chief Strategy Officer, Mayfair Equity Partners

Every business strategy book I have read has been based on a formula of starting with a long-winded theory and methodology and then repeating that theory and methodology in each chapter of the book. *Strategic Value Creation* provides an incisive and tremendously useful synthesis of multiple theories, illustrated with real human experiences, and then grounds them in applicable actions that can be taken by any business leader the very same day. It's a daily handbook to leading a business.
John Brown, Founder and CEO, Don't Cry Wolf

A must-read for everyone involved in strategy development and value creation. Rupert and Jon build on the existing know-how and skilfully enhance the body of knowledge. The book is a future classic full of wisdom, insights and actionable frameworks from authors who have not only done the research but created value for share- and stakeholders in the real world. In

particular, boards will see value in a well-structured strategy/value creation process, clearly established metrics, systematic tracking and the synthesis thereof in dashboards that provide the insights they need for their decision-making processes.
Sabine Dembkowski, Managing Partner, Better Boards

A must-read for anyone embarking on a private equity journey – whether as a manager, investor, chief of staff or NED. By bridging the theory with the practical, this book will help guide you through the challenges, avoid the pitfalls and make the most of the opportunities. It provides academic frameworks and real-life case studies to bring it all to life. Jon and Rupert have proven themselves perfectly placed to help readers navigate the minefield of high-growth situations.
James Hurrell, Partner, Bridges Fund Management

A comprehensive and important insight into the world of value creation. Both newcomers and experienced practitioners will find this an invaluable, accessible and practical reference tool.
Richard Swann, Partner, Inflexion Private Equity Partners LLP

They have actually cracked the code and developed the ultimate toolkit for CEOs, faced with jumping off the wooden plank and into the world of private equity. With all those board meetings to prepare for, strategy sessions, operational and financial reporting deadlines, sustainability reports (oh and running a business!) etc, I can tell you that you only have time to keep one guidebook to hand. And this book hits you straight out of the blocks – get the right culture, the right talent, all agree on a strategy, get the funding, develop a viable economic model and you're in good shape. As a team, you're all in the Māori waka, paddling in the same direction like your lives depend on it! Please read every page of this book, keep it in your bag at all times and if you're fortunate enough to meet Jon or Rupert, you'll probably be happy to acknowledge that you owe them that pint of ale!
David Fletcher, CEO, GEV Wind Power

Without a clear and well communicated plan and process for sharpening the team's focus on value creation delivering investor returns is impossible – this is a first-class guide to planning, implementing and monitoring value creation from Rupert, Jon and the team at Ārahi.
Sam Smith, Co-Founder and CEO, PEPTalks

This is the first business book I have read that creates a clear thread from strategy through to value creation and then to the contents of the board report. It is the reference book all ambitious board members should have in their briefcase.

Gary Flowers, Serial Chair including, NSW Institute of Sport, Rawson Group, RIGCOM

This practical and thoughtful work provides the structure to drive effective decisions, the tools that enable leadership teams to create a plan that delivers tangible value and shares the wisdom that Rupert and Jon have gathered through their own demonstrable business successes. We have applied value creation planning in our own business. It is a 'north star' for the whole business as well as enabling alignment with shareholders and the rest of the business.

Ruth Poole, CEO, Preventx

Jon and Rupert are the UK experts in the field of creating equity value for PE firms and the management teams they work with. If you want a guide on how to appraise your business and plot the path to maximizing its value, this book is essential reading.

Bernard Dale, Managing Partner, Connection Capital

An excellent fusion of some of the most powerful strategy concepts, brought together and overlaid with Jon and Rupert's broad and deep experience. Its guidance on starting with a focus on purpose and vision, while putting in place the foundations for growth will make this book relevant to businesses at any stage of their growth. With clear language and a practical and repeatable methodology, this book will be a useful tool for anyone interested in designing and implementing strategy.

Guy Bates, Cyfarwyddwr Portffolio/Portfolio Director, Development Bank of Wales

Jon and Rupert's passion for value creation jumps out of every page. They are inherently teachers with high degrees of self-awareness and reflection on just how difficult this is. To you, the reader, they are honest – this is an immensely challenging and never-ending process to build better organizations. With genuine care they have provided a guide of distilled wisdom that should be a constant friend and companion. This is a book that

needs re-reading, book marking, dog-earring and to be actively practiced. In doing so, you'll see the clear intent of the authors to pass on their accumulated wisdom and that of many others to give you the best chance of breakout success.
Tom Redpath, Senior Principal, TowerBrook Capital Partners

A challenging *and* thought provoking read that is a must have for any CEO in the PE environment. It is concise, factual and jargon busting. It contains a step-by-step guide to formulating your strategy, and most importantly offers the tools with clear insight in how to execute and deliver it. As the CEO of Nexgen, with Jon as our Chair, I have lived, tried, tested and executed our value creation plan based on the easily digestible and guiding principles set out in this book.
Mark Little, CEO, Nexgen Group

Strategic Value Creation

Design and execute a strategy for breakthrough returns

Rupert Morrison and Jon Andrew

KoganPage

First published in Great Britain and the United States in 2024 by Kogan Page Limited

2nd Floor, 45 Gee Street
London
EC1V 3RS
United Kingdom

8 W 38th Street, Suite 902
New York, NY 10018
USA

www.koganpage.com

Kogan Page books are printed on paper from sustainable forests.

ISBNs

Hardback 978 1 3986 1595 3
Paperback 978 1 3986 1593 9
Ebook 978 1 3986 1594 6

British Library Cataloguing-in-Publication Data

A CIP record for this book is available from the British Library.

Library of Congress Cataloging-in-Publication Data

A CIP record for this book is available from the Library of Congress.

Typeset by Integra Software Services, Pondicherry
Print production managed by Jellyfish
Printed and bound by Henry Ling Limited at the Dorset Press, Dorchester, DT1 1HD

CONTENTS

ABOUT THE AUTHORS

Rupert Morrison

Rupert Morrison is an entrepreneur, economist and visionary. He is the author of *Data-Driven Organization Design*, now in its second edition, and *Organizational Planning and Analysis*.

Rupert started life on a sheep station in the Wairarapa, New Zealand. After studying economics, he began his career in management consulting with a focus on supply chain, organization design and transformation work. This role saw him work with many of the world's largest companies in multiple sectors (automotive, FMCG, mining, government agencies, pharmaceutical and private equity). This work led him to found software solutions company Concentra Analytics Limited in 2008 and launch Orgvue, the organizational design and planning platform, in 2011. Under his steer, the firm became one of the fastest-growing technology companies in the UK (Sunday Times Tech Track 100, 2011). In 2018 Rupert secured $62 million in funding to further the expansion of the business.

Rupert stepped down as CEO in 2021 to co-found Ārahi with Jon but remains on the board. Rupert spends much of his time evangelizing the data-driven approach to both organizational design and strategy design and execution at conferences and in the media.

Away from professional life, Rupert lives with his wife and three sons in London. He's a rugby fanatic – both as a follower of the All Blacks and as a coach of his local junior team – and an IRONMAN competitor.

Jon Andrew

Jon Andrew is a private equity expert and long-time proponent of value creation planning. He began his career as an accountant and early member of the PwC transaction services team in the late 1990s. He has over 25 years of experience in value creation, working alongside CEOs and management teams. Jon has built more than 100 value creation plans and set up and run two value enhancement teams for two private equity firms. He has extensive experience as a Chair and Non-Executive Director.

Jon provides training on value creation for the British Private Equity & Venture Capital Association (BVCA). He is an Honorary Member and regular contributor to PePTalks, a peer-to-peer learning company dedicated to supporting private equity-backed leaders. In 2021, Jon co-founded Ārahi with Rupert.

Originally from Middlesbrough in the northeast of England, Jon now lives with his wife and cockapoo, Lola, in Surrey. His three daughters have just about flown the nest but are still very much part of the house. Outside work, Jon is a fitness nut, a football and cricket fan and a lover of music – never happier than when he's at a music festival.

FOREWORD

This is unlike most strategy books you will read. Most strategy texts take an academic, theoretical, often rose-tinted perspective. Yes, they might refer to a few real-world case studies, but strategy often looks neat and clear in the rear-view mirror, whereas the process of *actually defining it* is anything but. What sets this book apart is the intense focus on practical application; the pages contained herein are packed full of tools and techniques to help you not only design your strategy but go on and execute it too. This book brings theory to life.

Another differentiator is the sheer quantum of ideas contained within these pages. The research that has gone into this book is broad and wide, drawing inspiration from several domains. As you would expect, there is reference to the heavyweight, classical strategy thinkers, but this is combined with newer, more avant-garde business thinking. It covers topics as diverse as behaviour theory, productivity thinking, software development, microeconomics, game theory and many more. What the book does beautifully is draw this diversity of thought together into a narrative that is both insightful and practical. We call this 'connecting the dots'.

Talking of connections, the one between Rupert and Jon is unique and interesting, for, on the face of it, they could appear to be poles apart. On the one hand, you have Rupert, a swashbuckling entrepreneur who left a successful career as a management consultant to start a business that would disrupt the very industry from which he came. He is a rugby man, a proud follower of the All Blacks, and a father to three boys. On the other, you have Jon, a veteran of the private equity industry, a cerebral thinker and master facilitator whose natural habitat is the boardroom. He is a football man, a proud follower of Middlesbrough, and a father to three girls.

Jon and Rupert united over a shared passion. A passion borne out of frustration with current practice and a deep-seated belief that there must be a better way. Their initial focus was board reporting, both having felt the frustration of ineffective and inefficient board materials and meetings. But this soon broadened to cover strategy design and execution more generally, with the ultimate intent being value creation.

Passion is the appropriate word when it comes to describing Rupert and Jon's approach. Having worked with the two of them for a combined total of 66 years (and counting!), we have observed first hand the energy, enthusiasm and dedication that they each apply to their work. The energy is impressive. The enthusiasm is infectious. And the dedication they exhibit daily is downright inspirational; each is a master of his craft. What's equally important is their insistence that hard work should be enjoyable, with success celebrated in meaningful ways.

This is the book that crystallizes Rupert and Jon's thinking after a combined six decades of advising, leading and growing businesses. We know they've loved writing it. We hope you enjoy reading it. And most importantly, we hope you enjoy *using* it.

Bill Atkinson and James Don-Carolis
London, December 2023

PREFACE

The two of us have dedicated our careers to growing businesses and creating shareholder value – Rupert as a CEO and management consultant and Jon as an expert in value creation and private equity. This book stems from our desire to distil our knowledge into a playbook for a new generation of CEOs, Chairs, board members, leaders, and strategy and value enhancement experts.

Almost everything we have done over our 30-year-long careers has been about devising and executing strategy to create value. I (Rupert) have done this at the coalface – as a CEO working tirelessly to grow two businesses from the ground up. Before founding and becoming CEO of my first company, Concentra Analytics, I worked as a management consultant, helping both young and mature companies across various sectors and industries to overcome their challenges.

I (Jon) have spent over 20 years in the world of private equity. I built my first value creation plan in 2002 at PwC (although, back then, it was framed as 100-day planning rather than value creation planning). As value creation planning gradually began to enter the business lexicon, I was inspired by the new ideas and thinking and became an early proponent of the practice. I moved to LDC, a London-based private equity investment firm, to build their value enhancement team. From there I went to Inflexion, where I developed their portfolio reporting and value creation approaches. I am now a consultant, Chair and Non-Executive Director (NED). Value creation is in my blood. At the time of writing, I have built 104 value creation plans. I have helped hundreds of CEOs and their management teams navigate the various challenges that arise as they move towards their value creation goals.

Our experience combines breadth and depth, as shown in Figure 0.1.1. Jon's experience is wide while Rupert's is deep, having lived through building a company from top to bottom through most stages of growth. We meet at the intersection of the T. We hope that our combined experience will make this book invaluable for all those tasked with creating value, either in their organizations or as a board member or investor.

FIGURE 0.0.1 The breadth and depth of our combined experience

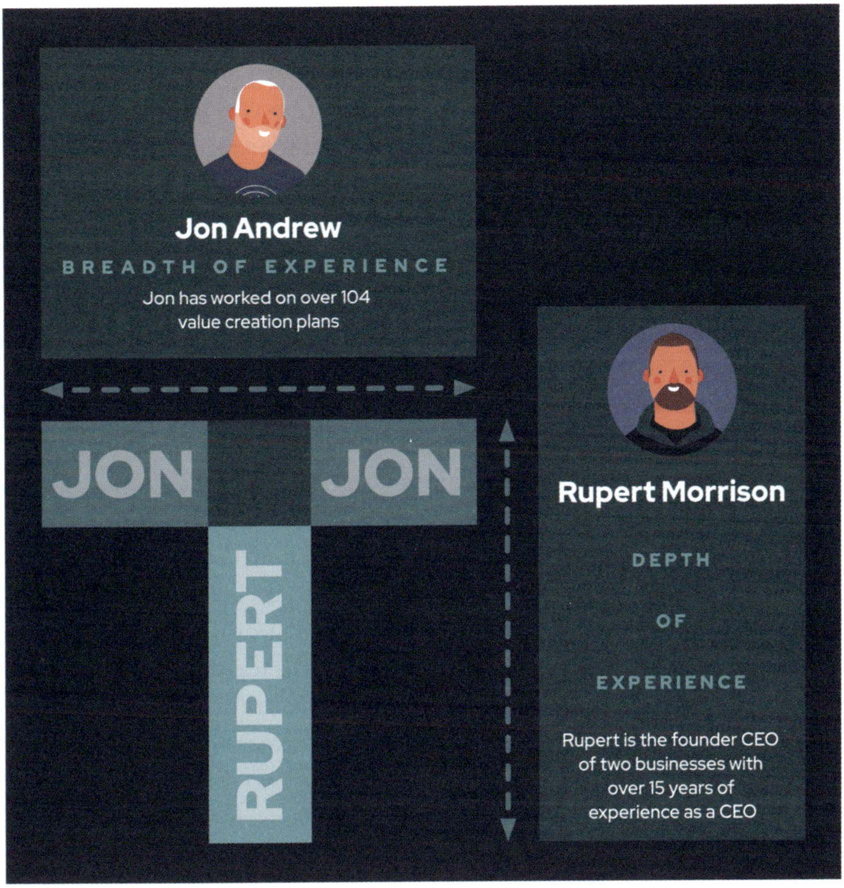

We met in 2015. At the time, Rupert was CEO of Orgvue, an organization design SaaS platform he had launched in 2011 after founding Concentra Analytics in 2008. Jon was at Inflexion working as their Value Enhancement Director. Our friend Bill (remember Bill's name – he has co-written the Foreword and appears later in the book) introduced us. We went for a beer after a successful meeting where Rupert had demoed his product to Jon. While Bill was at the bar, the two of us started talking about board meetings and, in particular, board packs. We had a lot to say. We had similar frustrations about the inefficient and unproductive nature of board meetings. We both felt that while they should be the pinnacle of corporate standards, they were anything but. We scribbled our ideas on napkins and beer mats. Board meetings got us onto board packs – how they were written and produced and how, ultimately, they didn't drive necessary actions. We couldn't stop. It was pouring out of us. Bill checked out, quite understandably. Drinks became dinner. Dinner became a nightcap at a hotel, which was the only place we could find still serving. They let us have one drink but said to have more we'd need to be paying guests. So, Rupert booked himself a room (he didn't end up using it but Jon did, to get changed for a meeting the following morning). We talked until the sun came up, putting the world to rights about strategy and the vital role that board pack reporting plays. It was the beginning of a very productive and deep friendship.

Over time, our conversations led to how we could help solve the pervasive problems we encountered every day. Then one day, I (Jon) was neck-deep trying to get a board pack out when Rupert rang. I had to decline his call and send a quick text to explain that I was up against it. We finally caught up later in the day and we had the same old conversation about what a time-sink board meeting preparation is. Rupert's response? 'Let's stop talking about this. We know there has to be a better way. Let's do something about it. Do we want to fix this problem or not?' I answered with an emphatic 'yes'.

We started to develop ideas for Ārahi, the platform we co-founded in 2021 that helps companies design and execute strategy, so they can refine their value creation plans and track progress against them. Ārahi has led to this book. We aim to unite the knowledge and experiences of a CEO and private equity value enhancement expert to give two different perspectives on how to grow businesses successfully. Between us, we've seen it all – the good, the bad and the ugly. We have extensive insight into how to get it right, as well as how to get it wrong. We hope this book will help others who are treading a similar path.

Throughout the book, we use our personal experiences to enliven the narrative and help make the lessons relatable for our readers. We mainly write using 'we' but we sometimes use 'I'. 'I' might be Rupert or 'I' might be Jon. We usually clarify who is talking as we have done in this Preface. Our more substantial stories are included in boxes throughout. We hope that these boxes will give you extensive insight into our different perspectives – as a CEO and a Chair, NED and private equity expert.

You'll find that we draw extensively on numerous sources throughout the chapters. We have read a huge number of books, some four or five times over, and learned something new every time. We are also podcast devotees. The Bibliography lists our sources of inspiration. We encourage you to read as many of these books as you can. As Marc Andreessen is thought to have said: 'For very little money and a few hours of time, you can learn from someone's accumulated experience...'

While this is Jon's first book, it is Rupert's third. *Data-Driven Organization Design* (now in its second edition) and *Organizational Planning and Analysis* are my (Rupert's) answers to the questions I encountered in organization design. We refer to them throughout this book at pertinent points where we think it might be helpful for you to know more. This might be concerning a certain framework or to help understand organization design principles to aid strategy execution.

We want to be clear that the thinking behind the book's content has been developed as a team. We've had endless debates with our Ārahi colleagues to refine the frameworks and methods described in these pages. These include the aforementioned Bill Atkinson, James Don-Carolis, Chris Wood and Alex Logvynovskiy. We have developed training courses and tested the theories and methods with numerous clients. Together, we have produced content that we can all get behind and truly believe in. We hope you enjoy it, learn from it and, one day, perhaps tell us what you think.

ACKNOWLEDGEMENTS

We have so many to thank for helping this book come to life.

To our early adopter clients and key partners: Martin and Anna at Horizon Capital, Julian and Pascal at Ethos, Jonathan and Simon at Liberation Group with Tim at Caledonia, Ruth at Preventx, Guy and Leanna at Development Bank of Wales, Ross at Red Global, John and Sarah at Don't Cry Wolf and the training team at BVCA. Thanks to PepTalks, particularly Sam, Joe and Lucy for your fantastic partnership and support. Thank you all for placing your continuing faith in us.

To Ārahi's early founding team. To the developers and UX/UI: David Kinross, Alexander Kachkaev, Bartek Laskowski, Sajad Jabari, Kyle Mcintosh and Ramiro Medina. A special mention to our lead developer, Alex Logvynovskiy, our first employee. We are so grateful to you for your leadership, trust and support. Alex, you are our anchor. Ārahi would not be Ārahi without you. You don't realize your impact and just how good you are. And to our Ārahi Method and Content team: Chris Wood, James Don-Carolis and Bill Atkinson. Thank you for everything, including your support with the writing of this book. Your meticulous chapter reviews at various stages of the writing process have been invaluable. A special mention to James Don-Carolis and Bill Atkinson who have been with us for so many years. Thanks, Bill, for introducing us and James for being with Rupert from the earliest days of Concentra Analytics. And thank you, so much, for writing the Foreword to this book.

Thanks to Vanessa Morrison for your unwavering and practical general counsel support in getting Ārahi off the ground.

Thanks to Henry Makansi for being our anchor investor and for your trust, support and friendship.

To Benji Strickland, of Ngāti Kahungunu, Ngāi Tahu, Ngāti Whātua o Kaipara tribes. Thank you for educating us on the Māori worldview foundations of our company name that we have vested. Thanks too for your advice about Māori culture which has helped us to find our pūtake – our why.

To John Brown at Don't Cry Wolf, for helping us to get going, driving our brand and always being so supportive. Thanks too for your advice throughout the writing process, we owe you a great deal.

Thank you to Ian Kantor for being the inspiration behind QFOR-A and for providing us with passages of wisdom for this book. I (Rupert) would like to thank you for your exceptional mentorship. I'd also like to give a special mention to Richard Thompson for his mentorship and for being such an extraordinary role model as a Chair. Richard's words of wisdom appear throughout this book. I would also like to thank the Orgvue board and team.

I (Jon) would like to thank the GEV and NexGen Group boards plus Phil, Michelle and James et al at Bridges Fund Management. I'd also like to thank Darryl Eales, Paddy Sellars and my entire Value Enhancement team at LDC, Grant Berry at North Edge, and Carl Wormald and Richard Swann at Inflexion.

To Isabelle Cheng and Charlie Lynn at Kogan Page. Thanks to you, Isabelle, for spotting the potential in our book project and for your expertise, support and advice in the early days. Charlie, thanks for your invaluable feedback throughout the writing process. It has made the book so much better.

To Annie Cope and David Kinross for your ingenious images. We are indebted to you for your ability to turn our whiteboard sketches into elegant graphics that are easy to understand. Thank you for all your advice. You have been a joy to work with and have made this book ten times better than it otherwise would have been.

Special thanks to Katherine Hartle for your tremendous writing support. You have been our rock; you have held this all together with such patience, charm and a constant smile. Your contribution has been outstanding and we owe you so, so much. We can't thank you enough.

Finally, to our families. First, Rupert's. To my father, who passed over 30 years ago, and my mother. To Henk and Alexandra, my four brothers and dear sister, my special Uncle Erik, Aunt Marg and dear Gran. To my three gorgeous boys, Hugh, Alec and Peter, who bring me so much joy and pride. You are growing way too fast. And to my dear wife, Vanessa. Everyone who knows me well knows that none of this would have been possible without you. To you, Vanessa, the biggest thanks of all.

Second, to Jon's family. To my mother and father and my twin brother David with whom I have shared so much. To the four wonderful ladies in my life. You make the early mornings and late nights all worth it. Thank you for your constant laughter and love. To my girls, Ellie, Issy and Scarlett, thank you for your joie de vivre and for making me so very proud to have you as my daughters. To my wife, Sally, thank you for everything, for your constant and unwavering support and for believing in me. I will be forever indebted to your patience, calmness and kindness.

ABBREVIATIONS

BHAG Big Hairy Audacious Goal

BRAG Blue, Red, Amber, Green

BROP-A Bridge, Risks, Objectives, Plan and Action

COD Capture, Organize, Do

CRASI Capture, Responsible, Approver, Supporting, Informed

5S Action Framework Stop, Shrink, Stay, Stretch, Start

4D Framework Diagnose today, Design tomorrow, Draw the plan and Deliver the plan

KOD Key Organizational Dimension

PACCTACC Purpose, Ambition, Challenge, Critical value factors, Target segments, Arranged capabilities, Competition and Cash generation

PAID Problem-solving, Actioning, Information sharing and Deciding

POAP Plan on a Page

QFOR-A Questions, Facts, Opinions, Recommendations and Actions

SOAP Strategy on a Page

TAF Target, Actual, Forecast

3T Framework Treat, Tolerate and Terminate

WAVS Weighted Average Value Score

PART ONE

Introduction

1.1

Introduction to strategic value creation

The premise of this book is simple: businesses that fail to create value won't survive

We wish we could have read this book 15 years ago. It would have helped us both, immeasurably, in our careers. We have written it to help those like our younger selves, who are tasked with driving **value creation** in business.

Back then, I (Rupert) was a young entrepreneur embarking on my journey as a business founder and CEO. If I could give the 33-year-old me the advice contained in these pages, I would have got to where I wanted to go faster, with less angst along the way. I was a bright (if I say so myself) young guy who was full of energy, ideas and hope. I'd been a management consultant for ten years and I had a dream to start my own business. I left my job and followed my dream. I co-founded Concentra Analytics. Like any founder, the pull to take such a risk was strong. I was driven. I had a vision. I wanted to create something – a product that would provide unique value to the clients I was currently serving. This book would have helped me to articulate that vision and communicate it to the people who mattered. It would have made it easier to take them on the journey with me. We had some great times. But it wasn't without significant stress. I led Concentra Analytics (which became Orgvue) as CEO for 13 years and grew the Annual Recurring Revenue (ARR) by many multiples of the 2018 ARR. (ARR was used as the basis for the valuation of the Series C $62m investment round).[1] I stepped down as CEO in 2021 to co-found Ārahi with Jon but remain on the board. My learnings were immense, which made things a lot easier the second time around. I've distilled them into this book in the hope that they can help others like me.

While Rupert was busy founding Concentra Analytics, I (Jon) was working in the private equity industry, helping CEOs and management teams grow their businesses and create shareholder value. This book is a distillation of my approach to value creation which I have honed over the last 20-plus years in various roles. I have implemented value creation strategies at two leading mid-market UK private equity houses. I have worked with CEOs and management teams to build 104 (and counting) value creation plans. I've been involved in over 50 change programmes. I am now co-founder of Ārahi and take Chair roles for various private equity-backed companies. This book would have helped me better advise the numerous CEOs I have helped in my career and give them more structure to drive effective discussions and decision-making with the board. It would have helped me to adopt a longer-term mentality with them and build value creation plans that were more linked to **strategy** and focused on sales-led profit growth.

The premise of this book is simple: businesses that fail to create value won't survive. Value creation sets a business apart from its competitors, secures repeat purchasing from customers and makes it stand out to investors. This introductory chapter sets out our approach to strategic value creation. We explain why companies struggle with it and introduce our overarching method for applying strategy theory to practice: **The 4D Framework**: Diagnose today, Design tomorrow, Draw the plan and Deliver the plan.

What is strategic value creation?

Successful businesses make value creation their lifeblood. They realize it is the reason they exist and why they leave competitors eating their dust, or even make the competition irrelevant. An in-depth understanding of the value you create, and for whom, versus the value you need to create in the future can make the difference between success and failure for any organization. Value creation work often means capturing and recording data in the form of people's opinions. How do different groups define value? What specific things do they place value on? We call these **value factors**. They are the reason people buy from you, the reason people work for you and the reason people invest in you. Value comes in many shapes and sizes, and it's likely to mean a different thing to each of us than it does to you. But if one thing's for sure, value doesn't just exist. It has to be created.

Value creation happens through the **value chain** – the end-to-end steps of how a company transforms inputs into outputs to deliver value for specific groups of people and, increasingly, into outputs that benefit society or the environment. Your value factors are the outputs from your value chain. The transformation of inputs into outputs is achieved by a unique set of activities you perform as a business. As a general rule, businesses create value for four groups or reasons:

1 Customers (who you may call your clients, patients, members or consumers).
2 People (these could be employees on your payroll or other stakeholders such as contractors or suppliers).
3 Shareholders (or investors).
4 Impact (on the planet, society and people).

It is important to understand how the value you create through the chain is perceived by your customers, people and shareholders, compared to their perception of the value created by your competitors. If customers believe they would get better value elsewhere, they will buy from there. If shareholders believe the same, they will invest in someone else, and if people believe the same, they will up sticks and work for someone else.

Throughout this book, we frame value creation in the context of the **Four Cornerstones of Corporate Health**, as shown in Figure 1.1.1. It's important to track both **leading** and **lagging indicators** to predict future outcomes and make proactive adjustments if necessary. These Cornerstones also form the basis for our recommended board pack dashboard (see Chapter 4.2):

1 Customer health: Simply reporting on customer churn (a lag indicator) is not enough. Proactive analysis of customer health based on what they value and how happy they are with your provision of that value is necessary to keep your current customers and gain new ones. We understand this through value factors, as described in Part 2.
2 People health: Many companies simply report on the rate of employee churn and employee engagement statistics. This is not enough to maintain loyalty over time. Like customers, the people who work for you (employees and contractors) have value factors. The same methods used to analyse customer health can be applied to people.
3 Financial and operational health: Many organizations focus almost exclusively on financial health and providing financial value to shareholders and investors. This is the easiest data to collect because it is transactional and collected by internal systems. But financial performance is often a lag indicator. It considers measures or outcomes that have

already occurred, such as a previous year's profit or revenue. Look instead at lead input measures. For example, don't just look at sales, look instead at sales conversion rates and which lead sources have the greatest impact.

4 Impact health: The world is in deep trouble. We could achieve all of the above and it could all be for nothing. We can believe we have no meaningful impact. We can put our heads in the sand like many governments. We can pretend that the science isn't real. Or we can lead. We can be the example, the role model, the catalyst. We don't go deep on impact health in this book. It could take a whole book to itself. But we have to commit. We have to make it one of the four things we prioritize. If we don't, there's no point in any of the work that we do for the other three Cornerstones.

Improving the odds

Value creation is all about increasing the chance of success. Improving the odds. A value creation plan sets out what the business is trying to achieve over a specific timeframe as well as the measurable initiatives that will help them reach this goal.

FIGURE 1.1.1 The Four Cornerstones of Corporate Health

Numerous research studies paint a gloomy picture of the survival rate of companies, both large and small. We've all heard statistics about the alarming failure rate of start-ups. In the UK, 750,000 companies are incorporated every year, and 600,000 are dissolved.[2] Nine to 18 per cent of companies are dissolved within 24 months of incorporation and 30 to 40 per cent are dissolved within 36 months of incorporation.[3] The reasons for the companies' demise are many and varied. They range from insufficient market need to being beaten by the competition, having a flawed business model, or a poor-quality, badly timed product. These reasons all have something in common: they all relate to strategy.

At the other end of the spectrum, the average lifespan of companies on the S&P 500 index has been tumbling for some time either because of a decline in market value or acquisition. The index, brought to life in the 'Corporate Longevity Report' from Innosight, shows that in the late 1970s, S&P 500 companies had an average tenure of 30 to 35 years. According to Innosight's 2021 report, this is likely to drop to 15 to 20 years by 2030. Added to this, in 2015, there were 12 US-based, venture-backed private companies valued at $5 billion or higher, but in 2020, there were 28.[4] This is all thanks to what the economist Joseph Schumpeter termed 'creative destruction' in 1942. He argued that the constant evolution of industries revolutionizes the economic structure they are part of, continually destroying it and creating a new one.

Businesses that survive do so because they create the necessary conditions. None of these conditions is sufficient by itself. Survival depends on creating the right value for the right customers, as well as the right culture, recruiting the right talent, designing the right strategy, finding funding and a viable economic model. But the right talent without the right culture is not enough. If company politics are horrible and no one is aligned, the most talented people in the world will struggle to effectively execute strategy. Drucker is thought to have said that culture eats strategy for breakfast. But a first-class culture won't get you far if you're not giving your customers what they want, or if you don't have the right economic model or sufficient funding.

JON

Two major sources have inspired my value creation philosophy and approach over the past 13 years. The first was a report published by McKinsey in 2005, 'Why some private equity firms do better than others' by Joachim Heel and Conor Kehoe.[5] Heel and Kehoe cited factors that differentiated investor returns that were better than those of industry peers. They concluded that in nearly two-thirds of the deals sampled, the main source of value creation was not due to market or sector growth or sophisticated financial leveraging. It was not due to **arbitrage** because of a below-market purchase price. It was because of company out-performance, i.e. the ability of management teams and boards to achieve results better than set targets and budgets. In the article, Heel and Kehoe went on to highlight the importance of investors actively involving themselves with the senior team in crafting value creation plans that were ambitious and challenging yet achievable. Following this is the importance of the effective execution of these plans. They noted that the most successful investments came from boards that continually review and revise the plan and use **key performance indicators (KPIs)** to monitor progress. Such an approach was present in 92 per cent of the best-performing deals and only half as often in the worst. It is safe to say that this article had a profound effect on my career. It was published the year I joined LDC, and I subsequently founded the firm's value enhancement team. I have probably been one of Heel and Kehoe's biggest evangelists since.

Five years after joining LDC, I came across my other key source of inspiration. In 2010 Hugh MacArthur, Head of Global Private Equity at Bain & Co., published the first *Global Private Equity Report* which identified trends in the private equity industry based on the company's experience and research undertaken across investors, fund managers and management teams.[6] Released in the first quarter of each year, the report has become my go-to source for insight, themes and trends. Like McKinsey before it, this canon of work has inspired me to continue to shout from the rooftops about the importance of developing a structured approach to value creation.

What do we mean by breakthrough returns?

The subtitle of this book is 'Design and execute a strategy for breakthrough returns'. For us, a company that triples its enterprise value in five years, generating a 25 per cent return, achieves breakthrough returns.

What is this definition based on? We have triangulated three sources and two measures. The two measures are the **Internal Rate of Return (IRR)** and the **Money Multiple** (**MM**). IRR is expressed as a percentage. The IRR is a discount rate that makes the **Net Present Value** (**NPV**) of all cash flow equal to zero. My (Rupert's) first Chair was Richard Thompson. He was one of the founders of the value creation industry in the UK. He had ten funds over roughly 30 years, focused on the tech and healthcare sectors. He was incredibly proud to achieve over 16 per cent IRR in his lifetime. Warren Buffett and Charlie Munger achieved an average of 20 per cent over the 45 years that Munger was involved in Berkshire Hathaway.[7] But these percentages relate to funds, not companies. They are reduced by underperformers. We believe that breakthrough companies have to achieve a higher percentage than this.

The MM is typically referred to as the return. Sometimes referred to as the **Multiple on Invested Capital** (**MOIC**), it measures the value generated by an investment relative to the initial investment. I (Rupert) am proud that in April 2018 I gave my investors over ten times their investment from December 2009. The MM is the realized cash proceeds divided by the total invested proceeds. If you invest at a value of $100 and receive $150 on exit, your MM would be 1.5. We tie the MM back to the IRR by looking at what compounded annual return is needed to hit that number. For instance, an MM of 1.5 requires a 22 per cent IRR if the timeframe is two years. If the timeframe is five years, it requires an 8 per cent IRR.

The third source comes from Jim Collins and the S&P 500. In *Good to Great*, Collins performed research to determine whether it's possible to transform a good company into a great company. He examined the performance of 1,435 good companies over 40 years. He used case studies of 11 companies that went from tracking the market (i.e. good companies) to exceeding it by over three times (i.e. becoming great companies).[8] The great companies ranged from delivering 3.4 greater returns than the stock market (Circuit City) to nearly 19 times (Kimberly-Clark) and sustained their performance for over 15 years. The average rate of return for the S&P 500 for the 20 years from 2002 to 2022 was 8.14 per cent.[9] Times that by three and you get 24.4 per cent. To achieve an MM of three times over a five-year hold period, you need a 25 per cent IRR.

So, 25 per cent is our breakthrough return number. Does achieving less than this mean you are a failure? Your success or failure depends on your ambition. You may just want a lifestyle business, or you might be in the public or third sector. These measures might be irrelevant to you, but much of this book should still be helpful. It depends also on the company's stage and maturity. The bigger and more mature the company, the harder it is to achieve these numbers. And then there's your risk appetite. As we explain in this book, the greater the risk, the greater the potential upside.

Some go further. We can learn a lot from the tech world, where ambitions are off the charts. Investors in Silicon Valley look for technology businesses that can drive ten times growth in a four- to five-year period. Unicorn status can be achieved in the right market with the right business model. The focus is on driving value from building significant multi-year licence revenue. In these cases, where the revenue is extremely predictable and recurring, **Annual Recurring Revenue** growth is used instead of **EBITDA** to value businesses. Many businesses are tech businesses. All businesses can leverage tech for growth. In *Zero to One*, Peter Thiel, PayPal's co-founder, articulates four ways to establish natural monopolies. We love the mindset that this gives. The four Thiel tests are:

1. Proprietary technology – your product needs to be 'ten times better' than the competition.
2. **Network effects** – the more people who use a product or service, the greater the value for all of the users. LinkedIn is a good example, or Uber. The more people who use LinkedIn, the more connections people make and the more useful it becomes. The more people who use Uber, the greater the number of drivers on the road and the quicker the pickup times.
3. Economies of scale – this means that the cost-per-product falls as production and sales increase. Bulk purchasing is a good example of economies of scale.
4. Branding – this is the hardest trait to cultivate but the one that has the potential to contribute the most to the creation of a monopoly. Brands can form part of people's identities. Think Apple and Samsung, or Volvo and BMW. The latter two are priced similarly, but Volvos are all about safety while BMWs are all about driving performance. That's how they differentiate, and that's how they win their customers.[10]

We would add a fifth test to Thiel's four:

5. Size of your **Total Addressable Market** (**TAM**) and **Serviceable Available Market** (**SAM**) – your TAM relates to the number of potential customers in the world. You multiply that number by your average price. 10,000 customers with an average price of $50,000 means your TAM is $0.5 billion. Your SAM is the portion you can service. If you can only reach the UK market and there are 500 customers in the UK, all of whom you can serve, your SAM is $25 million. We explain TAM further in Chapter 3.2.

There are some important considerations for businesses seeking breakthrough returns, which go to the very heart of this book:

- Growing organically is often supplemented by growth through acquisition. There is an inherent value in scale and size. Value creation plans typically include a mergers and acquisitions strategy.
- The business will likely need to transform itself to achieve its ambition. It will look and feel different. It will be more complex and require more people, structure and discipline. Doing this and retaining the culture and the ethos of the business that was started around a kitchen table or in a garage is incredibly difficult.
- Most value creation plans are grounded in one key ingredient: sales growth. While it is essential to improve cost management and increase the productivity or efficiency of your workforce or production line, the greatest source of value creation is sales growth. There is rarely sufficient clarity about where the sales growth will come from, the shape of the sales team and how it's going to win against the competition. Many boards do not clearly understand how their business generates leads and converts them to sales. This hinders their ability to understand their customers and make effective decisions. So, as an investor, CEO or business leader, ask yourself whether the plan for sales growth is sufficiently clear. We discuss this in depth in Chapter 3.2.

In summary, breakthrough returns come from building value creation plans that set targets to at least triple organic profits over five years. This profit growth should be anchored in sales growth. Once the value creation plan has been built, everyone from the board downwards will be focused on knocking the lights out of it. Overperformance is the aim.

Why businesses struggle with value creation

Value creation is close to impossible if you don't have the right strategy and an integrated, action-focused plan to execute it. Designing and executing a winning strategy is hard. The majority of businesses don't get it right if they do it at all. Companies can lose weeks and months embroiled in strategy planning, only to find that it has failed to deliver 12 to 18 months or even five years down the line. The truth is that strategy rarely lives up to the hype.

Designing a winning strategy is difficult, but it often seems simple in hindsight. It boils down to asking the right questions to get to the core of an issue. Shall I do A or B? Edwin Land was an American inventor born in the early 1900s. He had a dream to invent an instant camera that people could put in their pockets. To do this, he needed to find a way to mimic light polarization using synthetic crystals, not natural ones. Once he discovered how to do it, he couldn't believe how blindingly obvious it was (excuse the pun). He was so incredulous that he furiously documented everything to prove that he got there first. No one else managed it, and the Polaroid camera was born.[11]

Hitting on the right strategy is vital, but it's only half of the puzzle. The *execution* of that strategy is equally important. In many organizations, people put their energy into the wrong things. They are stressed and overwhelmed by overflowing inboxes, pointless meetings and to-do lists. Despite all the activity, people's actions can achieve very little of actual value. Actions that arise from one month's meeting aren't completed, or even started, when the next month's meeting comes around. Information is everywhere, but it doesn't translate into actionable insight and purposeful decision-making. Companies, leaders, managers and teams consistently fail to meet goals and objectives. Under these circumstances, it doesn't matter how good your strategy is, it's highly likely to crash and burn.

The 4D Framework: Diagnose today, Design tomorrow, Draw the plan and Deliver the plan

We've drawn on thinking from many inspirational books and podcasts. The bibliography gives a full list. We have found the work of six specific authors (or author partnerships) particularly helpful when building our framework for value creation. They are all complementary. There are no contradictions between them. We've done our best to distil them into one method for designing and executing strategy to create value:

1. Jim Collins
2. Simon Sinek
3. Michael E Porter
4. Richard Rumelt
5. W Chan Kim and Renée Mauborgne
6. A G Lafley and Roger L Martin

These books provide ideas, frameworks and methods which have shaped thinking about strategy formulation and execution. Collins told us about the importance of disciplined people, thought and action and the need to confront your brutal facts as a first step to designing strategy.[12] Sinek told us to start with 'why', not 'what'.[13] Porter gave us three generic strategies for competing and frameworks such as the activity system map.[14,15] Rumelt taught us the importance of identifying the kernel of good strategy and the need to follow a guiding principle.[16] W Chan Kim and Renée Mauborgne introduced us to the idea of creating uncontested market space so that you can swim in a blue ocean rather than vying with the rest of the sharks in red waters.[17] Lafley and Martin gave us a five-step strategy model for making an integrated set of choices to find a unique position within your industry.[18]

Brilliant as these ideas and frameworks are, the practical application is often missing. As practitioners with many years of experience designing and executing strategy, we have often found ourselves frustrated that they don't go far enough. To this end, we have spent many years reading and re-reading these books. We have painstakingly analysed and annotated them. We have spent hours wrestling with the ideas and whiteboarding. We have discussed them over many cups of coffee and glasses of wine with colleagues and friends. We have ruminated about what they mean, what they *really* mean, for those of us tasked with creating value in our organizations. We have drawn out the key learnings and used them to form a method called the '4D Framework': *Diagnose* today, *Design* tomorrow, *Draw* the plan and *Deliver* the plan, as shown in Figure 1.1.2.

1 Diagnose today

Diagnosing today is about doing a holistic assessment of your business in the present day. It's like being a forensic scientist. You ask questions, collect information and analyse. It involves confronting your brutal reality and asking fundamental questions such as:

- Why do we exist?
- What do we sell?
- Who do we sell it to?
- Why do customers buy from us?
- What are we good at?
- What are we *not* good at?
- Do we have the right people in our organization to achieve our goals?

FIGURE 1.1.2 The 4D Framework

This involves understanding what value you currently provide to whom, what your customers value the most and how they score you against the competition. It helps you to see where you win, where you lose, and why you lose in a scenario where you want or need to win. Here, we draw heavily on the work of W Chan Kim and Renée Mauborgne in *Blue Ocean Strategy*. We also draw on the work of Jim Collins. He talks about the need to confront the brutal facts of your business to achieve greatness.

2 Design tomorrow

Designing tomorrow is all about grand designs. You're an architect, designing and drawing your vision of an ambitious and desirable but achievable future state. Then, you distil this vision down to one page so it can be communicated and easily understood. You ask questions like:

- What is the vision?
- What will the business look like?
- What will our main activities be? How will these differ from our competitors' activities?
- What would we be selling, to whom, and where?
- What would our key measures and metrics look like?
- What is our economic model?

It's all about asking what value you can deliver tomorrow that will differentiate you from the competition and make customers choose you. You identify the customer segments you most want to focus on and why, which value factors need to be increased the most and any new ones that need to be added.

This is all about designing your strategy, and to help, we draw on some of the most well-known strategy ideas and frameworks. But a strategy, contrary to a common belief, ain't a plan. Therefore, to improve the odds of success, you Draw the plan.

3 Draw the plan

You can design the best strategy in the world, but there's little point if you don't also have a plan for how to execute it. Here, you're an engineer. You build a step-by-step, logical plan that stipulates tactics and timing. You factor in risk. You think about which actions are needed, by when and who needs to do them. Is it realistic enough? Is it challenging enough to allow you to break through?

The plan is drawn using our framework, **BROP-A**, which stands for Bridge, Risks, Objectives, Plan and Action. The bridge represents a multi-year planning arc and is a useful metaphor for visualizing how you're going to reach your designed future. The bridge could represent sales or enterprise value. Private equity-backed businesses are likely to have a planning arc which spans four to six years.

Objectives and risks are opposite sides of the same coin. While objectives tell us what we need to achieve, risks tell us what we need to avoid. Objectives tell us what we need to start, risks tell us what we need to prevent. A plan that doesn't include your objectives and risks isn't viable.

4 Deliver the plan

You're a delivery driver, on the road. You've planned your route. Now you've got to drive your route and deliver the parcel. This can be an emotional ride. Stuff can go wrong. There will be problems along the way that delay you. You'll constantly have to re-route. Despair will creep in when you realize there's another roadblock up ahead. But there will also be moments of euphoria. You'll see the happy faces when you do deliver the parcel and you'll celebrate those moments.

Objectives and risks in the plan are linked to defined actions. Agreement is needed on who is responsible for delivering those actions and by when. Objectives are cascaded to people in different forums. This is a team sport. Working effectively as a team to deliver the plan is another prerequisite. We meet in a range of forums to review progress, understand and address issues and agree on what needs to be done. The board is an example of a forum that we discuss in detail. It sets the tone for the rest of the organization and should be the exemplar for all meetings.

The arrows in Figure 1.1.2 show the feedback loops. The whole thing requires a lot of back and forth. Diagnosing and designing are done together. One informs the other. There are also constant feedback loops between planning and strategy, and between execution and planning. Is the strategy doable? Is the plan deliverable? What should you prioritize? The figure shows a lighter arrow between execution and strategy. How the strategy is executed informs strategy design, but the feedback loop is not as constant.

Our reasons for writing this book

This is an ambitious book which covers a lot of ground. We've written it for ambitious people. It is the culmination of two lifetimes of hard work. We've seen success and experienced multiple failures, and we're not afraid to share what we've learned. We have distilled our combined 60 years of experience into a practical field guide packed with frameworks, stories and insights. As we say above, so much has been written about strategy, but nowhere near enough has been written about how to make it happen. We joke that this book is a mini-MBA.

Think of a magazine article about your future business. What would the article say? Think about your culture, your team and the customers you serve. Imagine the very best version of yourself. What would it be about you (your product or service, values, team or culture) that your customers love? Why do they keep coming back to you? Why do they ignore competitor offerings? What is it about *what you do* that is so valuable to them? We've written this book to help you achieve the vision in your head. We want to help create greatness.

You are unlikely to be able to read this book in one sitting. It contains around 120,000 words and includes a lot of detail. We want it to be your companion, constantly by your side, so you can dip into it time and again. You'll find our personal stories peppered throughout. We want to show what it's like behind the curtain of a software CEO, Chair and private equity investor. This is a human story. We have created a special bond by writing it together. We have a love and respect for each other, but we don't always agree. We occasionally fight like brothers. But the best insight comes from wrestling with ideas and emotionally charged moments of conflict.

As we write this sentence, having a cleansing ale at the Eel's Foot pub in Suffolk, England, we are nearing the end of our final three-day writing retreat. The publishing deadline is just a fortnight away. We ask ourselves, what is our ultimate goal in writing this book? It is to meet you one day and for you to tell us, with a tear in your eye, and holding your well-thumbed copy, that our book was a meaningful part of your journey to greatness. Hearing that would make it all worthwhile: the pain, endless iterations and 4 am wakeups. If this book makes a difference to just one person, we will have succeeded.

How this book will help you

We have written this book primarily for ambitious CEOs and anyone who supports them with driving growth and trying to create an over three times return within five years (or 25 per cent IRR). You might be an investor, founder, Chair, Non-Executive Director or leader. We see the book being particularly applicable for executives in the Chief of Staff role. We hope this might be the Chief of Staff's bible. It sets out how to design your strategy and then build and execute the value creation plan to achieve those ambitions.

All CEOs need good mentors and we hope that this book might go some way to fulfilling this role. It will help you to answer the questions 'What is my job here?', 'What should I be doing?', 'What should I be thinking about?' and break down your role into more manageable chunks.

We have written it with private equity-backed businesses in mind, but the frameworks and thinking can be applied no matter what your business. We often reference our private equity experience. If you're new to this world, don't be put off by it. Private equity has its detractors and critics, but it does give many entrepreneurs and leaders access to risk capital they would otherwise not get. It has helped businesses bring discipline and rigour to their approach to growth. This book is a summary of all those approaches. The term private equity has many facets – from earlier-stage venture funding to growth capital through to full-scale management buy-out. With the rise of the private debt fund, access to debt packages is now much greater than a corporate bank. In essence, the concepts and frameworks in this book appeal equally well to any type of private capital-funded business, however financially structured.

Our goal is to help you achieve greatness. For you, greatness might mean creating **breakthrough returns**. But it could also mean setting up a successful not-for-profit or charity. It might mean creating a healthy lifestyle business. At the end of the day, every business has goals and every business needs a strategy. It's always helpful to articulate what you want to achieve, by when, and be able to communicate that clearly and succinctly to the people who need to know.

Structure of the book

The remainder of Part 1 consists of two chapters. The first focuses on the common challenges you are likely to face. The second outlines the core foundations of this book: our five truths, five frameworks and five communication pillars.

Part 2 is concerned with the first two of the 'Four Ds'. It explains the importance of diagnosing your current situation before designing where you want to get to in the future. This is the part of the book that focuses on strategy. We draw heavily on the wisdom of *Blue Ocean Strategy* and introduce value factors, the **value landscape** and the importance of identifying your niche to target the right customers.

Part 3 looks at how you're going to get to your designed future. This is the third 'D' – Draw the plan. This is the part that relates to your value creation plan. There are four chapters. The first is on how to bridge the gap between where you are today and where you want to be tomorrow, using **landmarks** and **stepping stones** to break down the task. The second is on risk management (which could be framed as risk-taking). The third is on objectives management and the fourth describes how to create an integrated plan that pulls everything together.

Part 4 looks at delivering the plan (the fourth 'D'). First, we look at how to run effective board meetings, including how to put together a board pack which drives the right actions. The board meeting is the pinnacle of all meetings and it's important to get this right first. The next chapter looks at the role of forums and other meetings aside from the board. It also considers the importance of healthy and productive team dynamics. The following chapter focuses on action management. We look at the different types of actions and different approaches to managing them. The final chapter in the book gives our concluding thoughts. It looks at the difficulties you might encounter as you grow and how to navigate predictable crises as you reach different stages.

Throughout, we give examples and case studies from a range of different businesses to help connect the theory to real-world applications. You'll notice that certain words are emboldened within the text, as they are in this chapter. This denotes a glossary term. The glossary can be found at the back of the book.

Final thoughts

As Peter Drucker is thought to have said, 'Good strategy is strategy that is executed'. But strategy can't be executed by itself. Too often, executives devise promising and exciting strategy for their business, but the thinking stops there. No one considers how that strategy is going to be translated into actions, let alone how to measure progress against strategic goals. Employees' daily actions are rarely tied to an overall business plan showing how the organization's strategy is going to be achieved.

The practical frameworks and methods proposed in this book focus on the design of good strategy and its execution in equal measure. This reflects a consistent theme, that of integration and evolution. Strategy is integrated with its execution, the board is integrated with action, theory is integrated with practice, ideas evolve into results. As this chapter has shown, this book is predicated on three foundations.

1 Theory

The theory we draw on hails from some of the most influential strategy and action management books ever written. We hope to bring a new understanding to theory which you are likely to already know by connecting the dots and pulling it into one overarching method.

2 Practice

This book is predicated on our practice as well as the practice of the whole Ārahi team and our clients. We have coached, mentored and, in Jon's case, trained many CEOs. We have heard about their successes and failures and listened to what they are up against every day. This combined knowledge of what it's like to be on the frontline brings a perspective to this book that many strategy books lack as they are written by academics or consultants. They are not written by people with the breadth and depth of our practical experience.

3 Experience

We have benefited from the wisdom of many individuals. Our team and our mentors have been hugely influential and generous in sharing their experiences with us. I (Rupert) have been lucky enough to gain from the mentorship of two extraordinary people. One was Richard Thompson, who we mentioned above. Richard sadly passed in 2022. You will find some of his words throughout this book. You'll also find contributions from my second mentor, Ian Kantor, co-founder of Investec. Ian built the company from nothing and led it throughout its transition to a global multinational. His experience is vast. He has a boundless thirst for knowledge and is one of the most fascinating people I have ever known. He has generously shared some of his wisdom with us for this book. You will find his words in Chapter 1.3.

We have learned a huge amount from many different sources. We've leveraged the experiences of those who have also written about designing and executing strategy. For instance, Ben Horowitz recounts his experience as co-founder and CEO of Opsware in *The Hard Thing About Hard Things*.[19] Kevin and Jackie Freiberg discuss how Herb Kelleher reinvented air travel when he founded Southwest Airlines in *Nuts!*.[20] Colin Bryar and Bill Carr, two top-level former Amazon executives, give an insider's account of Amazon's approach to culture, leadership and best practices in *Working Backwards*.[21] In *Playing to Win*, Roger Martin and A.G. Lafley describe how they applied their framework incorporating a set of five essential strategic choices during their time at Procter and Gamble.[22] In *Only the Paranoid Survive*, Andrew Grove shows us how to exploit moments of change using his experience of transforming Intel into the world's largest computer chip-maker and the seventh most profitable company in the Fortune 500.[23] Over 40 books have informed the thinking of this one.

Another notable example is a podcast called *Founders*, which David Senra hosts. Senra is an extraordinary guy who studies history's greatest founders and entrepreneurs in incredible depth. He re-reads biographies multiple times so that he can learn from them and extract common themes. We have learned about many books from Senra, have gone on to read them ourselves, and been inspired by his podcast.[24]

Each one of you reading this book will have different goals. You might want to solve an environmental or societal problem, double your value within the next year, reach unicorn status or break into the Fortune 500 list. Whatever you want to achieve, you will succeed only if you create value for distinct groups of people who have the power to determine your success or failure.

REMEMBER THIS

1. Businesses that fail to create value for the right sets of people won't survive.
2. Ambitions can be realized only if forged from a distinctive and coherent strategy translated into the right decisions and actions.
3. Success depends on businesses creating several necessary conditions, none of which is sufficient by itself.
4. A company that triples its profits in five years and grows IRR by 25 per cent has achieved breakthrough returns.
5. Throughout this book, we apply theory to practice and give one overarching method for designing and executing strategy: The 4D Framework.

Notes

1. Orgvue was founded as Concentra Analytics, forming a software development business with analytical consulting. It grew as a services business. £1m Series A funding meant we could develop Orgvue. Orgvue grew to such an extent that the rest of the business was either spun off or discontinued.
2. Official company incorporations and dissolutions data according to Companies House and Gov.UK reported by resolvefinancial.co.uk

3 Official company incorporations and dissolutions data according to Companies House and Gov.UK reported by resolvefinancial.co.uk
4 Viguerie, P, Calder, N and Hindo, B (2021) 2021 Corporate Longevity Forecast, Innosight Available from: www.innosight.com/insight/creative-destruction/ (archived at https://perma.cc/8ZBB-9ZSY)
5 Heel, J and Kehoe, C (2005) Why some private equity firms do better than others, McKinsey Quarterly, 1 February, www.mckinsey.com/capabilities/strategy-and-corporate-finance/our-insights/why-some-private-equity-firms-do-better-than-others (archived at https://perma.cc/68Z4-PRUS)
6 Bain & Company (2023) Global Private Equity Report, https://www.bain.com/insights/topics/global-private-equity-report/ (archived at https://perma.cc/GHE6-L7TT)
7 Khalaf, R (2023) Charlie Munger: Compounding the power of US enterprise over 99 years, *Financial Times*, 29 November, www.ft.com/content/70e84213-7267-4c98-b6ef-cc98e48b328b (archived at https://perma.cc/M5MC-839V)
8 Collins, J (2001) *Good to Great: Why some companies make the leap… and others don't*, HarperBusiness, New York
9 S&P 500 Data (2023) S&P 500: $100 in 2002 – $517.66 in 2022, www.officialdata.org/us/stocks/s-p-500/2002?amount=100&endYear=2022 (archived at https://perma.cc/6RR8-6P2S)
10 Thiel, P with Masters, B (2015) *Zero to One: Notes on startups, or how to build the future*, Virgin Books, London
11 Founders (2022) The story of Edwin Land and Polaroid – number 264 [podcast], 24 August, www.founderspodcast.com/episodes/34860270/senra-edwin-land-the-story-of-polaroid (archived at https://perma.cc/6SZU-3D2U)
12 Collins, J (2001) *Good to Great: Why some companies make the leap… and others don't*, HarperBusiness, New York
13 Sinek, S (2011) *Start with Why: How great leaders inspire everyone to take action*, Penguin Books, New York
14 Porter, M (2004) *Competitive Strategy: Techniques for analyzing industries and competitors*, Free Press, New York
15 Porter, M (2004) *Competitive Advantage: Creating and sustaining superior performance*, Free Press, New York
16 Rumelt, R (2011) *Good Strategy/Bad Strategy: The difference and why it matters*, Crown Currency, New York
17 Kim, W C and Mauborgne, R A (2015) *Blue Ocean Strategy: How to create uncontested marketspace and make the competition irrelevant* (Expanded edition), Harvard Business Review Press, Boston
18 Lafley, A G and Martin, R L (2013) *Playing to Win: How strategy really works*, Harvard Business Review Press, Boston

19 Horowitz, B (2014) *The Hard Thing About Hard Things: Building a business when there are no easy answers*, HarperBusiness, New York

20 Freiberg, K and Freiberg, J (1998) *Nuts!: Southwest Airline's crazy recipe for business and personal success*, Broadway Books, New York

21 Bryar, C and Carr, B (2021) *Working Backwards: Insights, stories and secrets from inside Amazon, Macmillan*, London

22 Lafley, A G and Martin, R L (2013) *Playing to Win: How strategy really works*, Harvard Business Review Press, Boston

23 Grove, A (2022) *Only the Paranoid Survive: How to exploit the crisis points that challenge every company and career*, Profile Books, London

24 David Senra, Founders, www.founderspodcast.com (archived at https://perma.cc/WSB2-Q2KC)

1.2

Challenges and paradoxes

Achieving breakthroughs requires grit, passion, discipline, hard work and the desire to embrace a challenge

Introduction

Marc Andreessen, one of the big names from Silicon Valley, told his friend and business partner, Ben Horowitz (another big name), a 'not-so-funny-at-the-time' joke: 'Do you know what the best thing is about start-ups? You only ever experience two emotions: euphoria and terror. And I find that lack of sleep enhances them both.' Ben Horowitz recounts his trials and tribulations in his best-selling book, *The Hard Thing About Hard Things*.[1] He gives an honest and at times brutal account of the harsh realities of starting and scaling a business. Much of what he says chimes with our experiences and we expect it might chime with many of our readers' experiences too.

Most start-ups fail. We gave the stats in Chapter 1.1. To succeed, lots of things need to go right – the thinking, the strategy, the execution of the strategy, the planning and the governance through the board. You need the right people working on the right things – forums of just the right number of people who hold just the right number and type of meetings to stay on track and keep identifying the right actions that will build momentum.

How to get these things right is the focus of this book, but the last thing we want to do is draw a picture of a simple recipe and suggest that if you follow it, you will become hyper-successful. It just isn't that easy. This is about improving the odds of success, not guaranteeing it. It's about facing the challenges and finding a way through, around, under and over them.

It's crucial to think about what could stop you. What headwinds will you face as you head across your sales bridge? Some of these headwinds can be articulated in terms of risk events that can lead to business failure (see Chapter 3.3). Many of these reasons relate to poorly designed strategy (see Chapters 2.1 to 2.3) or execution (see Chapter 3.1 to the end of the book). But there are many other generic challenges. These might not kill you, but they might make you less efficient. They might be the cause of irritation, or stress. They might seem contradictory and make you question yourself. They might keep you awake at night and make the journey a bit less fun than it could otherwise be.

This chapter highlights seven of the most common challenges you are likely to face when designing and executing a strategy to get breakthrough returns. It also highlights seven key paradoxes that you are likely to have to understand and navigate. We have both come across these challenges and paradoxes many times, in our different roles at numerous organizations. The seven key challenges are:

1 Not putting culture first and hiring people who embody it.
2 Trying to grow too quickly.
3 Dealing with spreadsheet strategists.
4 Having too much of an internal, operational focus.
5 Lack of focus and chasing the 'shiny-shiny'.
6 Lack of alignment.
7 Focusing on operational risk at the expense of strategic risk.

We outline the nature of each challenge and suggest possible solutions for each one. The seven paradoxes are:

1 To listen or not to listen.
2 Being evidence-driven when the most important stuff is unmeasurable.
3 Disciplined thinking versus free moments of creativity.
4 Benign dictatorship versus democracy.
5 Benchmarking versus thinking for yourself.
6 Learning from failure versus trying not to fail.
7 Playing it safe versus risking it all.

Seven common challenges on the path to success

Challenge 1: Not putting culture first and hiring people who embody it

The steps we describe in this book are predicated on fostering tight-knit relationships between people who engage in ongoing discussion and debate to drive the right actions. If you can't do this within your organization, you will struggle with the task ahead of you. This is not an easy thing to achieve and can be done only if the team dynamic allows for it. Teams need people who dare to stand up for what they believe in. They need people who are ready to unite behind company culture and values and call out any decisions or behaviours which do not align. Teams perform best when there is extreme trust. In Chapter 4.3, we look at Patrick Lencioni's *Five Dysfunctions of a Team*.[2] For a team to perform well, there needs to be a culture of allowing healthy conflict and encouraging team members to show their vulnerabilities.

Commitment is also important. This means people being accountable. In Professor Damian Hughes' book *The Barcelona Way*, he draws similarities between business models and football teams, citing the total commitment model, championed by Barcelona as *the* only cultural model that creates success every time. It focuses on steeping everyone in the organization in the legacy, history, culture and values of the business from the moment they walk through the door. It also focuses on only hiring those who embody the established culture and will even improve it.[3]

The starting point to building great teams is to hire the right people. Jim Collins famously says that organizations should start with 'who'. He writes about how great organizations think first about having the right people 'on the bus' (and in the key seats) and the wrong people 'off the bus' *before* they figure out where to drive it. According to Collins, if you have the wrong people, you'll never have a great company. The right direction can never compensate for having the wrong people on board.[4]

Figure 1.2.1 shows the importance of starting with the right people in the right seats. Build the foundations first. Those people are needed to put the right systems and processes into place. People, systems and processes together form the right capability to produce the data, insight and key performance indicators (KPIs) necessary for driving value creation. Parts 3 and 4 discuss KPIs in detail. As Figure 1.2.2 shows, if the management team is not well rounded and experienced enough to drive growth, it is difficult to scale. There's a lot to do before you can drive value creation. However, once the foundations are well set, you can scale quickly and immediately.

With the right people, organizations are better able to adapt. If people join the bus only because of where it's going, they will be less likely to accept a change in direction. If people join because of who else is on the bus, change becomes much easier. The right people are self-motivated by their inner drive to produce the best and to be part of creating something great. How do you attract the right people? A good place to start is with your culture and purpose.

Get your culture right. Start with 'why'. Then start again with 'who'. So much of getting your culture right comes down to purpose. Nail this and you'll have a much better chance of attracting the right people to your organization and making sure that the good people stay. In *Start with Why*, Simon Sinek investigates why some people and organizations are more inventive, pioneering and successful than others, and what it is about them that means they can repeat that success over and over again. The trick, he

FIGURE 1.2.1 Take time to set the foundations

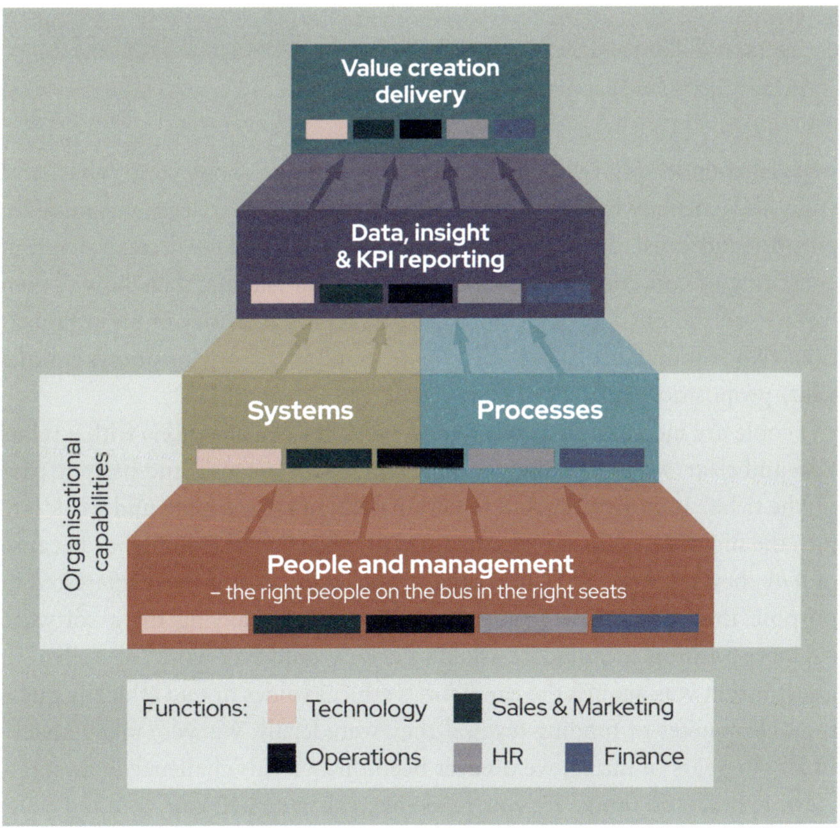

FIGURE 1.2.2 Setting the foundations well means you can scale fast and straight away

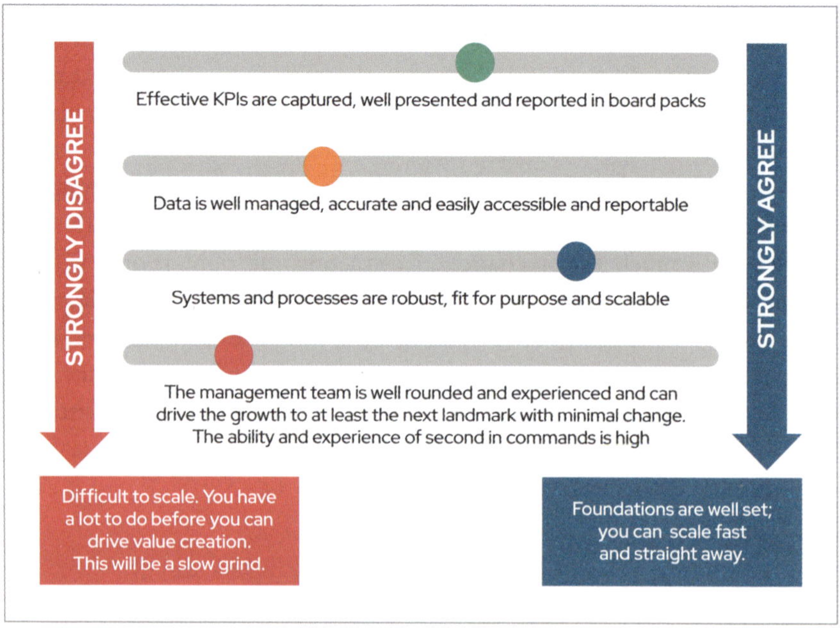

says, is to understand your 'why' before you think about your 'what' and your 'how'. Your 'why' is the organization's reason for existing – its mission, purpose and cause. He explains this through the Golden Circle, a diagram consisting of concentric circles with 'why?' in the middle, then 'how?', then 'what?' on the outside.[5] The 'what' relates to the activities of an organization: 'We manufacture x, we sell y.' The 'how' is the organization's unique value proposition, process or USP.

People are increasingly motivated to work for organizations with a relatable and clear 'why'. It enables them to unite over 'a cause' and become part of 'the tribe'. It motivates them to get up early in the morning and work late into the night. They do this not because of *what* they are doing but because of *why* they are doing it. Generations Z and Alpha are far more interested in purpose than their predecessors were. While interviewing for a software engineer position, a candidate asked us if we would ever work for a client in a sector that was against the candidate's ethical values or had ethically questionable sources of funding (even if they were legal). We were taken aback. In all our years of hiring, we'd never been thrown this challenge in an interview. It made us think. As you read this, ask yourself, can you and your management clearly and consistently articulate your purpose? Does that articulation permeate through your organization from your website to your proposal materials to your town hall messages? Be brutally honest with your answers.

We recognize Sinek's Golden Circle and the importance of starting with 'why?', but we believe there is a stage immediately after this: 'start again with who'. This fits with Collins' mantra of getting the right people on the bus. The two notions are linked. Get your 'why' right and you'll find it easier to hire the right leaders – those who fit the model of Level 5 Leadership, another concept developed by Jim Collins in *Good to Great*. Collins describes these level 5 leaders as hugely ambitious people who have an unswerving belief in the company's purpose. They put the organization's needs and ambitions before their own. They help to drive the company's purpose and create a culture which retains people and inspires others to join.[6]

JON

In my value creation plan work, I hold an initial kick-off meeting with management which includes a session on how well the team can articulate its purpose. Why does it exist and what problems does it solve for customers? What is the ambition of the business? This often forms part of the commercial due diligence report during the pre-deal assessment, so it should be front of mind, but I am often underwhelmed by how poorly management teams can articulate it. It's rarely crisp and clear. It sometimes even seems like it's the first time the question has been asked.

In *The Hard Thing About Hard Things*, Horowitz is pretty scathing about management books. One of the questions he asks is, what if you are struggling and A players don't want to come and work for you? You're unlikely to attract the 'right people' if you're tanking. Should you give up and go home?[7] This book is also written by guys who have been there, done it and felt the pain. We know how hard it is to get the right people on the bus and we have huge amounts of experience in the kinds of things that can go wrong once these 'right people' are sitting in their seats. The truth is that many hiring decisions turn out to be mistakes. We all want A-team players, but we often fail. All you can do is recruit the best people you can afford and aim to hire on culture. The biggest risk, as John Doerr, the famous Silicon Valley venture capitalist, points out, is hiring mercenaries instead of missionaries.[8] Missionaries are there for the 'why'. They're there for the challenge and the journey. Mercenaries just want to maximize their return. They will be focused on the short term, sharp elbowed, polished in promoting themselves and as political as Kevin Spacey's character, Frank Underwood, in *House of Cards*.

Another significant risk is the common practice of hiring for the busi ness you aspire to be rather than the business you are. You will build a stronger organization if you nurture the people who have been with you from where you are today. These are the people who are building the capability and are invested in the company. If they don't fully recognize what it takes to grow and deliver in a more complex organization, find an external coach or consultant to help them. Don't just replace them and hire for that endpoint. Those hires often don't want to get their hands dirty and go on the journey again.

RUPERT

In *Data-Driven Organization Design*, I wrote about many of the mistakes I made early on when designing my organization. Even though I was the CEO, had consulted in organization design and had built an organization design product, I still made mistakes. What was my Achilles heel? It was dealing with the politics between senior people who wanted, and even demanded, certain roles. I focused the design too much on what people wanted and not enough on what the strategy dictated the business needed. This is a classic mistake. I went for short-term compromise over long-term effectiveness. That short-term 'peace' turned out to be very short term and, in the end, issues remained. We got there, but it cost us time and our momentum suffered.

SOLUTION

- When hiring, look internally first. The best person might already be in the organization. Aptitude and cultural alignment are the most important things. Focus on training to fill any skills gaps. The best people are often the worst at self-promotion, and vice versa. Be mindful of the 'shiny shiny'.
- Nail your culture and recruit to that. Distil it and create a screening process. What are the signals? This takes rigour.

- Promote those who align with your culture. Make exemplars of them.
- Focus on hiring missionaries, not mercenaries. Look for the red flags – people who are obsessed with job titles and reward or who have moved around organizations a lot throughout their careers.

Challenge 2: Trying to grow too quickly

Too often CEOs and management teams go through the gruelling process of fundraising and go straight into 100-day planning without giving themselves time to rest and think. This is dangerous. You're exhausted and it's easy to make mistakes. Our advice is to take some time to rest and consolidate before jumping in. This is difficult advice to take. We know, we've seen it often enough (in Rupert's case, I've experienced it myself). It will feel counterintuitive to take time out to consolidate and settle, but believe us when we say you need it.

This is very often reflected in the numbers. CEOs and management often plan their spreadsheets to achieve fast growth, as shown in the top half of Figure 1.2.3. This figure shows the investment plan in terms of profit over time. It shows a common scenario where the actual line dips down immediately post-investment, so you're already on the back foot with a gap to close. It's far better to plan for slower growth in year 1 during the foundation phase, as shown in the bottom half of Figure 1.2.3. Accelerate through the growth phase. You'll end up in the same place.

Taking the time to consolidate also allows you to build a strong balance sheet in time for the growth phase. Fast-growing companies need enough cash to absorb working capital requirements and deal with shocks. It also means that they can be bolder and take bigger bets.

RUPERT

In the summer of 2017, the Concentra Analytics board decided to raise **Series C funding**. Our analytical services business was growing modestly and our ARR business was seeing stellar growth and very solid unit economics. We had one person in marketing and, at most, three people selling our SaaS platform. I was one of the three. We appointed corporate finance help, wrote the investment memorandum and pitched to over 40 firms in London, New York and the Bay Area.

Eight offers came in throughout November. Each offer involved lots of negotiation. We worked out who to go exclusive with. Then detailed due diligence started, which involved lengthy legal documents and more negotiation. During this process, the numbers changed. By late November, our ARR had stopped growing and many investors became concerned. One even pulled out. This stalled growth became known as an 'air pocket'. That year our revenue had more than doubled and ARR had been a rocket ship. But ARR sales growth stalled from July to November. It wasn't surprising, I was our top salesperson and was 150 per cent allocated to the Series C round. I had no time to sell and the numbers reflected this.

The deal was done in early April 2018. I didn't realize how exhausted I was. I'd spent so much time raising the money and talking about our growth aspirations that I forgot to take a break. I needed to relax, sleep and recover. The business was exhausted too. It seriously needed time to rest and then lay the foundations. Looking back, I made more mistakes in the first three months after investment than at any other stage of my career. None was fatal. We did well. But I wish I had laid the foundations instead of imposing growth targets on myself. Jon has seen this pattern repeatedly. It is so common. So please, take our advice. Give yourself time. An extra three to four months in the heat of the moment feels like an eternity. But it isn't and it can make all the difference.

SOLUTION

- The idea of advancing and consolidating comes from the military. Once you have advanced, take some time to consolidate.
- Take time to put the foundations in place (see Challenge 1).
- Do things in the right order. Why scale a sales team if you can't feed them qualified leads or train them effectively? Don't throw away hard-earned money.

Challenge 3: Dealing with spreadsheet strategists

This relates to plugging a set of assumptions into a spreadsheet and then believing those assumptions are real. Spreadsheets give the illusion of certainty where there is none. For example, some investment firms only focus on buy-and-build and it can work. But it's easy to overdo it or think it is too easy, based on what your spreadsheet is telling you. For any type of

FIGURE 1.2.3 Allow time to put the foundations in place

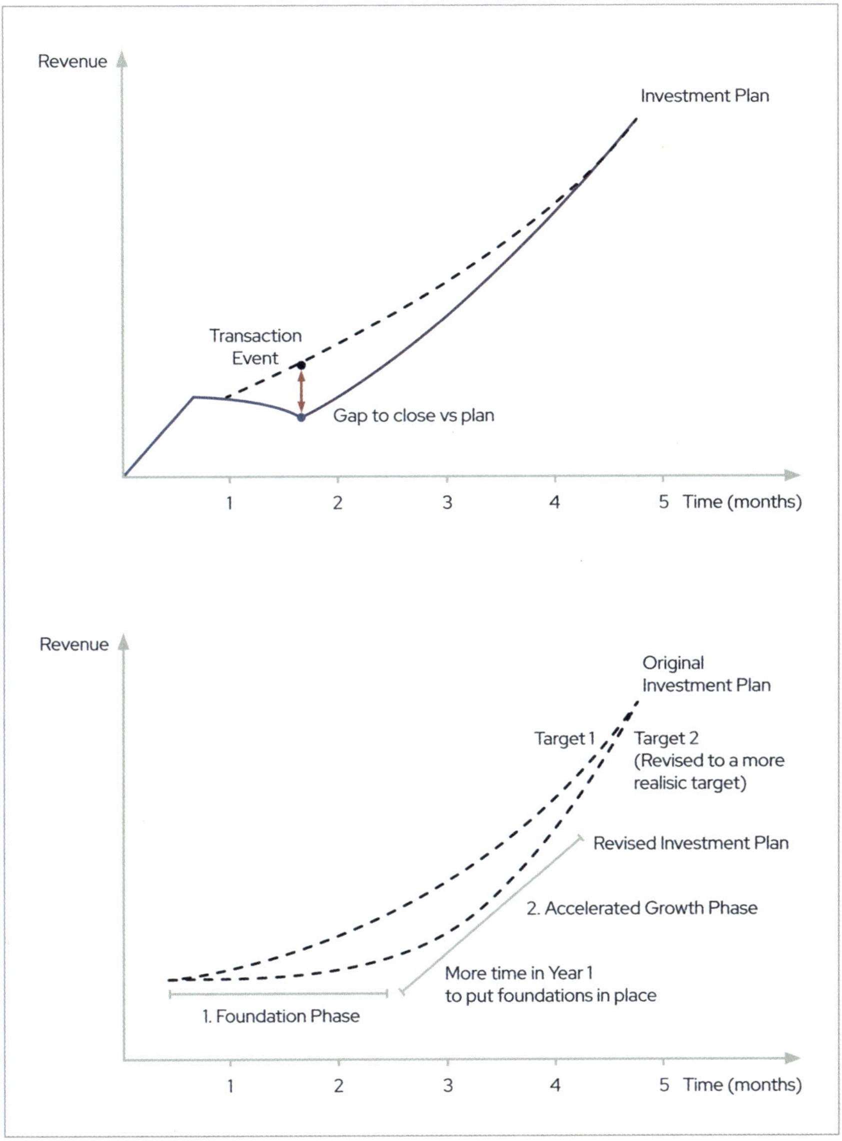

investment, it's trivially easy to build a model, plug numbers into a spreadsheet and show something. You can demonstrate growth just with a few simple calculations. This is where a lot of investment professionals go wrong. They invest based on their spreadsheet and think that their Excel plan is the plan. But spreadsheets such as these just reflect assumptions for a moment in time. Almost as soon as you've plugged it all in, it goes out of date.

In *The Hard Thing About Hard Things*, Ben Horowitz quotes Peter Thiel talking about calculus versus statistics in answering determinate and indeterminate questions: 'In a determinate (certain) world, calculus dominates. You can calculate specific things precisely and deterministically... But the indeterminate future is somehow one in which probability and statistics are the dominant modality for making sense of the world.'[9] You can think of this as the difference between economics and engineering. Economics is like poker: it's a game of chance. Shocks happen that you can't control. It is statistical. Engineering is determinate. You calculate using known formulas. A spreadsheet strategist thinks like a determinist because a spreadsheet is just calculus. You can use calculus when you are looking back, but not when you are looking forward. When you are looking forward, you need a statistical mindset.

JON

As Chair, I had a furious row with an investor who wanted to cut 55 per cent of the headcount in the business because the actual numbers were behind budget and he was worried that a banking covenant would be breached. 'We need to scale back hard and then go again,' he said. My response was equally brutal: 'If you do that, we won't have a business. You will rip the heart and soul out of it. It won't survive. I'm not signing up for that.' The discussion escalated. 'Well, if you won't do it, I will find a management team that can,' he shouted. 'Good luck with that approach,' I said, before the line went dead. I lost the battle but stood my ground. As a result, I lost my job as Chair. The CEO survived and did not scale back as far as the investor wanted. The business is now flourishing.

I turned out to be right, but only after I was made the scapegoat for underperformance against budget. That's life. Don't be a slave to the business plan just because it's in a model. Business problems aren't solved that way.

SOLUTION

- Understand sensitivities and run scenarios.
- Don't solve strategic questions using spreadsheets and calculus. Don't confuse a plan and set of objectives with a well-thought-through, designed strategy as we describe in Chapter 2.3.

- Numbers aren't just numbers, they represent real things. Don't cut costs because you've missed the budget. Think about the capabilities you will lose. Think about what you will destroy.
- Don't set your next year's budget based on a trajectory back-solved for an endpoint.

Challenge 4: Having too much of an internal, operational focus

Lack of time is a perennial problem for most professionals in most industries. Companies, leaders, managers and teams consistently fail to meet goals and objectives because they spend too much time in meetings and responding to emails. Most meetings, from the boardroom to the shop floor, are sub-optimal, but no one has time to change how things are done.

Against this backdrop, it's easy to see how you can get bogged down in operational detail and the day-to-day grind. To formulate robust strategy, executives need time and space for deep thought. They need to look outside the organization and think deeply about customers and competitors. We live in a volatile and uncertain world. We need to constantly scan the horizon, spot megatrends and external risks and be ready to adapt and change as necessary. This space won't simply present itself – we need to create it. We advise blocking time in your calendar for deep thinking work. Warren Buffett famously sits in his office for hours and reads – newspapers, books, anything that will help him learn and grow.

SOLUTION

- Use the Four Cornerstones of Corporate Health described in Chapter 1.1 to ensure a focus on external as well as internal issues.
- Use the value landscape work in Chapter 2.2 to gain a deep understanding of your customers and competition.
- Follow our advice about meetings given in Chapter 4.3.

Challenge 5: Lack of focus and chasing the 'shiny-shiny'

Invariably, plans include too many initiatives. This just means that teams get overstretched and fail to deliver. Plans go from sizzle to fizzle. Many CEOs (particularly, in our experience, founder CEOs) like to pursue ambitious side projects (we call it chasing the shiny-shiny). This leads to a diversion from the core focus. Resources are allocated to pet projects and the important, **key initiatives** suffer.

I (Jon) have found time and again that CEOs take on too much, while I (Rupert) have been that overenthusiastic CEO in need of taming. In my early years at Concentra Analytics, I fell into this trap repeatedly. As part of some research for a whitepaper in 2010, we interviewed 15 value creation professionals from 15 different investment firms. We asked all of them an open question: 'What's your biggest challenge?' The response was unanimous: trying to do too many projects at once. We asked a follow-up question: 'What's the optimal number of projects?' Again, everyone gave the same answer: four. It was only once we started following this advice that things started getting done.

RUPERT

It took me a while to realize that while everything is possible, it just takes longer than you might at first think, or hope. If I'm critical of myself, trying to do too much too quickly is one of my less helpful traits. If you're an entrepreneur who has had lots of success in life, you can see that it's all possible and you have an optimism bias. This is something that Richard Thompson, my mentor and Chair at Concentra Analytics, said to me many times: 'Keep your head in the cloud and your feet on the ground'. Urgency is great, but it can come at a price. I like to fill my plate up, both literally and figuratively. Let's start building this new product *and* get a foothold in the US with our analysis business. Why not? Let's go!

Back in 2010, I did both of these things. If I was going to achieve our goals, I needed to build a software product. I built an analytical piece of software based on my expertise (in organization design). I was, at the time, running a successful analytical services business and we had quite a few Americans in the team. We were committed to opening a US office, which we did, in 2010. We built the product and started to win some great clients in 2011. But in the summer of 2012, during the London Olympics, we were hit by three risk events at once (we describe this in detail in Chapter 3.3). Any one of these events would have been reasonably easy to deal with. Two would have been hard, but three, at the time, was enormously concerning. They were tough times. We had to lay off staff, pull the plug on many strategic initiatives and close the US office (we would return in 2014. North America became our largest region and, by far, the highest growth region by 2018). At one stage, I was watching cash daily. I secured a funding pipeline, just in case, and in the end didn't need it.

There is a reason why Chapter 3.3, on risk management, is so important. In the real world, painful things happen.

SOLUTION

- Don't let the bling blind you.
- Focus on a small number of key initiatives that you can deliver well. Don't spread your resources too thinly.
- From our experience, a good rule of thumb is to have no more than four key initiatives per forum (see Chapter 4.3 for more on forums).

Challenge 6: Lack of alignment

This challenge might sound like an obvious one, but it is an easy trap to fall into. In our experience, lack of alignment occurs for four main reasons:

1. Different motives and values. Missionaries and mercenaries are two types of people with different motives and values.
2. Different time horizons or objectives. Many disagreements occur because people maximize a given set of objectives for different time frames. Someone might maximize for three months while someone else is maximizing for three years.
3. Different interpretations of the facts. This can come through a lack of understanding, different experiences, or someone ignoring certain facts completely because they don't fit their agenda.
4. Different risk appetites. Different personalities are likely to have different approaches to risk-taking. For example, while we don't want to generalize, CEOs and founders are often more open to taking risks than finance professionals are.

SOLUTION

- As Stephen Covey said, 'Seek first to understand, then to be understood.'[10]
- Follow our advice in this book and particularly our Five Communication Pillars (see Chapter 1.3) to articulate strategy and minimize lack of alignment.

Unfortunately, there are times when differences can't be reconciled. Our advice is as follows:

- If the lack of alignment is due to reasons 1 or 2, our recommendation is to part ways. This is especially true for number 1. Certain challenges are insurmountable.

- If the lack of alignment is down to reasons 3 or 4, work out how to bridge the gap. In Chapter 1.3, we include a piece from Ian Kantor (whom we introduced in Chapter 1.1) on the power of using questions to reconcile differences of opinion. It can sometimes take practice to understand things from other people's point of view. Build trust and find a way.

Challenge 7: Focusing on operational risk at the expense of strategic risk

People tend to focus on what is in front of them. Operational risk is easy to quantify. It's tangible. We direct our attention towards things that are easy to understand. As we explain in Chapter 3.3, too much time and focus on operational risk can leave us wide open to more unpredictable, and potentially more ruinous, strategic risk.

Nassim Nicholas Taleb is a Lebanese-American essayist and mathematical statistician. He presses home the need to be paranoid about 'ruin risks', which, he argues, are more prevalent than you might think. Black swan events fall into a category of risk that Taleb calls 'fat tails'. Tail risk refers to 'irregular' risks – unpredictable, highly improbable events that have a big impact. In the world of statistics, normal distribution suggests that tail risks are very, very rare. The tail, therefore, is thin. Most events (99.7 of them) happen close to the mean – within three standard deviations of it. According to normal distribution, the probability that events will occur beyond these three standard deviations is very low. Taleb argues that the world isn't normally distributed and the tail is much fatter than we think. These catastrophic, black swan events happen far more than people realize.[11]

No one likes to think about events that could kill them. And yet, it's clear how many businesses go to the wall every day, especially during times of crisis. You only need to think through the last 25 years – 9/11, the financial crisis, the Covid pandemic – to understand that 'once-in-a-lifetime events' occur more than you might at first realize. We should all heed Taleb's advice and try to imagine unpredictable strategic risks that could take us down. As we explain in Chapter 3.3, this isn't just about having a plan to deal with these risks, it can be about turning risk on its head and creating an upside opportunity.

SOLUTION

- Focus on strategic risk and understand that these risks can sometimes become strategic opportunities.

- Make time to think through the possibilities so you are more prepared (see Chapter 3.3).
- Ensure your environment is conducive to creative thought (see Chapter 4.3 for tips on meeting hygiene).
- Don't let a failure of imagination end it all. Only the paranoid survive.[12]

Seven common paradoxes

Building organizations requires steely determination and grit. It also requires you to navigate a whole host of paradoxes.

Paradox 1: To listen or not to listen

There's a tension between listening to your customers and then ignoring them altogether. In Chapter 1.3 we talk about Amazon's leadership principles. The first of these is 'Customer Obsession'. It's described as 'Leaders start with the customer and work backwards. They work vigorously to earn and keep customer trust. Although leaders pay attention to competitors, they obsess over customers'.[13] In Part 2 of this book, we talk about the importance of nailing your niche and creating 'value factors' so that customer segments buy from you and no one else. You ask them what they value and then ask them to assign scores to show how you deliver on that value versus your competitors. You are there to serve them, and they are always right.

But then we hear about Steve Jobs, who famously didn't trust conventional customer research. He never asked customers what they wanted because: 'Our task is to read things that aren't yet on the page'.[14] Jobs came from the Henry Ford school of thought, who allegedly said: 'If I had asked people what they wanted, they would have said faster horses.' There's a lot of literature in product development that backs up these assertions. Asking customers what they want results in incrementalism. Your product will only change by small degrees. Customers won't tell you how to design an entirely new and innovative solution that solves a problem they didn't even know they had.

The important thing is that you understand your customers inside and out. Our favourite example of this is the story of the Citroën 2CV. It is brilliantly captured in Cameron McAllister's novel *The Tin Snail*.[15] The 2CV stands for 'deux chevaux', meaning 'two horses' or 'two taxable horsepower'. The car was originally conceived in 1936 as the TPV, the 'Tout Petite Voiture' or 'Very Small Car'. At the time Citroën was under the control of Michelin following the death of its founder André Citroën, in 1935. Pierre-Jules Boulanger, the chief design engineer, wanted to mobilize the rural communities of France and replace their bicycles, pony traps and horse-drawn carts with a small car. Boulanger had no interest in the look of the car, he was focused only on its functionality for the rural French population. He was obsessed with giving them what they needed. He wanted a car with seats for two peasants and space for 50 kg of potatoes or a small cask of wine. It needed good enough suspension to travel across a ploughed field without breaking the eggs on the seat. Production planning began in 1939. The aim was to launch the 2CV at the 1939 Paris Motor Show, but the outbreak of World War II postponed these ambitions. Indeed, Michelin dismantled all prototypes and hid the parts to prevent the design from falling into German hands. Eventually, the 2CV was previewed at the Paris Car Show in 1948, nine years later than planned. And the rest, as they say, is history.

Paradox 2: Being evidence-driven when the most important stuff is unmeasurable

We all know that our actions should be grounded in evidence, but in a saying attributed to Peter Drucker, you can only manage what you can measure. In Chapter 1.1 we introduced the Four Cornerstones of Corporate Health: customer, people, financial, impact. Each of these cornerstones has associated measures which can be tracked and monitored. But some of the most important things are unmeasurable. For example, how do you track how happy your customers or people are? How do you know about the true impact you're having on society? For example, at Ārahi we are involved with the Longford Trust, an organization that believes in giving a second chance to people who have served a prison sentence. They do this by helping them get into education and/or employment. How is it possible to measure the impact of these interventions? It's not just about the person's life. The impact extends to their family, friends and the generations that follow. The fact that these consequences are unquantifiable does not mean it's an unworthy pursuit.

Similarly, culture is vital to the success or failure of a business, as we discussed in Challenge 1. Culture is incredibly difficult to measure. You can feel it and try to describe it. But it's very hard to articulate and put it into words. Tracking how close you are to an ideal, defined culture is close to impossible, and yet it trumps everything. If you've got the wrong culture, you're dead in the water.

Paradox 3: Disciplined thinking versus free moments of creativity

We advocate taking a disciplined approach – disciplined thinking and disciplined action. This implies that defining moments or kernels of insight come linearly – so long as you apply a disciplined approach, they will happen. But that's not how it works. Inspiration comes in a brief moment in the shower or walking the dog. Divergent thinking is essential. Insight is gained from making mistakes, from failing and digging into the reasons why. We both agree that our best ideas haven't come from being disciplined, they've come when we've created space to think, had a walk with someone and felt inspired.

Paradox 4: Benign dictatorship versus democracy

Many successful businesses stem from a founder or founders with a strong vision. These individuals can often tend towards being autocratic. That's their natural inclination. They have a strong vision and they know how to succeed. But building a successful business is all about alignment. It's about taking people with you on the journey. A paradox exists between having a vision and making autocratic decisions to achieve it and getting everyone aligned. Committees are very bad at creative decision-making. You need someone to drive things forward. If you ran every decision by a committee, you'd get little done. When do you trust your gut and go for it and when do you have to listen?

Paradox 5: Benchmarking versus thinking for yourself

Benchmarking has its place. It can help us to learn. It can be a useful indicator of the art of the possible at an operational level. We'll give you an example. A key finance metric we refer to in this book relates to the period between closing accounts at month-end and finalizing board materials. It's important to do this quickly so that the board can have a relevant discussion based on the most up-to-date information. It takes many companies nearly 21 days, but we've seen large, complex organizations manage it in six to eight. In a situation like this, benchmarking can show you what is possible.

How come a complex organization can do something in seven days that it takes far smaller organizations 21 days to accomplish?

But benchmarking can be too limiting. There's a great story about Herb Kelleher, one of the founders of Southwest Airlines, hiring someone to run an advertising campaign. The person said it would take nine months as this was the standard timeframe, widely accepted in the industry. Kelleher told them they had less than nine days.[16] Industries often do things in a certain way, just because. Asking what a benchmark *could be* unlocks creativity.

In Chapter 2.1 we discuss how it is critical to design a unique and distinctive strategy to achieve breakthrough returns. You have to create your business model, your solutions and your way. Continental Lite folded after just two years because it tried to copy Southwest Airlines. It was an airline in the same market but it was different, for example it had a hub. It wasn't point-to-point. It tried to be something it wasn't, so it failed.

Paradox 6: Learning from failure versus trying not to fail

The best lessons come from failure. And yet, you spend all your time trying to succeed. We're all in it to win it. This is why it's so helpful to read avidly, listen to podcasts and learn from other people's failures. When I (Rupert) was at Kearney, I learned the value of debriefing. We created a T-account of What Went Well (WWW) and Even Better If (EBI). We use this religiously at Ārahi. Every moment is a learning moment.

Paradox 7: Playing it safe versus risking it all

Fortune favours the brave. Hollywood movies celebrate the bold. The biggest breakthrough returns belong to those who risk it all, often many times over, to conquer all who came before them. Think Musk, Jobs or Bezos. Think Sam Zemurray. His story is told brilliantly in Rich Cohen's book *The Fish That Ate the Whale*.[17] Otherwise known as 'Sam the banana man', Zemurray was an entrepreneur who arrived in the US aged 15 with no personal connections and not a dollar to his name. He decided to make money in the banana business, which at the time was extremely competitive. He took bananas that the United Fruit Company thought were too ripe to sell and sold them himself for profit. As the story progresses, we learn about Zemurray buying land in Honduras to grow bananas and finding a way not to pay taxes so that he could undercut the United Fruit Company. He put everything on the line multiple times over. He even staged a coup to overthrow the President of Honduras. By the time he died, he was one of the richest men in America. This is an example of someone who risked it all time and again.

Sam Zemurray is an example of a runaway success. His is an extraordinary story that warrants being written down. There is a survivorship bias in the stories that we hear. For every Musk, Jobs, Bezos or Zemurray, there are countless John and Jane Does who don't make it. Lives can be ruined and their stories are forgotten. If we were fed a more complete picture of the number of entrepreneurs who succeed and fail, we might think twice before risking it all.

There is also a paradox in the fact that as you become more successful, you also become more risk averse. This aversion, as we discuss in Chapters 3.3 and 4.5, can become your biggest risk. In Chapter 4.5 we focus particularly on a concept called The Founder's Mentality, developed by two Bain & Company executives, Chris Zook and James Allen. They look at whether companies can maintain their unique strengths and values as they grow. The authors analysed companies that managed (and didn't manage) to achieve their growth ambitions over a sustained period. Those that didn't manage it rarely cited the markets as the cause. Instead, they cited internal issues, such as a culture of risk aversion as the main barrier to growth.[18]

Final thoughts

We briefly mentioned David Senra's podcast *Founders* in Chapter 1.1. He recounts stories of focus and passion. They describe people who found a niche and succeeded against the odds. Ralph Lauren broke through by selling ties at five times the normal price. He was the first designer to focus on men. He came from humble beginnings and built a brand on aspiration – the preppy elite world of polo. It was a world that he didn't come from.[19] Then there's Coco Chanel. She was an orphan from rural France. She started by selling hats with a feather in them for double, if not more than double, the price of other hats.[20] Dyson, one of Senra's favourites, broke through for the first time by creating a new sort of wheelbarrow using a ball at the front instead of a wheel. He sold directly through advertising in newspapers and magazines rather than losing all his margin through trade like everyone else. But then he lost it all because his investors wanted to bring in professionals who adopted the 'best practices' of their industry and therefore sold through channels.[21] Dyson's success embodies another theme from the stories told in *Founders* – the great founders found their own way. They didn't copy someone else's model, they created their way own, from first principles and often out of necessity.

Many, if not most, success stories take a long time. Dyson worked for over a decade in his shed to turn his idea of a vacuum cleaner without a bag into a reality. Achieving breakthroughs requires grit, passion, discipline, hard work and the desire to embrace a challenge.

REMEMBER THIS

What you take away from this chapter is personal to you. Please take a moment to write your five points to remember.

Notes

1 Horowitz, B (2014) *The Hard Thing About Hard Things: Building a business when there are no easy answers*, HarperBusiness, New York

2 Lencioni, P (2002) *Five Dysfunctions of a Team: A leadership fable*, Jossey-Bass, San Francisco

3 Hughes, D (2018) *The Barcelona Way: How to create a high-performance culture*, Macmillan, London

4 Collins, J (2001) *Good to Great: Why some companies make the leap... and others don't*, HarperBusiness, New York

5 Sinek, S (2011) *Start with Why: How great leaders inspire everyone to take action*, Penguin Books, New York

6 Collins, J (2001) *Good to Great: Why some companies make the leap... and others don't*, HarperBusiness, New York

7 Horowitz, B (2014) *The Hard Thing About Hard Things: Building a business when there are no easy answers*, HarperBusiness, New York

8 Taylor, B (2016) 'The best entrepreneurs are missionaries, not mercenaries,' Harvard Business Review, 11 April, https://hbr.org/2016/04/what-separates-high-impact-entrepreneurs-from-those-who-dont-make-a-big-difference (archived at https://perma.cc/74L9-GH6N)

9 Horowitz, B (2014) *The Hard Thing About Hard Things: Building a business when there are no easy answers*, HarperBusiness, New York

10 Covey, S (2020) *The Seven Habits of Highly Effective People* (Reissue edition), Simon & Schuster, London

11 RiskMindsTV (2018) Nassim Nicholas Taleb: 'You should study risk taking, not risk management' [online video], www.youtube.com/watch?v=4P47UTF0tZA (archived at https://perma.cc/FYJ8-TTMS)
12 Andy Grove is credited with coining this phase. He wrote a book with it as the title.
13 Bryar, C and Carr, B (2021) *Working Backwards: Insights, stories and secrets from inside Amazon*, Macmillan, London
14 Goodreads, Steve Jobs Quotes, www.goodreads.com/author/quotes/5255891.Steve_Jobs?page=2#:~:text=%22%20People%20don%27t%20know%20what,not%20yet%20on%20the%20page (archived at https://perma.cc/3VVR-8DHA)
15 McAllister, C (2015) *The Tin Snail*, Corgi Childrens, London
16 Freiberg, K and Freiberg, J (1998) *Nuts!: Southwest Airline's crazy recipe for business and personal success*, Broadway Books, New York
17 Cohen, R (2013) *The Fish That Ate the Whale: The life and times of America's banana king*, Picador, New York
18 Zook, C and Allen, J (2016) *The Founder's Mentality: How to overcome the predictable crises of growth*, Harvard Business Review Press, Boston
19 Founders (2023) Ralph Lauren – number 288 [podcast] 31 January, www.founderspodcast.com/episodes/69912643/senra-ralph-lauren-the-man-behind-the-mystique (archived at https://perma.cc/RHU8-7JQG)
20 Founders (2019) Coco Chanel (her life and secrets) – number 64 [podcast] 24 March, www.founderspodcast.com/episodes/34741537/senra-coco-chanel-her-life-her-secrets (archived at https://perma.cc/6TWN-KDFE)
21 Founders (2023) James Dyson (against the odds) – number 300 [podcast] 24 April, www.founderspodcast.com/episodes/88384801/senra-james-dyson-against-the-odds-an-autobiography (archived at https://perma.cc/8XGN-B5KU)

1.3

Core truths, frameworks and communication pillars

Never stop thinking, questioning... and learning

Introduction

All buildings need deep foundations. Value is built on deep foundations. This chapter lays out the foundational building blocks for this book. You are likely to find yourself returning to it as you read through the chapters to refer to the concepts we describe. We've tried to keep things simple by describing five truths, five frameworks and five communication pillars.

There are five core truths which underlie our approach to strategic value creation:

Truth 1: Never stop thinking and questioning.
Truth 2: Value creation requires an integrated and connected system. It is not linear.
Truth 3: Value creation is always evolving and always on. It is not a 'one-and-done' process.
Truth 4: Value creation requires disciplined action.
Truth 5: Value creation is [insert expletive] HARD so you had better love it.

The practical and visual frameworks we propose in this book will help you to instil a disciplined approach to driving action, align action management with your value creation strategies and track and monitor progress towards your business goals. Our five core frameworks for designing and executing strategy are as follows:

Framework 1: QFOR-A (Questions, Facts, Opinions, Recommendations and Actions).
Framework 2: TAF (Target, Actual, Forecast).

Framework 3: BRAG (Blue, Red, Amber, Green).
Framework 4: KODs (Key Organizational Dimensions).
Framework 5: CRASI (Capture, Responsible, Approver, Supporting, Informed).

There's no point in having a great strategy or plan if no one knows about it. Communication is everything. It can make the difference between success and failure. Value creation can happen only if you get everyone aligned and travelling in the right direction. For this reason, we define five communication pillars intended to help you communicate your strategy and plan:

Pillar 1: The power of the one-pager.
Pillar 2: Visualize to optimize.
Pillar 3: Make things as simple as possible but no simpler.
Pillar 4: Refine, refine, refine.
Pillar 5: Repeat, repeat, repeat.

The five core truths of strategic value creation

Truth 1: Never stop thinking and questioning

Numerous research studies have been done into the questioning mindset of the child. One such study came from Paul Harris, a child psychologist at Harvard, who found that a child asks about 40,000 questions between the ages of two and five, which averages out to around 100 questions per day.[1] Gradually, as we age, our curiosity wanes and the number of questions we ask falls dramatically. We get out of the habit. We stop asking 'why?' and too often simply accept things for the way they are.

We hope that this book demonstrates the importance of having an inquiring mindset. In business, as in life, we can never know enough. Just like children, we should always seek to question what is in front of us and understand more. And we should never stop thinking about what we learn and asking how we can use new information to help us progress towards our goals. When we fail or make mistakes, it's important to take time to reflect on how we could improve and use these moments as an opportunity to learn.

In his book *Good to Great*, Jim Collins talks about creating a Culture of Discipline. Through his research, he found that great companies rely on people engaging in disciplined thought and taking disciplined action. For him, disciplined thought means relentlessly searching for a deep understanding of the brutal facts of your reality. Brutal facts can be painful to take, but meaningful change can't happen unless they are acknowledged, accepted and addressed. Collins talks about how, throughout the Second World War, Churchill repeatedly asked for facts, with no filtering or veneer. He even set up a separate department called the Central Statistical Office 'with the principal function of feeding him – continuously updated and completely unfiltered – the most brutal facts of reality'.[2]

The 4D Framework explained in Chapter 1.1 encourages this continual process of disciplined thinking and questioning. Diagnosing today is a process of delving into your total truth. The aim is to achieve absolute clarity on your current position and why things are the way they are, before proceeding to design your strategy. Designing strategy means asking many questions about where you want to get to and how you're going to get there. Part of drawing the plan means understanding the risks you face. It can mean thinking outside the box to consider unpredictable events which could have serious consequences. It also means asking questions to get to the root cause of risk events, the likelihood of them happening and the impact they could have. Delivering the plan means monitoring progress using targets, actual and forecast data (see below). It means thinking about how to use this data to extract the facts you need to answer your questions and find a clear way forward.

In Chapter 4.3 we introduce a process to explain thinking and questioning in terms of percolating and distilling ideas and thoughts. It's similar to the triple distillation process used in the manufacture of alcohol. Letting ideas percolate is always worthwhile. The best ideas often come in our slower moments – when we're out walking, or on our commute to work. We touched on this in Paradox 3 in Chapter 1.2 when we discussed how free moments of creativity do not necessarily flow from disciplined thought – they come from divergent thinking. But the process of percolation and distillation is a disciplined one – you give yourself time for thoughts to percolate and you distil them. You nail down the key matters that need attention or the key questions that need to be asked.

In Chapter 1.1, we talked about the importance of mentorship. I (Rupert) introduced two individuals I have been incredibly lucky to have as mentors. One is Ian Kantor, who is most well known for co-founding Investec and leading it through its transition to a global multinational. Ian is a master of conversation and of building fruitful working relationships. He has an innate ability to get to the nub of an issue, draw out people's opinions, reconcile differences and find a way forward. In the box, he tells us his thoughts on the importance of asking the right questions to help you learn more. We return to him later in the chapter.

IAN KANTOR

I have always been fascinated by what I don't know. I became captured by the phrase 'the more you know, the less you know', which dates back at least to Socrates. Of the many translations of that, my own is to visualize all our knowledge, from nanoparticles and microcosms to galaxies and the universe, where everything is connected, communicating and interacting in a cosmic soup. I visualize all that knowledge residing in a multi-dimensional cloud in some form or other. On the surface of that cloud, extending infinitely, is what we don't know. As the knowledge and so the cosmic cloud increases, exponentially, in size, so does the surface area, which is where so much examination, research and development are currently happening.

This applies to each of us individually, to groups or organizations, and even to the entire world. For me, this is one of the most exciting times in our history. What grabs me the most is the idea that everything is connected, communicating and interacting. What does this mean for us, on our little planet, and how we as individuals are structured and governed and how we interact with each other within the interlinked organizations that dominate our world? I guess that is why I find Rupert's book so prescient right now.

I have been fortunate to pick up some amazing teachers throughout my life, from a rabbi who taught me many years ago, to a friend who is a leading behaviourist, to the former Chairman of Investec, Bas Kardol, who was an extraordinary human being. Of course, I also learned a huge amount from my parents as well as from many books and other people that I have interacted with, from our children and their friends to the hairdresser. All these people have helped to hone my understanding of things around me, particularly of human behaviour and how we interact. I've learned that it's possible to work together to reconcile differences and reach a higher place.

It starts with how you ask a question. Direct questions can sound accusatory. Compare 'Why did you do that?' with 'That's interesting, can you elaborate on that for me?' or 'I like what you're saying but I don't understand it, can you help me?'. You're asking the same question in a far more open, inviting way. You're asking it in a way that will help you to learn more.

Truth 2: Value creation requires an integrated and connected system. It is not linear

Realizing value creation ambitions relies on the integration of strategy design with planning and action management. Within this system, everyone, from the board downwards, works consistently towards the same end value creation goals. There is a clear plan for how these goals will be achieved, which everyone understands. Day-to-day actions are tailored to the plan and value creation goals. Risk management is tied to objectives and both are included in your planning so that you know how you will mitigate risks and challenges that get in the way of where you want to go. The thinking and the data are connected. They are not siloed.

This integration starts with the board and its input into the design and execution of strategy. This involves tracking metrics related to key initiatives and monitoring progress towards goals. It involves supporting and productively challenging management to encourage them to think critically about decisions. The discussion in the boardroom is tightly connected to the day-to-day actions taken in the company.

FIGURE 1.3.1 We describe a linear process but in reality it is divergent and messy

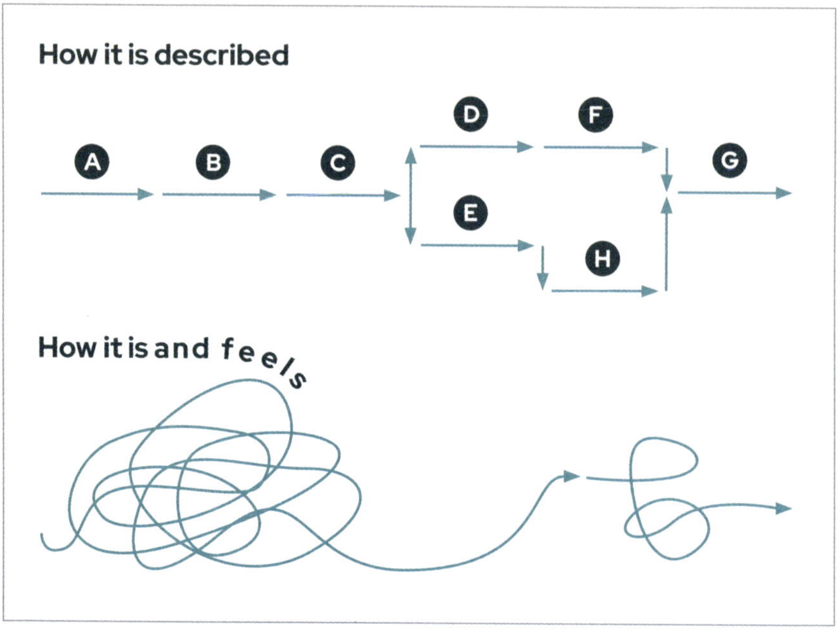

While everything is integrated, it does not mean it is linear. We have linearly written this book. It was the only way to do it. We have presented value creation as a process that you step through sequentially. First, you diagnose your current situation, then you think about where you want to get to, then you draw the plan and finally you execute the plan. But this isn't how it works in reality. The world isn't linear. As you address new aspects and progress through the steps we describe, you will find that you need to go back and rethink. It's like building a jigsaw. Diagnosing today and designing tomorrow is an iterative process. You have an 'as-is' (today) and a 'to-be' (tomorrow). Your understanding of one informs your understanding of the other. You will find yourself constantly going backwards and forwards between the two. The planning process will make you rethink aspects of your strategy design. You might still be designing your strategy when you start to execute it. You might have an integrated plan in place, or you might not. You might have thought through risk, or you might only have thought about objectives. As Kevin and Jackie Freiberg say in *Nuts!*: 'Reality is chaotic; planning is ordered and logical. The two don't square with one another.'[3] You might want to first focus on making your board meetings as productive as possible and improving your board packs and work backwards from there. A process that is described along the lines of the top half of Figure 1.3.1 feels very much more like the bottom half.

INTEGRATION OF THE FOUR CORNERSTONES OF CORPORATE HEALTH

Systems thinking is a problem-solving approach that cuts through complexity by considering how things relate to each other and the impact that a change in one part of the system can have elsewhere. A great example of systems thinking is a phenomenon called Dutch Disease. In 1959, natural gas was discovered in the Netherlands. This appeared to be a positive thing, but unemployment in the Netherlands increased. The discovery led to an appreciation of Dutch currency, exports became uncompetitive and the markets stopped buying. Dutch businesses started to struggle and job losses followed. A positive thing that happened in the economic system (discovering natural gas) had an unexpected negative impact on the manufacturing and agricultural sectors. People lost their livelihoods. While it's not hard to make those connections in hindsight, no one pre-empted it at the time.

The point of systems thinking is to think through the possible connections within an integrated whole so that you can pre-empt what would otherwise be unexpected events. So how can we apply it to value creation?

The Four Cornerstones of Corporate Health can be viewed through a systems thinking lens. The interests of these four cornerstones are linked. If one corner is sick, it's likely to impact the other three. For example, if you're not creating value for the customer, they won't buy from you, so you won't be able to give shareholders the returns they need, employee bonuses will shrink and impact objectives will likely suffer because of diminished budgets. Similarly, if you're mistreating employees or contractors, they will be unlikely to go the extra mile for the customer, so you'll no longer be creating value for the customer and the cycle will continue. Increasingly, a disregard for your impact on the environment and society can make not only the planet but also customers, people and therefore shareholders very unhappy. If your finances are healthy, you can have a greater impact on the environment and society, and you can make your people happier too.

Creating value for your customers should always be your top priority. Without customers, your business can't exist. Frederick F Reichheld hailed the importance of loyal customers in his 1996 book *The Loyalty Effect*.[4] He proved that just a small improvement in customer retention has the potential to double your company's profits. The overriding message is therefore as relevant as it was almost three decades ago: ignore the customer at your peril.

Truth 3: Value creation is always evolving and always on. It is not a 'one-and-done' process

The Forth Bridge is a cantilever railway bridge in east central Scotland, UK. It spans the Firth of Forth estuary to connect Edinburgh to Fife. The 1.5-mile-long bridge opened in 1890 and at the time had the longest single cantilever bridge span in the world. It was often said that the bridge needed perpetual maintenance. The story went that no sooner would painters finish at one end of the bridge than they would need to return to the start and begin all over again. This has been contested, but myth or not, what is clear is that the bridge has needed fairly constant attention. Or at least it did until 2011, when painters finally applied the last stroke of heavy-duty paint, which was expected to last for 25 years. At last, maintenance could stop. The bosses of Network Rail, which owns the bridge, didn't need to give it another thought. But alas, in 2020, photos showed the paint peeling off. What had been expected to last for 25 years was failing after just nine.[5] We can learn a lot from this tale of woe. It doesn't pay to take your eye off the ball.

Value creation is a dynamic, living and breathing process. It is not something to do once and then forget about. The world constantly evolves. New threats and opportunities emerge continuously. Breakthrough returns happen only to companies that evolve alongside the world and constantly scan the horizon. In *Nuts!*, Kevin and Jackie Freiberg discuss how Southwest Airlines constantly tried to anticipate competitive airlines' next moves, assessing how they altered their approaches and what was dominating their thinking. In *Data-Driven Organization Design*, I (Rupert) wrote about an exercise called 'Imagine your nightmare competitor'. It involves thinking beyond your obvious competitors to imagine who might be able to take you down. The military call this 'red team planning'. Think about what Apple did to Sony or Tesla did to the automotive sector. It's all part of horizon scanning and scenario planning. Southwest did it constantly. They asked 'what if' questions around what would happen if they opened new airports. How would the competition respond? How many planes would they need and where would they get them? Thinking things through in this way enabled them to act quickly when new opportunities presented themselves – they'd already role-played it in their minds so could make quick decisions.[6]

Companies that take the same approach as Southwest can pivot from the plan as necessary to take advantage of new opportunities. They are the ones to spot threats and, sometimes, turn them on their head and convert them into opportunities. Companies that create breakthrough returns keep their eyes open. They continually question what is in front of them and move fast when required, changing direction if necessary. This ability to move fast gives a real competitive advantage.

In Chapter 3.2 we describe the bridges of BROP-A and how to break down the time it takes to reach your long-term goal into stepping stones. We explain how metrics related to the key initiatives are tracked and monitored. This monitoring can give you early warning signals about potential problems so that you can move quickly to head them off before they negatively impact progress.

Truth 4: Value creation requires disciplined action

The need for disciplined action is a fundamental belief underpinning everything in this book. BROP-A (introduced in Chapter 1.1) ends in action. **QFOR-A**, a framework that we introduce below, ends in action. Leaders need a relentless focus on making the right decisions and taking the right action. Everything should lead to action – all of the thinking, questioning and decision-making. If it doesn't, there's very little point to any of it. As mentioned in Truth 3, ideally the impact of these actions would be monitored to ensure that they are having the desired effect. This is part of our disciplined approach.

A focus on disciplined action is particularly important as companies grow. Complexity heightens, meetings proliferate, bureaucracy increases and organizational hierarchies are put into place. Actions whirl out of meetings. Without a disciplined approach, they can fail to be recorded, which therefore means they often don't get done. This can make meetings – the thing that many of us spend most of our time doing – a total waste of time.

Actions need people to be responsible for them. It's often helpful to understand where and when actions were captured and by whom. Other people may need to be involved – to approve the action before it can be considered complete or to support the person responsible for it. And others may need to be kept informed of progress. Below, we introduce **CRASI** as one of our five primary frameworks.

Truth 5: Value creation is [insert expletive] HARD so you had better love it

This isn't an easy game. Think back to Marc Andreessen's words at the beginning of Chapter 1.2. Several of the books we have read as part of our research relay people's lived experiences of growing successful companies (see the Bibliography). No one finds it easy. It's hard. Any number of things can and will go wrong. While we try to illustrate some of these in Chapter 1.2 (on challenges) and Chapter 3.3 (on risks), we've just scratched the surface.

Ben Horowitz is particularly candid about the difficulties he's faced. He found that there is no playbook (although, dare we say it, we hope that this book goes some way to providing one). Many of the truly amazing books out there are not written by practitioners who have toiled at the coalface. They don't say what to do when things don't go to plan and when difficult decisions need to be made.

Value creation is hard no matter what role you are in – a member of the executive team, board member, chair, investor. But the CEO bears the brunt of it. In the words of Stanford Professor Nick Bloom: 'It's frankly a horrible job... Being a CEO of a big company is a hundred-hour-a-week job. It consumes your life. It consumes your weekend. It's super stressful. Sure, there are enormous perks, but it's also all-encompassing'.[7] We discuss the role of the CEO, particularly in relation to the role of the board, in

Chapter 4.2. As a CEO, the buck stops with you. If employees are unhappy, it's because of you. If the culture is toxic, it's because of you. If customers are unhappy, it's your fault. If the brand promise is confusing or contradictory, that's you too. You get the blame if you are too aggressive and overshoot, or if you are too conservative and miss the boat on a big opportunity. People scrutinize your every move – who you speak to, who you don't speak to. Your mood or a throwaway comment can get analysed to death. A random idea that you verbalize (perhaps unintentionally) can lead to a flurry of activity.

It's truly exhausting. It's truly hard. So, you do have to love it. You have to get a kick out of it. You have to believe completely in what you're doing. Your passion will get you through. It will carry you through the hard times and motivate you like nothing else. It will help you to motivate others when they are feeling the pain.

This is a good place to note the importance of celebration. Reaching stepping stones and milestones along your bridge will be tough. Nothing is ever straightforward. It will involve incredibly hard work and dedication from several people. It's vital to celebrate the wins. Celebration is restorative. It can reinvigorate and renew energy stores. It can also renew enthusiasm and passion. Celebrations give us permission to pat ourselves on the back and acknowledge our achievements. They can lift us and prepare us for the next stage. We talk more about the importance of celebration in Chapter 5.3.

The five core frameworks used in strategic value creation

Framework 1: QFOR-A (Questions, Facts, Opinions, Recommendations and Actions)

Many years ago, Ian Kantor introduced me (Rupert) to a process called information–opinion–suggestion–action–review to encourage fruitful discussions. He tells us more about the process and how he uses it to reach better answers in the box below.

We have honed his process into QFOR-A, which stands for Questions, Facts, Opinions, Recommendations and Actions (as shown in Figure 1.3.2). There are four types of statements – questions, facts, opinions and recommendations. In the context of any business conversation, but particularly in the boardroom, the purpose of these statements is to drive action.

FIGURE 1.3.2 QFOR-A

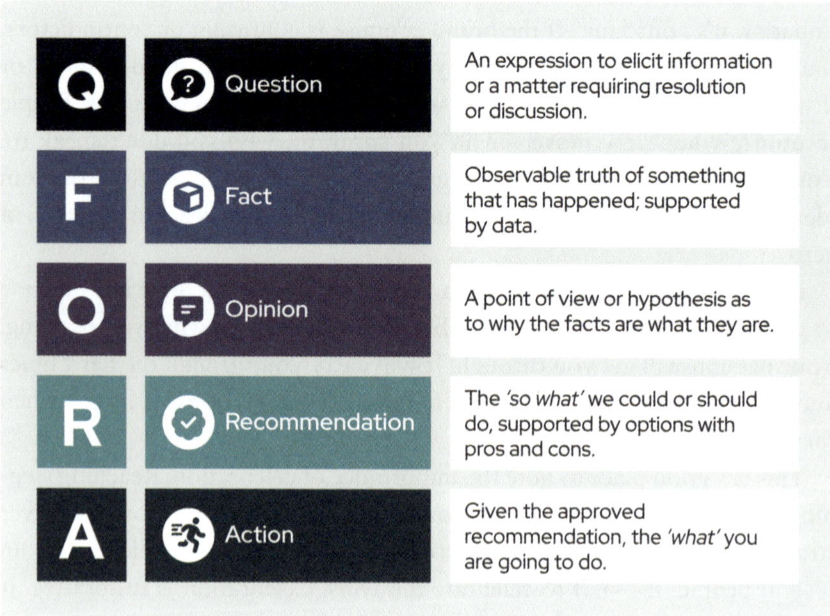

- Questions are a gateway to learning. They invite dialogue and information exchange. Is there such a thing as a bad question? Yes, there most certainly is, in the boardroom at least. We delve into the good, bad and ugly types of questions in Chapter 4.2. Questions have answers and these answers come in the form of facts, opinions and recommendations.
- Facts are things that have happened. Facts are established using data. 'Where are we against budget?', 'Which rep sold the most last month?', 'Who failed to hit their target?' and 'What is our NPS and how does it compare to last quarter?'
- Opinions give people's perspective on why certain events or outcomes have occurred. They are often found by asking open 'why' questions (for more on this, see Chapter 4.2). For example, 'Why do you think we are behind budget in the US?', 'Why do you think so many people are leaving our sales team?'
- Recommendations offer a particular type of opinion. Ian Kantor typically uses the term 'suggestion' as a lighter way of making a recommendation. They tell us what someone believes should be done in a particular set of circumstances. One of the Chair's key roles in a meeting is to steer the

conversation in the direction of recommendations. Facts and opinions are all very well, but they amount to nothing if they don't result in a recommendation that leads to action. Recommendations answer the 'So what?'. Facts overlaid with opinion can give you valuable insight, but there's no point in insight for insight's sake. It's what you do with the insight that matters. Management consultants ask the 'So what?' question all the time. Their job is to use insight to solve organizations' problems. What does the insight mean? What conclusions and therefore recommendations can you draw from it?

- The dash between the R and the A in QFOR-A shows that everything leads to action. Actions result from agreeing and approving a recommendation.

QFOR-A helps to structure thinking and writing. It also helps to structure conversations in meetings. It keeps everyone focused on the main aim – to ask the right questions to get the right insight and use that insight to reach the right recommendations and actions.

For a full explanation, we will hand over to Ian Kantor, who, as mentioned above, explained his process to me (Rupert) many years ago as a method he used at Investec.

IAN KANTOR

On their own, opinions are worthless. Everyone has them, by the dozen. If you don't understand the information that someone's opinion is based on, it's very difficult to engage with it. Having all the relevant information is crucial. As we have seen, how you ask the question can have a huge impact on the information you receive in return.

In a court of law, many decisions are based on facts. Judges base their opinions on information and then suggest a course of action. If you want to change a ruling, your only hope is to change the judge's references. Legal reasoning in a court of law will most often follow a deductive process. It uses the available information to form a specific conclusion.

Our perception – how we see things – dictates the way we respond or behave. With the information–opinion–suggestion sequence, your brain takes in data. Your perception dictates the opinions you form and the suggestions you make. But to get a more complete picture, it's sometimes helpful to change perception. You can do this by reversing the sequence. Instead of starting with the information, you can start with a suggestion. For example, say there's a question about the performance of an employee. If you lead with the facts, someone's opinion will be based on those facts and their suggestion might be that the person should be let go. But what if you lead by putting the suggestion on the table:

'What do you think we should do about this person?'

'I don't think he's great, we should let him go.'

'Ah, that's interesting. How much do we know? I agree he's not great, but have we factored in the consequences of getting rid of him? Can we replace him? Does he have strong allegiances here?'

You're asking for a new set of facts to learn more. You're changing perception. The question about this person's performance and whether he should be let go or not isn't just about the individual. The relevant information doesn't only relate to them and their performance. It's about the consequences that that decision might have. Here, the sequence suggestion–opinion–information is used to make a better-informed decision.

At Investec, we worked hard to instil a culture of reconciling our differences to reach better answers. The chances that six people in a room will share the same opinion are close to zero. Not even two people will share the same opinion. People can fight vigorously for their ideas. This conflict can provide us with a powerful ingredient which can usefully be mobilized in an open and transparent culture of reconciling differences. You can say things like, 'I get the feeling that you're very wedded to this idea. Can you explain it a bit more?' Eventually, you find that you get to a solution that no individual in the team could have come up with by themselves. It's about trying to find a space where people can agree.

I started by explaining the deductive reasoning process in a court of law. Deductive thinking allows you to be more conclusive, but it is in attempting to reconcile differences that you enter into a process of inductive group thinking that allows the group to find new answers. Often, the only place members of the team or group can meet is in the inductive space. Linearly and deductively, people might always disagree. It's about coming up with better answers, which are then, almost by definition, also innovative.

By focusing on resolving differences, we create a process which is itself inductive, allowing us to find answers that no one member of the group would have found on their own. This is the whole reason we meet. The value created in our meeting should be greater than anything anyone could do on their own.

Framework 2: TAF (Target, Actual, Forecast)

Targets, actuals and forecasts. These three data points are central to so many elements of strategy execution described in this book. As Figure 1.3.3 shows, targets are what we aim to achieve by a point in time. They hold us to account. Actuals are what we did achieve. Forecasts are what we think we will achieve.

Figure 1.3.4 shows **TAF data** in relation to revenue. Actual revenue is lagging far behind the target set and three separate forecasts performed at different moments in time show how the gap will be closed.

FIGURE 1.3.3 TAF data

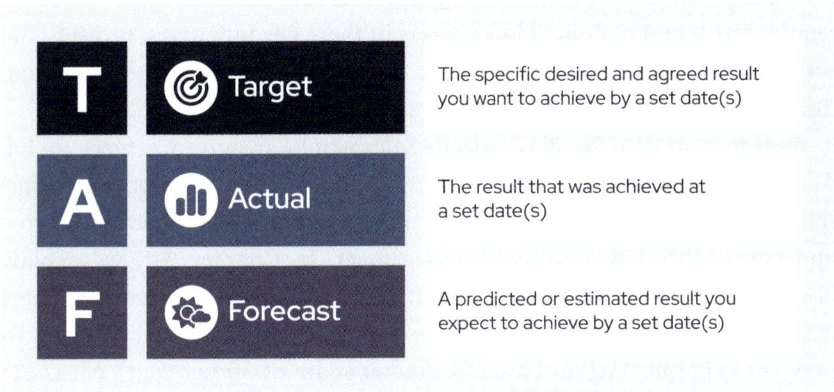

FIGURE 1.3.4 Target, actual and forecast data in relation to revenue

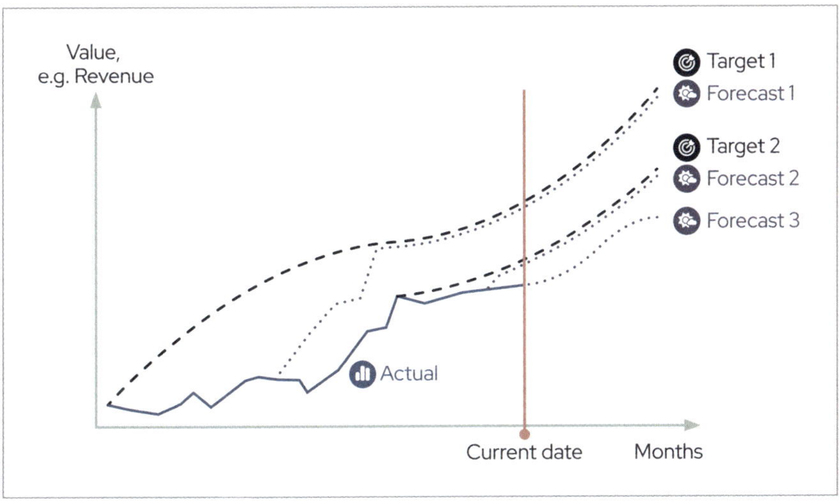

The TAF data points are all connected. Comparing targets to actuals shows us how well we're performing. Comparing targets to forecasts shows how well we think we're going to perform. Comparing actuals to forecasts gives us a window into the accuracy of our predictions. Comparing and triangulating this data provides us with a constant feedback loop so that we can learn and improve. How close are we to hitting target? How far off was our forecast? Most forecasters don't get high-quality feedback on their forecast accuracy. TAF provides that feedback.

You'll find TAF used as a verb throughout this book. Many elements of what we discuss can be **'TAF-arized'**. In Part 3, we explain how to break down large, long-term goals into smaller stepping stone goals. These, in turn, can be broken down into key initiatives and projects. These key initiatives and projects can be broken down further into different types of actions required to get them done. The progress of these key initiatives, projects and actions can be tracked using target dates, our best-guess expected dates and then, the truth. When did we complete it?

Budgets can also be TAF-arized. Salespeople are given targets to hit. Actual revenue can be tracked against these targets and forecast revenue shows the expected outturn. TAF-arizing, planning and budgeting is often understood through objectives management. In Chapter 3.4, we explain how objectives have different types of targets. Some are milestones. These denote a need to complete a certain task by a certain date. Others are measures, for example, 'Achieve a net promoter score of 50 per cent'. Measures can either be static, as in the example just given, or moving, for example sales targets by quarter.

In Chapter 3.3, we explain how to TAF-arize risks by calculating the weighted average impact on the enterprise value at the next landmark. By aggregating risk scores to one metric, you can create a target level of risk (this is the level of risk that the organization can tolerate). The forecast shows the amount of risk that you think you might have to take and actuals are the actual figures related to impact if risk events occur.

TAF data changes over time and it's important to keep track of this and understand what your targets were at any given point in time, as well as actuals and forecasts. Actuals and forecasts change all the time. Targets don't change as much, although they can do so if priorities and realities shift or you have been blown so off track that they've become demotivating.

There are different ways to determine forecasts. You can provide two – a pessimistic one that can be committed to and a best-case one. Revisit your forecasts frequently. In theory, your forecast could change every day as the world evolves. John Maynard Keynes is thought to have said, 'When the facts change, I change my mind. What do you do, sir?' The more you question and learn, the better your forecasts will be. In Chapter 3.3 we talk about the practice of 'superforecasting' concerning risk management. This practice, introduced by Philip E Tetlock and Dan Gardner in their book of the same name, proves that individuals can improve their forecasting accuracy by learning certain methods and techniques.[8] The book demonstrates how it's possible to predict in small increments and update forecasts continually, improving accuracy all the time.

Actuals can also change. You could record something as true only to discover at a later date that it wasn't. For example, you might think you've completed an action, only to find out later that you still had more to do. Financial numbers such as revenue or costs are often restated.

Framework 3: BRAG (Blue, Red, Amber, Green)

The **BRAG** framework is related to TAF. Board packs can contain an overwhelming amount of information – too much for most of us to consume quickly and easily. Many of the techniques and methods we discuss in this book are aimed at reducing cognitive load. BRAG is one of them. It is very similar to RAG, the red, amber, green traffic light system. Colour is used to signify when a project is way off target (red), a little off target (amber) or on target (green). It therefore relates to the actual and target data of TAF.

We have added blue to signify overachievement. If something is coloured blue, it means you're smashing it. You've surpassed the target. This insight might mean that you can increase your ambition. While we realize this breaks the **Rule of Three** (see below), it's worth it to recognize and celebrate overachievement.

When board pack dashboards display key metrics and milestones in their BRAG colour, it enables readers to scan the page quickly and immediately see which ones are a concern. The aim is for board members to 'catch falling knives' and understand which metrics might be leading indicators of your key risks. Chapter 4.2 gives an example of a dashboard that uses BRAG colours to direct focus.

THE ĀRAHI ARROW

BRAG colour status gives only a third of the picture. Trend and volatility complete it. Say you are green, at 101 per cent of the target. Are you happy?

Most would say 'yes'. But what if you were at 111 per cent in the previous period? And 121 per cent, 131 per cent and 141 per cent over the preceding three? How happy would you be then? You are trending down. But even worse than this alarming trend, what if you just have no idea – if the numbers feel random and if there is no process control? If you were 40 per cent of target last quarter, 110 per cent the previous one, 75 per cent before that and a whopping 150 per cent before that? You have no idea where you will be next quarter. This is volatility. It makes it hard to plan and impossible to know.

We bring these three statistics into one visual, the **Ārahi Arrow**, as shown in Figure 1.3.5. It shows the BRAG colours and four different arrows. Arrows can be straight, squiggly or wavy. A straight arrow as shown in the top-left hand box of the figure signifies consistency. A squiggly arrow, as shown in both of the bottom boxes, signifies erratic performance. A wavy arrow, as shown in the top-right amber box, signifies high volatility.

Imagine the following scenario. A board pack shows actuals versus target metrics for two sales reps. One rep is green with a squiggly downward arrow as shown in the bottom-right box of Figure 1.3.5. They are on target, but their performance is erratic and dramatically worsening. The other rep's

FIGURE 1.3.5 The Ārahi Arrow

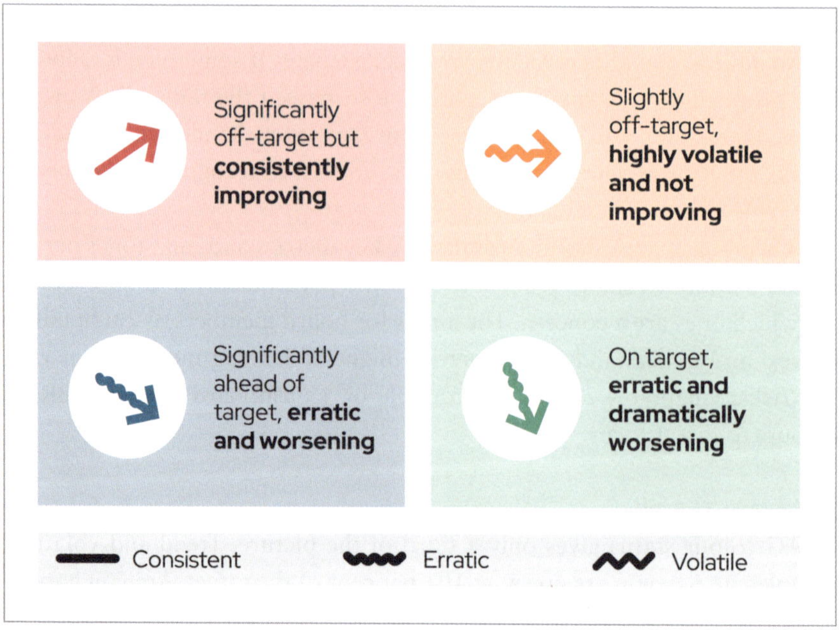

metrics are represented by the arrow in the top-left corner. They are in the red, so they are significantly off target, but they are consistently improving. Who should you be more worried about?

Framework 4: KODs (Key Organizational Dimensions)

Key Organizational Dimensions are the key lenses through which you can view your organization and measure performance. They relate to the different ways that you can slice the organization and therefore the data used to report on it. Targets can be broken down by KODs. Each KOD has an owner who is responsible for that slice of the organization. This owner is likely to have a leadership team. These leadership teams are examples of forums, which we discuss in Chapter 4.3.

There are five KODs that organizations commonly slice by:

1. Function.
2. Geography.
3. Business unit or product.
4. Segment (industry that you sell to).
5. Channel (this can be direct to the customer or indirect through a distributor).

As a rule of thumb, if the board is interested in slicing by something, it means it's a KOD.

One of the main points we make about KODs throughout this book is: complexity kills. As organizations grow, the number of KODs and the number of dimensions within each KOD can proliferate. More targets are set and it can become overwhelming. As an example, think about the board pack and board meetings. Imagine you have two KODs: product and segment. Within these, you have three products and three different segments that you sell to. This means you have nine slices to report on. This translates to nine dashboards in the board pack, nine separate profit and loss accounts and nine pipelines. Say each page takes five minutes to discuss, that's 45 minutes. Now imagine you have three KODs, product, segment and channel, and within these you have four products, four segments and two channels (both direct and indirect). This means you have 32 slices, or 32 pages in the board pack. At five minutes a page, that's 2 hours and 40 minutes' worth of discussion.

There are many examples we can draw on that illustrate the power of keeping things simple. One is Southwest Airlines. The company has two KODs. It operates one type of plane, the Boeing 737, and it has one clear customer segment. Another is Apple. When Steve Jobs took over as CEO in 1997, he famously stripped it right back. The company was on its knees. It had too many products with no clear differentiation strategy. Instead of adding new and advanced products, Jobs started to cut. He got rid of almost everything. He slashed the product portfolio by almost 80 per cent, cutting a list of 15 desktop computers to one and all portable models back to just one laptop. He did this so that he could focus attention on what mattered – bringing innovative, breakthrough products to market.[9] The leadership team at Nokia, who allegedly knew about Jobs' divestment strategy, did not opt to do the same. They chose to maintain the number of product SKUs (stock-keeping units) and customer segments.[10] Complexity pretty much killed the company. They had too many KODs to respond to Apple effectively, even though they knew what was on the horizon.

Framework 5: CRASI (Capture, Responsible, Approver, Supporting, Informed)

CRASI is our accountability framework used to instil a disciplined approach to action management. Many of you will be familiar with the acronym RASCI, an accountability matrix which stands for Responsible (R), Accountable (A), Supporting (S), Consulted (C) and Informed (I). CRASI is similar, but we've adapted it to make it more applicable to action management.

CAPTURE (C)

The person who records the action is the one who captures it. That person owns it until they assign responsibility to someone else and that person accepts it. It's worth noting that often, the Secretary of a meeting will capture all the actions. This doesn't mean that they own all the actions! In this circumstance, the meeting members collectively own the actions until each one is accepted by an individual.

RESPONSIBLE (R)

The responsible person owns the action and is accountable for getting it done. As above, in-out actions tend to be captured and owned by the same person. People responsible for governed actions need to accept the ownership – it can't just be given to them (more on this later).

APPROVER (A)

This is the person or group of individuals (for example, a forum) that needs to approve that the action is done or a decision associated with the action should be taken. If a group of people has approval rights, it can be helpful to introduce a per cent threshold. For example, could a decision go ahead if 50 or 60 per cent of the group agree or do approvers have veto rights? Clarity is everything.

SUPPORTING (S)

A supporting person helps the owner to complete the action. If support is needed to do a specific task within the broader action, you might want to break this out and give the person responsibility for that task with a clear dependency (see Chapters 3.5 and 4.4 for more on dependencies).

INFORMED (I)

Other people might need to be kept informed of progress, key decisions and outcomes. These may be individuals or forums. Some documents need formal updates, for example updates on key initiatives.

RUPERT

I've written about accountability frameworks before in *Data-Driven Organization Design* and *Organizational Planning and Analysis*.[11] In those books, I put forward RAD as an alternative methodology to RASCI for use when designing an organization. RAD simplifies RASCI. It combines the R and A (what's the difference between being responsible and accountable? It's not clear). It adds in a new A for 'Approve' to help clarify the governance. RAD also throws out the C and I of RASCI. In the context of designing an organization, the responsible person can determine who needs to be consulted and kept informed. It takes a lot of effort to define this, and in the context of design, it isn't always necessary. RAD also adds a D for 'Do'.

So why are we proposing yet another accountability framework? Because executing strategy is very different from designing an organization. RAD is too simplistic to be used in the context of action management. But I still believe in the principles that led to its inception. RASCI is still insufficient. CRASI, like RAD, combines the R and the A of RASCI. It adds a C at the beginning for 'Capture' so you have an audit trail and an A for 'Approve'. These are both vital elements to understand. The person who accepts responsibility for an action needs to know who captured it, when it was captured and which meeting it was captured in. They also need to understand who has approval rights. It's helpful for the action owner to know who can help them complete the action, as well as who needs to be kept in the loop.

The five core communication pillars for strategic value creation

Pillar 1: The power of the one-pager

How often have you used the expression 'Let's get on the same page'? It's something that many of us say when we need to agree with others. It means ensuring that everyone has the same understanding of a situation. Everyone has the same facts. In 2003, I (Rupert) was helping with a big government programme worth hundreds of millions of pounds (I describe it in detail in Chapter 3.5). At the time, we asked a dozen of the senior leaders what milestones they were working towards. They all said different things. So, we created a single-page milestone map to get everyone 'on the same page'.

We both strongly believe in the power of distilling a host of information down to one page to make it easy to communicate and understand. This is the goal of a well-designed dashboard and it's also a big goal of this book. It means that all the key information is available at a glance. It provides an easy reference tool and minimizes the chance of misunderstandings. Far too often, strategy and plans exist only in people's heads or are filed away somewhere without being communicated beyond the boardroom. A core, underlying theme of this book is the need for the strategy and plan to be visible, easy to communicate and easy to understand so that decisions taken at the top of the organization can filter down to the day-to-day actions of those on the 'shop floor'.

To this end, we give you a range of single pages, some of which we've designed ourselves, like the **Strategy on a Page (SOAP)** and **Plan on a Page (POAP)**, the **Value-Cap Map** or the **Ārahi Arrow Dashboard.**

JON

One of my first transformation programmes involved running an integration programme for an aerospace business that had just acquired a competitor. I wanted to produce a status report for the CEO, a tough Scotsman whose engineering background had led him to become a rising star in aerospace. I was talking him through the collated information for the numerous workstreams when he stopped me. 'Jon, don't build a monster. We don't want these guys spending so much time reporting. That will kill us. Let's just keep it simple. Just have a one-page summary for each key initiative.' This one-page summary took out the complexity. It was easier to put together and easier to communicate and understand.

The CEO was John Ferrie. He went on to receive the CBE for services to the defence and aerospace industry in the Queen's Honours list of 2004. His statement about not building a monster has stayed with me for over 20 years.

Pillar 2: Visualize to optimize

A picture tells a thousand words. According to statistics, 65 per cent of people are visual learners.[12] This book is intentionally visual with full colour. You represent your perspective by the picture you draw on a page. If you want to give another perspective, draw another picture. Visualizing things in different ways helps you to see things from different angles and points of view. It can broaden your understanding and help you to retain information. There are so many different ways to do it. Simplicity is key. Elaborate visuals lose audiences fast. Even just three lines on a line graph are hard to read.

Stories help you to get to the crux of the matter. Visual stories – cartoons if you like – reduce cognitive load, create connections and elicit emotion. The goal is for the visual to tell a thousand words, not for you to need a thousand words to explain the picture. This is why the combination of a bar chart and a good old-fashioned table is so powerful. The bar chart gives a simple, overall picture while the table shows the details. Visuals help us spot patterns and see outliers. They facilitate debate, questioning and enquiry. They tell a story or perhaps start the process of discovering a new story.

Sometimes, other infographics are helpful, for example interactive bubble charts that change with time. Sankey diagrams show the flow or change from one state to another over time. The key is to use colour and different shapes and sizes to gain a range of perspectives.

We believe in creating a visual language that is easily recognizable and reduces cognitive load. The one-page communication tools we describe in Pillar 1 are designed to be visual. There's a reason why '*Draw* the plan' is in the 4D Framework. You're drawing it. You're creating a visual way for people to understand a wealth of information. Many other tools in this book are also designed as visual aids. Key initiatives are broken down into single-page charters as described in Chapter 3.5. These, in turn, are broken down into integrated Gantt charts and dependency maps. In action management, we use the **Kanban**, another visual tool, for organization actions. Mind maps provide a way to break down an idea or question. The 'why tree' is a particularly useful version of a mind map. It is so simple. All you do is ask a series of 'whys?' and write down the answers, as shown in Figure 1.3.6. For example: Why did you lose the deal? Because service was below par, there were security concerns and you had a poor sales process. Why was service poor? Because the service level agreement (SLA) for inbound query was only four hours. Why? Because the process map wasn't clear and it looked like it had been cobbled together. The winner had a branded process with credible data showing their 98.4 per cent performance within the hour.

In Chapter 4.2, we explain how consistent use of colour in board pack reporting can help the reader quickly understand and absorb what they are looking at. We also advocate adopting a language for line graphs. These might show actuals or forecasts. We draw a monthly actual line more thinly than an LTM (Last Twelve Months) line. We use a solid line for actuals and a dotted line for forecasts. The key is to find a simple language that works and stick to it. This links nicely with our next communication pillar – to make things as simple as possible but no simpler.

Pillar 3: Make things as simple as possible but no simpler

Einstein came up with the idea that things should be as simple as possible but no simpler. This pillar runs through all five of our communication pillars. The one-pager aims to make things as simple as you can. The most effective visualizations are the simple ones. Pillars 4 and 5 relate to refinement and repetition. One goal of refinement is to whittle things down to their simplest form. Repetition involves stating simple, key messages again and again and again. It's not always simple to reach simplicity. As Steve Jobs is thought to have said: 'You have to work hard to get your thinking clean to make it simple. But it's worth it in the end because once you get there, you can move mountains.'

FIGURE 1.3.6 A 'why' tree

This pillar started life as the Rule of Three. We try to adhere to this rule as much as possible. It is a well-known communication tool for writing and speaking and relates to how humans absorb information. We are hardwired to remember things in groups of three. If a list is longer than three, most people will struggle to remember it. This starts in childhood with fairy tales and myths. Think *The Three Little Pigs*, *Goldilocks and the Three Bears* and *The Three Blind Mice*. Jack climbs up the beanstalk three times, the boy cries wolf three times. There were three Musketeers. It's not just the preserve of childhood. The Rule of Three is everywhere – sex, drugs and rock and roll; Father, Son and Holy Ghost; liberté, égalité, fraternité. We could go on…

Interestingly, in *The Bezos Blueprint*, Carmine Gallo discusses a study that found the rule pervades the world of start-ups and venture capital investing. The survey, conducted by DocSend, found that investors spend an average of three minutes reviewing a pitch deck. During those three minutes, they focus on three slides: solution, product and team. They also put more money into start-ups with three founders.[13]

We love the Rule of Three and we advocate sticking to it wherever you can. But there are caveats. While three is an easy number of items to remember, one is even easier. When communicating ideas and thoughts, consider whether there is one key message you want to get across. If there is, start with this. You can always use the Rule of Three to give three supporting points to back up this key message. This idea is advocated in Barbara Minto's *The Pyramid Principle*. The book focuses on the fact that ideas in writing should form a pyramid under a single, key thought. This pyramid is a tool to 'help you find out what you think' before you start to write. The key message at the top of the pyramid is followed by layers of arguments and supporting evidence in a logical order.

Our second caveat is that sometimes, three is just not right. There will be times when try as you might, you really can't whittle things down to three key points. In *The Pyramid Principle*, Minto talks about 'The magic number seven, plus or minus two', which she borrows from George A. Miller, the American psychologist. Miller's point is that the mind cannot hold more than seven items in its short-term memory. Some people will be able to hold up to nine items, and others as few as five. Most of us, as we have seen, like three or, ideally, one.[14] We've tried to stick to this principle in this book with one exception – Chapter 2.3 lists eight components of strategy design. We tried extremely hard to get it down to seven, but it was impossible. So, in summary:

- Isolate the one key thing.
- Find the three next most important things.
- If you really can't stick to three, do your best not to go over seven, plus or minus two.

We delve into this further in Chapter 4.2 in relation to how to write commentary for the board pack. To get it as simple as possible takes iteration and refinement, which is Pillar 4.

Pillar 4: Refine, refine, refine

How often do you strike gold with your thinking first time? Hardly ever? Us neither. Getting things right takes time to understand things better. It takes iteration, refinement and improvement. In this pillar, we focus mainly on the importance of refining language, but refinement applies equally to thinking. The percolation and distillation process described above is all about refinement, as the process of drawing and redrawing, modifying and editing, rethinking and redrawing. It took round after round of iteration and debate before we were happy with our SOAP and POAP.

In Chapter 4.2, we delve into detail about the importance of refining language when writing commentary. But we don't need to watch our words only when writing them down. Words matter in all communication. They drive how you think and act.

One of our favourite books is *Legacy* by James Kerr.[15] It presents fifteen lessons in leadership that can be learned from New Zealand's national rugby team, the All Blacks. We love this book so much that we give a copy to all new starters at Ārahi. The book uncovers what it takes to create a high-performance culture and maintain it over time. Kerr discusses the importance of language at length. In 2003, the All Blacks, by their standards, were failing and losing their way. Rugby had gone professional in 1995. Some players were beginning to believe and act like they were greater than the team. To fix this, they convened a group of six great former and existing players who codified what it meant to be an All Black. One of these was Sir Brian Lochore, a former All Black captain, World Cup-winning coach and the manager of the team during the 1995 'Mandela' World Cup. In his words: 'Great people make great All Blacks.' The statement has stuck with the team ever since. It has become the bedrock of the team's culture. It implies that raw athletic ability and skill are not enough. It was clarified by the introduction of a policy which we can't repeat here because it uses a common expletive for someone who is unpleasant, arrogant and prioritizes themselves. The word used immediately conjures up the image of someone who believes they are greater than the team. Institutionalizing this policy and using this specific language went to the heart of the culture the team wanted to create. Humility became the name of the game. Players were expected to 'sweep the sheds' after games. These New Zealand stars and icons came off the field and didn't leave their changing room until it was as clean as when they found it.

We'd love to know how long it took to come up with this precise language. Messages need to go through a process of refinement before you can nail them. This is particularly important when writing your strategy. There's a lot of language to nail down. In Chapter 2.3 we take you through a process of articulating your passion, ambition, overriding challenge and critical value factors, among other things. There are lots of terms and words to define and it's critical to be precise and to communicate your ideas in a way that can be easily understood by everyone.

Working Backwards, by Colin Bryar and Bill Carr, gives an insider account of what it's like to work at Amazon. At one point in the book, the authors, who were top-level Amazon executives, describe how Amazon's head of human resources, Mike George, and his colleague Robin Andrulevich wanted to nail Amazon's leadership principles. They wanted to achieve this by creating a leadership programme and codifying what it meant to be a great leader at Amazon. They describe how a process that they thought would take two months ended up taking nine. By the time they had finished, they had a list of 14 principles. Each one was drafted based on interviews with effective leaders at Amazon. Each draft was debated. The list was constantly refined, as was the language used within each definition. The result was 14 principles written in tight language that could be understood by everyone throughout the organization. They are listed on Amazon's website (but interestingly, they now have 16, which shows they have continued to refine the list). It's interesting to note that the ninth principle is 'Bias for action'. This principle is particularly aligned with our thinking and philosophy. It is defined as 'Speed matters in business. Many decisions and actions are reversible and do not need extensive study. We value calculated risk-taking.'[16]

These three, punchy sentences articulate exactly what 'Bias for action' means. Any existing or aspiring Amazon leader can immediately see how to use this principle to inform their decision-making and action.

JON

When we founded Ārahi, we knew we needed to nail the language that we used. We spent a week off-site in Cornwall debating and honing our key messages. We percolated and distilled (we went for walks and planted hedgerows with a local charity to help this process along).

One thing we wrestled long and hard about was how we would describe our platform, which we call a console. Rupert said it had to be beautiful, but others didn't agree, particularly our lead developer, Alex. He pushed back and the debate became quite heated. 'How can you argue with beauty?' Rupert cried. 'We want to live in a beautiful world. Nature is beautiful and relaxing. Sunsets are undeniably beautiful. We want our console to make people feel as relaxed as they do when looking at a sunset or walking in autumnal woods.' Alex just didn't agree. The word didn't sit right with him. He pointed out that you *can* argue with the notion of beauty: 'Beauty is subjective. It's in the eye of the beholder. It can mean many different things to many different people. It can be superficial. Maths, on the other hand, is elegant. You can't argue with elegance.'

Boom. We all got it. Elegance it was and is. Elegance is our aspiration. Every time we look at the design of the console we ask: 'Is this elegant?'

Pillar 5: Repeat, repeat, repeat

In *Working Backwards*, Bryar and Carr describe at length how Bezos repeated mantras to get them at the forefront of people's minds. The 16 leadership principles are one example. The authors describe how they are repeated over and over again through different mechanisms. For example, a 'Just Do It' award is given to employees who best exhibit the Bias for Action principle. The prize is an 'abnormally large, well-worn Nike sneaker'.

We mentioned another book about Amazon, *The Bezos Blueprint*, earlier in the chapter. In it, Carmine Gallo describes how Bezos turned Amazon's mission of customer obsession into a mantra. He repeated it relentlessly in interviews, shareholder letters, speeches, and memos until everyone internalized it. It became part of who they were.[17]

In Chapter 4.3 we talk about the importance of the notion 'Tell them what you're going to tell them, tell them, tell them what you told them'. There, we talk about it in relation to chairing meetings, but it's useful advice for all communication. It's a way of repeating key messages and ensuring that they end on the points that you want people to remember. Repeating key messages, missions and principles in well-defined and consistent language ensures that, over time, they will start to drive culture and frame how people get things done. People (staff) generally need to be told a key message at least three times before it begins to resonate and take hold.

Final thoughts

The truths, frameworks and communication pillars described in this chapter are very much connected. They go to the heart of the key themes penetrating the chapters of this book. The need to continually ask good questions to reach the right action is key. QFOR-A helps with this discipline, as does visualization. Seeing things in different ways provokes new lines of inquiry. Questioning also helps the refinement process. The more you question, the more you improve your thinking and the more you refine.

Another key point is discipline. Here, we are very much aligned with Jim Collins and his concept of a Culture of Discipline. Collins talks about disciplined people who engage in disciplined thought and take disciplined action. We couldn't agree more. We hope that the five frameworks we provide go some way to encouraging such a culture. QFOR-A helps to structure thoughts and keep meetings on track. It ensures that all questions result in a 'So what?' – a recommendation that leads to action. TAF encourages a disciplined approach to target setting and forecasting. By comparing forecast and actual data, you can get feedback on your forecast accuracy and constantly seek to improve. Both BRAG and KODs encourage a disciplined approach to board pack reporting. CRASI is our answer to how to be disciplined in your action management.

We hope that you find the truths, frameworks and communication pillars helpful in designing and executing strategy in your organization. The ideas we have described will help you to navigate the rest of this book.

REMEMBER THIS

1. Never stop thinking, questioning and learning.
2. Everything is connected and nothing is linear. Be ready to follow the tangled path.
3. Value creation is a dynamic, living and breathing process.
4. The questions you ask are important. Use them to reconcile differences and reach better answers.
5. Think about how you communicate your messages. Communicate them again and again and again.

Notes

1 Papadopoulos, N (2020) The question is the answer part 2: Why we stop asking questions and how to start again, Metalearn, 9 March, www.metalearn.net/the-question-is-the-answer-part-2-why-we-stop-asking-questions-and-how-to-start-again/#:~:text=Research%20by%20Harvard%20child%20psychologist,day%20but%20then%2C%20something%20happens (archived at https://perma.cc/3XAD-85W6)

2 Collins, J (2001) *Good to Great: Why some companies make the leap... and others don't*, HarperBusiness, New York

3 Freiberg, K and Freiberg, J (1998) *Nuts!: Southwest Airline's crazy recipe for business and personal success*, Broadway Books, New York

4 Reichheld, F (2001) *The Loyalty Effect: The hidden force behind growth, profits, and lasting value*, Harvard Business Review Press, Boston

5 Shipley, A (2020) Photo shows paint peeling off Forth Bridge nine years after '25-year paint job', Daily Record, 21 July, www.dailyrecord.co.uk/news/scottish-news/photo-shows-paint-peeling-forth-22386716 (archived at https://perma.cc/ZZ5H-A9K8)

6 Freiberg, K and Freiberg, J (1998) *Nuts!: Southwest Airline's crazy recipe for business and personal success*, Broadway Books, New York

7 Mattu, R (2023) Who would want to be a CEO?, The New York Times, 14 May, www.nytimes.com/2023/05/14/business/dealbook/ceo-politics-chatgpt.html#:~:text="It%27s%20frankly%20a%20horrible%20job,It%20consumes%20your%20weekend

8 Tetlock, P E and Gardner, D (2016) *Superforecasting: The art and science of prediction*, Random House Books, New York

9 Srinivasan, R (2022) How did Steve Jobs save Apple using the Law of Elimination?, LinkedIn, 19 April, www.linkedin.com/pulse/how-did-steve-jobs-save-apple-using-law-elimination-srinivasan-/ (archived at https://perma.cc/6K9K-AV6E)

10 Rumelt, R (2022) *The Crux: How leaders become strategists*, Profile Books, London

11 When doing organization design and assigning accountability to roles, I prefer to use RAD: who is Responsible, who Approves; who actually Does the work. There should only be one 'R', i.e. a single point of accountability. But there might be multiple approvers and doers. See *Data-Driven Organization Design* for a more in-depth explanation of what should be done with the 'ASI' letters.

12 Zopf, R, Giabbiconi, C M, Gruber, T and Müller, M (2004) Attentional modulation of the human somatosensory evoked potential in a trial-by-trial spatial cueing and sustained spatial attention task measured with high density 128 channels EEG, PubMed, 20 (3), pubmed.ncbi.nlm.nih.gov/15268926/ (archived at https://perma.cc/G4CG-6BTK)

13 Gallo, C (2022) *The Bezos Blueprint: Communication secrets that power Amazon's success*, Macmillan, London

14 Minto, B (2021) *The Pyramid Principle: Logic in writing and thinking* (3e), Pearson Education, Harlow

15 Kerr, J (2013) *Legacy: What the All Blacks can teach us about the business of life*, Constable, London

16 Bryar, C and Carr, B (2021) *Working Backwards: Insights, stories and secrets from inside Amazon*, Macmillan, London

17 Gallo, C (2022) *The Bezos Blueprint: Communication secrets that power Amazon's success*, Macmillan, London

PART TWO

Diagnose today and Design tomorrow

2.1

What is strategy?

Strategy is the way you design a unique set of capabilities to deliver differentiating value factors, overcome your key challenge and economically fulfil your purpose and ambition

What do the words 'literally', 'genius' and 'random' all have in common? All of them have been abused, so much so that they have literally (yes, literally) lost their meaning. 'Literally' no longer means 'actually'. Sometimes it does, but it's often used as a throwaway intensifier: 'Did you literally just say that?' 'Genius' is the same. It's not uncommon to call someone a 'genius' for doing something as everyday as recommending a good sandwich filling. In the past, 'random' just referred to something unpredictable. Now, it's used to describe people who don't conform: 'She's a bit of a random' or people you don't know: 'I got chatting to some randoms on the train.'

What does this have to do with strategy? 'Strategy' is another word that's lost its meaning. The business world adopted it from the military, where it was well understood. Once it became subsumed into the day-to-day business lexicon, it came to mean many different things. Try Googling 'meaning of strategy'. It returns about two billion answers. How can this be? How can this one word, which in essence signifies whether a company is destined to thrive or fail, mean so many different things?

This observation is not new. Most management books make it at some point. Richard Rumelt, in his book *Good Strategy/Bad Strategy*, refers to the word 'strategy' as a 'verbal tic': 'A word that can mean anything has lost its bite... To begin the journey toward clarity, it is helpful to recognize that the words "strategy" and "strategic" are often sloppily used to mark decisions made by the highest-level officials.'[1] Rumelt first wrote about this in 2011. As we write this, nearly 13 years later, nothing has changed.

This confusion means that true strategy is very hard to find. You don't see it very often. You see other things or activities labelled as strategy, and there are huge numbers of strategy 'experts' and consultants, but what they're doing can't always be described as strategy. Important and high-impact work, yes. But strategy? No. I (Rupert) found this in my work as an organization design consultant. Organization design stems from a firm's strategy. Time and time again, when I asked clients to show me their strategy, I'd be handed a list of objectives or goals: 'We want to be number one.' Their 'strategy' was almost always centred on what they wanted to achieve, not how they were going to achieve it. When I asked the 'how' question, I was often met with stunned silence. If you don't know how you're going to do it, the 'what' has very little context or meaning. It's easy to fall foul of this. Grand statements are exciting. They make you feel good. It's exhilarating to think about your vision, mission statement, your 'why' and your biggest, most exciting goals. But there's little point in any of it if it doesn't get to the 'how'.

It only takes a little digging to reveal a total lack of consistency between definitions of strategy. Here are two examples:

- 'A general plan or set of plans intended to achieve something, especially over a long period' (*Collins Dictionary*).[2]
- 'An action that managers take to attain one or more of the organization's goals' or 'A general direction set for the company and its various components to achieve a desired state in the future. Strategy results from the detailed strategic planning process'. (*Management Study Guide*).[3]

These definitions agree that strategy is about achieving something in the future. The *Management Study Guide*'s definition describes strategy as 'an action'. This is another helpful point that will be developed throughout this book.

Look to the best: the strategy greats

The chapters in Part 2 draw heavily on the work of several great strategy thinkers: Michael Porter, Richard Rumelt, Jim Collins, Simon Sinek, Roger Martin and Alan G Lafley, Renée Mauborgne and W Chan Kim and Michael D Watkins. Each of these thinkers defines strategy in a slightly different way, using different vocabulary and frameworks. But, as we hope to demonstrate, the underlying messages and key themes running throughout this huge body of work are very similar.

- Michael Porter, a professor from Harvard Business School, is regarded by many as the father of the modern strategy field. He has authored 19 books, including *Competitive Strategy*, *Competitive Advantage* and *On Competition*.
- Richard Rumelt is a professor emeritus at Anderson School of Management, University of California, Los Angeles. His 2011 book *Good Strategy/Bad Strategy* redefined strategy as a form of problem-solving. He went further in 2022 with his book *The Crux*, in which he developed his idea of 'challenge-based strategy'. This involves identifying your most critical challenges and devising policies and concrete actions to resolve them.
- Jim Collins is a researcher and consultant focused on business management, company sustainability and growth. He has authored six books based on his research. In these chapters we use concepts from two of his best: *Built to Last* and *Good to Great*. We discussed his Culture of Discipline in Chapter 1.3 and touched on his concept, Confront the Brutal Facts. We pick up on these again in Part 2 as well as looking at the Hedgehog Concept and the BHAG.
- Simon Sinek is the author of five books, including *Start with Why* which we introduced in Chapter 1.2. This is an important concept to understand when designing strategy. He is credited with the fourth most-watched TED Talk of all time (with more than 60 million views).[4]
- Alan G. Lafley is a businessman who led Procter & Gamble as chairman, president and CEO. He worked in partnership with his strategic advisor, Roger Martin, professor emeritus at the Rotman School of Management at the University of Toronto. Lafley led the company from 2000 to 2009 and in that time doubled sales, quadrupled profits and increased market value by more than $100 billion.[5] Together, they wrote *Playing to Win*, which describes their five steps for developing successful business strategy.
- Renée Mauborne and W Chan Kim are professors of strategy at INSEAD and creators of Blue Ocean Strategy. They authored a book of the same name which describes how to stop vying with the sharks in red oceans and instead create new demand and swim in blue oceans of uncontested marketspace.

- Michael D Watkins is a professor of leadership and organizational change at IMD. He is the author of several books, including *The First 90 Days*. In this chapter, we draw on his definition of strategy given in a 2007 *Harvard Business Review* article 'Demystifying strategy: The what, who, how and why'.[6]

Defining strategy

We believe that the most helpful definitions of business strategy come from Michael Porter, Richard Rumelt, Alan G. Lafley and Roger Martin, and Michael D Watkins.

In 1996, Porter published a seminal article in *Harvard Business Review* called 'What is strategy?' In it, he defined strategy as 'the creation of a unique and valuable position involving a different set of activities'.[7] For him, strategy is all about competition. He gives us Three Generic Strategies for how to differentiate from the competition. He discusses the importance of creating an economic moat to protect a company's profits from competitors.[8]

In *Good Strategy/Bad Strategy*, Rumelt defines the 'kernel' of good strategy as 'an effective mixture of thought and action with a basic underlying structure'. The kernel contains three elements, which answer the 'why', 'what' and 'how':

- Diagnosis of the problem (why): a good diagnosis defines or explains the nature of the challenge. It simplifies the often overwhelming complexity of reality by identifying certain aspects of the situation as critical.
- Guiding policy (what): a guiding policy is an overall approach that guides decision-making so that the obstacles identified in the diagnosis can be overcome.
- Coherent actions (how): a coordinated set of actions carries out the guiding policy.[9]

In *Playing to Win*, authors Alan G Lafley and Roger Martin define strategy as 'an integrated set of choices that uniquely positions the firm in its industry so as to create sustainable advantage and superior value relative to the competition'. Specifically, they say that strategy is the answer to five interrelated questions:

1. *What is your winning aspiration?* The purpose of your enterprise, its motivating aspiration.

2 *Where will you play?* A playing field where you can achieve that aspiration.
3 *How will you win?* The way you will win on the chosen playing field.
4 *What capabilities must be in place?* The set and configuration of capabilities required to win in the chosen way.
5 *What management systems are required?* The systems and measures that enable the capabilities and support the choices.

These questions are connected. Lafley and Martin emphasize that you can't answer any individual question until you've addressed all of them.[10]

Michael D Watkins defines strategy as 'a set of guiding principles that, when communicated and adopted in the organization, generates a desired pattern of decision making'. He explains that a strategy is how people 'make decisions and allocate resources in order to accomplish key objectives'.[11]

As well as providing the best definitions of strategy around, these great thinkers are fairly aligned on what strategy is not. Watkins, in the same article, explains how strategy is often confused with mission (what the organization's leaders want to accomplish), goals (what missions get turned into), value network (the web of relationships within which organizations co-create and capture value) or vision ('an inspiring portrait of what it will look and feel like to pursue and achieve the organization's mission and goals'). (It's worth noting that many of these are vital ingredients in a good strategy, even if they don't constitute a strategy by themselves.)

Rumelt agrees. In *Good Strategy/Bad Strategy*, he explains how organizations have become caught up in the concept of Management by Objectives. Many organizations become so laser-focused on their objectives that they mistake them for their 'strategy'. When asked about their strategy, they give a list of goals or aspirations: 'We want to grow by X amount', 'We want to increase our profits by X' or 'We want to keep our customers happy.' Great objectives, not-so-great strategy.

Porter articulates 'flawed concepts of strategy' where strategy is mistaken for one of three things:

- An aspiration: 'We want to be the best in the world', 'our strategy is to grow'.
- An action: 'Our strategy is to internationalize', 'our strategy is to outsource'.
- A vision: 'Our strategy is to provide superior products and services', 'our strategy is to advance technology for mankind'.[12]

What can we learn from this? This book aims to give you the frameworks to implement strategy according to the key points in these definitions. Some frameworks are provided by the authors of these definitions, but not all of them. Considered as a whole, four main points emerge from the definitions of what strategy is. Strategy involves:

1 The diagnosis of your problem (see Chapter 2.2).
2 The creation of a unique and valuable position (see Chapters 2.2 and 2.3).
3 The construction of a guiding policy or set of principles to steer decision-making (see Chapter 2.3).
4 Linking decisions to coherent actions or activities so that you can accomplish your objectives (see Chapter 2.3).

These defining ideas have informed the first two 'Ds' of the 4D Framework: 'Diagnose today' and 'Design tomorrow' (for a full explanation of the 4D Framework, return to Chapter 1.1). Rumelt's diagnosis is central to 'Diagnose today', the subject of Chapter 2.2. You can't design your future unless you know where you're starting from. Diagnosing your problem involves understanding why you exist, what you sell and who you sell it to. It means articulating what you're good at as well as what you're not so good at. It forms the baseline from which you can determine the activities going forward that will help you to win tomorrow. It involves understanding your total truth.

The other three points form the essence of 'Design tomorrow', the subject of Chapter 2.3. The primary point is the need to create a unique and valuable position. You create this by doing something different. Success often comes with doing the polar opposite of what everyone else is doing. Take Southwest Airlines. When it was incorporated in 1967, all the other airlines were full-service operations. Southwest did the opposite of everybody else. Instead of providing a full service, it provided almost no service. It stripped everything back. Rather than operating out of hub airports, it was point-to-point. This strategy set the airline apart. By definition, that's what a strategy should do. If your 'strategy' doesn't do this, it isn't a strategy.

Do something different (and be careful about benchmarking)

Be careful about benchmarking against the competition at the exclusion of anything else. It can be a helpful practice and a large part of 'Diagnosing today' involves collecting data on your competitors to understand how you compare. In Chapter 1.3 we wrote about the need to continuously scan the horizon and understand how competitors might be able to take you down. This is all part of benchmarking.

However, it can be equally as dangerous to focus exclusively on what your competitors are doing. If all you do is benchmark against them, it can give rise to copycat strategy. Over time, companies that only take this approach can lose their competitive edge. Continental Airlines formed Continental Lite to compete with Southwest. It copied certain elements only (such as low-cost fares and no meals); it didn't copy all of them (it kept baggage transfers and travel agents, for example). It wasn't good enough to compete in the same market space and folded after just two years.

Copycat strategy often constitutes nothing but a willing engagement in a race to the bottom on price. As Lafley and Martin state: 'Sameness isn't a strategy. It's a recipe for mediocrity.'[13] To understand this, it's helpful to think in terms of Michael Porter's framework, Three Generic Strategies.[14] Porter asserts that strategy is about positioning; specifically, creating a unique and valuable competitive position. He lists three ways companies can choose to position themselves to create a 'moat' – a protective layer around the business.

1. Differentiation (provide a unique set of value factors)

For Porter, businesses can differentiate themselves by creating a unique product or service which is perceived by customers as better than competitor offerings. This tallies with Renée Mauborgne and W Chan Kim's Blue Ocean Strategy, which we draw on in Chapter 2.2 to describe how to design your value landscape. This is a process for differentiating. The authors discuss the need to create 'uncontested market space' which makes the competition irrelevant. They talk about the importance of defining the 'factors' that make companies unique. In this book, we refer to these as 'value factors'. Value factors are features of products and services that customers value and that influence initial and ongoing purchase decisions. They should form the bedrock of any company's differentiation strategy. If you adopted a differentiation strategy, you would aim to have a unique set of value factors that a broad range of segments value. This is in contrast to a 'differentiation focus', which we explain below.

2. Focus (target a niche)

Focus includes both cost focus and differentiation focus. If you decide to compete based on cost focus, you become the lowest-cost producer in a niche market. If you decide to compete based on differentiation focus, you provide customized products for a niche market. Either way, you're targeting a niche – a tightly defined customer segment you can own and that matches the relative strengths of your value factors. You do this by identifying the needs of the customer segment and developing products or services to meet that need. If you do organization design for government, you do a generic activity (organization design) for a niche (government). If you're an environmental, social and governance (ESG) consultant for oil and gas, ESG consulting is your generic activity and oil and gas is your niche. In the context of the value landscape, a group of customers that values the same factors, in the same way, forms a market segment or a niche which you can target.

For example, the architecture firm Populous has a big focus on spaces, from stadiums and arenas to airports, with one question in common: How do you keep people coming back time and again? Their website is full of images of crowds having huge experiences together. They cite expertise such as 'wayfinding' (getting people to where they want to go) and 'event design'.[15] They focus on targeting a niche. Foster + Partners has also designed stadiums, e.g. Wembley Stadium in London, but their website talks about a vast and diverse portfolio of architecture from the Mayo Clinic to the Kingdom of Saudi Arabia's Pavilion. They cite services from engineering to industrial design to workplace consultancy.[16] Foster + Partners is differentiated through the services they provide, but they are not targeting a niche.

3. Cost leadership (operational excellence)

Cost leadership requires a business to become the lowest-cost manufacturer or provider of a product or service. In effect, this means competing on operational excellence – companies aim to be more efficient, faster and slicker so that they can win on price and achieve higher margins. If you win in your marketplace through operational excellence, you'll do the same things as everyone else but quicker, or cheaper. In Porter's words, you'll be 'performing similar activities better than rivals perform them'.[17] Price will be your only point of differentiation. While this might work in the short term, choosing this path is not a long-term strategy for success. A new entrant could replicate

FIGURE 2.1.1 Long-term value comes from carving a unique and sustainable competitive position

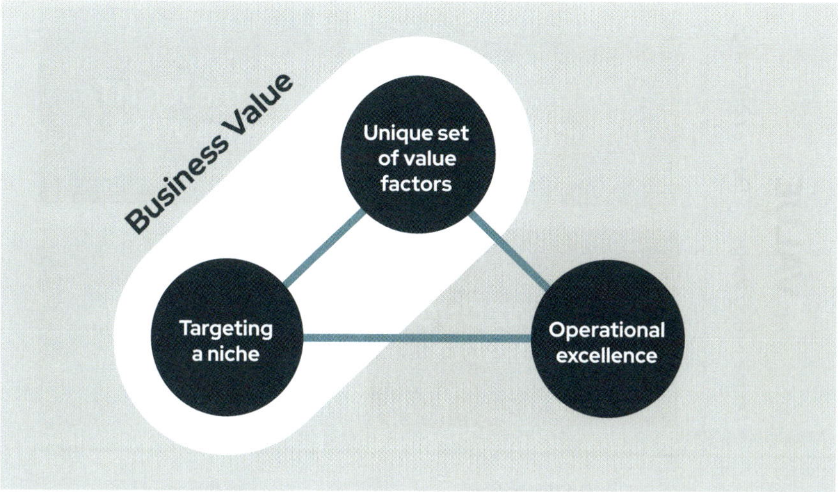

what you're doing but do it more efficiently than you. The longer you try to hold this position, the greater the chances that your technology or infrastructure will become out of date and superseded by a newer, faster and cheaper innovation. Companies that take this approach find themselves in a race to the bottom on price. As Porter says, 'few companies have competed successfully on the basis of operational effectiveness over an extended period'.

Within the context of the terminology we use in this book, these three ways of competing can be understood as shown in Figure 2.1.1. As the figure shows, we like to think of determining a 'unique set of value factors' and 'targeting a niche' as a continuum of how you're winning and making the competition irrelevant. Operational excellence is how you're driving profitability. It's important to note that it's not an either/or trade-off. Operational excellence is still something to aim for, even if you plan to win by targeting a niche and/or creating a unique set of value factors.

Figure 2.1.2 shows that value creation isn't just about doing the right things. If you do the right things well, you'll create value, but if you do the right things badly, profitability will suffer. The bottom-right quadrant is a likely best-case scenario for a company that chooses to compete solely on operational excellence. If they make it to the top-right, it'll be a fluke. As a CEO or leader, ask yourself, are you close to operational excellence? Are you doing the right things well? Are you measuring the right metrics so that you know?

FIGURE 2.1.2 Do the right things well

MOUSETRAP STRATEGY

Another way to think about how you want to compete is to frame strategic decision-making in terms of three choices: do something cheaper, do something better or change the game. Imagine you're in the pest control business. You have lots of competitors who all produce mousetraps. What should you do?

1 You could simply produce another mousetrap which is the same as everyone else's but cheaper. You could make everything about cost and efficiency by simply taking the standard design, offshoring the production and distributing in a low-cost way. If you want the cheapest mousetrap that can be produced at scale, this is the direction you could take. But you're not going to change the world and you'll always be looking over your shoulder in case someone's about to find a cheaper and more efficient way to produce their mousetrap than you.

2 You could opt to produce a better mousetrap than your competitors' mousetraps. Perhaps this could be a trap that catches multiple mice at one time or comes with irresistible food inside it. Or it could be one where the mouse enters and gets trapped inside so that you can't smell it.

How about an Internet of Things mousetrap that records the number of mice you've trapped? It could tell you which part of the house and at what time of day they were caught. It would collect all sorts of data to tell you how effective you are at capturing mice. The device would do the same thing but do a better job, which would mean you could charge more. But your competitive landscape would look quite similar to the landscape for Option 1.

3 Your third option is to change the game and create your own space, so you can forget about the mousetrap competitors. You could create a pest control solution that doesn't trap mice – it stops them from entering a property in the first place. This could be an electronic device that emits an ultrasonic sound. This device would eradicate the need for mousetraps and it would also deter rats and squirrels.

Apple is an example of a company that changed the game. The iPhone wasn't just a phone. It was a music player, camera and satellite navigation system all rolled into one. When it was launched in 2007, things became very difficult for TomTom, Sony and its very own iPod. Chapter 3.3 discusses risk. Risk management should always consider how someone might change the game on you. Breakthroughs happen only when you are the change-maker, not the other way around.

How to be different

For Porter, if operational effectiveness means performing similar activities better than rivals perform them, strategic positioning means 'performing different activities from rivals and performing similar activities in different ways'. In other words, to be strategic, you need to do something different. Entrepreneur and venture capitalist Peter Thiel agrees. In a 2014 lecture given at Stanford Center for Professional Development titled 'Competition is for losers', he stated, 'All happy companies are happy because they are unique… doing something in their own way.'[18]

Lafley and Martin talk about where to play and how to win.[19] Where to play is about selecting the right playing field – which regions, customers, products, channels and stages of production will you choose? Ryanair's strategy was to be the same as Southwest but in a different region of the world. Lafley and Martin describe their work with Procter & Gamble to turn around the failing Oil of Olay brand by tightening up its 'where to play' choices. They previously played in the category of women aged 50 and above, whose main concern is hiding or reducing their wrinkles. But Oil of Olay was becoming known as an 'old woman's cream'. They made Olay different by shifting to target women aged 35 to 50. These women had different concerns – they wanted to prevent ageing, not hide it. They might have been experiencing the first signs of ageing but also had other concerns such as dry or oily skin. This segment wasn't being targeted by anyone else.

How to win is about choosing how you will win on the field. Richard Thompson, who we introduced in Chapter 1.1, liked to invest in companies that integrated different worlds. He invested in Concentra Analytics because it integrated the management consultancy and tech worlds in the organization design space. Another way to create difference through the 'how' is to do what someone else is doing via a different mechanism. Workday and Salesforce replicated the 'on-premise' leaders (PeopleSoft and Cyborg) but did it via a different mechanism – the cloud. And then there's vertical stages of production. Apple famously uses a vertical integration strategy, when a company controls everything from manufacturing to distribution. Apple designs and manufactures its products and then sells them online and through physical Apple stores. The same is true for the automotive industry. Companies like Ford produce components and vehicles and sell them to customers. Other companies in other industries do the opposite. There is no formula or recipe. Anything could be possible. The important thing is that you don't simply copy someone else.

Differentiation comes from an insight. It often comes from the crux of a question. Rumelt developed the concept of the diagnostic question in his 2022 book *The Crux*.[20] It's probably the hardest thing to identify and often comes from felt pain. My (Rupert's) pain of trying to do organization design work in Excel and PowerPoint led to me founding Concentra Analytics. In Chapter 3.3 we talk about the circumstances that led to Zoom Communications. This company was also founded by someone who had felt customers' pain and wanted to create something more suited to their needs.

Sometimes, differentiation is born out of necessity. Logic will get you from A to B. Imagination will take you everywhere.[21] But necessity is the mother of all invention. IKEA is a case in point. The company's story is told by Jérôme Barthêlemy in his book *Myths of Strategy*.[22] Ingvar Kamprad, IKEA's founder, started the company as a mail-order business and quickly decided to focus on his most popular offering: home furnishings. But at that point, the company did not produce furniture, it simply sold it, at a very low price. These low prices angered some of IKEA's competitors, who put pressure on Scandinavian suppliers to boycott the company. The boycott meant that Kamprad had to make some changes. As the company could no longer buy the same furniture that others were buying, it started to design its own, but not in Scandinavia – in Poland. Barthêlemy points out that while many have interpreted this decision as astute and pre-planned, it was not. It was 'a desperate response to the boycott organized by the Swedish furniture sellers' cartel'. It had a happy ending, as it led to the distinctive design which is central to IKEA's success.

Barthêlemy also discusses the role that insurance companies played in IKEA's decision to transition to flat-pack, self-assembly furniture. While IKEA didn't invent the idea of shipping furniture in flatpacks, it took it to a whole new level by shipping directly to customers at scale. At this point, the company was still a mail-order business. The distribution process was complicated and expensive and many items, especially tables, were damaged in transit. The insurance companies weren't happy and put pressure on Kamprad (who was also annoyed about the expense of the distribution process) to find another way. So, IKEA flatpack furniture was born. As Kamprad put it: 'The more "knockdown" we could produce, the less damage occurred during transport and the lower freight costs.'

The Ārahi definition of strategy

For us, the following summarizes the fundamental aspects of a winning strategy. We have three different versions of the definition, **'full-fat'**, **'semi-skimmed'** and **'skimmed'**. (In the UK, these are the three main types of milk you can buy. For our US readers, they are the equivalent of 'whole', 'reduced-fat' and 'low-fat' milks.)

Our 'full-fat' definition of strategy:

> The way you design a unique set of capabilities to deliver differentiating value factors, overcome your key challenge and economically fulfil your purpose and ambition.

It is based on the following seven convictions:

1 Good strategy meets your purpose and ambition. If it doesn't, it's not going to work. This is similar to Martin and Lafley's winning aspiration.
2 As Collins notes, who you are is vital. The top team shapes the culture and it must be embodied in everything you stand for and everything you do.

3 Arriving at a winning strategy involves articulating your key challenge, which changes with time, as described by Rumelt.
4 Strategy should differentiate you from the competition in the eyes of your target segment(s). Aim to make the competition irrelevant. This idea is central to Porter's thinking as well as Mauborgne and Kim's.
5 Customers should be at the heart of everything you do. It's all about adding value for them. This is embodied in Peter Thiel's *Zero to One* and the way that Amazon grew to greatness.
6 You can't think about the 'what' if you don't also think about the 'how' or the 'why'. The 'why' is your purpose. We put particular emphasis on the 'how' – on augmenting certain value factors and capabilities to find points of differentiation so that you don't have to compete solely on price.
7 Strategy can work only if you have the right cash engine to enable it. Jim Collins discusses this with his Hedgehog Concept (see Chapter 2.3).[23]

We appreciate that our 'full-fat' version is a bit of a mouthful. Our 'semi-skimmed' version is therefore 'The way you design a unique set of capabilities to deliver differentiating value factors'. If you want a 'skimmed' version we would advocate going with Lafley and Martin's 'Where to play and how to win'. This simple phrase sums up the essence of strategy, though it does miss a lot of elements which allow for a more nuanced understanding.

Structure and logic for Part 2

This part of the book takes you through the first two of the Four Ds (see Chapter 1.1). This is where you Diagnose today and Design tomorrow before Drawing and Delivering the plan (the subjects of Parts 3 and 4). Chapter 2.2 looks at Diagnosing today. The process involves quantifying the value you currently deliver and comparing it to that which your competitors deliver. It's a way of achieving absolute clarity on what you are good at and what your competitors are good at. It's also about understanding the importance of that value to the people that matter. This is a vital first step in strategy design and provides a baseline from which you can 'Design tomorrow'.

Once you understand your current situation you can Design tomorrow – the second D in the 4D Framework and the subject of Chapter 2.3. Designing tomorrow is about determining how you are going to deliver value to your customers in the future so that you can beat your competitors and win. It's about articulating an ambitious and desirable yet achievable future state. In this chapter, we introduce **PACCTACC**, our process for designing tomorrow. It stands for Purpose, Ambition, Challenge, Critical value factors, Target segments, Arranged capabilities, Competition and Cash generation. These are all crucial elements to nail down when designing strategy. PACCTACC is derived from our definition of strategy.

We draw on two case studies throughout this part. The first is a relatively mature B2B branding agency which we use in Chapter 2.2. This case study shows how value factor work can trigger a dramatic rethink about why you do what you do and what you are ambitious for. The second case study is a fairly new consumer retail business with huge ambition. It's a grocery store in Rupert's neighbourhood. We use this case study in Chapter 2.3 to demonstrate how to use PACCTACC to Design tomorrow. We hope to demonstrate through these two businesses that our methods for Diagnosing today and Designing tomorrow have broad applicability.

These chapters are written linearly, but it is far from a gated process. The last thing we want to do is imply that either diagnosing or designing is a 'one and done' activity. In reality, you diagnose and design iteratively without clear boundaries between the two. While we describe PACCTACC as a mechanism for Designing tomorrow, you also need to understand where you are today for each of the elements, so it forms part of the diagnosis. This is the process we use in our work alongside CEOs. It's necessary to understand how you currently answer each element of PACCTACC before determining how you want them to evolve. It's a great way of diagnosing your current situation.

Note that in these chapters we focus on just one of the Cornerstones of Corporate Health (see Chapter 1.1). We do a deep dive into diagnosing who your customers are and the value proposition for your customers. A complete diagnosis and design would involve performing a similar exercise for all four Cornerstones – people health, impact health and financial and operational health.

In hindsight, strategy is almost always obvious. Once you get there, you won't believe that it took you years of thinking, wrestling and debating to reach it. But that's the beauty of it. If it's too complicated or feels uncomfortable in any way, you might want to question whether it is the right strategy for you.

Notes

1 Rumelt, R (2011) *Good Strategy/Bad Strategy: The difference and why it matters*, Crown Currency, New York

2 Collins Dictionary, Strategy definition, https://www.collinsdictionary.com/dictionary/english/strategy#:~:text=A%20strategy%20is%20a%20general,especially%20over%20a%20long%20period (archived at https://perma.cc/WG22-S9H6)

3 Management Study Guide, Strategy – definition and features, https://www.managementstudyguide.com/strategy-definition.htm (archived at https://perma.cc/SA2U-UA73)

4 Fleck, A (2023) The most popular TED Talks of all time, Statista, 17 April, https://www.statista.com/chart/29742/most-popular-ted-talks/#:~:text=TED%20Conference&text=In%20first%20place%20comes%20Sir,with%20almost%2075%20million%20views (archived at https://perma.cc/DXE9-XWF5)

5 Harvard Business Review, This is A.G. Lafley's guidebook. Shouldn't it be yours as well?, https://hbr.org/books/playing-to-win (archived at https://perma.cc/PE5C-VY7A)

6 Watkins, M D (2007) Demystifying strategy: The what, who, how, and why, Harvard Business Review, 10 September, https://hbr.org/2007/09/demystifying-strategy-the-what (archived at https://perma.cc/VDP2-LSL3)

7 Porter, M E (1996) What is strategy? For starters, it's not the same as operational effectiveness, Harvard Business Review, November–December, https://hbr.org/1996/11/what-is-strategy (archived at https://perma.cc/Z9AL-W5YU)

8 Porter, M (2004) *Competitive Strategy: Techniques for analyzing industries and competitors*, Free Press, New York

9 Rumelt, R (2011) *Good Strategy/Bad Strategy: The difference and why it matters*, Crown Currency, New York

10 Lafley, A G and Martin, R L (2013) *Playing to Win: How strategy really works*, Harvard Business Review Press, Boston

11 Watkins, M D (2007) Demystifying strategy: The what, who, how, and why, Harvard Business Review, 10 September, https://hbr.org/2007/09/demystifying-strategy-the-what (archived at https://perma.cc/G8ZV-52DG)

12 Porter, M E (1996) What is strategy? For starters, it's not the same as operational effectiveness, Harvard Business Review, November–December, https://hbr.org/1996/11/what-is-strategy (archived at https://perma.cc/52ZD-JFJT)

13 Lafley, A G and Martin, R L (2013) *Playing to Win: How strategy really works*, Harvard Business Review Press, Boston

14 Porter, M (2004) *Competitive Strategy: Techniques for analyzing industries and competitors*, Free Press, New York
15 Populous website: https://populous.com (archived at https://perma.cc/DU48-J5UM)
16 Foster + Partners website: https://www.fosterandpartners.com (archived at https://perma.cc/6Q5F-8LRW)
17 Porter, M E (1996) What is strategy? For starters, it's not the same as operational effectiveness, Harvard Business Review, November–December, https://hbr.org/1996/11/what-is-strategy (archived at https://perma.cc/H676-YJUC)
18 Stanford Center for Professional Development (2014) Competition is for losers with Peter Thiel [online video] https://www.youtube.com/watch?v=3Fx5Q8xGU8k (archived at https://perma.cc/W4K7-UEUX)
19 Lafley, A G and Martin, R L (2013) *Playing to Win: How strategy really works*, Harvard Business Review Press, Boston
20 Rumelt, R (2022) *The Crux: How leaders become strategists*, Profile Books, London
21 Einstein is thought to have said this.
22 Barthêlemy, J (2022) *Myths of Strategy: Dispel the misconceptions and deliver a winning strategy*, Kogan Page, London
23 Collins, J (2001) *Good to Great: Why some companies make the leap… and others don't*, HarperBusiness, New York

2.2

Diagnose today: confront your brutal truth

Become obsessive about knowing your customers and what they value

Introduction

One of Shakespeare's most famous pieces of advice is 'to thine own self be true'. Do you know thy true self? Do you know what you stand for, why you do what you do, what you're good at and what you're not so good at? Reflecting on these questions at a business level is just as important as reflecting on them at a personal one. Sometimes, the boundary between the two blurs, especially for founders. But if you're not the founder? Do you have a clear sense of your strengths relative to the competition? Is there much to differentiate you? Can you articulate your organization's 'why'? Businesses started with clear purpose and passion can become corporatized, diluting the 'why' over time. Professional managers are brought in and they impose practices from other contexts. Messages that were once at the core of the business start to ebb away. No single specific action can dismantle a company's 'why', but the accumulation of different values, tactics and ways of doing things can erode who you, the collective business, are, over time. It's like having hundreds if not thousands of actions cutting away at your core.

Understanding your current situation requires a holistic diagnosis. A full diagnosis would incorporate all four Cornerstones of Corporate Health, which could fill an entire book. In these chapters, we focus on customer health. We explain how to quantify the value you currently deliver for which customer segments and the value those segments receive from your competitors. It is a way of achieving absolute clarity on why you exist and your strengths and weaknesses versus your competitors. We also explain a method for diagnosing customer segments in terms of the strength of your value proposition and whether or not it's worth the effort to try to win those customers. This means looking at the size of the market and profit potential. It results in a complete understanding of which segments are worth investing in.

This is where you gather what Jim Collins calls your brutal facts.[1] Like assembling military intelligence, diagnosing today involves collecting as much data as you can from a range of sources to feed your analysis and provide rich and nuanced insight. You want the full gamut of internal and external opinions – the good, the bad and the ugly. The ugly is particularly important to understand as you work to get to the nub of why your customers make the decisions that they do.

In this chapter, we introduce Blue Ocean Strategy and apply it to market segmentation. We explain how to first determine the list of value factors you compete on before collecting data on your performance and your competitors' performance against each value factor as well as the importance of the value factors. The chapter concludes with analysis. Where do you win or lose versus the competition? Which value factors could you improve upon to make your competition irrelevant? Which segments provide the most potential in terms of market size and margin? These questions result in an understanding of where to direct your focus, which you can carry forward to the design phase.

To illustrate how the theory can be put into practice, we include a case study of a B2B branding agency. It demonstrates how performing a diagnosis can make you step back and think. The data might surprise you. Other people's perceptions of what you do and what you're good at might not align with yours or with your passion and ambition. As we will demonstrate, it can instigate a dramatic rethink.

The value landscape

In Chapter 1.3 we wrote about Jim Collins' concept of confronting the brutal facts. A diagnosis is about understanding your total truth which can, at times, be brutal and hard to hear. It comes down to asking the right questions, a crucial one being 'why?'. Why do you exist? Why do customers buy from you? Every purchasing decision is driven by individual preference, affordability and the value people place on certain things provided by a brand. Some people like Nike and others prefer Adidas. Some people choose to fly with Southwest Airlines, others choose American Airlines and others choose NetJets. What makes McKinsey win over Deloitte or Salesforce win over HubSpot? Why do some people go for a Samsung Galaxy and others an Apple iPhone? Nike's innovative design might win over Adidas's comfort. Low-cost flying might win over driving or taking the bus. An Android camera and value for money might win over the iPhone. Knowingly or not, discrete factors such as these combine to influence a person's decision to buy. They are what W Chan Kim and Renée Mauborgne term 'factors' in their highly influential book *Blue Ocean Strategy*.[2] In this book, we call them 'value factors'. They can be defined as the features of products and services provided by organizations that customers value and that influence initial and ongoing purchase decisions.

Blue Ocean Strategy focuses on gaining a nuanced understanding of the factors your industry competes on so that you can find your own market space. We call this the 'value landscape'. Understanding it creates a foundation to consider how you can shape your strategy to compete in areas where you are strongest and your competition is weakest.

Kim and Mauborgne use the idea of red and blue oceans to explain the notion of creating your own market space. Red oceans are contested waters where companies compete fiercely against one another on similar things. In red oceans, it's difficult to differentiate one company from another. According to Porter's Three Generic Strategies (see Chapter 2.1), companies in red oceans compete on operational effectiveness alone. The water is red because the companies are like sharks, only competing on price and vying for blood. Blue oceans, in contrast, are calm, uncontested waters. They provide enormous potential for opportunity and growth. Winning companies swim in blue oceans: unexplored, uncontested market space with new customer bases. Finding a blue ocean requires a company to provide a unique set of value factors to its target segments that can't be matched by competitors.

Kim and Mauborgne famously use Cirque du Soleil as an example of how to create uncontested market space. When it arrived on the scene, large national-level circus productions such as the Barnum & Bailey Circus were competing against smaller regional circuses. Both offered the same value factors, but on a different scale and at a different price. For example, they both had star performers and animals and offered aisle concessions. They were both fun and humorous and included an element of thrill and danger.

At first glance, this would appear to be a red ocean with limited profit and growth potential. Not a wise place to go and compete. But Cirque du

Soleil differentiated itself by crafting an entirely new value landscape. It didn't provide star performers, animal shows and aisle concessions. But it did maintain factors that customers of traditional circuses valued most highly, such as fun and humour and thrills and danger. It also added new value factors to the traditional circuses' offering:

- The shows were based around themes and storylines, so customers came back for different productions.
- It added intellectual stimulation; the shows were like a Broadway musical or night at the opera.
- It refined the environment, doing away with the tired old tent and instead putting on performances in an impressive venue.
- It introduced dance and acrobatics, with intricate and varied choreography.
- Each production was visually stunning, with high production values, unique musical scores and high-tech lighting.

The result was an entirely new kind of show that appealed to a new customer segment.

Cirque du Soleil offers us just one example of how to create a blue ocean. It's easy to think of more. Steve Jobs' strategic moves continuously helped to keep Apple's waters blue. First came the iPod, which was far more user-friendly than any other MP3 player on the market at the time. Then came iTunes, which allowed people to purchase individual songs as opposed to an entire album. And then the iPhone, which created an entirely new market space where design and ease of use were paramount.

Using the value landscape to demystify market segmentation

We love Blue Ocean Strategy and we have developed it further to help with the practical application and measurement of the process. The authors suggest scoring companies against value factors using a scale of 'high', 'medium' and 'low'. These things are open to interpretation. In workshops, we have found them difficult to define. What does 'high' look like relative to 'medium', or 'medium' relative to 'low'? As we explain later in the chapter, we advocate using a scale which assigns numbers to value factors on a **swing rating scale** of zero to 100.

FIGURE 2.2.1 A set of customers that places the same weighting profile on the same mix of value factors constitutes a market segment

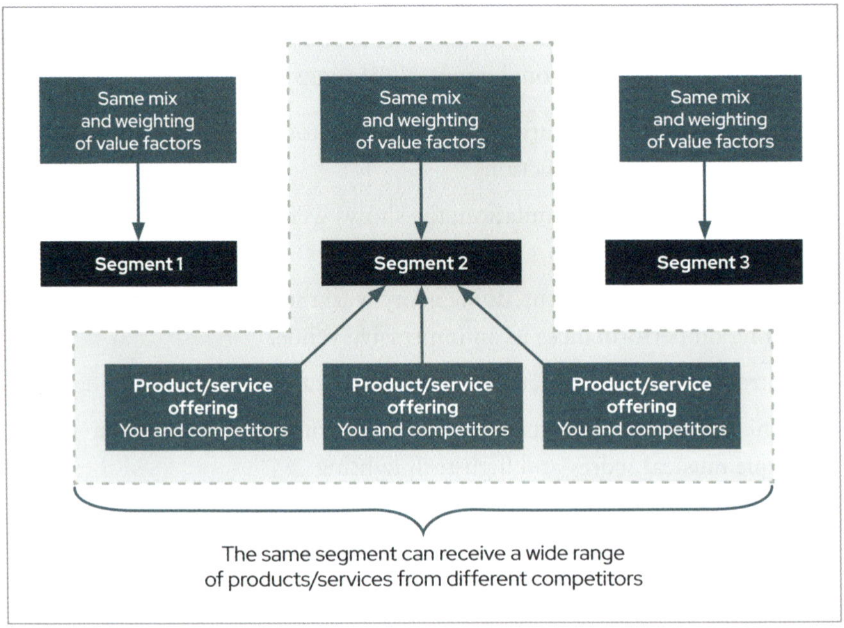

We also advocate using a similar scale to understand how customers rate the relative importance of value factors. Whole books have been written on customer segmentation. Whole modules are dedicated to it in business and management courses. You'd be forgiven for thinking it's a complicated business. Framing it in terms of value factors makes it crystal clear. Value factors exist because you serve customers. Customers put different amounts of importance on different things. Some might favour responsiveness, others brand. As Figure 2.2.1 shows, a set of customers that places the same amount of value on the same value factors is a **market segment**. It's that easy.

Collecting data to diagnose today

There are three stages of data collection involved in diagnosing today. All three can incorporate both quantitative and qualitative research:

1 *Preliminary research*. This takes the form of desk research, workshops and, sometimes, a few customer interviews. By the end of this stage, you

should have a draft taxonomy of value factors across the landscape, appropriate descriptions for each one and know how you're going to collect your data in the next stage. The draft taxonomy and descriptions can be verified throughout the next two stages.

2 *Collect your performance scores against each value factor and the weightings.* Interviews, workshops and surveys can be used to collect data about the importance of value factors and how you score against each one. This stage deepens your understanding of the value landscape and serves to sense-check your draft taxonomy.

3 *Collect your competitors' performance scores.* The same process as Stage 2 can be used to understand how your competitors score against each value factor.

Stage 1: Preliminary research

The starting point is to agree on the list of value factors that form your industry's value landscape. These are the things that make people decide who they want to buy from. By the end of the preliminary research, the aim is to have a draft taxonomy of value factors in place.

This requires much debate and iteration. We recommend performing the work in four stages:

1. Work individually or in pairs to brain dump onto sticky notes to create a long list.
2. Organize the long list into groups or key themes. Sticky notes are particularly helpful because you can arrange the ideas in clusters on a wall and move them around as necessary. Identify which are main value factors and which are sub-value factors within them. Refine as a team. Debate and iterate.
3. Define each term – debate and iterate until you have them right.
4. Review your agreed draft list of value factors as a team.

Individual desk research helps understand how you are positioning yourself and the value factors across your landscape. Anyone doing this exercise should record all their thoughts as input into workshops. Here are a few ideas:

- Review your website. What does it tell customers about the services you currently provide? How does it compare to your competitors' websites? Does the value they provide come across differently from the value you provide?

- Look at your sales collateral. How does your organization position itself when pitching to clients? What are you saying about yourself?
- Review customers' 'Request for proposal' documents. What are they asking for? How much consistency is there between customers? What are the key themes? How well can you respond to these key themes? Where are you strongest and where you are weakest?

INTERNAL WORKSHOPS AND CUSTOMER INTERVIEWS

Workshops are an excellent way to garner opinions from across the organization and provide an ideal space to start structuring your findings into a draft taxonomy. But a word of warning: workshops can give rise to groupthink. Somebody says something that sounds sensible and everyone else agrees, without giving alternatives very much thought. To avoid opinions merging across the group, participants should first work by themselves, writing down the company's value factors as they see them. This is where initial desk research comes in handy – it means that people can come prepared. Ask participants to write their ideas onto sticky notes so that they can later be arranged in clusters on a wall. Think carefully about who to involve. If you are a small organization, it may suffice to simply involve the management team. In larger organizations, it can be helpful to include people from different functions and levels. This may mean running several different workshops. The larger the organization, the more data there will be and you will need watertight processes in place to ensure the range of opinion is adequately recorded.

There are several ways to prompt people in this scenario. Encourage participants to think from the customer's perspective as well as the company's. Ask how they pitch for work. What are the three biggest win themes they aim to get across? These are the top three things that communicate why you should be chosen over anyone else. Ask participants what they are most proud of – what do they tell their friends about the company? What are they particularly good at? What's the best thing about working for the business, in their eyes?

Then ask for the flip side. What are they not so proud of? What do they feel the company isn't great at? Which competitor do they think is hurting you the most? Why? What specific things does this competitor do to cause this pain? A **win-loss analysis** can be a particularly helpful way to answer some of these questions and tease out value factors (see later in the chapter for an explanation of this method).

Note that while there is no need to do too many customer interviews at this stage, a select number can help to give you a precursory understanding of the external view of the value landscape, and how you fit into it. They can also help to validate the assumptions from your preliminary research.

ORGANIZING THE LONG LIST OF VALUE FACTORS INTO GROUPS

At the end of this exercise, you are likely to have a long list of overlapping value factors. Some might mean the same thing but be expressed in a slightly different way. It can help to cluster the ideas into groups so you can refine the long list to form the beginning of a draft value factor taxonomy. Ideally, aim to have no more than ten value factors. Any more than this can make the exercise too cognitively demanding. This is a **Goldilocks problem.** Too few value factors will be meaningless, but too many can be overwhelming. Ten is about the right number. It isn't always possible to stick to this (you'll see in the 'Defining value factors' case study box that we settled on 12 for the branding agency).

To demonstrate how this can be done, see the branding agency case study, 'Organizing ideas into groups'.

BRANDING AGENCY CASE STUDY

ORGANIZING IDEAS INTO GROUPS

Preliminary research for the branding agency involved desk research, interviews and workshops. Desk research included a review of the agency's website as well as its sales collateral, including case studies, sales presentations and responses to 'Requests for proposals'. One-to-one interviews were conducted with members of the agency's leadership team alongside three customer interviews. The desk research and interviews centred around the question 'What services does the agency provide?'. The analysis highlighted a degree of confusion – 25 different services were mentioned and 15 unique words.

Many of the unique words naturally came together into four groups:

1. Creative
   - Creative
   - Content
   - Production
   - Design
2. PR & Comms
   - PR
   - Comms
   - Comms strategy
   - Creative comms

3 Brand
   - Brand
   - Branding
4 Other
   - Activation
   - Brand activism
   - Campaigns
   - Execution
   - Strategy

Now that the branding agency has grouped these words, they can start to refine and define their value factors.

DEFINING VALUE FACTORS

The next stage is to define each value factor. Three definitions are needed:

1. An overview definition of the value factor for that market.
2. A description of best practices in the market.
3. Descriptions for anchor points on a swing rating scale related to your market.

Once again, language is critical. This is an iterative process and it can take a great deal of effort to get these definitions right. The descriptors should make the scoring easy. Draw on multiple sources – your management team, customers, competitors and non-competitor exemplars, web research and even books or articles. For a more detailed idea of how to create descriptions, see the branding agency case study, 'Defining value factors'.

BRANDING AGENCY CASE STUDY

DEFINING VALUE FACTORS

After much debate and iteration, we agreed on the following draft list of value factors:

1. Strategic and creative
2. Brand personality

FIGURE 2.2.2 An example of the value factor 'Trusted advisor'

Value Factor: "Trusted Advisor"

For: Founder / Partner in a UK-based Branding & Creative Agency

Overview

The extent to which you are considered a strategic partner with expert skills that the client sees as an asset to achieve their goals in the branding and creative domain

Best practices

- Regarded has having the leading perspective in this domain
- Completely trusted and known to be reliable; always delivers what the client needs, when they need it
- Develops outstanding branding and creative concepts, and delivers the assets that bring them to life
- Is prepared to deliver tough messages; gives advice that the client needs to hear, not wants to hear

Relative scale (for my market)

100	**Trust-based relationship** focuses on client as an individual, spends energy on understanding the client Delivers consistently outstanding advice in the creative domain. Exceeding expectations	123 Partners
50	**Relationship-based** focuses on the client organisation, spends energy on providing insights, provides ideas Delivers good creative work that always meets and sometimes exceeds expectations and impact	XYZ Ltd.
10	**Needs-based relationship** focuses on the business problem, spends energy on problem-solving, provides a solution Delivers satisfactory creative work that meets expectations and impact	ABC Inc.

Best in the world

2x	**Trust-based relationship** focuses on client as an individual, spends energy on understanding the client, provides a safe-haven for hard issues Is completely trusted to advise on all aspects of the client's life, professional and personal	CEO performance coach / mentor

Best practices

- Regarded has having a trusted perspective across a broad range of domains
- 100% holistic advice, not limited to industry or function, covers both professional and personal domains
- Can be contacted at all times for any reason
- Clinical psychology-style training
- Completely trusted with the most sensitive information
- Is prepared to deliver tough messages; gives advice that the client needs to hear, not wants to hear

3. Pitch theatre
4. Insight
5. Results
6. Trusted advisor
7. Client experience
8. Media landscape
9. Sector specialism
10. Breadth of offering
11. Geo coverage
12. Environmental, social and governance

These things are open to a lot of interpretation. What exactly did we mean by 'brand personality', 'pitch theatre' or 'trusted advisor'? This needed to be clear before we asked people to provide scores and weightings. The next step was to assign descriptors to each value factor in the form of an overview and what best practices in the industry looked like. The result for the 'Trusted advisor' value factor is shown in Figure 2.2.2. We drew on numerous sources to define it, including an excellent book, *The Trusted Advisor* by David Maister, Charles Green and Robert Galford.[3]

DESCRIBING ANCHOR POINTS ON THE SWING RATING SCALE

As mentioned above, we prefer to score value factors using anchor points on a data-driven scale rather than using 'high', 'medium' and 'low'. Having a collective understanding of scoring and what scores mean is the only way to reach a clear consensus on the diagnosis. Turning opinion into hard numbers means we can use maths to track progress, set targets and make actions tangible.

The best way to do this is with the swing rating method. The best performer is given a score of 100 and all other scores are understood relative to this top score. When we perform this exercise with management teams, we can find a huge divergence in scores. This can be because people think on different scales. CEOs often give lower scores than many because they're thinking on a global scale, and sometimes outside of their industry. They compare themselves to the best in the world. Others are likely to think about the market that they compete in (in terms of industry sector and geography). There are two scales to be aware of:

1 Relative (best in the market).
2 Absolute (best in the world).

We suggest using a relative, best-in-the-market scale most of the time. This is shown in the middle of Figure 2.2.2. Descriptions for anchor points on this scale should be relative to best practices in the market. Respondents are then asked to assess performance compared to competitors in your market. The market in which you compete is defined by both industry sector and geography. This is an important measure because the market represents the natural pool of competitors that buyers select from when procuring the goods or services that you provide.

Writing descriptions for anchor points is not an easy thing to do. It always requires a great deal of debate to get it right. A score of 100 is twice as good as a score of 50 and 10 times better than a score of 10. A score of 10 is equivalent to a credible offering. It's 'table stakes' in your industry. It is the Ford Fiesta of the car industry. For the business traveller, it might be a Premier Inn. In a procurement process, a score of 10 would mean that when asked if you provide 'X', or if your product offers 'X', you can credibly answer 'yes'. If, and only if, your segment wants only the bare minimum and is very sensitive to price, you might choose to score 10 across the board and price as low as you can. This is Southwest's strategy.

In the car industry, a score of 100 for the value factor 'driving experience' might equate to a McLaren or Lamborghini. A score of 100 for the value factor 'luxury' might equate to Rolls-Royce. At the other end of the scale, a score of zero is easy to understand. It means that a company has no capability in that value factor. This isn't a bad thing. Your zeros are key – they mean you have made a choice. You can't be all things to all people. For example, Cirque du Soleil scores zero on 'animal shows' and 'aisle concessions'.

Above all, see this as a journey. Scores evolve. Something that would have scored 100 ten years ago would not get the same score today. At one time, Nintendo's Game Boy would have been the best mobile game device around. Like so many things in this book, this is an ongoing process.

THE VALUE OF AN ABSOLUTE SCALE

An absolute scale compares performance to the best providers in the world, which could come from any industry in any geography. This is a useful measure because it encourages 'outside the box' thinking. It makes you think about the art of the possible and how you could develop your offer to differentiate yourself from any other competitor in your industry, making the competition irrelevant. The danger of solely working to a relative industry scale is that you'll end up the same as everyone else and find yourself competing only on price.

This can be a difficult thing to imagine so it can help to use real examples that most people know about. If you want the best packaging, think about the finest bottle of cognac or champagne. If you want the best design, think Versace or Chanel, Norman Foster or Zaha Hadid. At Ārahi, one of our value factors is providing a concierge service for our clients. It relates to the practices we put in place to take care of our clients' needs and desires. When articulating what this meant, we looked to the best – those we could think of from across industries who were the best in the world at looking after their customers. We thought particularly about private members' clubs or exclusive hotels such as the Four Seasons. If staff at the latter know that you love theatre, they might suggest booking a show for you. They want to make you feel at home. They want to take away the noise and give you space to relax and enjoy yourself.

FIGURE 2.2.3 Relative to market versus absolute scores

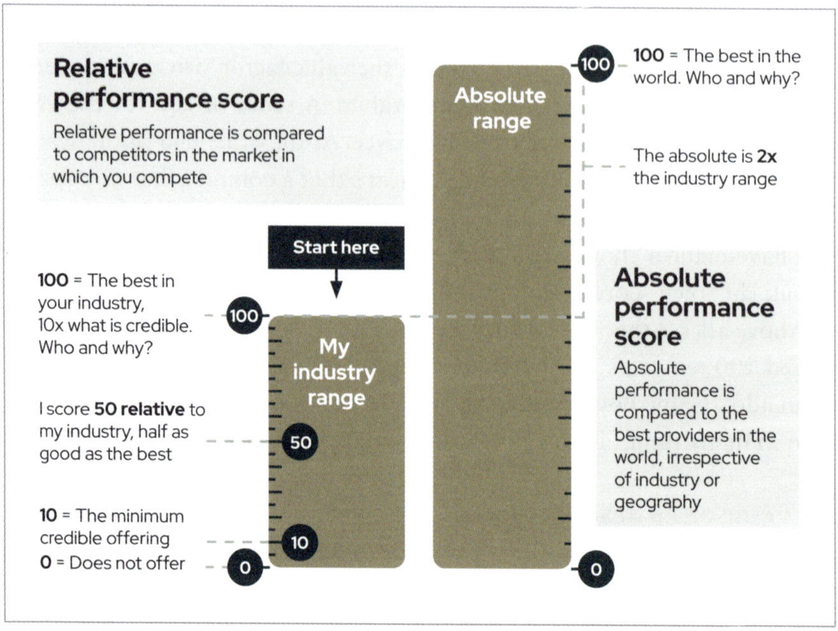

Figure 2.2.3 shows how a score of 100 on the relative best-in-the-market scale can differ from a score on an absolute scale. Let's return to the value factor 'trusted advisor'. The best trusted advisor in the world could be a CEO performance coach or mentor. They offer CEOs holistic support on both professional and personal matters and receive clinical psychology-style training. They are prepared to deliver tough messages and give advice that their clients need to hear, not want to hear. A score of 100 on an industry range may only be half as good as a score of 100 on an absolute range. It can be helpful to understand what 100 looks like on an absolute scale, as shown in the top-right-hand corner of Figure 2.2.3.

STAGE 1 OUTPUTS

- Draft taxonomy of value factors.
- An overview and best practices descriptions for each value factor, done at a market level.
- Descriptions for anchor points on the relative best-in-the-market scale for each value factor.
- Description of a 100 score for each value factor as well as best practice descriptions on an absolute scale.

Stage 2: Collect your performance scores against each value factor and value factor weightings

Quantitative data is collected in the form of scores and weightings. This is what helps you to plot your value curve in the landscape and ultimately compare it to your competitors so you can decide how to compete. This is, essentially, a benchmarking exercise. The weightings tell you how important the value factors are to your customers and employees. This is crucial to capture so that you can draw your value curve and understand how it differs from that of your competitors. You learn the most from interviewing customers and employees and running workshops. The qualitative data can lead to valuable insight, helping you to understand the reasons behind the scores and opening the door to your total truth.

When interviewing people using the relative scale described above, remember to be clear about what the scores signify. Be clear that you are primarily collecting scores relative to the best in the market (in the industry on a global scale). Use your intuition to decide whether to veer away from this to explore the absolute scale. Some respondents will be more able to conceptualize this than others, largely dependent on their experience. People with less experience may simply think in terms of what they know, which can mean their industry within their locality. While conducting interviews with a management team, we received hugely divergent views about the value factor 'insight'. Person A compared their capability to management consulting firms, investment banking analysts and deep thinkers who produce podcasts and write articles and books. They had a view of those who were the best in the world. Person B compared their insight capability to businesses they knew about in the town where they operated. A score of 50 from Person A was therefore not the same as a score of 50 from Person B. This experience taught us about the need to be clear about the scales.

TRIANGULATING DATA FROM DIFFERENT SOURCES

So much value factor work involves capturing and recording data in the form of people's subjective opinions and perceptions. There is huge value in this data, but it can be dangerous to apply too much data science to perceptions obtained by a single means. For increased rigour, we advocate collecting opinions and perceptions via different methods and triangulating the data to increase the validity and reliability of the results. In this chapter, we mainly describe collecting data through relative scoring using the swing rating method. There is enormous value in this approach. It is important, however, to combine this methodology with others such as those mentioned below. There is no ideal method. The aim is to understand people's true preferences as fast and quickly as you can.

Allocate 100 units Tell participants to imagine they have 100 units (e.g. $100) to spend. Next, tell them to allocate those 100 units across the value factors based on how they would prioritize them. For example, someone might give value factor 'A' 25, 'B' 10 and 'C' only 2, etc. We then rebase the highest score to 100. Value factor 'A' is given a swing rating score of 100 because it was allocated the most, 'B' gets a swing rating of 40 and 'C' gets a swing rating of 8, or (100/25)*2 = 8. It's a process of normalizing to the 100 swing rating scale. This method works well because it is gamified and tangible and participants are forced to make choices. It involves an allocation of finite resource and therefore requires participants to actively engage in thinking about trade-offs between each value factor.

Win-loss analysis This is a great method to use when working with employees in workshops or as a format for a customer interview after you have pitched for work. Think about the last big customer you won. Why did you win it? What about the last time you lost? Why did you lose? Who did you lose to and why? Talk to clients directly after pitching for work to understand the reasons behind their decisions. This is a golden opportunity to learn. If you lose, ask who you lost to. Ask what would have swung it in your favour. Ask if there is a particular value factor that you could improve to ensure you win the next time.

A fantastic question to ask is, 'What made you almost say no to us?' If you're told consistently that you're winning on price, that's food for thought. What if someone else can do the same as you but cheaper? Sometimes you lose because it's not the right time and no one gets the contract. Ask why that is – it might help you in the future.

Win-loss analysis can help you to build a picture of which customer segments are working best for you. Someone might tell you that you lost because you don't know enough about their industry. Over time, you can start to see which industries you're winning in and which you're losing in. This helps when understanding your niche and where to direct your focus.

Pulse surveys People often wonder which is more effective: surveys or interviews. Surveys are the less expensive option. They are good for getting a pulse from a large sample size (a quick view given in two to three minutes).

For a quick survey try converting your score descriptions (described above) to yes/no questions. For example, returning to our 'trusted advisor' value factor, simple questions could include:

- Do you feel valued and understood as an individual?
- Do we deliver outstanding advice in the creative domain?
- Are we consistent in our delivery of outstanding advice?
- Do we exceed your expectations?
- Do we exceed your expectations every time we deliver work?

'Yes' answers to the above four questions would result in a score of 100 for that value factor. The 'no' answers would give a clear indication of where and how to improve, which could be linked to specific actions.

Pulse surveys can be useful, but, like all the methods described here, don't do them at the exclusion of everything else. You'll miss the qualitative detail you get from an interview, whether that's a win-loss analysis interview or one to capture scores and weightings on the relative scale. Your target buyer (in the B2B world) is likely to be senior and time-poor. They are also likely to be surveyed out. They are more likely to say yes to an interview, particularly if the interviewer is someone credible. It's also a great opportunity to build a relationship with them. There's value to be gained on both sides, even if it is more time-consuming, more expensive and harder to get a large sample size. Interviews also provide a useful way to sense-check the value factor taxonomy.

In *Playing to Win*, the authors passionately describe P&G's research activity, crediting the company's methods with its sustained growth and success. P&G leveraged anthropological research, which means going out into the real world of the people you are studying. After P&G acquired Gillette, one of their goals was to achieve global expansion for the brand. India was a key target. While sitting in Boston, the P&G team discussed the need to observe men shaving in India with their new Gillette colleagues. The 'Gillette guys' missed the point: 'Why not observe them in Boston? There are loads of Indians in Boston.' They would be selling to men in India and they needed to be observed in India. They made a simple observation which they would have missed if they'd stayed in Boston. In most of India, men weren't shaving with running water. They put a bit of water in a cup and used that to rinse the facial hair off the blade. To sell in this market, Gillette needed to offer a different blade type at a different price point. On the flight home, the designer had the workings of a highly successful product in a crucial target market.[4] This is a big part of effective diagnosis. It is getting to an insight or set of insights that can help drive the design of a more valuable way to address a need.

JON

One investment I was involved in was a branded cosmetic business selling into high street retailers and beauty salons. Five months after investing, a major conglomerate brought out a completely new product which had an immediate and disastrous effect on our sales. Value creation planning had identified the need for a robust product development pipeline. But this shock came too early in the plan and it took over a year to respond with a rival product. At this point, we were conducting focus groups with loyal customers on the branding and packaging of the new product.

> Following a board meeting, I went along with my CEO and Chair to listen to the focus groups from behind a screen where the customers couldn't see us. We hadn't been watching for very long when one young lady picked up the sample packaging and said: 'I don't know, it all looks a bit corporate, it just.....' She hesitated, then stated, '... it just looks like it has been designed by a bunch of men in suits.' I looked to my right and left and there we were. Three men in suits. She'd nailed it. Over 90 per cent of this brand's customers were female. We had no female representation at the senior level of the business. I was stunned by our ignorance. I subsequently hired a female brand expert to advise the board. She later became the CEO and successfully turned the business around. We eventually had a successful exit to a major cosmetics house. This story highlights the importance of everyone, including the leaders, tapping into the psyche of customers.

Collecting importance weighting scores for value factors The importance of value factors is understood through weighting, which again can be done by using a swing rating method. Weighting your value factors helps to see which ones are most important for your target segment and possibly, eventually, segments.

Take your list of value factors and ask internal and external respondents to designate the single most important one on the list. Which one do they value the most? It's important to have a clear understanding of your organization's purpose when performing this exercise. This is the start of defining your critical value factors so that you can design your strategy. We describe this in detail in Chapter 2.3. Your critical value factors are the ones that make you truly different. They inform everything that you do. Work your way through the list, asking respondents to determine each value factor's importance relative to this most important one. Collect data both internally and externally so that you can compare the two.

Scoring the importance of value factors might seem simple, but how you ask the question can change the outcome. Remember that the aim is to get to your customers' true preferences and how they are likely to act with their wallets. As with performance scores, there are other techniques you can use, aside from just asking for scores out of 100. It is important to triangulate the data to have confidence in the results:

1 Use the allocation of 100 units technique (e.g. $) as described above.

2 Use a Likert scale of, for example, seven levels: 'most critical'; 'critical'; 'important'; 'desirable'; 'nice-to-have'; 'a small benefit'; 'irrelevant'. Then, give a value to each level, for example 100, 60, 40, 20, 10, 5, 0.
3 **Conjoint analysis**, otherwise known as multiple variable correlation analysis, asks people to decide based on a range of value factors. Once someone has selected the most important, you can make subtle changes to the range and ask them to pick again. Eventually, you start to understand which factors are driving decision-making in the context of the full package.
4 Give them two options, A versus B, and ask them to select the most important one. Then give them two more at random – C versus D. And then two more – E versus F, etc. Then, pair more up at random – B versus D, A versus E, etc. From this, you can infer a mathematical score. This A versus B technique is a simplified version of conjoint analysis and assumes that everything else in the world is equal.

Statistically, Option 3 is the most scientifically robust method. It's much more realistic than the more artificial A versus B method. It is also, by far, the hardest and the most expensive as the sample size needs to be large for any conclusions to be relevant. Our aim is simply to make you aware of it. We don't have the space to delve into it in any detail. There are many other sources you can turn to for help if you want to go down this route. Start simple, gather views and triangulate. With time, you could mature into conjoint analysis if you think the increase in accuracy and refinement is worth the cost. For more about collecting weightings, see the branding agency case study, 'Value factor weightings'.

BRANDING AGENCY CASE STUDY

VALUE FACTOR WEIGHTINGS

Figure 2.2.4 shows four sets of value factor weightings – one from the point of view of the branding agency's customers and the other three from the point of view of their management team, given as minimum, maximum and average.

As the figure shows, 'insight' was the main value factor with a notably divergent weighting from the agency team. Here, the maximum given weighting was 75, and the minimum was 25. This required further discussion to explore the reasons for the lack of alignment. 'Trusted advisor' was consistently voted as important by customers and the agency team. Note that 'Geographical coverage' was seen as important by the agency whereas clients hardly valued it all – it was the lowest scoring value factor.

This simple exercise shows that the team was aligned on some value factors, but certainly not all of them. Once you understand this, you can do something about it. Below and in Chapter 2.3 we explain how, in particular, the divergence of opinion about geographical coverage dramatically changed the agency's strategy.

FIGURE 2.2.4 Importance weightings from the point of view of the client and management team

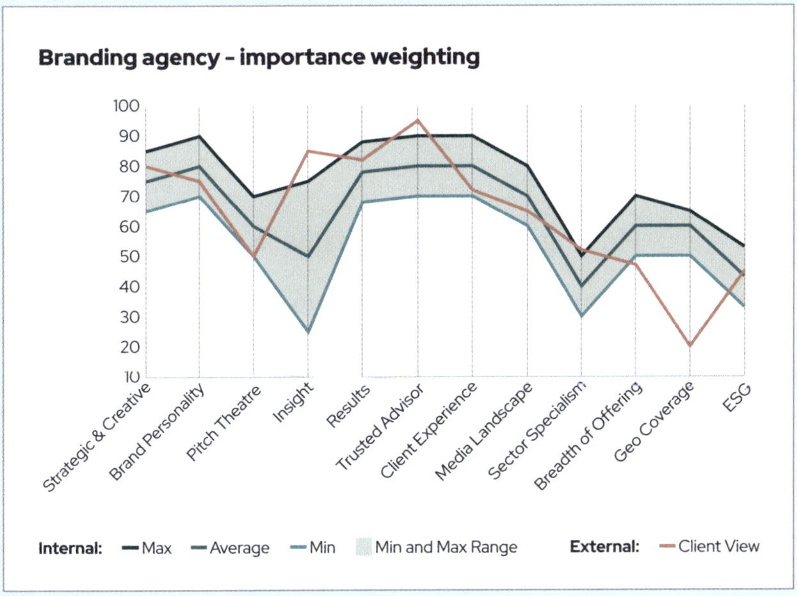

STAGE 2 OUTPUTS

- Customers' scores reflecting your performance for each value factor.
- Customers' views on the importance of each value factor.
- The management team's scores reflecting your performance for each value factor.
- The management team's views on the importance of each value factor.

Stage 3: Collect your competitors' performance scores

Understand how your competitors deliver against each value factor and whether they win over you or you win over them. Once you have collected data on yourself, ask participants to score your competitors one value factor at a time. It can be helpful to group competitors together into archetypes and ask people to score against them. For example, in the management consulting world, you may choose to group competitors as follows: A – the 'Big 4' (PwC, Deloitte, EY and KPMG); B – the 'Big 3' strategy firms (McKinsey & Company, The Boston Consulting Group and Bain); C – small boutique firms with 30–60 consultants; and D – tiny groups of individuals.

This process helps to refine the value factors and it may make respondents rethink how they have scored you. Triangulate your results against your competitors' results, as well as comparing your competitors' results to each other. This process can help you refine the taxonomy and may sometimes make you rethink descriptions and scores.

Plotting scores on the value landscape

Calculate average scores and start to plot them on the value landscape. This process starts to reveal commonality in views. One thing you may notice is that the average scores given by the customers are much higher than internal ones. This is clearly shown in the continuation of the branding agency case study, 'Plotting scores'.

BRANDING AGENCY CASE STUDY

PLOTTING SCORES

We are often harsher on ourselves than others are on us. Figure 2.2.5 shows the range of internal performance scores versus the average external performance score. The range of internal scores demonstrates a typical divergence in opinion within the management team, as discussed earlier. The founder CEO scored the agency much more harshly than less experienced members of the team. Interestingly, once these scores are plotted on the value landscape, you can see that the curves are broadly consistent, despite the customer interviews returning higher average scores.

FIGURE 2.2.5 Plotting performance scores on the value landscape

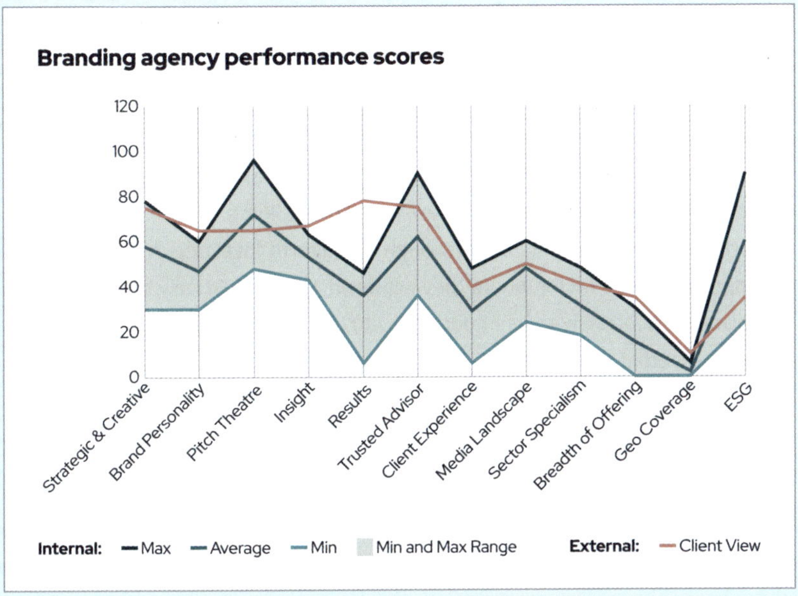

FIGURE 2.2.6 A scatter plot showing performance and weighting scores

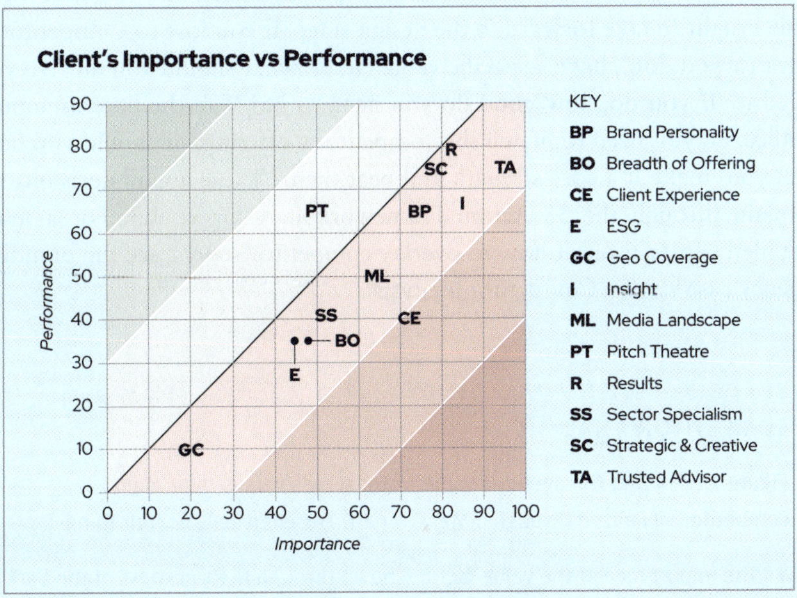

Figure 2.2.6 is an example of a scatter plot showing the client's importance and performance scores. This visualization is a helpful tool for diagnosing where you want to invest in improving your performance. For example, any value factors in the bottom right-hand corner might be a cause for concern. 'Trusted advisor' is an example of an important value factor that the agency performs well against. Their performance for 'Geographical coverage' is low, but they shouldn't worry because it's not important. They can exit this value factor and make their performance zero. They are excellent at 'Pitch theatre' but the importance rating suggests that it wouldn't be worth investing in it. 'Insight' is an important value factor where they achieved a fairly relatively high performance score. Given its importance, it could be worth investing further in this value factor.

Overlaying with competitor scores

You can overlay your value landscape with your competitors' value landscapes in various ways – compare yourself to a single competitor, an archetype or a manifest view of all of your competitors. Start to spot patterns. Which value factors do you compete on the most, which do you compete on the least and where might you be able to find your blue ocean? Who do you lose to? Which value factors are you losing on? This is all valuable insight to take forward to the design stage. If you lose to Competitor A because you don't have a specific value factor, what should you do? Do you need it? If you do, how good do you need to be? Will the bare minimum suffice, do you need to match the competitor's offering, or should you (and can you) make it a core strength and beat them? These are all decisions we explain through the 5S Action Framework in Chapter 2.3. For a more detailed explanation of how to overlay competitor scores, see the branding agency case study: 'Competitor analysis'.

BRANDING AGENCY CASE STUDY

COMPETITOR ANALYSIS

Figure 2.2.7 shows the agency's value factor scores versus their main competitor visualized through a Mekko chart. The chart tells us four things:

1 The importance of the value factor (shown through the thickness of the bar).

2 The average performance rating for the branding agency.

FIGURE 2.2.7 A Mekko chart showing average value factor scores versus a key competitor

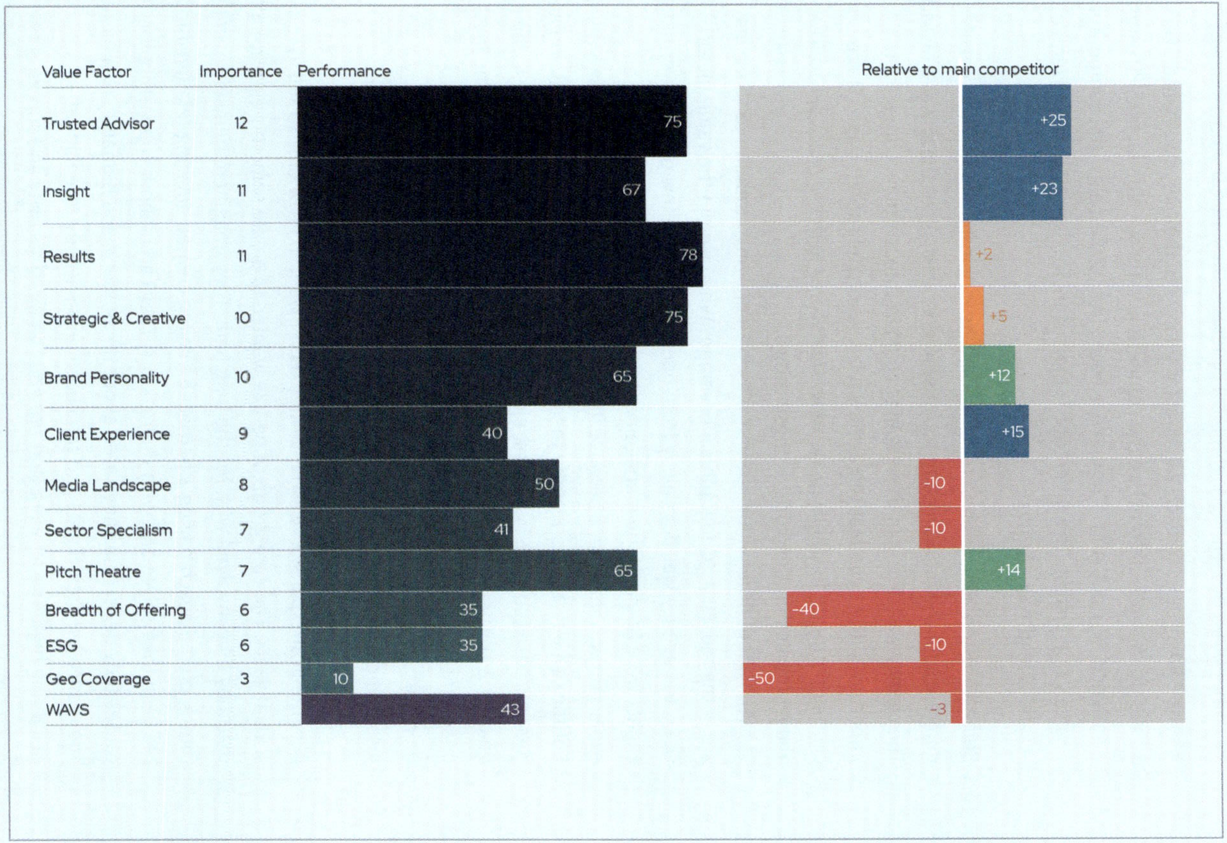

3 The performance for each value factor versus the main competitor. Taking the two extremes, with 'trusted advisor' they are 25 points above the competition but with 'geographical coverage' they are 50 points below.

4 The BRAG status of each value factor relative to their key competitor. They are significantly better than the competitor in three value factors: 'Trusted advisor', 'Insight' and 'Client experience'. They score below the competitor in five value factors. The difference is most stark for 'Geographical coverage' and 'Breadth of offering'.

Being a trusted advisor and providing high-quality insight are clear points of difference for the branding agency. Customers cared about these value factors. The agency was strong in these things compared to the main competitor. Importantly, the people at the agency felt passionately about them. There is a clear opportunity for them to increase their scores to get them closer to 100 and be the best in the world at these things.

What about other value factors? It's worth drawing attention to three that are in the red. First, 'Geographical coverage'. When we did the value factor work, the agency was days away from opening a brand-new office in Germany. Flights were booked. The management team believed that geographical expansion was important because it was what all their competitors were doing. But the value factor work made them stop and question both their passion and their purpose (purpose is the first element of PACCTACC, which we describe in Chapter 2.3). The Mekko chart shows that 'Geographical coverage' is the least important value factor on the list (customers consistently rated it as unimportant and the management team was split). It scored 10, so they were just credible, and they were 50 points away from the main competitor.

When we asked them about their purpose, the team realized that geographical expansion wasn't it. They didn't want to grow only to sell in several years. The core group of people wanted to create something meaningful that they'd be involved with for the long haul. They imagined themselves in the future, on the beach having a barbecue, having created amazing relationships between themselves and with their clients. They cared about supporting the causes they believe in. They cared about the emotion and humanity of a brand. They cancelled their flights and refocused on what they cared about – delivering high-impact work that provides financial security and supports the environment.

The other two red value factors worth noting are 'Media landscape' and 'Breadth of offering'. Their knowledge of the media landscape was 10 points below the main competitor. Their breadth of offering was 40 points below. This begged the question: did the media PR influencing side of the business make sense? Or did it make more sense to keep the breadth of the agency's offer tight and focusing solely on their brand agency work?

Assessing pricing as part of your value proposition

The term 'value proposition' often crops up in day-to-day business vernacular. Different definitions exist, but it is believed to have originated in a McKinsey research paper published in 1988, which defined it as 'a clear, simple statement of the benefits, both tangible and intangible, that the company will provide, along with the approximate price it will charge each customer segment for those benefits'.[5]

Kim and Mauborgne frame tangible and intangible benefits as 'utility'. For them, a value proposition is 'the utility buyers receive from an offering minus the price they pay for it'. Utility is a term in economics which refers to the total satisfaction received from consuming a product or service. In the context of this book, 'utility' can be defined as the weighted average sum of all the value factors. Importantly, we define price as the total cost of ownership (TCO). Not just the initial outlay, but any costs incurred over the lifetime of consumption of the product or service. For example, it costs more to buy an electric vehicle than a combustion engine car. However, the ongoing service costs for an electric vehicle are much less than those of a traditional petrol car. We have spoken to two taxi drivers in London who have worked this out. Overall, the TCO of an electric vehicle is less than that of a petrol car.

Your value proposition is strong when your **Weighted Average Value Score (WAVS)** minus price is greater than your competitors' equivalent. The WAVS is the distillation of your value proposition into a single number; your score for each value factor is weighted by the level of importance that buyers assign to it. The resulting number allows a direct comparison to your competitors. Peter Thiel would say that if your best competitor is an incumbent, you need to be ten times better than they are to disrupt them. Not just marginally better, but ten times (this is subjective, of course. You might not need to be ten times better, but you do need to be significantly better). The point is that there's a cost to switching – customers need to be persuaded.

Value factors give you a clear idea of the utility you provide. But what about the price? There is a positive correlation between your WAVS and price – the higher your WAVS, the more you can charge. Pricing is a difficult thing to get right. It's hard to estimate price elasticity, even with all the relevant data at your disposal. Pricing is a strange, psychological thing (think of Veblen goods where the demand increases the higher the price). Win-loss analysis and customer interviews can give you a good idea about your price. Ask customers how much more they'd be willing to pay if you increased a certain value factor from x to y. How much would that be worth to them? How much would it cost you? With triangulation and time, you'll get a good idea of your pricing versus the competition.

Figure 2.2.8 illustrates the value/price trade-off. Imagine you're Competitor A. You're stuck in the middle of a pool of competitors in a contested, red ocean. If the customers know about you, you don't need to worry about Competitor B. They're losing to you every time. You both provide the same value, but you charge customers less for it. But if the customer doesn't know about you (or Competitor D), Competitor B can still drive sales. Competitors C and D both give you something to worry about. You're being squeezed by Competitor C's lower price and Competitor D's higher quality. They don't compete with each other. They are both more differentiated than you. You can't be sure whether you will win or lose against either of them. It's hit and miss. You provide greater value than Competitor C, but not all customers will believe the price trade-off is worth

FIGURE 2.2.8 Stuck in the middle of a contested, red ocean

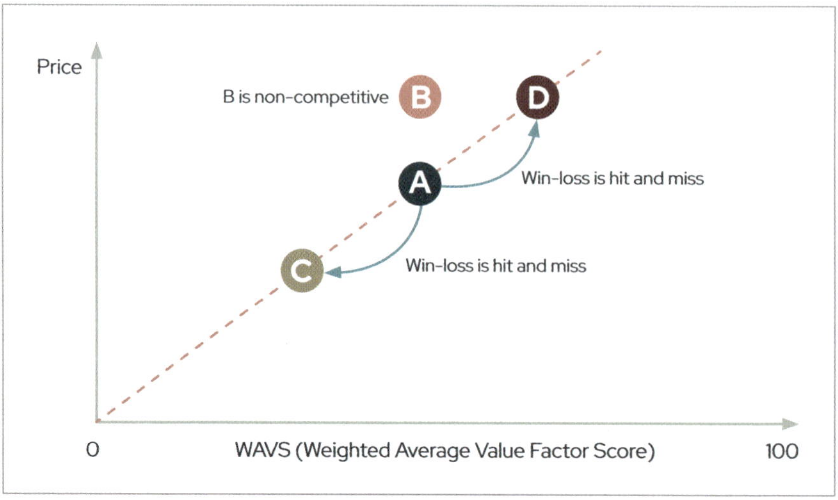

FIGURE 2.2.9 Options for Competitor A to differentiate themselves

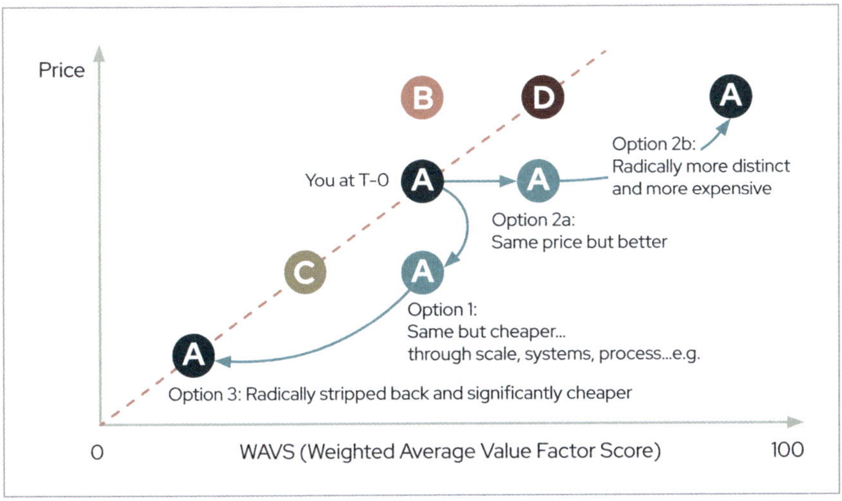

it. You're also missing value factors provided by Competitor D. Customers might be willing to pay for this extra value and choose D over you.

So what can you do? You can have a 'flight' to quality or price. This is your key challenge, which we explain in Chapter 2.3. Figure 2.2.9 shows the options:

- Option 1 is to do the same but cheaper, through scale, systems and processes. This constitutes competing on operational excellence and results in a race to the bottom on price (see Chapter 2.1).
- Option 2a would see Competitor A offering more value at the same price. You'd probably win against D, provided your brand reputation is strong enough (see below).
- Option 2b would make Competitor A radically more distinct and more expensive. This would make them truly differentiated and make the competition irrelevant.
- Option 3 represents another option for true differentiation. Competitor A could 'do a Southwest' and strip out all value. It could decide to give bare bones value factors, scoring 10 across the board (just credible offerings) and pricing as low as possible.

Understanding what to prioritize

A similar analysis can be performed to diagnose your current standing with specific customer segments. Figure 2.2.10 shows four scatter plot charts for three customer segments – A, B and C. To keep things simple, competitors are not included on the charts. Each chart has three pieces of data represented on the x-axis, the y-axis, and the scale of the bubble. Collectively, they include seven pieces of data:

1. Price
2. WAVS
3. Margin
4. Total Addressable Market (TAM)
5. Growth of TAM
6. Brand image
7. Brand awareness

FIGURE 2.2.10 Understanding what to prioritize

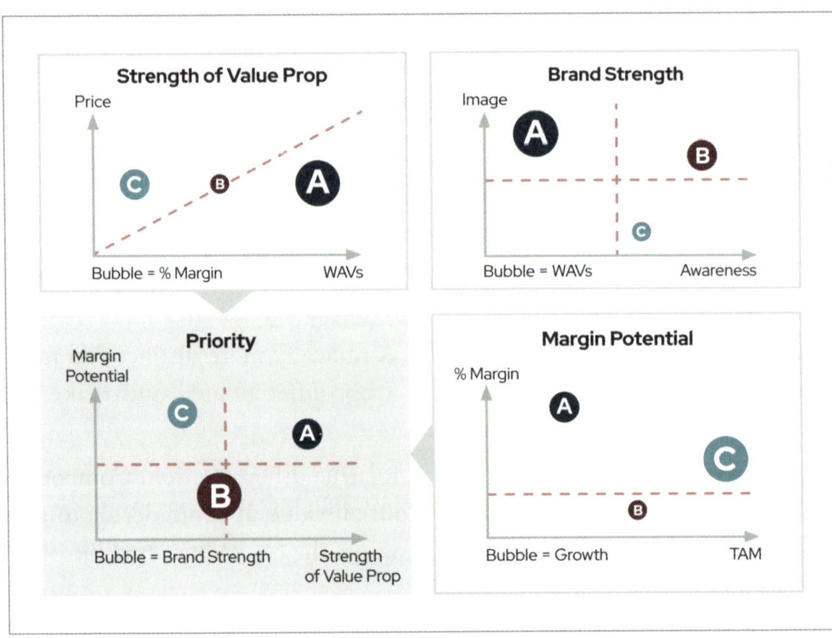

These charts contain a lot of information. Some pieces of data are used twice, i.e. the margin and WAVS. These charts allow you to see the connections between these seven important strategic measures. The dotted lines represent thresholds to help with your decision-making.

The top-left chart represents the strength of your value proposition in each of the segments. This is the WAVS versus price chart described above but with an extra piece of data added – the per cent margin. The bubble for Segment A is relatively large. This represents a high margin and therefore room to reduce the price to improve the value proposition. The smaller the bubble, the lower the margin. You might consider exiting the market for Segment B.

The bottom-right chart represents the margin potential. You might be able to win a segment, but do you want to? Is it worth your while in terms of market size, growth of the market and profitability? Segment B falls below the threshold. The margin isn't high enough for this segment and you should consider exiting it.

The top-right chart represents the strength of your brand in each of the segments. Is your brand strong enough to win? Does the segment know about you? Does it have a positive impression of what you do? The x-axis is brand awareness (how well-known you are within each segment) and brand image (the customer's perception of you – this could be positive, negative or neutral). The bubble is your WAVS. The bubble for Segment A is large. This represents a high WAVS score. For Segment A, this correlates with a high image score, which is what you would expect. If Segment A had a small WAVS bubble but a high image, that might indicate two things. Either the WAVS score is wrong, or you are not communicating your value sufficiently.

The bottom-left chart, called the 'Priority' chart, summarizes the other three. The x-axis shows the strength of your value proposition. The y-axis shows the margin potential. It's a combination of the profit TAM and the profit margin. The bubble shows brand strength. Let's focus on Segment A. It has a high margin and high WAVS. But there is an issue. Customers in the segment don't know about you. Those in Segments B and C have a far higher awareness of you (even if their image of you is lower). There's clear action – increase marketing spend and target marketing activity on Segment A to increase awareness. It might have a much smaller TAM, but you can own it.

STAGE 3 OUTPUTS

- Customers' scores reflecting your competitors' performance for each value factor.
- The management team's scores reflecting your competitors' performance for each value factor.

Final thoughts

Diagnosing is not a one-and-done process. The companies that consistently win constantly listen and diagnose. The value landscape is a living, breathing thing that evolves through time and requires constant attention. As the world evolves, your customers' needs change. New competitors may enter your space with innovative ways of solving your customers' problems.

Perhaps the most important thing to remember with this work is that you're dealing with subjective perception and opinion. Everyone will come to this exercise with a range of different life experiences which will affect their scores. Don't be blinded by false precision. A 10 per cent difference in how people score you versus the competition is not significant. True difference requires you to be demonstrably better than others. It requires you to knock it out of the park.

We ended this chapter with a diagnosis of lots of important factors – market size, margin, WAVS and how to determine your priorities. This is all key information to take forward to the design stage, the subject of Chapter 2.3.

REMEMBER THIS

1. Invest in getting to know your customers, how they are segmented and what they value. Seek to find high-value segments.
2. Have a clear, robust definition of all your value factors.
3. Understand your competitive landscape and what your competitors' strategies are.
4. Overlay your key metrics like TAM, margin and brand strength.
5. Understand your value for money and where you sit on the price/quality trade-off.
6. You're always on. This is your Forth Bridge (see Chapter 1.3). It never stops.

Notes

1 Collins, J (2001) *Good to Great: Why some companies make the leap… and others don't*, HarperBusiness, New York

2 Kim, W C and Mauborgne, R A (2015) *Blue Ocean Strategy: How to create uncontested marketspace and make the competition irrelevant* (Expanded edition), Harvard Business Review Press, Boston

3 Maister, D, Green, C and Galford, R (2002) *The Trusted Advisor*, Simon & Schuster, London

4 Lafley, A G and Martin, R L (2013) *Playing to Win: How strategy really works*, Harvard Business Review Press, Boston

5 Lanning, M J and Michaels E G (1988) A business is a value delivery system, McKinsey staff paper No. 41. July, www.scribd.com/document/191700424/A-Business-is-a-Value-Delivery-System (archived at https://perma.cc/4PYD-QXBL)

2.3

Design tomorrow

Your strategy should tell a compelling, consistent and coherent story

Introduction

Of all the reading I (Rupert) have done over the past three years, the one standout 'ah-ha' moment was during an early-morning reading session. Sitting in a comfortable chair, sipping my coffee, reading Richard Rumelt's *Good Strategy/Bad Strategy*. And bang. Rumelt said it. You design a strategy. At that moment, it became clear. Strategy is a design process. It's not a planning one or a goal-setting one. It's not analysis. It's design thinking.

Design is about creating something. It's about taking something from your head, putting it onto paper and then into some tangible format that people can use in the real world to make their lives better. As Peter Thiel has said, '"good design" is an aesthetic imperative... It's true that every entrepreneur is first and foremost a designer.'[1] Good design is elegant. It is functional. It is hard to do but amazing when you see it. The process takes iteration, reflection and debate.

This chapter shows you how to *design* a strategy. Part of this involves distilling strategic thinking down into drawn artefacts. A vision is important, but it isn't enough. Designing *how* you're going to achieve your vision is crucial for success. In this chapter, we explain how to nail your 'why', 'how' and 'what'. Designing tomorrow is your chance to define an ambitious, desirable but achievable future state.

- What is your purpose? What are you passionate about?
- What do you want to achieve and how will you do it?
- What's the one thing you need to overcome to achieve this?

- What value factors are most critical to your success?
- Who will you sell to?
- How will you arrange your capabilities to win?
- Who are your competitors? How can you win against them?
- How will you generate the cash you need to succeed?

We describe all this through our acronym, PACCTACC: Purpose, Ambition, Challenge, Critical value factors, Target segments, Arranged capabilities, Competition and Cash generation. You can think of PACCTACC as your set of guiding policies that help to steer decision-making throughout the organization (see Chapter 2.1).

This chapter is structured according to PACCTACC, stepping through each of the elements in turn. It ends with a visualization of Strategy on a Page (SOAP). This distils PACCTACC down to one page which can be easily communicated and understood throughout the organization. Throughout, we draw on a new case study of a corner shop called Grocery Post to show how PACCTACC works in practice. We'll begin by giving the necessary background.

Grocery Post

In my (Rupert's) neighbourhood, there is a corner shop called Grocery Post. It is no ordinary corner shop and very different from anything else in the area. When I go in, I often think about a case example given by Rumelt in *Good Strategy/Bad Strategy*. He introduces us to his friend Stephanie who runs a grocery store close to a university. She is losing out to a competitor that has recently opened nearby and she has a series of questions about what she should do and which customers she should target. Rumelt uses the example to illustrate his concept of a guiding policy to steer strategic decision-making (see Chapter 2.1).[2] From the day it opened, Grocery Post has felt unique. It's felt consistent, coherent and underpinned by clear, strategic thinking. The founders have nailed a niche.

We wanted to understand more about how the founders devised and executed their strategy and who they saw as their competition, so we asked if we could interview them for this book. We discovered that our hunches were true. The strategy was strong. It was underpinned by Blue Ocean Strategy. The founders, James and James, had learned about how to create a blue ocean and had put it into practice. In the interview, we stepped through the different elements of PACCTACC to both diagnose the current situation and understand the strategy design. Our findings are peppered throughout this chapter.

James and James are old school friends. Grocery Post is not their first business (in fact, for one of them, it's their fourth). It's the third business that they've founded together. All of their businesses have been driven by a desire to create something special and have a positive impact on the community. They love branding. They love events.

They opened their first store at the height of the Covid-19 pandemic. They found the perfect spot and signed a 25-year lease. It's in Highgate, an affluent neighbourhood in North London. It's on a corner, close to where people live, near a tube station and opposite a nursery. They got the store ready themselves, sanding down shelves and painting walls well into the early hours. They didn't have much money at that point – just £50,000. It wasn't enough to fill all the shelves and when they opened, half of them were empty. Their previous businesses had taught them some of life's hard lessons and their forecasts were conservative. But the business took off much more quickly than they were expecting. They achieved their 12-month run-rate target in a matter of weeks. Three years later, they opened their second store in West Hampstead. Again, it is on a corner in an affluent neighbourhood, where lots of people pass by.

Grocery Post is a special kind of corner shop. Everything about it shouts indulgence and luxury. Before they opened, when they were hard at work in their overalls, they spray-painted 'The Soho House of convenience stores' on the walls. Their vision was strong. If we asked them to articulate their 'best in the world' performer on an absolute scale, the exclusive members' club Soho House might be it. Grocery Post sells expensive groceries from high-end brands – brands that have loyal followings and that people don't mind paying over the odds for. They sell wine, beer, cheese, cured meats, pick 'n' mix, candles, olives, nuts and olive oil. They stock only one SKU per category. An online reviewer of the Highgate store calls it 'the most considered product selection in London'. Talented and friendly baristas serve delicious coffee. They sell freshly made cakes, sausage rolls, soups and sandwiches. They only offer a narrow range and things aren't available every day, but the quality is as high as you can get.

As we will see, they have two clearly defined customer segments. These customers value community, want to support small, local brands and care about the provenance of the goods they buy. The online reviews are interesting.

FIGURE 2.3.1 Grocery Post has ten value factors, five competitor archetypes and two customer segments

There are far more positive reviews than negative ones (the Highgate store gets an average of 4.5 stars out of 5 from 80 reviews. The West Hampstead store gets an average of 4.8 stars out of 5 with 16 reviews). Those who give high scores often acknowledge the expense but are not put off by it: 'It's local, independent and high-quality so you would expect to pay more.' They talk about the great community spirit and vibe. The more negative reviews tend to complain about waiting times, inventory management and often the cost of the products. Grocery Post might not be the best option for people who are in a hurry. It also doesn't work for those who are cost-sensitive. For some, the WAVS/price trade-off isn't worth it. (We introduced WAVS in Chapter 2.2. As a reminder, it stands for Weighted Average Value Score. It distils your value proposition into a single number. The score for each value factor is weighted by the level of importance that buyers assign to it.)

Figure 2.3.1 shows a summary of Grocery Post's value factors, competitor archetypes and customer segments. It might be useful to refer back to as you read the chapter.

Purpose

In Chapter 1.2, we talk about the importance of putting culture first. Part of this is understanding your purpose and, as Simon Sinek has so famously said, 'starting with why'.[3]

Your purpose is what drives you. It's informed by your passion and desire to do something remarkable. It has to be personal.

The Hedgehog Concept is an idea developed by Jim Collins in *Good to Great*. The concept is inspired by the philosopher Isaiah Berlin's 1953 essay 'The Hedgehog and the Fox', which is based upon an ancient Greek parable: 'The fox knows many things, but the hedgehog knows one big thing.' The idea is to be hedgehogs, not foxes, and simplify the world into one unifying idea. Collins discovered that good-to-great companies find their hedgehog concept by asking themselves three key questions:

1 What are we deeply passionate about?
2 What can we be best in the world at?
3 What drives our economic engine?[4]

We'll return to points 2 and 3 later in the chapter. At this point, we'll discuss point 1: passion. Collins reminds us that passion cannot be manufactured. It has to be real. It might not be immediately apparent and is often a voyage of discovery. But it is crucial to know what ignites your passion and the passion of those around you.

If your passions aren't in sync, it's difficult to align on anything. Success doesn't just depend on the alignment of behaviour and values. It depends on the alignment of purpose. When this clicks, beautiful things can happen. When it doesn't, relationships can break down and it can be the cause of huge amounts of stress. This is why you start with your purpose. You have to have this nailed. It is the foundation upon which you build your strategy.

As we discussed in the Preface, we bonded over passionate beliefs about board meetings and board pack reporting. We both also feel strongly about the importance of high-quality corporate training. We love passing on our experience and helping people learn new skills. I (Jon) have been training people throughout my entire career while I (Rupert) led the core corporate skills training in Kearney (I have also been training kids in rugby for 12 years and counting – different but related). We love codifying our methods (which is, in large part, the passion behind this book). Our passions led to us founding Ārahi with a strong common purpose – to improve our method and thinking and create a product and training materials to address our felt pain. Grocery Post has a strong sense of purpose which they have taken time to discover. They progressed through several failed businesses before their passions united over Grocery Post.

CASE STUDY

GROCERY POST: PURPOSE

Grocery Post's purpose is to 'create neighbourhood hangouts where people can come together with a shared love of food and drink'. James and James have passion oozing out of every pore. They care deeply about building something special to enhance communities. Their businesses have always had this at their core, whether that's a novel street food restaurant in the heart of London or an on-demand grocery delivery service that sourced products from the local high street. They are founders through and through. In their own words, 'We love making new things. We want to be able to say, "Look, look at what we've made."'

This passion has found a home in Grocery Post's purpose. They want to create a club feel, for both adults and children. They remember the excitement of going to the local corner shop when they were growing up with pocket money to buy a Slush Puppie. They want to create the same experience for kids and they sell pick 'n' mix for this reason. They hold Santa visits and free ice cream days for kids as well as cheese and wine tastings for adults. Their new running club was three times oversubscribed. All of it is driven by a common purpose – to be the hub of a community.

The extent of their care is shown in certain policies. For example, they charge the same price for decaf coffee because charging more (it costs them more to buy) would affect expectant mothers disproportionately. They also give free bottles of Prosecco to new mums to celebrate their newborns.

Ambition

Next comes your ambition. It's what Lafley and Martin call 'your winning aspiration'.

It's hard to design strategy without understanding the context of your ambition. As we explained in Chapter 1.1, achieving breakthrough returns depends on your ability to grow your Total Addressable Market (TAM). This is different for everyone. A lifestyle business will have different ambitions from a company hoping to achieve unicorn status. Be careful what you wish for. Our case study of the branding agency in Chapter 2.2 showed how value factor work made them realize that they had made assumptions about their ambition that weren't true. They realized that their ambition was being guided by what every other agency in their position does. It wasn't what they wanted. They wanted to create a lifestyle business and keep hold of it, not sell it.

There are different ways to think about your ambition and different frameworks to help you articulate it. One of the most commonly used and most helpful is Jim Collins's Big Hairy Audacious Goal (BHAG), which helps you to think about your ambition in terms of timescale and scope.[5] Your BHAG is an articulation of what the organization and the individuals within it are seeking to achieve over a long-term time horizon. BHAGs set a huge goal that drives progress, defines a vision for the future and gets everyone working towards achieving it. A BHAG is clear and compelling and should need little explanation.

A BHAG stops you from thinking too small, but it must still be doable. It should, at a minimum, have a 50 per cent chance of being achieved. A great BHAG sets a clear finishing line and creates a sense of urgency. It requires a long-term commitment – a minimum of ten years, but possibly even two or three decades. In most industries and contexts, it makes sense to work to a 15-year time horizon. John F Kennedy's 'Man on the Moon' speech is a famous example of a BHAG. In his address to Congress in May 1961, he famously said, 'I believe that this nation should commit itself to achieving the goal, before this decade is out, of landing a man on the Moon and returning him safely to the Earth'.[6] In July 1969, Armstrong set foot on the moon. Other prominent examples of BHAGs include Microsoft: 'A computer on every desk and in every home', Google: 'Organize the world's information' and Tesla: 'Accelerate the world's transition to sustainable energy'.

CASE STUDY

GROCERY POST: AMBITION

Grocery Post's BHAG is to grow to 40 stores across South-East England in the next ten years. They plan for each store to generate an average of £200,000 EBITDA, driving an Enterprise Value of over £100 million. In the near term, they are aiming to open five stores over five years.

They have bold ambitions. They want to become the LVMH of groceries with a portfolio of unique venture brands. They want to create their own branded products and leave behind a legacy.

Challenge

For Rumelt, the 'why' of good strategy comes down to defining and explaining the central challenge that needs to be overcome. This means boiling down what can be overwhelming complexity to a single problem. Rumelt develops this idea further in his 2022 book, *The Crux*.[7] The crux of a challenge is the fundamental issue where you should direct most of your energy and focus. Once identified, you can take decisive and coherent action to address it. Your challenge can change over time. Strategy is a living thing. Once you achieve it and reach a new stage of growth, you'll be on to the next one (see Chapter 3.2). Our case study helps to bring this concept to life.

CASE STUDY

GROCERY POST: CHALLENGE

At the beginning, Grocery Post's main challenge was to create a differentiated brand and capture a customer segment. At the time we did the interview, they had achieved that in spades. They were much more successful than their original targets. Their success had spurred on huge ambitions for growth and their challenge had therefore shifted to scalability and complexity. Their model and high-touch ideology worked for one shop, but they needed the processes and systems in place to make it work for 50 shops. They are unique, but how do they make that uniqueness repeatable?

Processes are needed for inventory management. They stock one SKU per category and have 180 suppliers. That's a lot of work. They had teething problems with the second store as they didn't have appropriate management processes in place. Great staff were too overworked and left.

Processes are also needed for training. Part of their brand is to offer high-touch service from engaging and friendly staff. They want to aim for a consistent level of staff product knowledge between shops. This is particularly difficult with wine, which takes up around 20 per cent of their shelf space. They might be able to find one wine expert for one shop, but it's not scalable. They therefore created a taxonomy of wines by taste rather than region.

Critical value factors

The second question posed through Jim Collins' Hedgehog Concept is, 'What can we be best in the world at?' In the context of Grocery Post, the 'world' is the neighbourhoods surrounding their shops. Your critical value factors are those that define your points of difference and make you the best in the world at what you do for your target customer segments. This exercise involves going through your list of value factors and identifying actions for each one that will increase or reduce your score and make you different from everyone else. It might also mean adding a value factor that you don't currently offer. The ultimate aim is to isolate the critical one to three value factors that define you. This helps to direct your focus. These are carried forward to your 'Value-Cap Map', which we explain later in the chapter.

Note that Collins talks about a crucial difference between what you *can* be the best in the world at and what you *want* to be the best in the world at. You might find that what you want to be the best in the world at is out of your reach, so you're better off not trying to compete in that space. To think all this through, we advocate using the 5S Action Framework.

The 5S Action Framework: Stop, Shrink, Stay, Stretch, Start

Designing strategy is effectively a series of decisions. What should we do less of? What should we do more of? What should stay the same? Your diagnosis should make the answers to these questions clear. To help you think it through, we've created the **5S Action Framework: Stop, Shrink, Stay, Stretch, Start**, as shown in Figure 2.3.2.

1. Stop – when you design your strategy, there may be value factors that you want to score 0 on. You want to cut them completely. Southwest cut concessions and hubs. Cirque du Soleil cut star performers, animal shows and aisle concessions. Our branding agency cut geographical expansion (see Chapter 2.2).
2. Shrink – 'Shrink' involves identifying the value factors that are not key differentiators for you and therefore reducing the amount of focus on them. This is a good way to take out costs. In the context of scoring, you might look to reduce a value factor from 25 to 10, so you're still credible in the industry. Note that dropping a value factor from 10 to 5 may not be worthwhile. This would take you to a status that is below credible and it might be better to drop the value factor altogether. Southwest shrunk a lot of value factors in their industry to save costs. For example, they did away with the need for a fancy, physical ticket. Air travel tickets in the 1970s were plush. They had layers and were printed using a special machine. Southwest's customer segment didn't care about these kinds of frills, so they printed 'This is a ticket' on the receipt and made do with that. That alone saved them $2 million back in the early Seventies.[8]
3. Stay – there will be lots of value factors that you want to continue just as they are.
4. Stretch – identify value factors that you currently have but could emphasize more. These value factors have the potential to be your core strengths. Think of them as your spikes, the things that make you famous. The reasons why people buy from you.

FIGURE 2.3.2 The 5S Action Framework: Stop, Shrink, Stay, Stretch, Start

5 Start – this involves thinking about the value factors that you don't currently have but could add. What new value factors can you bring to the table? You could start small and introduce the value factor with a score of 5 or 10. Alternatively, you could match the competition to nullify their strengths. This might involve going in at a score of 10 or 25. Or, you could bring something new to the industry and make the competition irrelevant. You could apply something outside your industry and make a big bet to create value that others haven't even considered. This is another example of how you could create a spike.

CASE STUDY

GROCERY POST: CRITICAL VALUE FACTORS

Grocery Post identified ten value factors on their landscape:

1 Broad range of delicatessen-quality products – high-end grocery categories, which are only premium quality.

2 Convenience – self-service, opening hours, location, short waiting time, stock availability.

3. Engaging staff with deep product knowledge – staff recruited for their personality and knowledge.
4. Exclusive bakery and bread – top-quality freshly baked bread and baked goods, with 'hero' products (products that they become known for and which bring people to the shop).
5. In-store events and occasions – community-building events that drive the neighbourhood feel.
6. Top-quality barista coffee experience –freshly brewed, handmade coffee.
7. Ready meals – convenience-focused to be cooked easily at home.
8. Mainstream branded snack products – classic mainstream snack brands at competitive prices.
9. Tables and table service – tables for those who want to sit, with table service for convenience.
10. Over-the-counter delicatessen service.

Figure 2.3.3 shows these factors in order of importance according to one customer segment (affluent local residents – we explain the segments in the next step). How might they apply the 5S Action Framework? There are two clear spikes – the broad range of delicatessen-quality products and the top-quality barista coffee experience. Performance scores for both of these are 100 and they are 90 points better than the national convenience chain. These would be labelled 'stay' – they would want to keep these as they are.

There are three value factors that they want to stretch. They currently score 70 for the value factor 'exclusive bakery and bread'. Part of their ambition is to start creating their own branded products, including their own baked goods. They aspire to have their own 'hero' products, for example the kind of cookies that customers will make a special trip for. They want to stretch this value factor to 90. (This will also help increase the margin of these products – see Cash generation later in the chapter.)

Linked to this is the value factor 'ready meals'. They currently score 10, so are just credible in the space. However, they intend to introduce their own branded ready meals, starting with Indian street food. They intend to stretch this value factor from 10 to 35.

The third value factor they plan to stretch is the product knowledge of their staff, taking it from 20 to 40. They plan to do this through training and creating playbooks so that it's not just the founders who can train new staff members –

FIGURE 2.3.3 A Mekko chart comparing Grocery Post to a national convenience chain

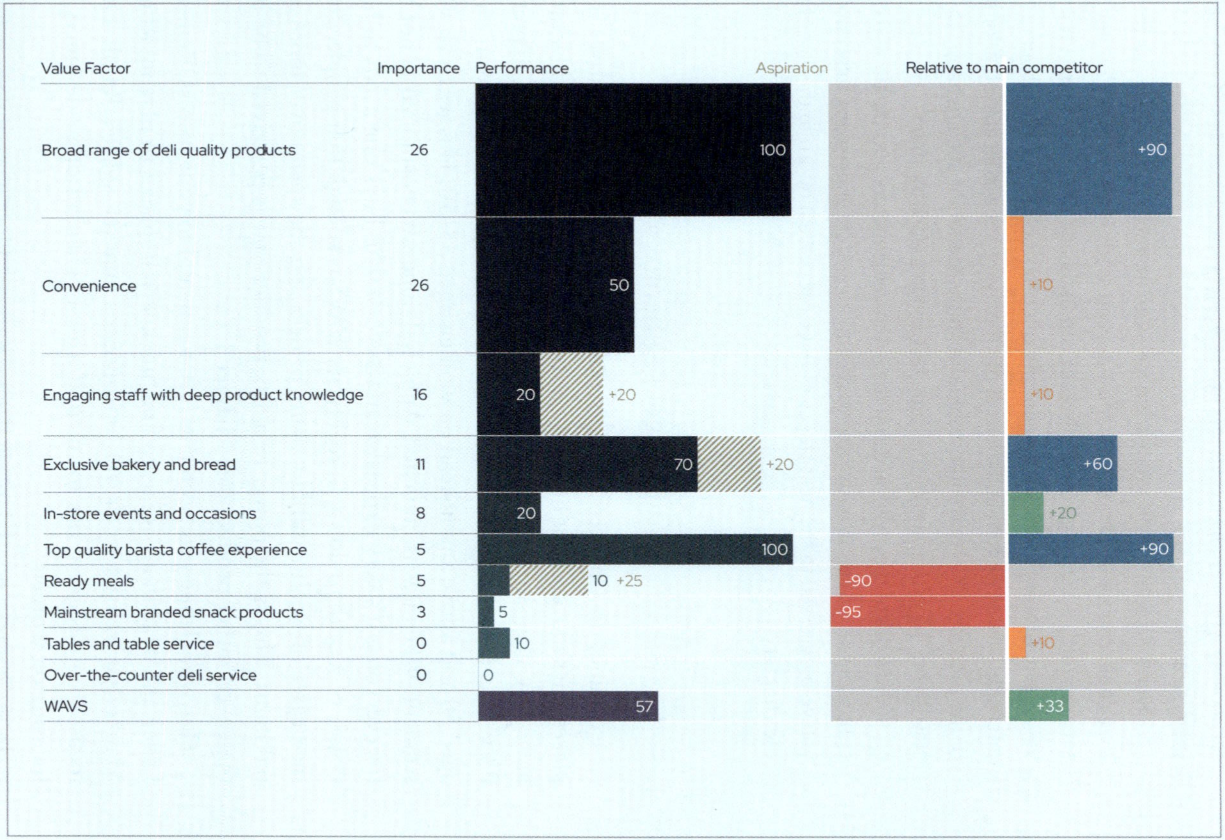

anyone can do it. This is partly how they plan to address the challenge of scalability. To help with wine knowledge, they plan to introduce in-store technology which enables customers to select a bottle of wine based on what they're eating.

'Over-the-counter delicatessen service' is an example of a value factor that they could choose to compete on. Most delicatessens have over-the-counter service which is very high touch. Queues can build and the stock doesn't turn very often. Grocery Post currently doesn't offer this because of the labour intensity, slow stock turn and the cost of employing knowledgeable staff for all of the products. They currently score 0 for this value factor and are happy to stay there. The economics of the value factor don't work for them.

So how might they whittle down these ten value factors into the three most critical ones? It's not an easy thing to do and it can't be understood fully until you've progressed to the next stages of PACCTACC. We'll return to this later in the chapter.

Target segments

As explained in Chapter 2.2, a market segment is a set of customers that places the same amount of value on the same value factors. Good strategies have very clear target segments. In the example we gave in Chapter 2.1, P&G decided to refocus Oil of Olay's target segment away from women aged 50 and above and instead on women aged 35–50. This was a very clear segment. When it was launched, Apple's iPhone was positioned as not being for everyone. It's very expensive and anyone who buys one needs to have a degree of wealth to do so. In reality, its WAVS is so high that people without the degree of wealth still buy them, prioritizing the spend over more essential items. This is the power of a 10× product that is perceived to be better than every other product (see Chapter 1.1).

How you define your segments is fundamental to your success. Remember Lafley and Martin advise us to find 'unexpected' places to play in. Kim and Mauborgne tell us to create 'uncontested market space'. Ralph Lauren focused on designing ties for men at a time when all other designers were focusing on women.

In the context of a relatively simple business like Grocery Post, it may be enough to understand your segments in a broad-brush way. In the Grocery Post case study, we explain how they have two main customer segments:

residents and people passing through the neighbourhood. In larger organizations that offer various products and services and may operate in numerous geographies, it's important to understand your segments on a deeper level. The clearer you can be about your target segment, the more you can hone your value proposition to tap into its needs. McKinsey suggests that the more you segment the market, the more successful you will be. They propose breaking down the customer universe into 30 to 50 segments, rather than the more typical five.[9] See this as a journey. Start broad. The more you understand your customers, the more granular you can be.

We don't have the space to delve into detail here (there are whole textbooks on it), but segments can be defined in terms of their attributes. In B2C, it's common to collect and analyse certain demographics – general characteristics about groups of people and populations, such as:

- gender
- age
- geography
- income
- education
- price sensitivity

In B2B, it's common to look at firmographics – a collection of descriptive attributes used by an organization to segment its target market. For example:

- industry
- location
- size
- status or structure
- performance

As well as collecting and analysing this data about your segments, bring them to life by giving them names and creating profiles for them. What does a day in the life of a person in a particular segment look like? What do they read? What do they listen to? How do they travel? What channel can you reach them through? It's about humanizing them and identifying common needs, pain points and behaviours.

The aim is to identify the one segment that you 'home run' on every time. This is your number one niche to target. Use the diagnosing techniques we described at the end of Chapter 2.2 to understand your ability to win in a segment and the attractiveness of that segment – the needs and behaviours of this niche help to steer your decision-making. Then, identify the two next most important segments. For each product or service that you offer, don't be tempted to target more than three segments. This is about prioritization and focus. Nailing a niche means zooming in where you know you can win. Stick to the Rule of Three (see Chapter 1.3).

CASE STUDY

GROCERY POST: TARGET SEGMENTS

Grocery Post has two main customer segments:

1. Affluent residents who live within walking distance and have high disposable income.
2. People on the move who are passing through, such as dog walkers, cyclists and parents picking up children from the nursery across the road.

Figure 2.3.4 shows the importance of value factors according to each of these segments. The people on the move value the bakery and coffee the most, whereas the residents value the broad range of delicatessen-quality products. Note that sometimes the data might look odd to you, for example this figure suggests that people on the move value in-store events and occasions more than the residents. Maybe this is the case, but this is an instance where you might want to increase the survey size and dig a bit deeper to find out whether it's true. The numbers are there to guide us. It's important to apply your judgement.

At the end of this chapter, we show a SOAP for Grocery Post, giving some metrics for each customer segment. Residents typically spend around £20 per visit and they are likely to visit the shop 50 times per year. There are around 3,000 residents in this segment. Knowing this data means we can calculate the Serviceable Available Market (SAM) per shop. The SAM represents the available market in the customer segment. The SAM for the 'residents' segment is £3 million. People on the move spend less per visit (£7) but visit more often (60 times per year) and there are more of them (5,000). The SAM for people on the move is £2.1 million. As we explained above, this segment data can be used to determine your critical value factors.

FIGURE 2.3.4 Importance weighting for Grocery Post's two customer segments

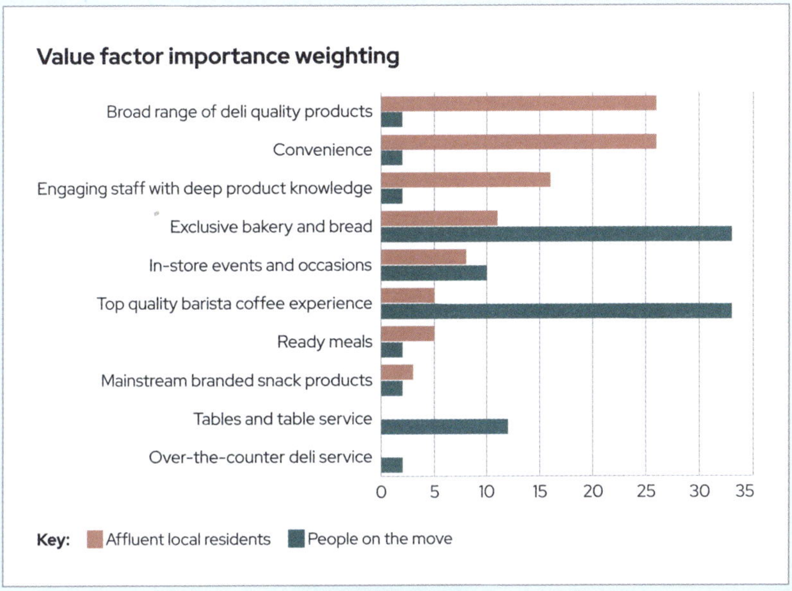

Arranged capabilities

Returning to Collins' Hedgehog Concept, we believe that understanding what you can be best in the world at requires consideration of both your critical value factors and your core capabilities. Together, they differentiate you from the competition. Lafley and Martin ask us in their fourth question to think about the capabilities that need to be in place to win.[10]

Organizational **capabilities** are often confused with competencies, which relate to the skills, knowledge, behaviours and cognitive abilities of individual people. Capabilities incorporate the processes, systems and people (with the right competencies) who come together to execute organizational strategy, as shown in Figure 2.3.5. People have competencies: behaviours, knowledge and skills. The process relates to the value chain – the end-to-end steps through which the company creates value. Company processes are how activities transform inputs into outputs. The systems are the protocols that are in place.

FIGURE 2.3.5 Organizational capabilities can be broken down into people, processes and systems

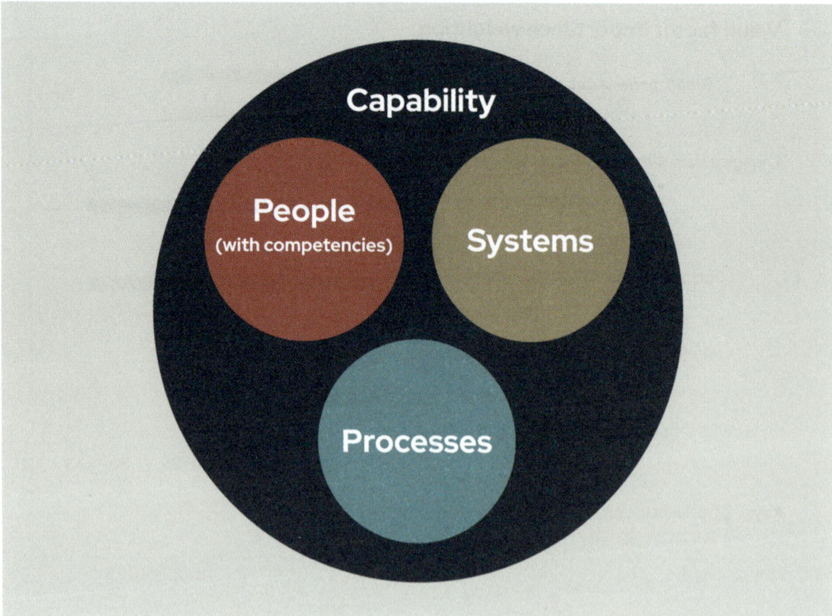

The Value-Cap Map

We like to visualize capabilities alongside value factors through a Value-Cap Map. This takes its inspiration from Michael Porter's Activity System Map. In *Competitive Advantage*, Porter asserts that a company achieves a sustainable competitive advantage by 'deliberately choosing a different set of activities to deliver unique value'.[11] Porter uses a graph structure to visualize the main 'strategic themes' or components of the value proposition alongside the set of activities necessary for putting it into practice. Lines connect the themes to the activities to show how they relate to each other. The beauty of it is that it distils a host of key information down to one page, enabling it to be articulated and communicated throughout the organization. He famously uses IKEA and Southwest to illustrate how strategy can be communicated in this way. For example, for Porter, IKEA has four strategic themes:

1. Self-selection by customers.
2. Modular furniture design.

3 Limited customer service.

4 Low manufacturing cost.

These four themes are linked to activities. For example, limited customer service is linked to having explanatory catalogues and informative displays and labels. They sell flat-pack furniture which customers assemble themselves. They are in suburban locations with ample parking, so customers can drive and transport the furniture themselves. The activities that allow customers to self-select include a high-traffic store layout. Customers are directed around stores via a one-way system, passing through different areas that sell different items of furniture. The suburban locations and car parks also link to this theme, as do the activities related to having inventory on-site.

Using Porter's strategic themes as inspiration, we have developed the concept further, breaking them down into five clearly defined self-reinforcing elements and highlighting the importance of capabilities:

1. Critical value factors (examples are 'modular furniture design' and 'limited customer service').
2. Core capabilities (examples are 'self-selection by customers' and 'low manufacturing cost').
3. 'How to' choices (examples linked to the value factor 'modular furniture design' are 'self-assembly by customers' and 'in-house design focused on cost of manufacturing').
4. Objectives (examples linked to modular furniture design are 'increased likelihood of future purchase' and 'ample inventory on-site').
5. Policies (an example linked to 'low manufacturing cost' is '100 per cent sourcing from long-term suppliers').

The Grocery Post case study shows how these can be visualized through a Value-Cap Map. The Value-Cap Map shows how you're going to win. You can use it to build your moat against future competitors.

CASE STUDY

GROCERY POST: CAPABILITIES AND THE VALUE-CAP MAP

The founders of Grocery Post need capabilities in place to enable their critical value factors and answer their current challenge – how to scale from 2 shops to 50. As mentioned above, a large part of this is inventory management. Lessons learned from opening the second store meant that they took this task away from the store manager and built a buying function, bringing in a professional to manage their 180 suppliers and be in charge of stock control. As we have also mentioned, they need processes and systems in place to enable training of new staff members and to plug any knowledge gaps of existing staff. Wine taxonomies and tech-enabled cheat sheets will help with this.

Figure 2.3.6 shows their Value-Cap Map. The three core capabilities are:

- sourcing of a wide range of high-quality products
- barista capability
- design and packaging

You can see that the three value factors that made it onto the map are:

- broad range of delicatessen quality products
- convenience
- top-quality barista coffee experience

The broad range of delicatessen quality products is a no-brainer. This is the most important value factor for their most valuable segment, the residents. They are outperforming the competition and they are the best in the world at it. 'Convenience' is also an obvious choice. It's second on the list for this segment and they are marginally outperforming the competition. What about the third? This is harder. Two value factors stand out – the artisan coffee and the bakery. These are both important value factors for the people on the move and the bakery is also important to the residents. They intend to stretch this one to 90. It is also a key vehicle for them to realize an important element of their ambition – to create their own-brand, hero products. To succeed, they will need the right capabilities in place and the right activities. But at the same time, they score 100 on the quality barista experience. It's valued highly. The scores show this as do the website reviews. They want to maintain their lead against the high-end bakery, which also provides good coffee. If people come in for the coffee, it might help to get the word out about their bakery's hero products. 'Top-quality barista coffee experience' makes it onto the map.

We'll end by focusing on the capability 'Sourcing of a wide range of high-quality products'. It is linked to one key objective 'Reliable availability of stock'. This capability feeds the value factors 'Full barista-style coffee offering' and 'Broad range of deli-quality products'. Various 'how to' choices feed this capability and these value factors, for example: 'Premium wine', 'High-quality

FIGURE 2.3.6 Grocery Post's Value-Cap Map

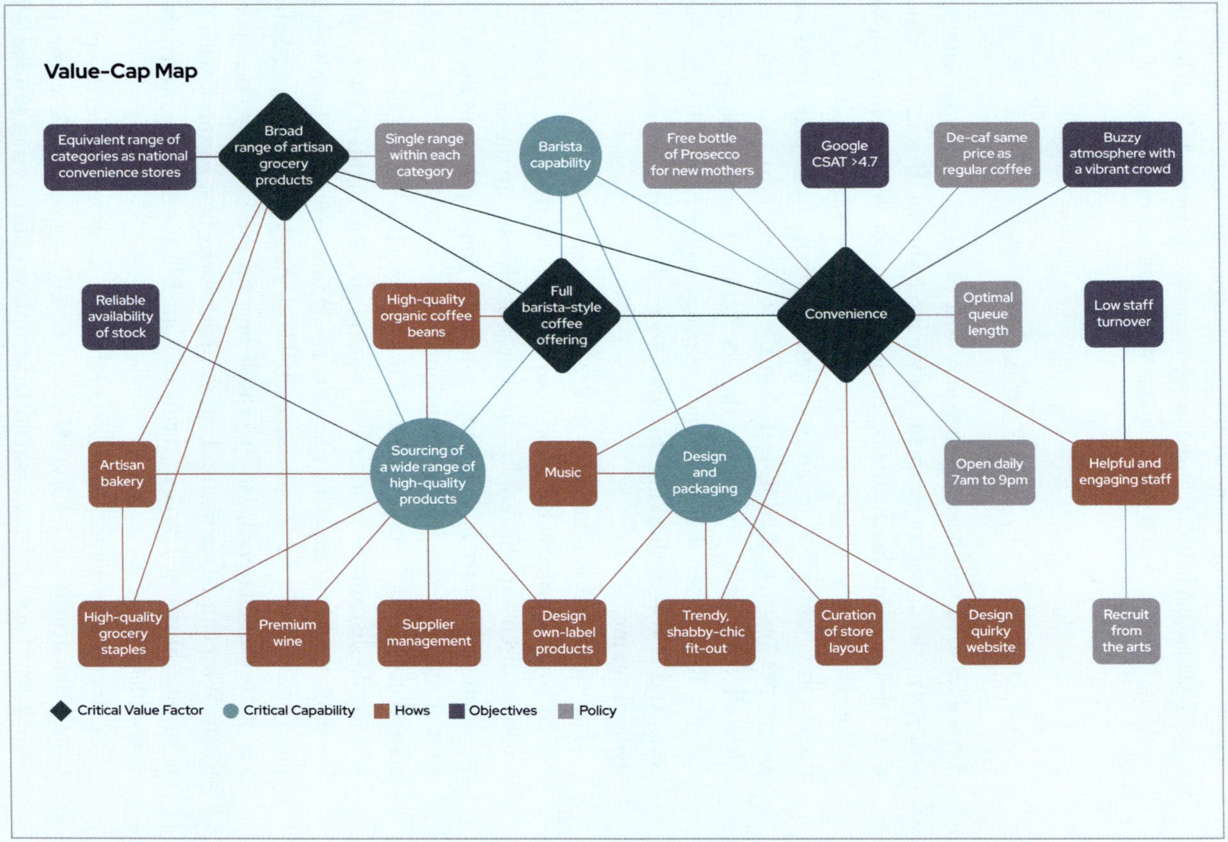

grocery staples', 'Artisan bakery' and 'High-quality organic coffee beans'. There are six policies on the map, one of which is to have a single SKU within each category. This policy is linked to the value factor 'Broad range of deli-quality products', which in turn is linked to the sourcing capability. This is an illustration of how the elements on the Value-Cap Map are all self-reinforcing.

Competition

Your diagnosis will have given you a host of data about your competitors and how you compare to them. As we have shown, this can be visualized through the value landscape or through Mekko charts, which show your performance versus your main competitors for each value factor. As we discuss in Chapter 2.2, it can be helpful to think of competitors in terms of archetypes (as also demonstrated in the Grocery Post case study below). This all feeds how you apply the 5S Action Framework to your value factors. Remember that different segments might have different competitors. And if you're thinking this way, so might your competitors. This is a dynamic game.

This diagnosis is crucial for understanding your present so that you can design your tomorrow based on your current situation. But like so much of what we discuss in this book, competitor analysis is an ongoing exercise. As we wrote in Chapter 1.3, winning companies constantly scan the horizon to spot competitor threats. We mentioned an exercise called 'The nightmare competitor'. This involves thinking outside the box to imagine challengers who could disrupt the market and destroy you overnight. It's not just about knowing the key competitors you are up against every day. It's about anticipating who could enter your market. Think Apple and Nokia or Sony. The key is to think laterally and to think beyond the industry you operate in today. Who can come in and beat you? It works best to think with a long-term time horizon. Think in terms of your BHAG timeline rather than the next milestone.

A great case example of a nightmare competitor is Zoom Video Communications and Cisco Webex. Cisco's biggest risk came from a competitor formed by a disgruntled employee. Eric Yuan landed a job at Webex when he was 27. A decade later, when Webex was sold to Cisco, he was made Vice President of Engineering and given a healthy six-figure salary. In an interview with CNBC Make It, he described how, after an initial period of happiness, he started to not want to go to work. He felt that the customers were unhappy and the product wasn't evolving sufficiently quickly to meet their needs. So what did he do? He left and formed Zoom, a product that happened to be in the right place at the right time when Covid-19 hit.[12] Had Cisco anticipated that someone with deep product knowledge and a real passion for the domain, like Yuan, might do this?

CASE STUDY

GROCERY POST: COMPETITION

When we first approached the founders of Grocery Post for an interview, we mentioned their competition. They looked surprised. 'We don't have any competition,' they replied. They later clarified what they meant. Usain Bolt didn't have competitors. He had people running against him. Grocery Post has consciously differentiated itself from any other shop in the neighbourhood. It runs against five competitor archetypes. These archetypes are shown in Figure 2.3.7 along with their WAVS for both segments. As the figure shows, Grocery Post wins for the residents, albeit marginally. They are competing primarily against high-end delicatessens and premium wine stores. For the people on the move, the high-end bakery café pips them to the post. This is clearly their main competitor for this segment. The various strengths and weaknesses of the archetypes versus Grocery Post are as follows:

1 High-end delicatessens, e.g. Italian deli

Strengths – high-quality deli products

Weaknesses – narrow range of products, often queues, poor-quality coffee

2 Premium wine stores, e.g. Borough Wines

Strengths – wide range of high-quality wines, highly experienced staff

Weaknesses – narrow range of products, only wine

3 High-end bakery and café, e.g. Gail's Bakery

Strengths – high-quality baked produce, in-store seating, comparable coffee

Weaknesses – narrow range of products, no wine, lack of club feel

4 National convenience chains, e.g. Sainsbury's Local

Strengths – wide range of produce at competitive price points

Weaknesses – poor service, low quality, no coffee

5 7-Eleven-style convenience stores, e.g. 7-Eleven

Strengths – extended opening hours, more snacks

Weaknesses – low-quality products, lack of club feel, no community spirit

Figure 2.3.8 shows their performance scores versus two archetypes: the national convenience store and the high-end bakery café. They are ordered according to the preference of affluent local residents No one can compete against them on the broad range of deli-quality products and they also win with the barista experience and convenience. The high-end bakery café

FIGURE 2.3.7 WAVS scores for both segments

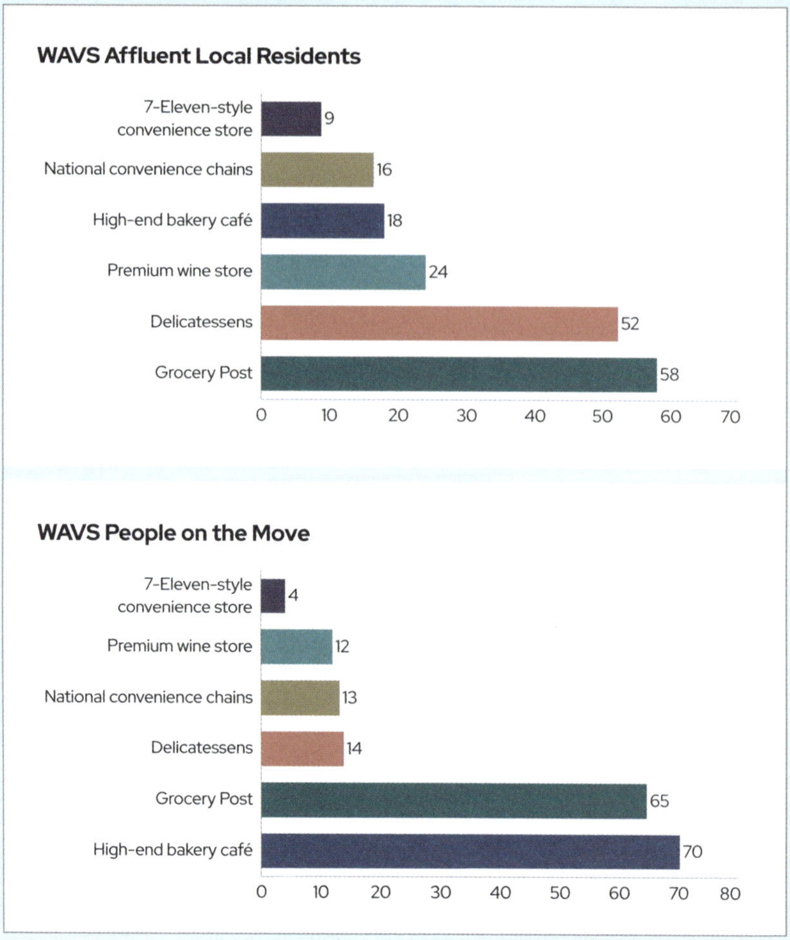

FIGURE 2.3.8 A comparison of Grocery Post with two competitor archetypes

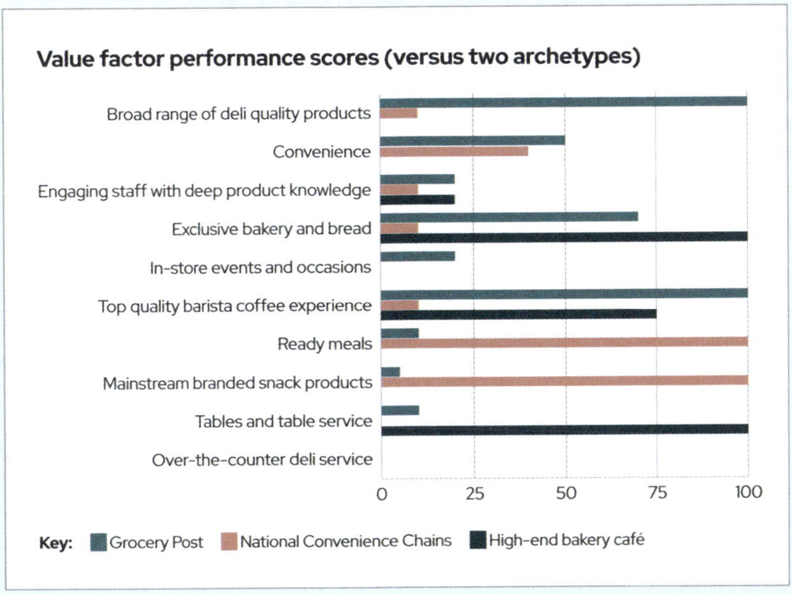

currently beats them on the exclusive bakery and bread and is not far behind them with the coffee. If people want to sit down, that's also where they'd go as Grocery Post has minimal seating. This is another reason for making the barista experience one of the critical value factors.

Cash generation

Cash generation relates to where your revenue comes from and, critically, your margin (the real top line). It has to make sense for your business model. Ultimately, it's how you deliver shareholder value. This relates to what Jim Collins calls your 'economic engine', which, he states, 'is measured by *one key metric* that defines the essence of your business model and is tied to your long-range goal'.[13]

Ultimately, we see the economic engine of a business through the lens of cash flow. Everyone views their cash generation through a different lens. It could relate to selling your product or service, memberships or subscriptions. In the restaurant industry, a Michelin Star restaurant might have only one cover per night, so their cash generation metric could be revenue or margin per cover. In contrast, a local pizza restaurant is likely to turn their tables as many times a night as they can – they might therefore look at revenue or margin per table. In the SaaS business, the Lifetime Value (LTV) to Customer Acquisition Cost (CAC) ratio is the commonly used metric. CAC relates to your efficiency in acquiring new revenue. This is expressed as Annual Recurring Revenue (ARR). It helps you understand subscription sales and shows the money that comes in every year over the life of a subscription. CAC tells you how much it costs to acquire $1 of ARR. An LTV/CAC of greater than 4 is good. In retail, you might look at the margin generated per square metre of floor space. This is one of the metrics measured by Grocery Post, as explained in the case study box.

CASE STUDY

GROCERY POST: CASH GENERATION

Grocery Post uses three metrics to measure its cash generation. These are shown in the bottom right-hand corner of the SOAP (see Figure 2.3.9). The metrics are:

- Revenue per square metre of retail space per month: they only have 68 square metres of floor space and they generate £2,000 per square metre per month. The aim is to get this to £2,500. They are very focused on cash and when people are likely to visit the shop. They aren't open for as long as many convenience stores. In their Highgate shop, their busiest period lasts for about 20 minutes and coincides with parents dropping their children off at the nursery opposite. They struggle to manage the queue for these 20 minutes and it often winds around the shop. While they do like to have a queue to help build a sense of community within the shop, the waiting time can't be so long that people give up. This comes back to capabilities and how they can manage this problem so that they can maximize their revenue during these peak periods.
- The number of times stock turns over in a year: this metric is linked to the one above. The more customers they get, the more they will turn their stock, which will mean their revenue per square metre can increase. They currently turn their stock 17 times per year. They aim to increase this to 25 times per year.
- Average margin on products sold: when they started, they were aiming for a margin of 35 per cent on products sold. A customer came in who just happened to be an expert and advised them to increase it to 40 per cent. So they did, the very next day. They have no plans to increase this.

The Strategy on a Page (SOAP)

We'll end this chapter with a visualization of the Strategy on a Page, or SOAP. The SOAP shown in Figure 2.3.9 includes all the key elements of PACCTACC on one page so that it's easy to communicate and understand. It's a great quick reference tool.

Final thoughts

Michael Porter has five ways of testing whether or not a strategy is any good:

1 A unique value proposition compared with other organizations.
2 Clear trade-offs and choosing what not to do.
3 A differentiated, tailored value chain.
4 Activities that fit together in a system and reinforce each other.
5 Strategic continuity with continual improvement.[14]

These chapters have given frameworks and methods to help with each of these five points. PACCTACC doesn't need to be stepped through sequentially. Arriving at your Value-Cap Map is an iterative, back-and-forth process. The most important thing to remember is that strategy is a living, breathing thing. Good strategies stand the test of time, but they evolve because the world evolves. No strategy work is ever set in stone. As our Grocery Post case study demonstrates, get your strategy working for you now and then think about how to scale. Nail value factors and add and improve them as you grow. As you scale, your key challenge will change. Think about how your capabilities need to evolve to address this shift. Your competitors will change. They will be watching you, seeing how they can differentiate from what you're doing and thinking of ways to change the game on you. Be ready for this, so you can respond quickly to their strategic moves. So much of this is about creative thinking and considering the possibilities. Don't let a failure of imagination be the reason you don't make it.

FIGURE 2.3.9 Grocery Post's SOAP

Strategy on a Page, Dec 2023

Purpose, Ambition, Challenge

Purpose	To create neighbourhood hangouts where people can come together with a shared love of food & drink.
Ambition	Grow to 40 stores across SE England in the next 10 years, each generating an average of £200k EBITDA, driving an Enterprise Value of £100m+. Become the LVMH of groceries with a portfolio of unique venture brands.
Challenge	Scaling complexity

Target segments

Name	Description	Spend per visit	Visits per year	Est. number	SAM	WAVS current	WAVS future
Affluent local residents	Affluent residents, and their families, who live within walking distance and have high disposable income	£20	50	3,000	3.0m	57	63
People on the move	People passing through the neighbourhood who do not necessarily live locally, such as dog-walkers, cyclists and parents	£7	60	5,000	£2.1m	64.6	68

Competitors

Name	Example	Strengths (vs GP)	Weaknesses (vs GP)	WAVS current
National convenience chain stores	Sainsbury's local	Wide range of produce at competitive price points	Poor service, low quality, no coffee	16.4
High-end bakery and coffee store	Gail's bakery	High quality baked produce, in-store seating, comparable coffee	Narrow range of products, no wine, lack of club-feel	18.0
Seven-11 style convenience stores	Seven-11	Extended opening hours, more snacks	Low quality products, lack of club-feel, no community spirit	8.8
Premium wine store	Borough Wines	Wide range of high-quality wines, highly experienced staff	Narrow range of products, only wine	24.0
High-end delicatessen	Italian Deli	High quality deli products	Narrow range of products, often queues, poor coffee	52.2

Critical Value Factors for Affluent Local Residents vs National Convenience Stores

Value Factor	Importance	Performance	Aspiration	Versus competition
Remaining Value Factors	32	46.7	+10.8	+15
Convenience	26	50		+10
Broad range of deli quality products	26	100		+90
Engaging staff with deep product knowledge	16	20	+20	+10
WAVS		57	+6	+33

Value-Cap Map

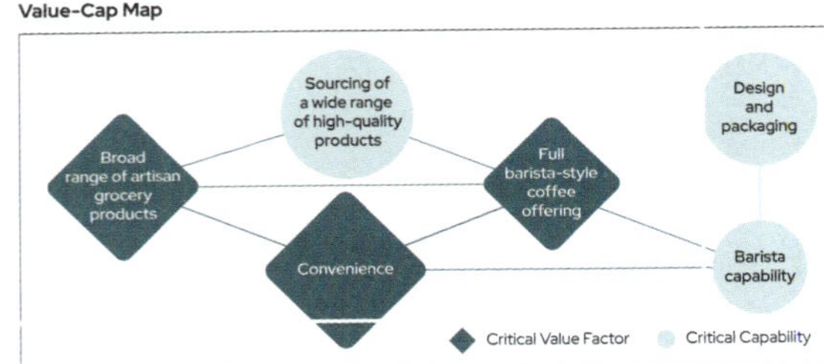

Economic engine

Name	Description	Metric T0	Metric T1	Metric Delta %
Revenue per metre squared	Revenue per square metre of retail space	£2,000	£2,500	£500 (+25%)
Stock turns (shelf products)	Number of times stock turns over per year	17x	25x	7x (+41%)
Margin	Average margin on products sold	40%	40%	0 (0%)

REMEMBER THIS

1. Answer the eight PACCTACC questions.
2. Create a compelling strategy story.
3. Use the 5S Action Framework to make your value proposition more compelling for your customers.
4. Your strategy is living. It isn't just about the long term and it evolves.
5. It is yours. Your trade-offs. Your choices. Your passion. It should be hard (near impossible) for anyone else to copy it.

Notes

1. Thiel, P with Masters, B (2015) *Zero to One: Notes on start ups, or how to build the future*, Virgin Books, London
2. Rumelt, R (2011) *Good Strategy/Bad Strategy: The difference and why it matters*, Crown Currency, New York
3. Sinek, S (2011) *Start with Why: How great leaders inspire everyone to take action*, Penguin Books, New York
4. Collins, J (2001) *Good to Great: Why some companies make the leap... and others don't*, HarperBusiness, New York
5. Collins, J (2002) *Built to Last: Successful habits of visionary companies* (3e), HarperBusiness, New York
6. Kennedy, J (1961) Excerpt from the 'Special message to the Congress on urgent national needs', 25 May, www.nasa.gov/history/the-decision-to-go-to-the-moon/ (archived at https://perma.cc/Q47T-3VJV)
7. Rumelt, R (2022) *The Crux: How leaders become strategists*, Profile Books, London
8. Freiberg, K and Freiberg, J (1998) *Nuts!: Southwest Airline's crazy recipe for business and personal success*, Broadway Books, New York
9. Bradley, C, Hurt, M and Smit, S (2011) Have you tested your strategy lately? McKinsey Quarterly, 1 January, www.mckinsey.com/capabilities/strategy-and-corporate-finance/our-insights/have-you-tested-your-strategy-lately (archived at https://perma.cc/8TG7-XYGK)
10. Lafley, A G and Martin, R L (2013) *Playing to Win: How strategy really works*, Harvard Business Review Press, Boston
11. Porter, M (2004) *Competitive Strategy: Techniques for analyzing industries and competitors*, Free Press, New York

12 Huddleston, T (2019) Zoom's founder left a 6-figure job because he wasn't happy – and following his heart made him a billionaire, CNBC Make It, 21 August, www.cnbc.com/2019/08/21/zoom-founder-left-job-because-he-wasnt-happy-became-billionaire.html (archived at https://perma.cc/2PAH-W4ZW)

13 Collins, J (2001) *Good to Great: Why some companies make the leap... and others don't*, HarperBusiness, New York

14 Porter, M (2004) *Competitive Advantage: Creating and sustaining superior performance*, Free Press, New York

PART THREE

Draw the plan

3.1

Introducing BROP-A

The idea of planning fills most of us with dread. It can be a laborious, fiddly process. And plans always change, so why bother? Just wing it. Besides, as Mike Tyson famously said, 'Everyone has a plan until they get punched in the face. Or put another way: 'No plan survives contact with the enemy.'[1] The World War II Allied Commander Dwight Eisenhower kind of agreed. He said that plans are worthless. But he clarified, 'Plans are worthless, but planning is everything.' For him, it was the process of planning that mattered, it didn't matter that the plan shifted and changed. The French writer Antoine de Saint-Exupéry probably said it best, 'A goal without a plan is just a wish.'[2]

So, we need to plan. And we need the ability to replan and then plan some more. We need to get good at it and, ideally, get to the point where we enjoy it. Planning is a continuous process and it's hard to do something well if you don't also enjoy doing it. As Picasso is thought to have said, 'Every child is an artist. The problem is, how to remain an artist once we grow up.' For us, planning is drawing. It is drawing a picture that tells a thousand words. It can be drawn in many different ways. Seeing it from different angles, just like seeing the world from different angles, builds a deeper understanding.

In this part of the book, we look at the third 'D' of the 4D Framework – Draw the plan. Here, we transition from strategy design to strategy execution. This is where you get proactive and start to plot your path towards your designed future. We say 'draw' the plan because this is about making the path to your BHAG visual so that you can understand it and communicate it to everyone who needs to come along for the ride. Except, they aren't just there for the ride. As we say in Chapter 1.2, they're there to help drive the bus. A good driver needs a navigator. A navigator needs a map. Your plan is your map.

Visualizing the path starts with top-level, big-picture thinking and transitions into more detailed plans needed in operational planning. In this part, we explain how to bridge the gap between strategy design and execution by showing how to draw up a plan to reach your designed future. To do this, we use our BROP-A framework, which we introduced in Chapter 1.1. It stands for Bridge, Risks, Objectives, Plan and Action, as shown in Figure 3.1.1. The hyphen preceding the 'A' serves as a reminder that everything, from the highest-order thinking downwards, leads to the day-to-day actions carried out by individuals in the organization. BROP-A is grounded in the belief that value creation is close to impossible without this kind of joined-up thinking.

BROP-A forms the backbone of your value creation plan. It provides a method for bridging the gap between the value you deliver as an organization today and the value you want to deliver tomorrow. The top-level, one-page bridge plans we explain in Chapter 3.2 are used as the basis for more detailed, operational planning further down the line – this planning is the P of BROP-A and is explained in Chapter 3.5. The top-level bridges are key strategic artefacts which emerge directly out of your strategy work.

BROP-A is your method for thinking through realistic timeframes and growth targets and how to phase the initiatives necessary to make things happen. It helps you to plot a concrete path to realizing your goals, measuring your progress along the way.

FIGURE 3.1.1 BROP-A

The difference between designing and planning

Designing and planning are distinct activities with different purposes, but they are so often thought of as the same. A strategy is not a plan and a plan is not a strategy. Planning flows from strategy and the two rely heavily on each other. You can't execute your designed strategy without a plan and you can't formulate a plan without strategic direction. In a blog post written in 2021, Roger Martin describes the difference: 'Strategy is the act of making an integrated set of choices, which positions the organization to win; while planning is the act of laying out projects with timelines, deliverables, budgets and responsibilities… instead of substitutes, strategy and planning should be complements.'[3]

The importance of time

In my (Rupert's) book *Data-Driven Organization Design*, I wrote about the concept of *ceteris paribus*. This Latin phrase means 'all other things being equal'. It's used to understand the economic system, which is too complex

FIGURE 3.1.2 Designing and planning are different activities that require different mindsets

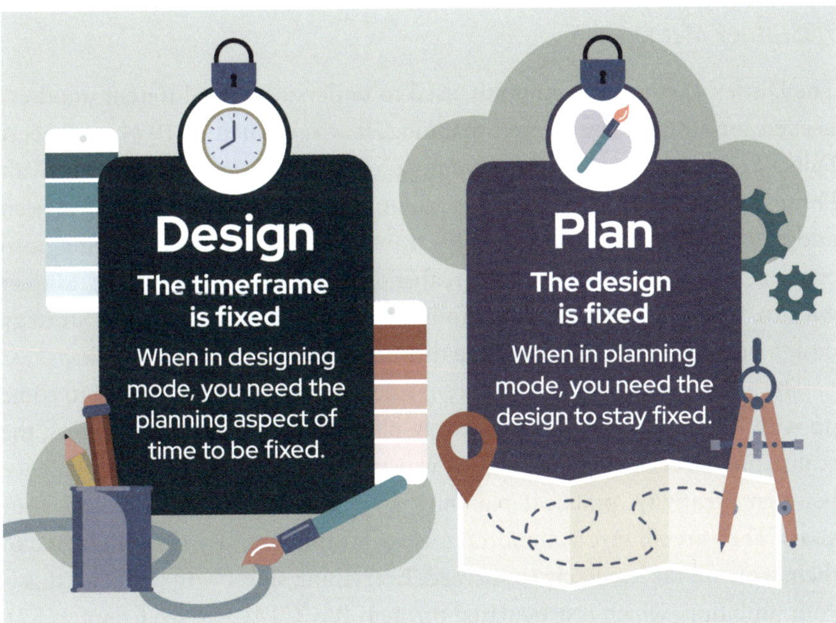

for the mind to comprehend in one go. You therefore make sense of it by zoning in on one variable at a time and ignoring the effects that other variables might have on it.

The same principle can be applied when designing and planning, as shown in Figure 3.1.2. The concept of time complicates strategy and goal design. You're designing for a point in the future – your 'to-be', which you are trying to change from your present – your 'as-is'. When designing strategic goals, you therefore simplify time and think only of two fixed points: today and tomorrow. This allows you to visualize your tomorrow without being distracted by the impact that time might have on the world and your organization. If you tried to account for that in your design, you'd tie yourself in knots. So, you make everything else equal and hold time fixed, effectively working with two photographic snapshots: today and tomorrow.

When you plan, it's a different story. Planning is a temporal activity and when doing it, you consider the design a done deal. You ignore the fact that the strategy might pivot over time. Attempting to think about all the different eventualities that might arise which could impact your goals would be like trying to nail jelly to a wall – a pointless endeavour. Some of us can struggle to switch between the different mindsets needed for designing and planning. The Disney Method provides a fantastic way to think about it.

The Disney Method

The Disney Method is commonly used to understand the different mindsets needed for strategy design and planning. It was created in 1994 by Robert Dilts, a neuro-linguistic programming expert. He modelled it on Walt Disney's methods for turning his dreams into reality. It has since been adopted in organizations to help transform imaginative thinking into concrete business strategy and a realistic plan for achieving it. It's a great way to think about how your ambition connects first with the strategy design and then the planning done through the BROP-A framework.

The basic idea is that three different roles (or mindsets) are needed to come up with a winning idea and effectively put it into practice: the dreamer, the realist and the critic. They are a great way to understand the necessary balance between creativity, practical planning and problem-solving to reach your goals. They are all just as important as each other and if you exclude one of them, you are far less likely to succeed. Everything starts with a dream (this is your ambition, which is articulated through PACCTACC – see Chapter 2.3). Without the dream, the realist and critic would have nothing to go on.

Each one of us will lean more towards one of the mindsets than the others and it might take a bit of effort to get into the ones we don't naturally inhabit. When we take participants through the Disney Method in a workshop setting, we wear different coloured hats to help get into the right mode (sometimes we do this physically). Green hats signify dreaming mode. Blue hats encourage realism and red hats make us think through everything that could go wrong.

- The dreamer – when you dream, you set yourself free to come up with the visionary, big-picture stuff. This is the mode to be in when you're thinking about your ambition and where you want to be in 15 years. You wore this hat when you came up with your BHAG (see Chapter 2.3). When you're in this mindset, it's important to let go and feel uninhibited.
- The realist – this is where you think about how things are going to work in practice. The realist and the critic are the mindsets most needed when working through the BROP-A framework. This is where you ask yourself whether or not what you are trying to achieve is realistic. Do you have too many initiatives? Do you have enough resources? How are projects going to work in practice? What are the workstreams? Are there dependencies to think about? What is the critical path for getting each project done?
- The critic – the final viewpoint is related to the realist, but it requires a greater level of scrutiny. The critic verifies the plan. They pay attention to the details. They think through the risks. We all need bold critics who aren't afraid to challenge big, exciting ideas. Critics and realists help to pull dreamers back down to the ground.

We believe we mostly fit into the dreamer and realist categories – Rupert is the dreamer and Jon is the pragmatist. At Ārahi, we're lucky to have Bill as our critic. We love Bill. He can't help but list all the reasons why we're going to fail. I (Rupert) have already written about my optimism bias. I often try to do too much and push too hard. I need Bill to pull me back. While I sometimes might not want to hear what he has to say, he's not afraid to challenge and, often, he has been proved right. For Bill, the 'i's need to be dotted and the 't's need to be crossed. (You should see his Christmas dinner preparation. The lists. The ingredients lined up in a row the night before in the order they will be used.) The three of us have worked together successfully for some time (in fact, Bill introduced us, as we explain in the Preface). We work so well together because we complement each other and naturally lean more towards one of these mindsets than the other. Of course, all three of us are capable of dreaming, putting together a realistic plan and thinking through risks, but we lean more naturally towards one of the mindsets than the others.

The three levels of planning: strategic, operational and tactical

Figure 3.1.3 shows three levels of planning: **strategic, operational** and **tactical.** Each of the levels requires a different type of thinking and a different amount of detailing.

1. Top-level, strategic planning

When it comes to drawing the plan, this is your starting point. It is the highest level of planning from which everything else follows. There are three top-level plans: the Plan on a Page (or POAP), the **enterprise value bridge** and the **revenue bridge.** We explain this level of planning further in Chapter 3.2. Each of these high-level plans fits on one page. This is important because they all serve as communication tools which help everyone in the organization understand top-level, strategic thinking. The space constraint forces prioritization, especially in the case of the POAP. Progress along each of the plans is easy to observe. In the case of the POAP, this happens via stepping stones between one landmark moment and the next. Reaching each stepping stone is a major cause for a pat on the back. The POAP contains the key initiatives, or major programmes of work, that need to be completed to reach each stepping stone.

2. Mid-level, operational planning

While strategic planning is done over multiple years, operational planning is done in year and per quarter. Mid-level planning requires you to think about the things that might stop you from reaching your value creation goals as well as the objectives that need to be achieved to get there. Risk management is a key component of mid-level planning. As discussed in Chapter 1.1, it's becoming increasingly difficult for companies to survive. We believe this is largely because organizations do not engage in meaningful and effective risk management.

FIGURE 3.1.3 The three levels of planning

The 'R' comes before the 'O' in BROP-A because until you understand your risks, you can't plan objectives to address them. A good way to plan is to eliminate your key risks first. At Ārahi, our biggest risk was our clients not getting their data into our product successfully. We needed the capability to connect and manage it. Without it, we would fail. So, one of our first objectives was to nail data management. Our second biggest risk was creating a product that was difficult to use. If it wasn't intuitive, we would fail. Our second recruit was the Head of UX/UI.

Once the risks and objectives for each key initiative have been mapped out, they are pulled together into an integrated plan which identifies the critical path to delivering the initiative. The integrated plan breaks down the objectives into projects (which might take months to complete) and sub-projects (which will take weeks or days to complete). We cover this level of planning in Chapter 3.5.

3. Detailed, tactical planning

Detailed and tactical planning is covered in Part 4, but we will explain it briefly here. It helps to understand how drawing the plan morphs into delivering the plan (the fourth 'D' of the 4D Framework). Detailed planning takes place over days and weeks. Projects and sub-projects identified in the **integrated plan** are broken down into actions. There are two different types of actions. **Governed actions** are more significant actions with more dependencies, more complicated workflows and more people involved. **In-out actions** are simple, quick things on people's to-do lists. They are called in-out actions because it takes as long to get them out as it does to get them in. Actions are monitored through forums of people who meet as required to get the work done.

If there is one key message we would like our readers to take away from this book, it's that there is a red line that runs from the BHAG all the way through strategy design and into strategy execution. That red line runs through the key initiatives identified in the multi-year plan, through to projects and sub-projects in the integrated plan, and finally to action management. Each stage requires work to be broken down into an extra level of detail until you reach the level of an individual's to-do list. In that way, every person in the organization works towards completing the key initiatives outlined in the POAP.

Boulders, rocks, pebbles and sand

Stephen Covey wrote one of the most successful management/self-help books in history, way back in 1989, *The Seven Habits of Highly Effective People*. In it, he observed that people focus too much on urgent tasks (even if they're not important) and not enough on non-urgent but important tasks. He framed this within the context of getting three different-sized objects into a bucket – a set of rocks, stones and sand. If you put the sand in first, you can't get the stones and rocks in. It's a simple metaphor that makes the simple point: sort the big stuff first. Put the rocks in, then the stones. Shake it about a bit so the stones fit around the rocks. Then, add in the sand.[4]

This metaphor is the inspiration for a framework at the heart of Part 3: **boulders, rocks, pebbles** and **sand**, as shown in Figure 3.1.4. The boulders are the big stuff. They are the key initiatives listed in your POAP. When you deliver a crucial set of them, you hit the next stepping stone. These key initiatives are big, so they have to be broken down into big chunks of work. These are the rocks – projects and sub-projects which, together, mean the key initiative gets done. (Note that many projects within a single KOD, such as a function like sales or HR, are rocks too, so not all rocks need to belong

FIGURE 3.1.4 Boulders, rocks, pebbles and sand

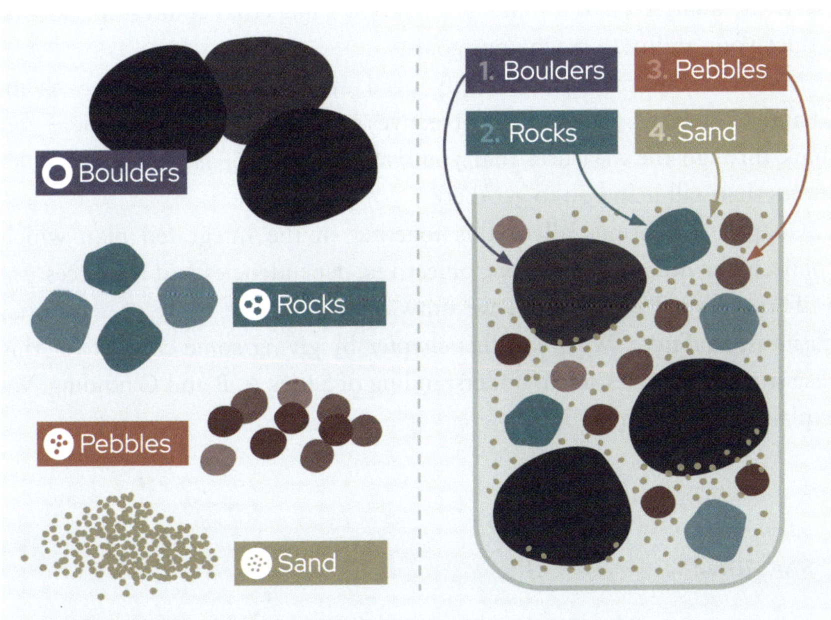

to a boulder. The complexity of large change programmes that cut across KODs and therefore require coordination is what makes them a boulder.) These rocks get broken down further into pebbles. Pebbles are a type of action that we call 'governed actions'. They are actions that others care about. They are tracked and people need to be kept informed about their progress. If you crush pebbles, what do you get? Grains of sand. The sand is another type of action that we call 'in-out' actions. These are the actions on individuals' to-do lists. It is the stuff that just needs to get done.

Structure and logic for Part 3

The chapters in this part follow the logic of the BROP-A framework. Chapter 3.2 kicks us off with the bridge. This chapter explains how to plot a clear path towards achieving your five- to ten-year value creation plan. It explains how to break time down into manageable chunks by using stepping stones, so you don't become overwhelmed. This is the highest level of planning, visualized through the POAP, the enterprise value bridge and the revenue, or sales bridge.

Chapter 3.3 looks at risk. Each way of growing our revenue comes with its risks and challenges. The key initiatives set out in the strategic multi-year POAP are analysed in the context of risk: the things that could stop, slow or reduce your ability to reach your goals.

Many of the risks you identify need an objective to address them. Chapter 3.4 takes you through objectives management. This is where you think through the measures that you want to achieve, as well as the milestones that will help you to get there.

Chapter 3.5 brings all of this together in the integrated plan which connects the dots between risks, objectives, dependencies and resources.

Throughout Parts 3 and 4 we draw on a new case study of a fictional business, SaaSurve. We'll end this chapter by giving some context for this case study (this relies on an understanding of Series A, B and C funding. We explain this in Chapter 3.2).

CASE STUDY
SAASURVE

SaaSurve was founded by high-school friends Adam and Bridget. Bridget has a PhD in qualitative research and Adam (who is CTO of SaaSurve) is a software engineer. After finishing her PhD, Bridget went into consulting, but she quickly found herself frustrated by the limitations of the technology for collecting and analysing people's opinions. Science was missing from the surveys. Structuring data for Python was cumbersome. Making the process repeatable, was impractical. She had an idea to create some new tech. She could do the science but not the code. She remembered her friend, Adam, the 'coding genius'. He was a fun guy that Bridget loved hanging out with. She made the call and SaaSurve was founded.

Bridget started by generating consulting revenue, helping marketing functions better understand the needs of their consumers. Devanshi, from a large consumer goods company, liked what Bridget was doing. She joined, bringing crucial industry knowledge with her. Caleb, who was slightly older, was a Principal at a strategy firm and a trusted advisor to Devanshi. He knew how to sell and how to set up and deliver a consulting project. He was a deep expert, his sponsor had just left and his firm felt he was specializing too much. He loved what Bridget was doing and believed in Devanshi. Caleb joined too. Together, with a few data scientists and fellow hackers, they grew their offering and their platform.

Ten years on, they got to 200 customers with $10 million in ARR. This was mostly bootstrapped with a bit of seed funding from friends and family, followed by a small $2 million Series B to scale Adam's R&D team. The Series B enabled them to build a highly differentiated platform providing real-time survey analysis with scientific insights.

In July 2022, having suffered from cutbacks during the Covid-19 pandemic and an inability to break the critical North American market (selling from London with a bunch of Europeans didn't work), they decided they should raise a Series C. They didn't have a sales force or even a sales model. Bridget and Caleb were still the key salespeople and Devanshi provided practical subject matter support. On the tech front, the platform was too slow and too manual. Every new tenant took two to three days to get live. The cost of managing the estate was prohibitive and they needed to automate. In other words, they needed DevOps. They had proven product market fit. They had proven there was a big market and that they had a unique, highly differentiated offering. It just wasn't scalable. They had been at it for ten years. It had been a slog. They had been paying themselves little and wanted to take a bit of money off the table to secure their families' futures. Serious tensions had been building between needing better pay and the acute need to invest in the business.

The team raised $36.5 million from Fitzrovia Capital – $21.5 million was primary capital (money going directly into the business) plus $15 million of secondary capital for their departing family and friends shareholders, and crucially for the early team members to derisk. They received a $100 million pre-money, $120 million post-money valuation. This gave their new investor a 30 per cent stake and a seat on a newly formed board. Bridget (CEO), Adam (CTO) and Felicity (CFO) agreed to an independent Chair (Chara). Felicity was newly appointed in conjunction with Fitzrovia and joined the team six weeks after the deal was closed on 4 May 2023. The team loved closing on Star Wars Day. The two speeches at the closing dinner were called 'Shooting for the stars' and 'Trusting in the force'.

Their investment plan showed that they were hoping to get to 550 customers and $41 million of ARR by May 2028. This gave them five years. The strategy was to leverage their deep expertise to bring critical, scientific out-of-the-box survey solutions to market for their marketing clients. Their purpose was to help their clients better understand their customers' needs, perceptions, fears and aspirations, so everyone would get more value.

A critical issue was employee satisfaction and churn. The team had suffered during the pandemic and felt disconnected. The nature of the work was also a problem. It was manual and boring work and had taken its toll. An **Individual Activity Analysis** was conducted using organization design software. It showed that 27 per cent of staff time was spent doing manual work that they could automate. Automation would also improve their ability to scale. The goal was to reduce manual work to 15 per cent within 18 months and to 6 per cent within five years. Improving the quality of work and the number of connections between staff was key. If this wasn't turned around, the plan was toast. It was still very much a people business.

SaaSurve's customers were broadly very satisfied (with an NPS of +25 per cent). Gross revenue retention was a healthy 90 per cent. But their superusers, the most intense users of the platform, were growing disgruntled. It was too slow, manual and complex. They were feeling neglected. Access to experts wasn't what it used to be. Learning to apply the science sounded cool, but if you didn't have a PhD in the topic it was difficult to get your head around it. If this wasn't addressed, it would limit the SAM. Better training was urgently needed. Jedi Padawans might learn 1-2-1 from their Masters, but SaaSurve needed a new approach. It would be great to have access to an online learning portal. The Jedi Master, on call 24-7 at the touch of a button. The due diligence from Fitzrovia confirmed all these issues.

So, the plan was to enter the North American market, but to do this they first needed to create a scalable sales process in the UK home market. Using the traditional methods didn't work. The thinking was typically flawed because the clients didn't have the know-how. Due diligence had also found that the platform was too cheap. They planned to provide a lot of extra value – improved customer service and access to the know-how through online training and new modules. That meant the platform could come at a higher price. In Chapter 3.2 we explain how they phased these things in the plan.

Notes

1 Oxford Essential Quotations (2016) Helmuth von Moltke 1800–91 Prussian military commander, www.oxfordreference.com/display/10.1093/acref/9780191826719.001.0001/q-oro-ed4-00007547 (archived at https://perma.cc/C5ZN-839D)

2 Good Reads, Antoine de Saint-Exupéry, www.goodreads.com/quotes/87476-a-goal-without-a-plan-is-just-a-wish (archived at https://perma.cc/FGF6-3EPD)

3 Martin, R (2021) Strategy vs. planning: Complements not substitutes, Medium, 15 February, https://rogermartin.medium.com/strategy-vs-planning-complements-not-substitutes-ea08e56809d6# (archived at https://perma.cc/GF6E-2P48)

4 Covey, S (2020) *The Seven Habits of Highly Effective People* (Reissue edition) Simon & Schuster, London

3.2

The bridges of BROP-A

The only way to eat an elephant is to do it one bite at a time

Introduction

Some of the most iconic architectural structures in the world are bridges. What would San Francisco be without the Golden Gate Bridge, Sydney without its Harbour Bridge or London without Tower Bridge? Bridges connect divided land.

Once you've designed your tomorrow, you know where you want to get to over the long term. But how do you get there from where you are today? This is the first stage of Drawing the plan in the 4D Framework: devising multi-year plans that fit on one page. They form part of your strategy documentation and are effectively your value creation plans. They make you think more deeply about which segments or geographies you're going to attack. They help you to phase your initiatives so that you don't try to do too much too quickly. The first is the POAP: the Plan on a Page. It breaks time down into stepping stones and lists the key initiatives that will help you reach your goal. The second is the enterprise value bridge. This shows how much you plan to grow your enterprise value over your timeframe and how you're going to do it. The third is the revenue or sales bridge, which shows where you expect revenue to come from. In Chapter 3.1 we discussed the levels of planning: boulders, rocks, pebbles and sand. These three plans are the boulders. They are your tools for top-level planning which form the backbone of your risk management and objectives. We bring this chapter to life by continuing the SaaSurve case study from Chapter 3.1.

Building bridges

As planning is a temporal activity (as opposed to designing – see Chapter 3.1), the first thing to determine is your timeframe. This is not the first time you'll have thought about timeframes. Everything described in Part 2 is done in the context of your BHAG – the ultimate goal that you want to reach.

The B in BROP-A stands for Bridge. This is a metaphor for the phase of time which connects today's reality to tomorrow's goal. Imagine standing on the edge of a cliff and looking across a chasm towards the peak of a mountain in the distance. You need to get to the peak. The first thing to do is build a bridge. The second thing to do is work out how you're going to get across.

How do you eat an elephant?

Getting across the bridge isn't as easy as it might sound. If the peak of the distant mountain represents your BHAG, that might be 15 years away, or longer. A lot can change in 15 years. Value creation goals need to be understood and tracked over shorter periods. When private equity firms acquire companies, most work to four- to six-year value creation plans (although they can span seven to eight years). Whether you are working in the context of private equity value creation or not, these are manageable time spans to plan over.

There is a famous saying that the only way to eat an elephant is to do it one bite at a time. Any daunting task can be accomplished little by little, one step at a time. As Gary Keller and Jay Papasan wrote in their book *The One Thing*, bringing a goal down into the steps needed to achieve it helps engage the thinking you need to plan for and achieve extraordinary results.[1]

Breaking time down into manageable 'bite-sized' chunks means that you can drill into a greater level of detail. Figure 3.2.1 shows how a 15-year timeframe can be broken down into three five-year periods. If your BHAG is 30 years into the future, your value creation landmarks might be ten years apart. **Landmarks** sit at the end of each period and each landmark represents a strategic goal. The dotted arrows represent the bridges or phases of time connecting today with tomorrow.

Five years may be less daunting than 15, but it is still a long period to plan over. So, we divide time further into stepping stones. Figure 3.2.2 shows a close-up of time between two landmarks. The landmarks are five years (or around 1,800 days) apart. There are four phases of time divided by three stepping stones. As we explain later in the chapter, stepping stones are typically

FIGURE 3.2.1 Determining your timeframes

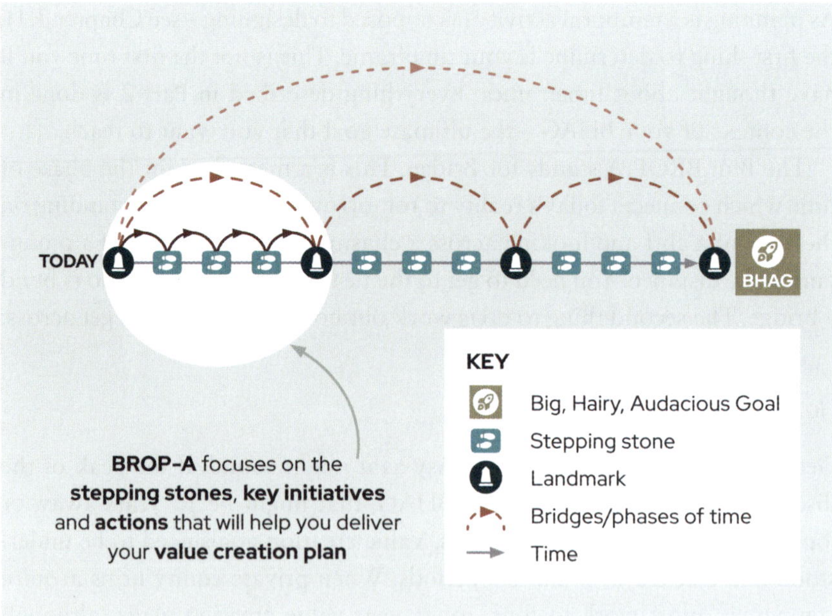

FIGURE 3.2.2 The stepping stones and phases of time in between landmark moments

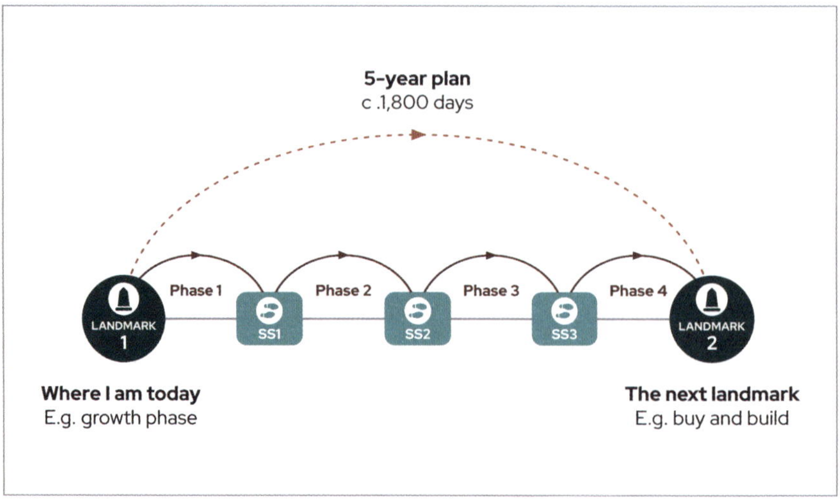

around 18 months apart, although there is far from any set rule. It is, however, important that these don't fit with your annual budget-setting process (see below).

The timeframe that you plan over depends on your context and your ambition. According to Amara's Law, we overestimate what we can achieve in the short run and underestimate what we can achieve in the long run. Roy Amara, a computer scientist in the 1960s, is thought to have said this when talking about the impact of technology in the short and long run.[2] We may need longer than we think to achieve our ambitions. As Richard Thompson was always telling me (Rupert), everything is achievable, it just takes longer. For most of us, that means planning over a longer time horizon than we might initially think is necessary.

The time horizon that you plan over can depend on market need. The Googles and Facebooks of this world manage to hit a moment in time with a product that fulfils an incredible unmet need, has a huge TAM and therefore significant potential to benefit from the network effect. We explained this in Chapter 1.1 in the context of Peter Thiel's conditions for creating a monopoly. In these rare circumstances, businesses (especially tech businesses) scale very quickly and can achieve a huge amount in a relatively short time. For these businesses, it makes sense to think more in the short term.

Whatever criteria you use to plan your timeframe, we can't emphasize enough how important it is to ensure that all stakeholders are aligned over the time horizons. Part of agreeing on your landmarks is agreeing when you expect to hit them.

RUPERT

We've given a general idea of the kind of timeframes that would make sense for many organizations, particularly those that have been acquired by private equity firms and have clear value creation plans to work to. I'll explain this briefly for those who are unfamiliar with how private equity value creation works and apply it to my experience at Concentra Analytics, which became Orgvue.

Private equity funding occurs in a series of rounds – A, B and C. These rounds typically follow initial 'seed funding' and 'angel investing', both of which help to get businesses off the ground. Each round signifies a point at which cash can be invested in exchange for equity. Series A funding might amount to about $2 million, Series B $10 million and Series C $50–$100 million. It varies a lot, but Series C is typically when you are offered big cheques to help you scale. In SaaS, the world I know most about, it often takes about seven years to get to Series C. At Orgvue, it took me eight years to get from writing the first line of code to Series C funding and a $62 million cheque. I got seed funding of $1 million (2009), which is usually what you would expect from Series A funding. Our Series B funding was $3 million (2015) and helped us to scale internationally and Series C funding came in 2018.

For Orgvue, the timescales we describe made sense. I planned to Series C. Once I got to that landmark and had new investors on board, I made another plan towards the next big landmark (in the context of private equity, landmark moments often signify a change of ownership or structure).

Avoid the planning fallacy

In his popular PsyBlog, psychologist Jeremy Dean has written about the power, but also the danger, of using visualization to help you achieve your goals. He claims that just dreaming about a goal 'may be worse than ineffective, it may reduce our performance'.[3] Dean distinguishes between outcome visualization and process visualization. He draws on a study by psychologists Pham and Taylor who looked at the role of visualizing goals in the context of students taking exams. They proved that simply visualizing your success is nowhere near as effective as visualizing the steps necessary to achieve that success. In the study, students who visualized themselves studying spent longer with their books. They therefore achieved superior results to those who simply imagined achieving the grade they wanted. Dean suggests that visualizing the process helped focus attention on the steps needed to reach the goal.

Simply visualizing reaching our landmarks is not going to help us understand the practical reality of getting there. If we understand exactly what we need to do and how hard we need to try to reach the landmarks, we're more likely to knuckle down and make it happen. We'll be more prepared for eventualities along the way and have more realistic expectations of the path ahead.

Dean talks about the planning fallacy, which he describes as our 'completely normal assumption that everything will be much easier than it really will be'. All of us consistently fail to anticipate how much of a plan can go wrong. For Dean, 'thinking about the process helps to focus the mind on potential problems and how to overcome them'.

The three bridges of BROP-A

As we wrote in Chapter 3.1, the whole point of drawing the plan is to visualize how you're going to get from where you are today (your as-is) to where you want to be tomorrow (your to-be). The three bridges of BROP-A are key strategic artefacts that connect strategic and operational thinking. They help you to plan your transition from the as-is to the to-be and visualize it in different ways – in terms of the key initiatives needed to reach each stepping stone and your expected enterprise value and revenue at each point. The three bridges are as follows:

1. POAP (Plan on a Page).
2. Enterprise value bridge.
3. Revenue (or sales) bridge.

The remainder of this chapter focuses on drawing these three bridges. All of them fit on one page. All of them are visual. They are linked and they can all be understood and communicated with ease. While we present them in a linear order, in reality you would work on them simultaneously as they all inform each other.

They feed the next two stages of BROP-A – risk management and objectives planning. Once you understand your key initiative, enterprise value and revenue targets, you can then start to consider the things that might stop you from reaching them (your risks) and the objectives you need to fulfil.

> JON
>
> I have reviewed over a hundred value creation plans in my time. They can vary considerably in length, quality and approach. They are rarely digestible, immediately understandable and easy to communicate. Commonly, they are either weighty, boring tomes that take hours to plough through or only exist in a few people's heads. The former means that it's virtually impossible to articulate the key points in the plan, let alone communicate these points to anyone else, and the latter usually indicates a lack of appreciation of the plan's importance.
>
> Both approaches result in confusion, misalignment, and ineffective execution. Value is pretty difficult to create if no one knows what they're aiming for or how they're going to get there.
>
> The best value creation plans are focused on a small number of well-phased key initiatives. Key initiatives are branded, have clearly defined milestones and everyone involved knows what they stand for and what needs to be done by when.

The Plan on a Page (POAP)

The POAP contains the key information everyone needs to know about the value creation plan. Unlike the other two bridges, it is not solely focused on financial metrics but articulates the key initiatives and Key Performance Indicators (KPIs) necessary to reach the next stepping stone. The POAP exists to ensure that everyone in the organization understands the strategic goals and the high-level plan for how the organization is going to transition from one landmark moment to the next on the road to the BHAG.

Nat Turner, the enslaved African-American preacher who led a slave rebellion in 1831, is thought to have said that 'good communication is the bridge between confusion and clarity'. The POAP is a compelling communication tool. It aims to distil a host of information in the value creation plan into one single page that is easy to understand. It serves as a north star for every individual in the organization, driving alignment through all levels of the business.

The POAP includes the following elements:

- landmark moments
- **swim lanes**
- stepping stones
- KPIs for each swim lane – these KPIs are specific metrics that, once met, signify that you have achieved a stepping stone or landmark moment
- key initiatives that will deliver the plan between each stepping stone. These are colour-coded according to their BRAG status (see Chapter 1.3).

You'll notice that the word 'key' keeps cropping up. The POAP is not exhaustive. Because everything needs to fit on one page, it forces you to be selective, choose wisely and prioritize. It lists only the *key* initiatives. It also forces you to articulate the performance indicators (metrics and measures) that are *most important to understand* to track progress to the next stepping stone – these are your KPIs. It also forces you to prioritize the critical lenses through which you view your business – your key strategic themes. These are the swim lanes on the plan.

It's important to remember that the POAP is not set in stone. It is a dynamic, living thing. Stuff happens that impacts your ability to reach your goals. You might think it's going to take five or six years to get from one landmark moment to the next, but you have no way of knowing what's going to crop up and challenge your ability to get there. In Chapter 3.3 we talk about uncontrollable, external risks – events like pandemics, entry of new competitors, cyber-attacks or climate emergencies. You can't control these risks. All you can do is take action to limit the impact if they do. The only thing you can be sure about is that things won't go to plan. Things will go wrong and your planned dates will change.

LANDMARK MOMENTS

Figure 3.2.3 shows SaaSurve's POAP. Their first landmark is named 'Today' and is dated May 2023. Their second landmark named 'Exit in 5 years', dated May 2028.

SWIM LANES

Swim lanes are the critical lenses you can view your business through. They represent the key value-driving strategic themes that need to be tracked over time to reach your landmarks. They can't be dictated, and how you determine them will depend on what you most want to change. There is only room for five to six swim lanes (SaaSurve has five). Adding any more would make the POAP too hard to read. Choosing them provides an excellent opportunity for debate and prioritization and it helps to structure your thinking.

Unless there are exceptional circumstances, three out of the Four Cornerstones of Corporate Health, introduced in Chapter 1.1, will occupy a swim lane spot – customer, people and finance and operations. That leaves space for just two more swim lanes. What are the two other things which are most central to your strategy that need to be tracked over time? You could combine finance and operations into one swim lane, as per the cornerstones, or you could break them out separately. It depends on the amount of attention each aspect needs. We like finance to occupy the bottom swim lane on the POAP. Finance is the outcome – the final set of output metrics. It starts with the customer and finishes with cash.

SaaSurve's two additional swim lanes are 'Revenue' and 'Product'. They are aiming to get to $41 million of ARR by May 2028 as per the investment plan so it makes sense to track this. Another big aim is to make their product less slow and cumbersome and turn their superusers around. The Product swim lane allows them to track the usability of the product.

RUPERT

For those who have read *Data-Driven Organization Design*, you may be interested to know that the process of choosing and prioritizing swim lanes is very similar to choosing and prioritizing design criteria. For those who haven't read it, design criteria are critical business goals which are used in the organization design process to evaluate design options. Choosing between design options involves prioritizing your design criteria and isolating the single most important criterion that matters more than the others. This top design criterion needs to be significantly more important than the second one on your list, which in turn needs to be significantly more important than the third. There are three commonly used methods to help a group of stakeholders prioritize a list:

1. Force list prioritization – ideas for swim lanes are put on a wall and the order is adjusted until a consensus is reached.
2. Voting by dots – each stakeholder is given two dots. They put them next to the two swim lanes they feel are most important.
3. A versus B – stakeholders trade one swim lane against another multiple times and the results are aggregated.

Each of these methods works well to encourage debate. It's important to hear everyone's opinions when running through the options. Get everything on the table and then choose your prioritization method (for more detail about how to do it, see *Data-Driven Organization Design*). It's not quick and easy, but eventually you will agree on the two most important swim lanes to prioritize alongside customer experience, people and finance.

STEPPING STONES

The names you give your stepping stones are important. You're branding them – turning a point in time into a meaningful, memorable and galvanizing target. Their names should evoke emotion and unite the team. Everyone should be able to visualize how they will feel when they get to that future point. When we reached our first stepping stone at Ārahi, we had a party, invited our clients along, demoed our product and celebrated our success. It was a meaningful moment in time that everyone had been working towards and we partied hard.

In Chapter 2.3 we talked about how to identify your key challenge in strategy design. This comes from Rumelt's idea of identifying a crux – the fundamental issue that requires your attention. Each stepping stone represents a new challenge. Once you overcome it, you move on to the next one. SaaSurve's stepping stones are 'Foundations for growth' and 'Welcome to America'. As we discussed in Chapter 1.2, companies are wise to give themselves breathing space immediately after investment rather than trying to scale too quickly. SaaSurve plans to take 17 months, until October 2024, to build the foundations for growth. Once those are in place, they'll spend the next two years and two months scaling and expanding into the North American market with a new platform module and training portal.

As this example shows, the phases of time between stepping stones do not need to be equal, but stepping stones are typically more than 18 months apart. We believe the strategic stepping stone cycle is just as important as the annual budget and planning cycle. Lafley and Martin talk about the importance of differentiating between strategic planning cycles and annual planning cycles in *Playing to Win*.[4] People are accustomed to thinking in terms of 12-month cycles and it may take some work to bring about a shift in thinking. Branding stepping stones helps to focus people on the timeframe. You could also pay bonuses when you hit stepping stones rather than at the end of the year. It makes a lot of sense to reward the achievement of outcomes, after all.

KEY PERFORMANCE INDICATORS

Performance indicators are the metrics (the measures or calculation of more than one measure) which provide insight into performance. There are likely to be hundreds of performance indicators to choose from but there is only room for a maximum of five per swim lane. Once again you need to prioritize. Use one of the methods described by Rupert to help you understand which ones are key. They should be strongly aligned to the strategic theme which informs the swim lane.

The first landmark is your starting point. Here you list the KPIs that you will use to monitor performance and that will ultimately signify successful completion. Achieving a KPI shows that you have solved your current challenge and that it's time to reflect, celebrate and move on to solving the next one. For example, among others, SaaSurve chose to track 'Number of customers' and 'Net promoter score' in their Customer swim lane. In revenue terms, ARR and CAC are important. For the product, 'Usability score' features, as does 'Employee churn' for the People swim lane. The Finance swim lane has five metrics, including EBITDA, the multiple and enterprise value. We explain the latter two below.

They start with 200 customers and plan to reach 500 customers by their second landmark. They want to grow their net promoter score by 25 points. ARR needs to grow from $10 million to $41 million and CAC from 0.8 to 1. The usability score needs to grow from 3.5 to 4.5 (out of a maximum of 5) and they want to get employee churn down from 20 per cent to 10 per cent. EBITDA needs to grow from $1.8 million to $11.6 million.

The stepping stones show how this growth will happen over time. For example, to complete the 'Foundations for growth' stage, customers need to grow to 350, ARR needs to grow to 17, the usability score needs to increase to 4.2 and employee churn needs to reduce to 17 per cent. The 'Foundations for growth' stage will not be complete until all the KPI targets for that stepping stone are hit.

KEY INITIATIVES

Stepping stones are reached by delivering key initiatives. Key initiatives are the most important, complex and significant initiatives that will drive a step-change to allow you to reach the next stepping stone. When initiatives cut across functions and silos and require coordination, they can be considered 'key'. All functions have initiatives, but not all of them are key. Key initiatives are listed on the POAP because of their critical impact on the value creation plan. They therefore require more governance than other initiatives.

Returning to the analogy of boulders, rocks, pebbles and sand, the key initiatives are the boulders. In the two subsequent levels of planning, they will be broken down into rocks (projects) and pebbles and sand (actions). This means that everyone can relate their actions to these key initiatives, providing a sense of ownership and spurring people on.

As Figure 3.2.3 shows, key initiatives are colour-coded according to their BRAG status. At the time of this POAP review, most key initiatives in the 'Foundations for growth' phase are going well – ten of the twelve are either green or blue. 'Review sales force effectiveness' is amber. This might be concerning because SaaSurve needs to prove it can create a scalable sales process in the UK home market before entering the bigger target market of North America. This initiative requires a new process, set of roles, team, sales ops and, fundamentally, a new organization. The key initiative 'Create licence to hire' is in the red.[5] As we discussed in Chapter 1.2, recruiting the right people is fundamental to setting the foundations, so the board is likely to be interested in why this is way off target.

FIGURE 3.2.3 SaaSurve's completed POAP

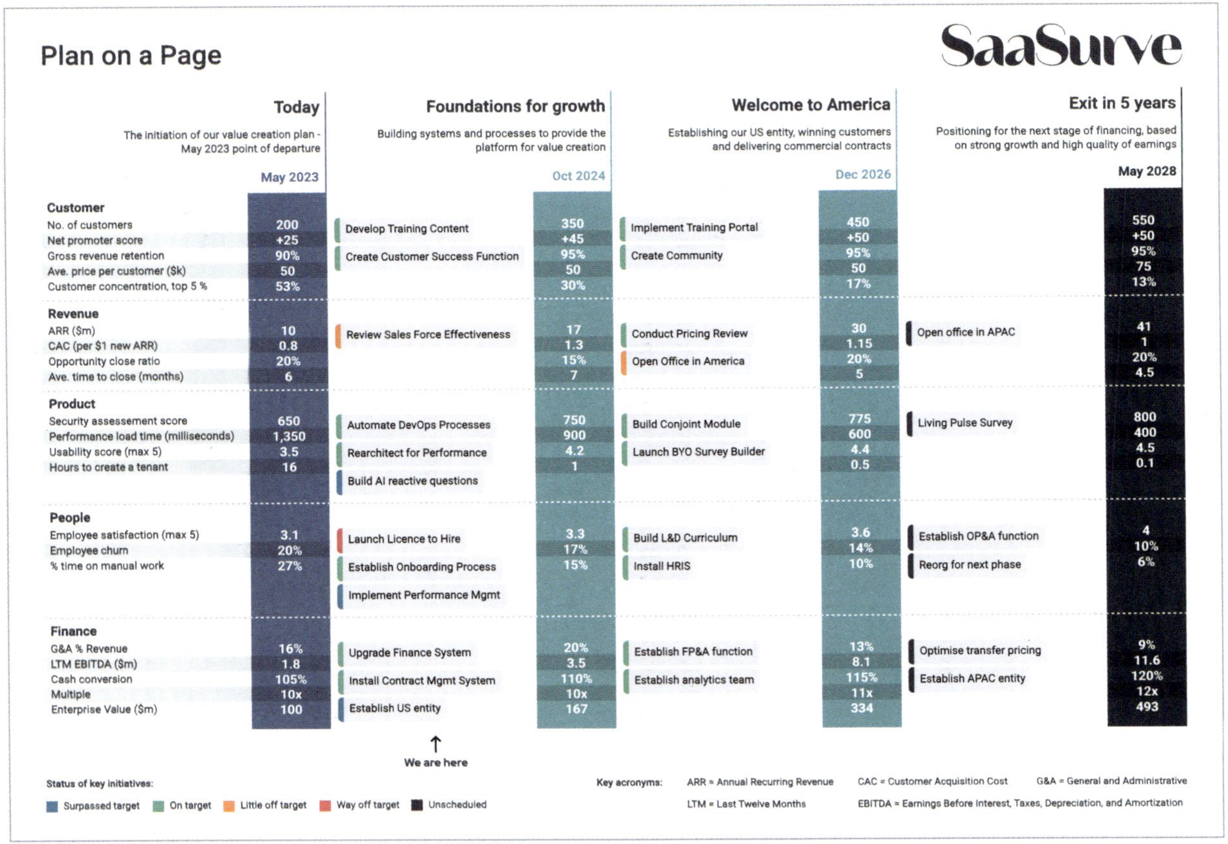

At the time of investment, due diligence found that the platform was being sold too cheaply. Providing extra value would mean they could sell it at a higher price. This included training content delivered through a portal and a new module on conjoint analysis. Given the number of key initiatives already planned, they decided to address this in the 'Welcome to America' phase. The key initiatives 'Implement training portal' and 'Build conjoint module' are therefore planned for a later date.

The enterprise value bridge

The next two bridges help you to think about your stepping stones in terms of enterprise value and revenue generation. They can be useful tools to help you determine what your stepping stones should be. Both are visualized through a waterfall chart to allow for an understanding of running totals as values are added or subtracted.

Figure 3.2.4 shows SaaSurve's enterprise value bridge. It shows their valuation today of $100 million and where they want to get to in five years: $518 million. It also shows how they expect to do it: $311 million through ARR growth, $82 million through **multiple arbitrage** and $25 million through cash generation (note that the figure on the POAP doesn't include cash). Multiple arbitrage relates to your ability to increase the value of a company without making any operational improvements to it.

FIGURE 3.2.4 The enterprise value bridge

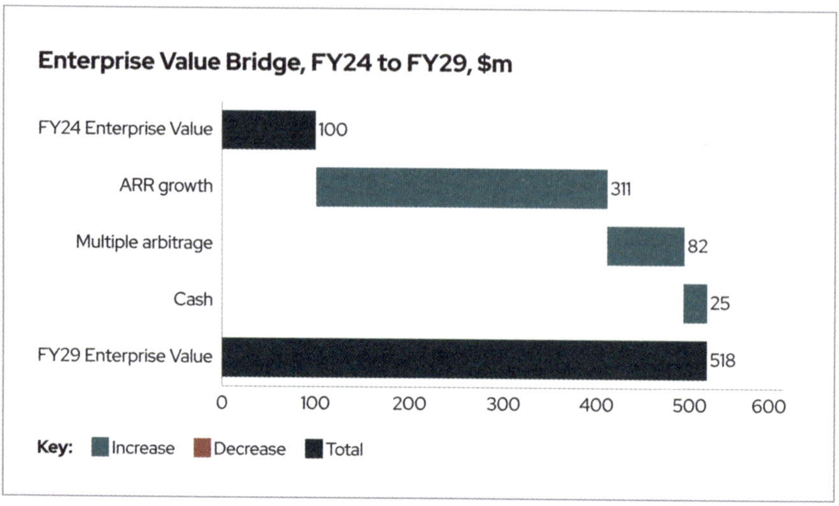

It's common practice to value companies based on EBITDA or ARR quantum and a **multiple**. EBITDA is the most used enterprise value multiple. It stands for Earnings before Interest, Taxes, Depreciation and Amortization. It's a useful metric to understand an organization's profitability before it pays interest and taxes and before depreciation and amortization are subtracted. Removing external accounting factors and non-operating expenses highlights the organization's operating performance and its ability to generate cash. This, in turn, gives a good idea of its growth potential.

There are many factors that drive the valuation multiple. These factors are referred to as **Quality of Earnings** (QoE). They are ostensibly an indication of the quality of the business. The valuation multiple is 10 times ARR for SaaSurve. By improving the QoE they can expect this to increase, conservatively, by 20 per cent to 12 times ARR. There are often threshold effects, where you get a leap in value. These threshold effects vary per industry. We've included some SaaS examples:

- Revenue quality. One-off revenue (e.g. project) is less valuable than repeat revenue which, in turn, is less valuable than recurring revenue. Hitting 80 per cent recurring revenue is a threshold. In recurring revenue businesses, Gross Revenue Retention (GRR) is a related metric where hitting 90 per cent is the target.
- Growth in revenue and EBITDA. In SaaS, hitting 40 per cent revenue growth plus EBITDA margin is another targeted level. For example, hitting 20 per cent growth and 20 per cent EBITDA has the same 'rule of 40' score as 60 per cent growth and a negative 20 per cent EBITDA loss.
- EBITDA quantum. As you go up in quantum, so does the multiple and the types of investors that are interested in investing. EBITDA thresholds for private equity are between $5 million and $10 million. A much bigger market opens up for those over $10 million with higher multiples. This applies to EBITDA-driven businesses as many SaaS, ARR-driven businesses are loss-making (although that has changed a lot since the high-multiple days of 2021).
- Customer and supplier concentration. A common target is to have the top five customers contributing less than 20 per cent of the revenue.
- Margin and cash generation. The benchmarks are industry specific. Gross margins in SaaS are expected to be over 90 per cent.
- Scale in terms of revenue or ARR. There are several threshold points, namely ARR at $1 million, $10 million, $30 million, $100 million.

- Professionalization. Smaller companies are more likely to have unsophisticated systems and other less desirable characteristics.
- Soft factors. Factors such as the quality of the management team and culture. You know this when you see it. This is a black art, not a science, and we haven't got the space to cover it in detail in this book.

SaaSurve has been valued at $100 million. To reach the target $518 million, it needs ARR to increase, the multiple to increase or both. This is when you can start to ask yourself questions about what seems feasible and realistic. Is the ARR growth achievable? If not, what's the alternative? What if ARR was less or stayed the same and the multiple increased? How much would the multiple need to increase to reach $518 million? To truly understand realistic ARR growth over time, you need to dig into a little more detail about where revenue growth is likely to come from – this is your revenue growth bridge. When putting this together, a good place to start is with your Total Addressable Market, or TAM.

Your Total Addressable Market (TAM)

As we explained in Chapter 1.1, the TAM refers to your maximum opportunity in the marketplace. It's a good indication of how much room you have to grow and where that growth could come from. It's an excellent tool for forecasting a realistic revenue growth goal through both ARR/EBITDA and multiple arbitrage.

To understand your potential TAM increase it's useful to break it down as shown in Figure 3.2.5. It shows how to bridge the gap between your as-is and to-be revenue in four different ways.

1. Sell existing products and services to existing customers, factoring in price increases.
2. Penetrate new customer logos within existing segments, products/services, geographies and channels.
3. Target new segments, sell new products/services, enter new geographies and sell through new channels.
4. Mergers and acquisitions.

The left-hand side represents methods to increase revenue. Realism is the name of the game. Think about new segments you identified in your segmentation work. Which ones could you add and when? Which new products

FIGURE 3.2.5 Your Total Addressable Market

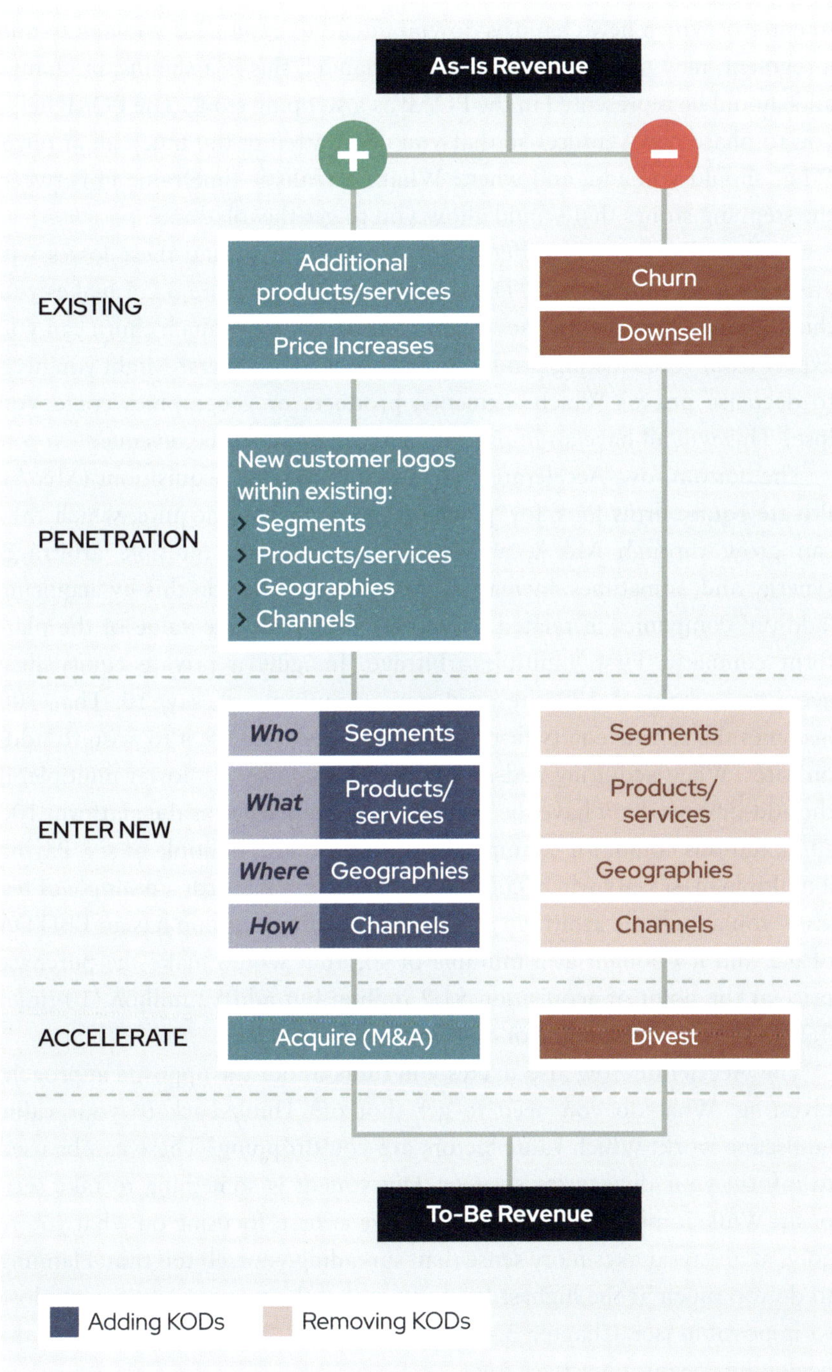

and/or services are you adding? Can you sell these to existing customers or do you need to target a new segment? Which new geographies do you intend to enter or which new channels do you intend to exploit? If you aim to add a segment, new product, geography or channel, this is a significant change and should be represented in the POAP as a stepping stone. The POAP helps you to phase new ventures so that you don't attempt too much all at once. What should you add, and when? What's a realistic timeframe in between the stepping stones that would allow you to get the job done?

Realistically, you will suffer losses in certain areas and these losses will affect your revenue growth. The right-hand side of Figure 3.2.5 makes you think about where these losses might come from. How much churn can you expect from your existing products/services and customers? Might you need to decrease prices? Which segments, products or geographies could you lose? This will all have an impact on achieving your to-be revenue.

The bottom row, 'Accelerate', refers to mergers and acquisitions (M&A). Private equity firms look for 'platform' companies to acquire, which they can grow through M&A, and specifically through multiple arbitrage, synergy and, sometimes, increasing the multiple. They do this by acquiring 'add-on' companies in related industries to increase the value of the platform company. First, multiple arbitrage. Imagine a private equity firm acquires a chain of 100 sites and pays a multiple of, say, 10. That 100 becomes the private equity firm's platform – they will use it to acquire 'add-on' sites. When acquiring add-ons, you look to do so at a lower multiple. If the add-on sites don't have the same scale and efficiency as the platform 100 sites, add-ons could, for example, be purchased at a multiple of six. Paying a multiple of, say, six when, collectively, the group is worth a multiple of ten gives you a multiple arbitrage of four. Say an add-on group has an EBITDA of 0.2 and it's bought at a multiple of six, that would make the purchase price at the point of acquisition $1.2 million but add $2 million (10 times 0.2) to the enterprise value or $0.8 million of arbitrage.

The 'Accelerate' row also makes you think about the opposite approach: divesting. What do you need to get shot of? Think back to your value landscape work. Which value factors are you dropping? These can be used to inform your divestment strategy. Divestment is something to take seriously. While it might seem counterintuitive at first, focusing on what you're good at always makes more sense than spreading yourself too thin. Planning to do too much at the highest level can make objectives management close to impossible (see Chapter 3.4). These top-level 'boulder' plans form the beginning of your objectives tree.

FIGURE 3.2.6 Managing complexity through Ansoff's Growth Matrix

Growth matrix	Existing Customer Segment		New Segment/ Geography
	Existing Customers	New Customers	New Customers
Existing Product	**Upsell, Downsell, Churn** MINIMAL R&CAC Key account management to maintain existing relationships to reduce churn	**New Logos** HIGH R&CAC Rinse and repeat existing sales approach to new, similar customers	**New Segment/ Geography** HIGHER R&CAC New sales approach with sector and local knowledge required to "speak the language"
New Products	**New Products** LOW R&CAC Key account managers to sell, although harder as no proven methodology	**New Products** HIGHER R&CAC Harder as no proven sales methodology or existing relationship	**New Product/ Segment/Geography** HIGHEST R&CAC Hardest approach as new product with new local/ sector experience required

Farming (Key Account Management) | **Hunting** (Dedicated Sales Team)

R&CAC = Risk and Customer Acquisition Cost

How much is too much? Managing complexity using Ansoff's Growth Matrix

Ansoff's Growth Matrix is a framework companies use to help plan growth strategies and understand the amount of complexity involved. Each stepping stone or initiative can be assessed by the degree of separation from existing competencies. Figure 3.2.6 imagines complexity in terms of six areas:

1. Upsell existing products to existing customers.
2. Sell new products to existing customers.
3. Sell existing products to new customer logos within existing customer segments/geographies.
4. Sell new products to new customer logos within existing customer segments/geographies.
5. Sell existing products to a new segment or geography.
6. Sell new products to a new segment or geography.

We have listed these in order of complexity and therefore difficulty of execution. For example, selling existing products to existing customers is easy.

This is the top-left-hand area. You already have all the customer information you need and you already have the product. You don't need to create anything new. Selling a new product to an existing customer is slightly harder (bottom-left-hand area). You have the customer information but no proven sales methodology for selling the new product.

As the figure shows, a different sales approach is needed once you start selling to new customer logos, even if they are in your existing segment. Selling to existing customers requires a 'farming' sales approach centred around key account management and relationship building. The intention is to 'cultivate' existing customers into higher-value propositions. Selling to new customers needs a different approach requiring a dedicated, 'hunting' sales team. The hunters focus on converting new leads and closing deals. It's far more complex than farming, but the degree of complexity varies. If you're selling an existing product to a new customer logo, you know who you're looking for and you can use an existing sales approach. If you're selling a new product to a new customer logo, this is harder because you have no proven sales methodology or existing relationship.

Selling anything to an existing customer segment, even if you need to find new customers within that segment, is far easier than selling into a new segment or geography. The hardest thing of all is to sell a new product into a new segment or geography. This is the bottom-right-hand corner of the matrix. Think carefully before you proceed with anything that fits the criteria of this corner. Finding new customers in a new segment or geography is challenging enough – as we said above, this in itself would be a stepping stone. Finding new customers in a new geography and trying to sell them a product for which you have no prior selling experience is risky. You would need local or sector expertise.

Once you've understood how you plan to reach your to-be revenue and checked that it's feasible in terms of complexity, you can bring it together into a revenue growth bridge.

The revenue growth bridge

In Chapter 1.1 we wrote that most value creation plans are grounded in sales growth. Sales are key. It's often the hardest thing to get right, the hardest function to hire into and the hardest area to forecast and evaluate. Without substantial sales growth, breakthrough returns are nigh on impossible to achieve. You may be reading this and thinking, 'Tell me something I

FIGURE 3.2.7 SaaSurve's revenue growth bridge

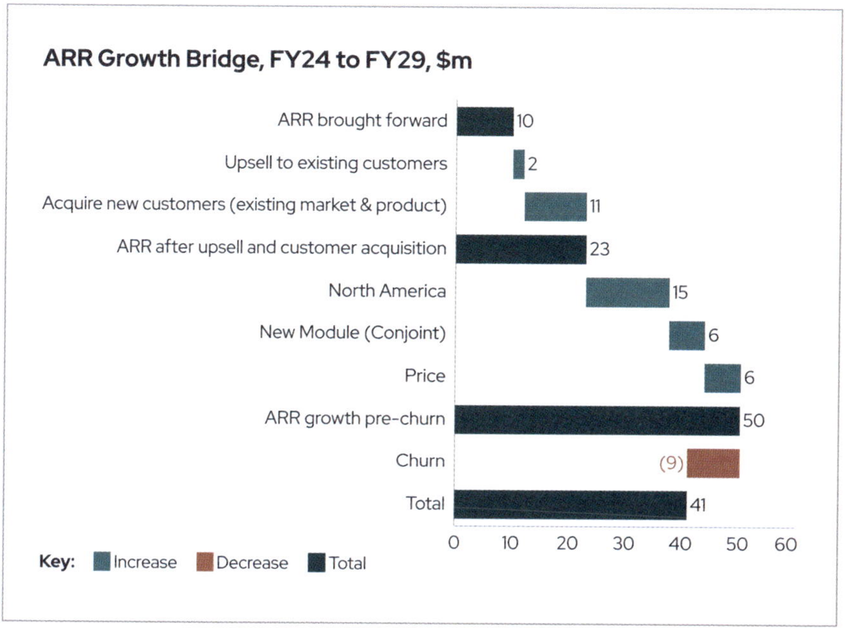

don't already know.' Our experience has shown us that many value creation plans are not sufficiently detailed and thorough regarding sales growth. Our answer is the revenue growth bridge.

The revenue growth bridge is a way of visualizing your understanding of Figure 3.2.5 over time. It breaks down the enterprise value creation bridge into greater detail and shows where revenue growth is expected to come from over the period. Each row shown in Figure 3.2.7 represents a method for revenue growth to measure and track. SaaSurve's starting point is ARR of $10 million. Their target is $41 million ARR in five years. The chart shows how they expect to get there:

- $23 million through upsell to existing customers and acquiring new customers in the existing market and with the existing product.
- $15 million through the North American market.
- $6 million selling the new conjoint analysis module.
- $6 million through price increases.

The red shows the decrease in ARR through customer churn.

Final thoughts

The POAP, enterprise value and revenue bridges are your starting point for risk and objectives planning. Figure 3.2.7 is a great example of how to break down an objective. Where are we today? Where do we want to get to? How are we going to get there? Remember that attempting to do too much can cripple you. You end up with too many initiatives, which compound risk and break down into too many objectives. Think of each potential way of growing your revenue as a boulder with its risks, challenges and rocks, which will need to be broken into pebbles and sand to get the work done.

As we've also said, this book is written linearly and you are likely to read it like that too. It makes strategy design and execution appear like a step-by-step process – you do one element, then you move on to the next and then the next. In reality, you will work on the three bridges of BROP-A simultaneously. They all feed and inform each other. Remember that none of them is set in stone. As you move forward you will refine your thinking and you'll refine your bridges too.

REMEMBER THIS

1. Break time down into manageable, bite-sized chunks.
2. Use the POAP to plan the key initiatives that will help you to reach each stepping stone.
3. Stepping stones are reached once all KPIs have been achieved. This is a huge moment for celebration and reflection before moving on to the next key challenge.
4. Use our enterprise value bridge to plan how you're going to reach the enterprise value target expressed in the POAP.
5. Dig into your TAM to forecast realistic revenue growth and use our revenue growth bridge to nail down where vital sales growth will come from.

Notes

1 Keller, G with Papasan, J (2019) *The One Thing: The surprisingly simple truth behind extraordinary results* (Revised edition), Bard Press, Austin, Texas

2 Farnam Street (2023) Gates' Law: How progress compounds and why it matters, https://fs.blog/gates-law/ (archived at https://perma.cc/FN5U-4LVX)

3 Dean, J (2023) Visualisation: How to avoid the planning fallacy, PsyBlog, 24 January, www.spring.org.uk/2023/01/visualisation-planning-fallacy.php (archived at https://perma.cc/K3CF-GPEE)

4 Lafley, A G and Martin, R L (2013) *Playing to Win: How strategy really works*, Harvard Business Review Press, Boston

5 A 'licence to hire' is a method and training given to those involved in interviewing to certify that they are trained to be effective. This key initiative would be appropriate when you expect to scale your organization significantly.

3.3

Risk taking... and management

Take risks

Introduction

It's 2012. London is hosting the Olympics. It's virtually impossible to get tickets for any of the events. I (Rupert) apply and I'm lucky, I get tickets for swimming, the sport I love and that I partake in myself. Before I know it, I'm there. I'm watching it. And I should be loving it. It should be completely absorbing me. But it's not. I can't focus. I don't care that I'm watching some of the world's best athletes compete right in front of me. All I can think about is the business I love and the fact it might be in ruins.

At that time, I was CEO of tech and analytical services business Concentra Analytics, which had been valued at just under $10 million. Within the space of about a week (if my memory serves), three of our top four clients dealt us a major blow. A global corporation pulled out of a major contract. We didn't have the means to sue them, even though we had contractual cover. At the same time, another fixed-price, fixed-scope project overran significantly. And then another major client informed us it was reaching the end of its life and winding down. Any one of those things by themselves would have been easy to weather. Two probably would have been okay. But all three? In the space of a few days? I was beyond worried.

We survived, but only just. I've never watched cash flow so closely. It was a level of stress that I hope never to repeat. We were fortunate. From the pain came renewal. Thanks to our strong balance sheet, we had some space for manoeuvre and could react. We maintained our strategy to develop a product with SaaS revenue which led to the eventual success of the business. But it so easily could have gone the other way. When three different events conspire against you, even the best-laid plans can come undone.

Risk management comes before objectives management in the BROP-A framework. Failure to manage risks properly can affect an organization's ability to achieve its objectives. In addition, any risks you identify should feed into the objectives you set so that they can be managed appropriately by individuals and groups.

In this chapter, we focus on the need to be a risk-taker. We start by explaining how most businesses have a dysfunctional approach to risk management. Applying a blanket approach to different types of risk makes no sense. We present a process for diagnosing the greatest risks you face and explain the need to understand risks in terms of those that can ruin you and those that will simply reduce your value. We discuss how to respond to risk using our **3T Framework** and introduce the **bow-tie framework** for treating risk.

We'll begin by providing some context about the suboptimal nature of most organizations' approach to risk management.

The problem with risk management

Risks – things that could result in events that impact an organization's ability to meet its objectives – are everywhere. There are a million things that could slow you down or stop you from getting to where you want to go. Some of them are obvious; some far less so. Some of them are serious. They can ruin you – wipe you out. Other risks are more regular – they might result in fluctuations in earnings and wipe out just 1, 5 or 10 per cent of your enterprise value. They might slow you down, but they won't take you down (at least not by themselves).

This chapter is founded on the belief that most organizations have a dysfunctional, unhealthy approach to risk management. Many *say* they do it (listed companies have to) but it's more of a tick-box exercise than a meaningful process aimed at achieving goals and breakthrough returns. Risk management is a key responsibility for management teams and the board and a core element of a board's fiduciary duty (as per the UK's Companies Act 2006) and yet most board packs don't feature it.

Consider, for a moment, how risk management makes you feel. Tense? Bored? You wouldn't be alone. Often, when we speak to CEOs about risk management, they clench up. For them, it's a way for others to prevent them from doing what they know is needed to create a breakthrough. It can also feel ineffective, superficial and overwhelming. You can spend hours assessing and reviewing the same risks month to month and then get blindsided by something you hadn't even considered. People can struggle to engage and something which should be high on the board's list of priorities is often ignored, marginalized or delegated.

It doesn't have to be this way. At its core, risk management should be entirely focused on improving the odds. A good strategy is fundamental for creating breakthrough returns but, by itself, is not enough. Framing risk in the context of getting to your next stepping stone will facilitate productive discussion. Ideally, all stakeholders would adopt a similar attitude towards risk and, as far as possible, align their risk appetites. This, combined with the right tools and methods, should make risk management an indispensable process for reaching your goals. We intend to equip you with these throughout this chapter. But first, we'll look at the top three reasons why risk management is failing.

Reason 1: Companies do not take and manage the right risk

You'll notice that the title of this chapter is 'Risk taking… and management'. The inspiration for this came from an interview given by the statistician and risk expert Nassim Nicholas Taleb at the RiskMinds International conference in 2018. In it, Taleb encapsulated the problem with risk management in two sentences: 'You should study risk taking, not risk management. You cannot separate the income-generating technique from the risks associated with it.'[1] And that is what this chapter is all about. Too many companies attempt to avoid all risk. But those companies will never generate sufficient income to achieve a breakthrough. Every stepping stone along your bridge is, in effect, a risk you've decided to take to realize your ambition.

This is the number one reason why risk management fails. It often focuses solely on eliminating operational risk and compliance. This pervasive and damaging approach misses the point. Addressing operational risk is important, but having this as your sole focus is wrong. Taleb argues that your focus should be on 'ruin risks' – those that can wipe out your enterprise value. He is well known for coining the term 'the black swan' to describe an unpredictable, rare and catastrophic event. He argues that the world isn't normally distributed and that these events happen far more than people realize. The tail is fatter than we think.

Ruin risks have the potential to wipe out your enterprise value. These are the risks that need the majority of your attention. In their influential article 'Managing risks: A new framework', Kaplan and Mikes identify three types of risk: strategy, preventable and external, explained below.[2] They use the former CEO of BP to illustrate the dangers of viewing risk management in terms of following a list of rules. When he took up his post in 2007, Tony Hayward drew up a list of dos and don'ts for his employees, down to minutiae like using coffee lids when walking down corridors. His focus was all wrong. An employee forgetting to put a lid on their coffee didn't have the potential to ruin the company. But a risk event that occurred in 2010 did. While his employees were safely navigating the company corridors burn-free, the BP Deepwater Horizon disaster happened. An oil rig exploded, causing loss of life and the biggest marine oil spill in history. This was one of the most dangerous risks facing the company. No one had predicted the likelihood of it occurring or the impact that a disaster of its kind could have. No mitigating action had been pre-emptively taken to reduce the significant impact of an explosion. People were too busy focusing on the small stuff. At the time of the disaster, the company was worth more than US$180 billion. It paid estimated damages of close to US$60 billion, which, it was said at the time, was thought to put it on the brink of collapse.[3] The Deepwater Horizon disaster didn't ruin BP, but the company was found to be grossly negligent and its reputation took a serious hit.

STRATEGY RISKS

Strategy risks are risks that are worth taking. They are a lever for value creation and a mechanism for reducing headwinds that the business faces in achieving its growth aspirations. Companies choose to run with them because they believe they will generate superior returns. The key word here is 'choose'. Taking strategic risk is a choice. It's like making a bet that could fail. You need to feel sure that it's more likely to succeed than not, but it may turn out you've made the wrong call. Taking this kind of risk requires courage.

Be a risk taker, not a risk manager. Entering a new geography is a strategic risk. So is targeting a new customer segment or channel, or mergers and acquisitions. Each stepping stone along your bridge is a strategic risk and should be viewed through the lens of the critic (see Chapter 3.1). What's going to stop you? Why aren't you going to make it? What's going to make your key initiatives fail or slow them down?

JON

I had the pleasure of being involved in a business chaired by Gary Flowers, a hugely experienced CEO and Chair. Gary was managing partner of Australian commercial law firm Sparke Helmore for 11 years, transforming the practice from a regional player to a top ten national practice. He has 25 years' experience as a leader, Chair and Non-Executive Director across a range of businesses and public institutions, such as Mirvac Group, Australian Rugby Union, Macquarie University and the NSW Institute of Sport.

Gary turns risk management on its head. He initiates an annual review to assess the board's appetite for risk in the coming year: 'The board needs to be comfortable with the level of risk it is prepared to tolerate over a range of scenarios. It might be what level of customer concentration is acceptable or the level of debt or minimum cash headroom that the board is not prepared to go beyond.'

We love this. By focusing on *appetite for risk* the board looks through an entirely different lens. It says it can tolerate or live with a level of risk. It also actively agrees on the parameters so that it can then set targets that it can measure to assess whether it is sailing close to those boundaries.

PREVENTABLE RISKS

Described by Kaplan and Mikes as 'risks arising from within the company that generate no strategic benefits', preventable risks are those that crop up on a day-to-day basis, i.e. they are operational risks. They normally relate to something simply going wrong, such as a server error or loss of data. Preventable risks are bad risks. These are the ones you want to eliminate. This is where rules-based risk management comes into play. A common mistake is thinking risk management starts and ends with preventable risk.

EXTERNAL RISKS

External risk refers to anything that could threaten your business from outside the company – a new competitor, an evolution in tech or a seismic shock like a pandemic, war or climate emergency. As they are driven by external factors, they are categorized as 'uncontrollable'. This means that they often don't make it onto the risk register. If you can't control it, why waste time thinking about it? What you can do is take action to control the potential impact. Thinking through 'what-if' impact mitigations will help you to move fast when the inevitable shocks happen.

Reason 2: Risk quantification is typically meaningless

Anyone who touches risk management has a method of scoring risk. But too often, the methods and language used fail to give a comprehensive understanding of probability and impact. Common practice involves assigning scores to specific risks by multiplying a risk impact rating by the probability of the event occurring:

$$\text{Risk Score} = \text{Impact} \times \text{Probability}$$

But impact is typically determined using a simple number scale attached to very basic descriptors. For example, 'minor', 'moderate', 'major' and 'extreme'. Put against a scale, 'minor' would be given a score of 1, 'moderate' 2, 'major' 3 and 'extreme' 4. But what might the impact look like in reality for each of these points on the scale? How would an extreme impact differ from a major one, or a moderate one from a minor?

And then there's probability. Typically, there might be three ways to assess this: 'possible', 'likely' and 'almost certain'. Does 'possible' mean a 1 per cent chance? Or a 5 per cent chance? A 10 per cent chance?

Reason 3: Risk management is performed in isolation and not adequately linked to action management

Typical risk registers are managed in Excel silos and the links between risks and actions are not sufficiently clear. Linking risks to actions is how you take charge. It's how you start controlling the risk. One action can impact multiple risks but typically, risk registers link risks to one and at most two actions.

Many different risks can be mitigated by many different actions. This means that in data terms, there is a many-to-many relationship between risks and actions (when many categories have relationships – or links – with many other categories). At Ārahi, we have a database of over 230 risks. We have identified that each action has an impact on an average of five risks and each risk has 13 actions to mitigate it. We have 150 actions, of which 25 impact 50 per cent of the risks. By understanding this many-to-many relationship, you can get more bang for your buck.

How to be a risk taker

A friend of mine (Rupert's) is the CEO of one of four divisions within a large corporate organization. It's a listed firm so they are obliged to discuss risk management. He avoids discussing it in the context of strategy for fear that it will scare his colleagues and derail innovation. He is ever mindful of his competitors snapping at his heels. Their obligations to risk management are therefore fulfilled by discussing the operational, compliance stuff. But dodging the discussion puts the company at the biggest risk imaginable. It's just as dangerous as not innovating at all. This is a prime example of a company that is allowing risk to control them, rather than the other way around.

We've witnessed this kind of extreme risk avoidance across countless businesses over many years. It is particularly common in organizations that punish failure. Making mistakes is an essential feature of any strategy with high expected returns. Penalizing people for making the wrong call creates a culture of fear – not a culture that values creativity, innovation, probing and discussion. Steve Jobs would never have had his breakthroughs if he avoided all risks. Willingness (or not) to take strategic risk can cause unhealthy dynamics in organizations. We discuss the need to balance different personalities in the boardroom in Chapter 4.2. This discussion applies particularly to risk taking as some personality types are more bullish about taking risks than others.

Diagnosing risk

Ruin risk is real. Research suggests that approximately 20 per cent of small businesses fail within the first year. By the end of the second year, 30 per cent will have failed. By the end of the fifth year, around 50 per cent will have bitten the dust and by the end of the decade, a whopping 70 per cent will have gone.[4] That's a pretty high failure rate. Diagnosing risk starts with understanding the reasons why there are so many casualties and appraising them within your context. This means digging into the root causes of risk events.

Reasons why start-ups fail can be many and varied, from running out of cash to a lack of market need or a flawed business model. It might come down to the quality of the team or a poor quality or mistimed product. Sometimes, it might be due to disharmony among the team and/or investors.

It's not just start-ups that fail. SMEs and larger businesses are also falling at an alarmingly increasing rate. A BBC Maestro article lists the reasons why businesses fail. The top three are lack of leadership, improper planning and ignoring customer needs. Unforeseen events are only tenth on the list.[5]

CREATING A RISK TAXONOMY

Diagnosing risk starts with brainstorming a list of all the things that could go wrong. On one level, this might sound easy. Coming up with a list of risks to your business isn't difficult. You can get specific by going through one key initiative at a time. You'll soon have a list of events that have the potential to derail you.

But the pressure to think of everything can be overwhelming. Don't try to make it perfect. It'll take multiple iterations with various stakeholders to get to something that you're happy with. There are many different frameworks and templates you can use to get you started. For example, the STOC model helps you categorize risks according to whether they are strategy, tactics, operations or compliance risks. This isn't too dissimilar to Kaplan and Mikes' model explained earlier. The PESTLE(E) model is used to establish sources of external risks: political, economic, sociological, technological, legal, ethical and environmental. The FIRM risk scorecard is used to identify risks across four areas: financial, infrastructure, reputational and marketplace. The first two are internal risks and the second two are external.

The point is, don't try to start from scratch. Either use a template that makes sense for you or build on something that already exists by using one of the many risk libraries (such as Ārahi's). It can save you a tonne of time. You just need to tweak it to make it your own. We favour Kaplan and Mikes' categories of strategic, preventable and external as they cover all the bases. And as we discuss in Chapter 1.3, things are easier to remember in threes.

The premortem The premortem is a useful exercise which can be performed alongside sourcing appropriate templates or libraries. First discussed by Gary Klein in 2007,[6] it uses a concept called prospective hindsight – imagining that an event has already occurred – to help diagnose all the reasons why a project might fail. The premortem is so called because it happens at the beginning of a project (as opposed to the postmortem, which happens at the end). Best performed in a workshop setting, participants are asked to imagine that a project or initiative has failed and then write a list of reasons why this could be the case. Crucially, Klein advises that participants write down the kinds of things they wouldn't ordinarily speak up about, for fear of being 'impolitic'. Participants need to feel safe to do this (see Chapter 4.3 for how to create a healthy team environment).

When we run this in a workshop we ask participants to complete the sentence 'We failed to achieve our stated ambition or objectives because…'.

And then we ask them to pick from the following: 'we didn't…' or 'we did…' Once everyone has their list, the reasons are read out and recorded. It's a great way to collect a variety of diverse views on how a project or initiative can be improved, some of which might otherwise have stayed hidden. To give it some structure, workshop participants can be asked to consider the following areas:

- the economy
- the market
- management
- investors and lenders
- customers
- suppliers
- products
- processes

It's key to think in terms of events. People often imagine a phenomenon rather than a specific event. We call this 'eventerization'. It means making phenomena SMART, i.e. specific, measurable, assignable, realistic and time-bound. For example, someone might say 'Supplier costs increase'. Actual events are more specific than this. Supplier costs increase to what? At what point would a cost increase become a problem? This kind of thinking could result in the following statement: 'Supplier costs increase more than 5 per cent versus budget.' This gives a far better idea of what has happened, which in turn will feed your ability to articulate the likely impact on the organization. For SaaSurve, an event is the North American team developing a different culture to the UK team and it becoming two firms, an 'us' and 'them'. This would result in unhealthy politics, lost time and inconsistent performance and service.

Get creative It's important to think creatively and look beyond the obvious when doing this exercise, particularly when you're assessing external risk. The most crushing situations often stem from threats in places where you'd never think to look. Former US Secretary of Defense Donald Rumsfeld brought attention to the concept of 'unknown unknowns' in his answer to a question about acting without concrete evidence during the Iraq war. There are known knowns - the things we know we know – and known unknowns – the things we know we don't know. But there are also unknown unknowns. These are our biggest risks. They are the events that have the potential to finish us, but we don't even know what they are.

In the aftermath of 9/11, many felt that the Pentagon should have thought about the possibility that a plane could be used as a bomb. Commentators were incredulous that someone hadn't considered it as a risk and taken steps to mitigate it. The disaster challenged people to be more inventive when imagining what the enemy could attempt. The Pentagon even got creative types from Hollywood to brainstorm possible terrorist attack scenarios and offer fresh perspectives on possible threats. These people were accustomed to imagining worst-case disasters for the films they produced – scenarios that you would hope would stay firmly in the realm of fiction. The message here is: don't suffer because you couldn't think of it. Listing your external threats requires input from many different people with varying experiences and perspectives.

Two methods for identifying your most urgent risks

At the beginning of this chapter, we said that one of the defining problems with risk management is the lack of an economic method for determining probability and impact. Here, we describe methods for making probability time-bound and quantifying impact in terms of enterprise value. These methods can be time-consuming. For this reason, we advocate using a forced ranking method initially as a quick and easy way to get an impression of the most urgent risks you face. You can then determine how you want to respond, get approval from the board and get to work on treating your most critical risk. As we explain later in the chapter, our favoured way to do this is by using the 3T Framework.

The forced ranking approach

The ultimate aim of this approach is to reach quick agreement on the high-level action you want to take. It's very likely that brainstorming your risks will result in a long list. We all have too many risks and only so much bandwidth. The first step is to isolate the ones that are most urgent and need your immediate attention – those that are most likely to occur and that are likely to have the biggest impact. Think of this stage as a triage. This is best done with a small group of cross-functional stakeholders. Give everyone the list of risk events and ask them to create two lists – one for impact and one for probability. Put the risk events in order from highest to lowest probability and highest to lowest impact. There will inevitably be some differences of opinion and this exercise can lead to considerable debate.

An economic method for scoring risk

The methods described below provide a more meaningful way to score probability and impact.

MAKING PROBABILITY TIME-BOUND

A probability score is meaningless unless it's contextualized within a timeframe. For example, the probability of a new competitor entering the market in the next three months might be less than 1 per cent, but the chance of it happening within the next five years could be closer to 90 per cent. The probability of a security breach happening in the next ten minutes is likely to be close to zero, but the probability of one happening in the next ten years is much higher. To improve our forecasting skills, we can look to techniques described by Philip E Tetlock and Dan Gardner in their book *Superforecasting*.[7]

Become a superforecaster Superforecasting is the result of research undertaken by Tetlock and others as part of an organization called 'The Good Judgement Project'. It recruited thousands of people between 2011 and 2015 and asked them to make predictions. Importantly, these people were not subject-matter experts on the topics they were asked to make predictions about. The recruits were given basic tutorials on best practices such as how to overcome cognitive biases. Their prediction accuracy was measured using a numerical approach called the Brier score. Those in the top 2 per cent became known as the 'superforecasters'. It was proved that they were capable of making predictions which were statistically more accurate than anyone else's, including experts in those fields.

At its core, superforecasting requires problem-solving and what Jim Collins refers to as 'disciplined thought' (see Chapter 1.3). Tetlock and Gardner highlight two important techniques:

1. Fermi-izing.
2. Anchoring.

1. Fermi-izing The Fermi problem technique is one of the most well-known estimation methods. Named after Enrico Fermi, the Italian physicist who was central to the invention of the atomic bomb, it uses simple logic to break down problems into individual components to find an answer. Tetlock and Gardner dub the technique 'Fermi-izing'. To explain it, they use a well-known example of the Fermi method (and a question often posed when interviewing for management consulting roles): 'How many piano tuners are there in Chicago?' To reach a viable answer to this question you break it down into sub-questions and attempt to answer each in turn:

1. What is the population of Chicago?
2. Roughly how many people live in each house? (This will give you the number of houses in Chicago)
3. What fraction of houses in Chicago has a piano? (Multiplying this fraction by the number of houses will give you the number of pianos)
4. How often do pianos need to be tuned? (Once a year?)
5. How many days a year does a piano tuner work?
6. How long does a piano take to tune and how many pianos can a tuner tune in one day?

Once you know how many pianos a tuner can tune in a day, you can multiply this by the number of days they work a year and you'll get the number of pianos they can tune in a year. So then divide the overall number of pianos in Chicago (worked out in point 3 above) by the number of pianos one tuner can tune in a year and you'll get the number of tuners needed in Chicago over one year.

Using this technique requires you to separate the knowns from the unknowns. The only question we can know the answer to for sure is the population of Chicago. To answer the remaining questions, it's necessary to find knowable proxies for the unknowns.

2. Anchoring Those who are good at forecasting probability start by finding an anchor: they baseline the risk according to what has happened before in their industry. The risk you are trying to predict may feel unique, but it won't be in most, if not all, cases. There will be something you can use as an anchor point. This minimizes the chance of an individual's biases or hunches influencing the forecast.

Quantify impact in terms of enterprise value Impact tends to be thought about in the context of the organization as a whole and described something along the lines of 'high', 'medium' and 'low'. But what, exactly, is likely to be impacted? Revenue? A major objective? It's unusual to find meaningful explanations behind these categories.

We prefer to link quantification to enterprise value at the next landmark as it's the single measure that everyone is shooting for. It therefore allows for objective prioritization and elevates risk management out of the land of high-medium-low theory. SaaSurve's enterprise value is expected to grow to $518 million within five years. Figure 3.3.1 shows a table of five one-off risks, (a), (b), (c), (d) and (e). In the context of deciding whether to treat, tolerate or terminate these risks, it also makes sense to consider how much it would cost to address each one and the benefit-cost ratio.

Risk (a) has a cash impact of $5,000 and a 10 per cent probability, making its risk score $1,000. If they do nothing with Risk (c), it could cost them $3.75 million. It will cost $1 million to treat, so they treat it. Risk (d) is expected to have a $10 million impact and has a 1 per cent probability. The risk score is $100,000 and it only costs $30,000 to treat it, so that's the decision. Risk (e) very small probability but it's a ruin risk – if it occurred, it would wipe you out. It would cost more than the risk score to treat it, so you decide to terminate it.

FIGURE 3.3.1 Determining risk scores, cost to treat and the benefit-cost ratio

Risk	Prob	Impact	Risk Score (Value)	Cost to Treat	Benefit - Cost	Decisions
a	10%	$5	$1	$2	0.3x	Tolerate
b	5%	$25,000	$1,250	$50	25.0x	Treat
c	25%	$15,000	$3,750	$1,000	3.8x	Treat
d	1%	$10,000	$100	$30	3.3x	Treat
e	0.10%	$500,000	$500	$600	0.8x	Terminate
Total			$5,601	$1,682	3.3x	
Treat actions cost: benefit			$5,100	$1,080	4.7x	

Key: Assumption 3T Actions *All values are in $'000*

The total cost of treating risks (b) to (d) is just over $1 million. The risk score for the 'treat' risks is $5,601,000 which is equal to a 4.7 benefit-cost ratio. It's a great return. Once you've treated and terminated risks (b) to (e), you'll only have to tolerate risk (a). There's a 10 per cent chance of risk (a) happening and it would only have a $5,000 impact.

TAF-arizing risk Expressing risk scores in terms of enterprise value provides a central metric which you can track over time. This allows you to gamify risk management while also putting the numbers into a real context – your enterprise value. Risk scores can be aggregated up the risk taxonomy to one metric which can be tracked over time using TAF: targets, actuals and forecasts. In this way, risk becomes another measure that you can keep on top of. Unless risk is distilled down to one measure, it's too abstract to manage. Cue the adage 'if you can't measure it, you can't manage it'.

The target articulates the acceptable level of risk to the enterprise value that you think your organization can take. The target is different from your forecast, which articulates the amount of risk you think you might have to bear heading into the future. Actuals can then be tracked against your forecasts. If a risk event occurs, record it along with an estimate of the impact on the enterprise value. This is where gamification comes in. How do the actuals compare to your forecasts? Are you beating them? Where do you need to improve? How can you use your actuals to improve your forecasting skills?

TAF-arizing risk can inform how you choose to respond. It may help you to identify which risks should be terminated to get your overall level of risk down to an acceptable figure, bearing in mind your mitigating actions. To help these discussions, we like to use the 3T Framework.

Responding to risk using the 3T Framework

Once you know the risks, what should you do? Taleb would tell you to worry like hell about the ruin risks. Be paranoid about those. Proceed with them if the returns are going to be high enough, but make sure you've done your homework first. Worry less about the non-ruin, volatility in earnings risks – the type of operational risks that might wipe out a small proportion of your EBITDA or even enterprise value. You will, in time, want to address these, but focus on the ruin and high-impact risks first. We advocate using the 3T Framework: Treat, Tolerate, Terminate to work out how to respond to different risks.

Treating risk

When you treat a risk, you attempt to control or reduce it. It makes sense to treat high-probability, high-impact risks first. This method of dealing with risk identifies actions that can be taken to either reduce the likelihood of the risk event occurring (probability) or minimize the impact that it would have if it were to occur, or both. One way to treat risk is to transfer it, for example through insurance. Once you have treated a risk, you have reduced it to an acceptable level and it can move to the bottom of the list.

You only have limited time, energy and resources at your disposal, so you can't treat all of your risks. Each risk that you treat will have several mitigating actions attached to it, so it's better to be realistic about what you can treat in the short term and focus your resources on getting the biggest bang for your buck. This inevitably means that some risks won't make the 'Treat' list, at least not initially. These are the risks that you will either tolerate or terminate. Focus particularly on ruin risks. The chances are you are underestimating their probability.

Each action reduces the risk score, which reduces the value of the subsequent action. At a certain point, you will move into diminishing returns. The Pareto principle is at play here. Do the top five to ten actions and then evaluate the next set of actions. It won't make sense to do all of the actions even if they all, on their own merit, make economic sense.

Certain metrics are leading indicators to help with decision-making. Customer concentration is a good example. Many investors won't invest if five clients represent 20 per cent of your revenue – it leaves you over-exposed to the top five clients, which, as evidenced by Rupert's story at the beginning of this chapter, is not a good idea. SaaSurve aims to reduce its customer concentration from 53 per cent down to 13 per cent over the five years. One of the company's key risks is losing more than two customers. Treating this risk takes time, so it becomes an objective with linked key initiatives and KPIs. You can treat this risk through sales growth and by setting up a customer success function.

Tolerating risk

Tolerating a risk means accepting it or retaining it in the short term. It's an affirmative, but not necessarily permanent, course of action. You decide not to take any immediate action to mitigate the risk. Once risks on the 'Treat' list have been mitigated, you may decide to move risks from the 'Tolerate' list across to 'Treat'.

Risks that can be tolerated are likely to have low probability and impact scores. Think twice before choosing to tolerate a ruin risk. You might also decide to tolerate a risk if you have a limited ability to do anything about it or if, after performing a benefit-cost analysis, you decide that the cost of mitigating actions is disproportionate to the benefit gained.

In the early days of Ārahi, we needed to assess the risk that someone might break into our office. We needed to decide between installing a fob system or giving everyone a set of keys. There's no doubt that fobs are more secure. If one gets stolen, you can disconnect the system. It would have cost us a few thousand pounds to install one. But was it worth it? When we brainstormed the impact a break-in would have on the business, we decided we didn't need to worry. Everything was stored in the cloud and we had no paperwork in the office that could identify our clients. The only things of value in the office were computer screens and wall-mounted monitors (and quite a nice coffee machine). The total cost to replace everything would be around £2,000. We then thought about the probability. The downstairs door wasn't particularly secure and there was no reception desk. We therefore estimated the probability to be around 5 per cent. So the impact could be worked out as:

$$5\% \times £2{,}000 = £100$$

Once we compared this to the cost of installing a fob system, our calculations showed us that it wouldn't be worth it. This was a risk that we decided to tolerate.

Terminating risk

Some risk events might be too severe to tolerate or treat by reducing the impact within your organization's risk appetite. These are likely to be low-probability, high-impact risks. Terminating risk is a big decision and it needs careful thought, particularly if it's a strategic risk. If it doesn't make sense to terminate your ruin risk, prioritize treating it.

Terminating a strategic risk takes courage. You would want to apply the more economic methods we describe before making a final decision. Delaying the launch of a new product or deciding not to enter a new market are examples of terminating strategic risk. As we wrote in Chapter 1.3, Steve Jobs removed KODs at Apple in 1997. Terminating a risk like this can be a huge relief. It gives you less to think about and the opportunity to focus your attention on what's left.

It's often obvious which risks need to be treated and much of the 3Ts discussion is likely to centre around whether to tolerate or terminate risks. Remember that if you tolerate a risk now, it doesn't have to be forever. If you terminate it, you may (but not necessarily) be closing the door on something for good. Once you've got to the end of this process, you'll have a list of risks on the 'treat' list that need immediate attention – these will be the ruin risks and the ones with the highest risk value score. The next stage is to determine mitigating actions and then allocate the risks to different forums for ongoing management. Enter the bow-tie framework.

Using the bow-tie framework for the risks you want to treat

The bow-tie framework is a useful method for understanding how to treat risks. It reduces the biggest risk of risk management: doing nothing. It is a graphic tool that helps you to identify and prioritize necessary actions to reduce the probability of the risk event occurring and the impact it could have. As you might expect, it is shaped like a bow tie with the risk event in the middle. Causes and actions that will reduce the probability are to the left and effects and actions that will reduce the impact are to the right.

FIGURE 3.3.2 The semi-skimmed bow tie using an office burglary as an example

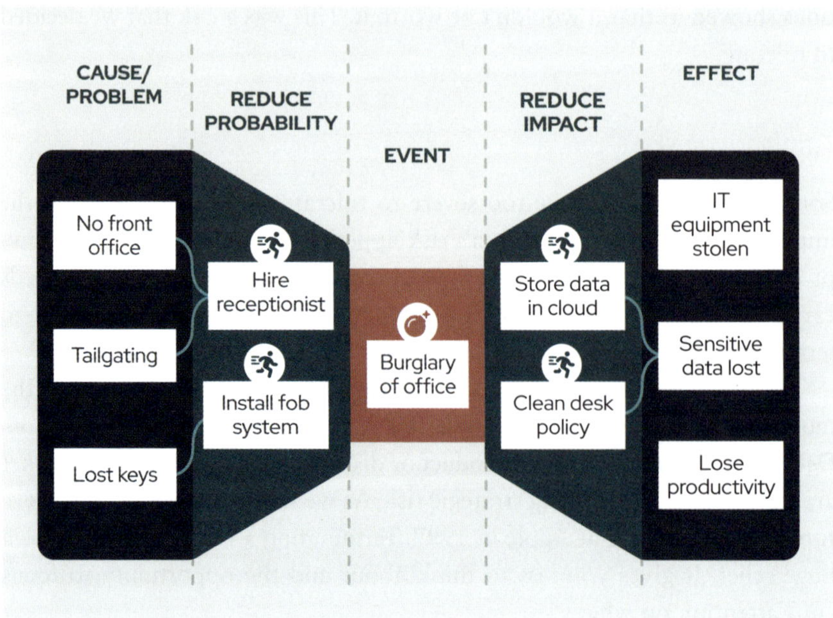

In Chapter 2.1 we introduced our analogy of 'full-fat', 'semi-skimmed' and 'skimmed' kinds of milk as a way to signpost different levels of detail. The 'skimmed' way of treating a risk is simply to write a list of actions that you could do. This can result in a long, paralysing list and no sense of where to begin or what to prioritize. Figure 3.3.2 shows the 'semi-skimmed' bow tie. For some risks, this version may be enough to understand what actions you need to take. But sometimes you may want to dig deeper to understand the economic benefit of those actions. Then, it can be useful to use our full-fat bow tie, shown in Figure 3.3.4. Be aware that each risk event takes between 15 and 30 minutes to put into a bow tie. This is why you can't treat all the risks at once: it's too cognitively demanding.

Note that both versions use a fictional event – an office burglary – to illustrate the workings of the framework. We mentioned above that in the early days of Ārahi, we assessed the risk that someone might break into our office. This had happened to me (Rupert) before, which was partly why we considered this risk as a priority. In the very early days of Concentra Analytics, our office was broken into. We were a start-up. We had an old and inexpensive office near the trendy Borough Market near London Bridge. The office was due to be demolished shortly so the landlords were reluctant to spend any money on it. It showed.

There was a guy in his eighties (let's call him Rob, not his real name) who was part receptionist, part janitor. He didn't take either role particularly seriously. The toilet seats were detached from the toilets (it worked wonders for our balancing skills) and the front desk was frequently left unattended. Even when he was sat there, he rarely checked who was coming and going. And so, we were burgled. The impact was minimal, compared to what it could have been. We lost a few of the designers' high-end Apple computers. But it made us sit up and take the risk seriously. We could have lost client data and suffered the accompanying reputational damage. We could have been sued. We could have had our infrastructure stolen, including our developer servers which a large proportion of our staff relied on. This would have resulted in losing weeks of productive time and had an impact on service delivery. We set about mitigating the risk. This included physical mitigations such as funding a fob system, installing visible cameras and improving the protection of the windows.

Figure 3.3.2, the semi-skimmed bow tie, identifies three causes for a burglary. Our inept 'receptionist' meant that there was virtually no front office. People could tailgate others to get in. Staff also had keys rather than fobs. We risked keys being lost alongside other items which identified the company. If a burglary occurred, three things might happen, as described above. Equipment might be stolen, data might be lost and the business might lose productivity. The bow tie identifies two ways to reduce the probability of a burglary. Hiring a (good) receptionist would provide a front office and stop people from tailgating. Installing a fob system would mitigate the lost keys risk as the system could be disabled. It also identifies two ways to reduce the impact. The first is to store data in the cloud. The second is to operate a clean desk policy so that no sensitive papers are left lying around.

JON

At first glance, the bow-tie framework looks like any other tool to flush out ideas and drive action. Increasingly, I find it's rather special and can lead to real standstill moments. The most memorable was the time I worked with a CEO and her management team in the technology health sector. Having used the premortem tool to identify all the risks that would stop the team from realizing its growth ambitions, we began to debate which risk we thought was the most significant. Many team members were emphatic – the biggest risk was losing key talent, particularly at the senior levels. This energized the team the most, so I went to the flipchart to begin the process of facilitating the bow tie on losing key talent. As I started, the CEO broke the flow and said that this wasn't the biggest risk. She saw failing to deliver on their tech transformation programme as the biggest obstacle to achieving their goals: 'We need to bow-tie the tech transformation programme.' Despite some chair shuffling, we changed tack and considered this risk. The CEO turned out to be right.

Once we had flipcharted the bow tie, we looked at what I'd written down. If the team allowed the tech transformation to fail, it would be perceived in the market as just another health business providing lab-based services to NHS trusts and end patients. It would not be perceived as a tech business with proprietary software that would revolutionize patient access to digital health services. The difference in the end valuation of the business was palpable. The business was private equity backed so the short-term goal was to realize an exit valuation for all shareholders. The bow-tie exercise had drawn out the fact that without the success of the tech transformation programme, the business would be half as valuable on exit. The management team was left with no doubt about what the priority focus was.

Reflecting on this session the CEO said, 'It crystalized everything I intuitively knew, but it wasn't until all the team saw it written down on the flipchart that I realized the importance of the programme. What was even more enlightening for me as CEO was that I'd always let the CTO and his team get on with the technology transformation programme as they are more tech-focused than me. It made me realize that I couldn't do that. It was our biggest risk and as CEO I had to spend more time on it.'

THE FULL-FAT BOW TIE

Our semi-skimmed bow tie identifies four possible actions you could take to reduce the probability and impact of an office burglary. Should you do them all blindly? How do you know which actions will provide the greatest impact on the enterprise value? Which ones will give you the biggest bang for your buck? Which ones should you do first? Which ones should you leave until later? Which should you not bother with at all? We aim to show how to understand the economic impact of your decisions using our full-fat bow tie.

Before delving into it, it is useful to first understand Figure 3.3.3. It demonstrates that with each action you take, you get diminishing returns. Imagine that you have identified seven possible actions to treat the risk of someone breaking into the office. Each one reduces the risk by 25 per cent and costs $50,000. If you do nothing, the risk score is $1 million. If you do the first action, this score reduces the probability to 15 per cent and the risk

FIGURE 3.3.3 A bow-tie explanation chart

Action	Reduction	Cost of action $k	Event Probability	Event Impact $k	Risk Score $k	Benefit of action $k	B:C Ratio
Do Nothing			20%	$5,000	$1,000		
Do '1'	25%	$50	15%	$5,000	$750	$250	5.0x
Do '2'	25%	$50	11%	$5,000	$563	$188	3.8x
Do '3'	25%	$50	8%	$5,000	$422	$141	2.8x
Do '4'	25%	$50	6%	$5,000	$316	$105	2.1x
Do '5'	25%	$50	5%	$5,000	$237	$79	1.6x
Do '6'	25%	$50	4%	$5,000	$178	$59	1.2x
Do '7'	25%	$50	3%	$5,000	$133	$44	0.9x

Key: Assumption B:C = Benefit Cost Ratio

score to $750,000. The benefit-cost ratio is 5.0. The second action reduces the probability to 11 per cent and the risk score to $563,000. The benefit-cost ratio is 3.8. By the time you get to the seventh action, the benefit ($44,000) is less than the cost ($50,000). It probably doesn't make sense to take all seven actions. We can only do so much, so where should we focus? The full-fat bow tie demonstrates that by applying some maths, we can quantify the economics of the whole risk event to understand the cost and benefit of the actions to help us prioritize and commit.

The full-fat bow tie adds another level of complexity by factoring in one-off and recurring costs and the impact that these have on the enterprise value. It comes with a health warning: don't try to reproduce these numbers using a calculator. There is a complex set of calculations behind this bow-tie framework which would take too much space to explain (and it wouldn't add much value to our readers to do so). It's a fictitious illustration of how to understand the economic impact of risks more accurately. This helps you to work out where to invest.

The three impacts are shown on the right-hand side, alongside the impact on the enterprise value. The total impact of the risk event on the enterprise value can be calculated by adding these together: $3m + $0.3m + $0.75m = $4.05m. This is shown in the bottom right-hand box.

The framework shows ten possible actions. Five of these reduce the probability of the risk event happening and five reduce the impact. The biggest impact on the enterprise value is the loss of sensitive data. This will have a likely impact of $3 million. The thickness of the lines between the actions and causes and impacts indicates the extent to which the action reduces the cause or impact. The thicker the line, the greater the reduction. For example, insurance completely eradicates the impact of infrastructure being stolen, which is demonstrated by the thickest line. Having a clean desk policy and moving IT services and data to the cloud significantly reduce the impact of losing sensitive client data (the clean desk policy more so than moving to the cloud), but these actions don't completely eradicate the impact. The actions are colour-coded according to the order in which they will be done. They are broken into waves. Wave 1 is dark green and Wave 2 is light green. Both waves include four actions. The second and fourth boxes along the bottom summarize the total cost by wave.

In this example, the management team has determined that if they take no action, there is a 25 per cent probability of the office being broken into before the next landmark. Remember that this example is inspired by what happened to me (Rupert). The security for that office was a joke. There were no proper locks on the windows and Rob was either absent or asleep most of the time. In addition, staff had keys, not fobs, so there was limited security at the front door. With this real-life example in mind, a 25 per cent probability seems like a reasonable assumption to make. The expected loss with this probability is just over $1 million.

It's worth noting that this example makes a series of simplifying assumptions. One of them is that the enterprise value multiple is 8× EBITDA. The biggest impact on the enterprise value would be the loss of sensitive data at $3 million. There are two actions identified to reduce this risk. One of them is a clean desk policy. There is a one-off cost of $10k for things like lockers and no recurring cost. The impact on the enterprise value is a $10k reduction in cash. The other action is moving IT services and data to the cloud. This is assumed to cost a one-off $1 million with an annual saving of $100k. Therefore, the impact on the enterprise value is $1m – 8×$100k = $200k.

These two actions form part of the first wave. Implementing a clean desk policy is inexpensive and easy. It has a big impact on the risk of losing sensitive client data. Moving everything to the cloud is a significant investment but it's worth it. These two actions almost halve the impact from $4,050k to $2,175k. Returning to the start-up office, the nature of it meant that it was harder to prevent the risk from occurring. You could reasonably estimate that installing cameras and putting a fob system in place would reduce the probability from 25 to 20 per cent. The benefit-to-cost of Wave 1 is therefore a 9× return. It fits into the no-brainer, 'just do it' category.

The actions in Wave 2 focus primarily on reducing the effect of having infrastructure stolen and losing productive time. The impact on the enterprise value of having infrastructure stolen is $300k. There is a recurring cost of $5k for insurance. Implementing remote working capability only has a one-off cost of $50k. This would involve providing everyone with laptops so that they can work remotely. In the end, at Concentra Analytics, this is what we did. It was too hard to effectively prevent a break-in, so as we grew and professionalized, we decided to find a new office in 2015. Everything was moved to the cloud and remote working was fully enabled for everyone. This had an additional benefit, as when the Covid-19 pandemic hit in 2020, we didn't miss a beat.

It doesn't always make sense to take all actions. As the example shows, awareness training and investing in reception don't have sufficient economic benefits, so the management team decided not to do them.

Part of the point of this exercise is to think through what could happen. What would the real costs be and what would it take, in reality, to address

FIGURE 3.3.4 The 'full fat' bow-tie framework

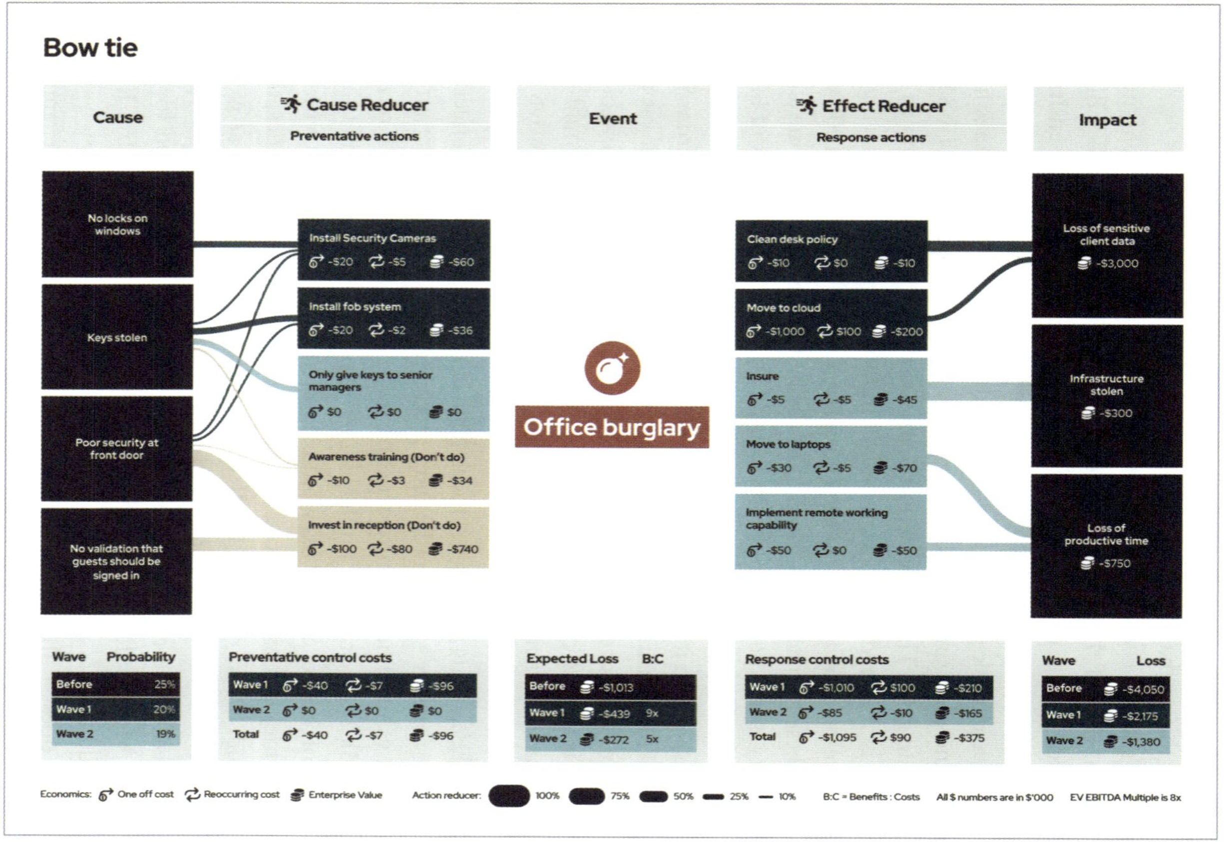

the risks? There are a lot of assumptions. As part of the process, you would question these and play with them. For example, what if the probability wasn't 25 per cent but 10 per cent? Would that affect your decision-making? Would you take different actions? If the answer is yes, perhaps you should spend a little longer thinking about the probability. If, however, it isn't material to your decisions, apply GEMO – Good Enough, Move On. We are all time-poor and most of us are cash-constrained. There is only so much we can do. We hope that the full-fat bow tie helps to quantify the cost and benefits of actions to help you commit to doing them. A 9× return is a great return in anyone's language. This is about prioritization and getting things down to simple numbers, all on one page.

Final thoughts

The adage of 'no risk, no reward' is a cliché for a reason. Return on investment is an easy thing to calculate and understand. Return on risk is harder. People can struggle to make it real – to make it tangible. But as we hope this chapter has shown, it can be done.

What's the risk that someone's going to change the game on you, like Apple did for Nokia? These are your ruin risks. Address them first. Companies tend to focus too much on value reduction risk and not enough on those that could take them down. As Taleb told us, the probability of these happening is far greater than we think.

Risk management activities should be embedded into business processes through the board pack. Specific risks are delegated to and owned by forums. BROP-A helps to ensure that risk management is seen as part of a connected whole and that the risks a company faces are continually reviewed and revised by forums set up to manage them. As the world moves on, a company's understanding of the risks it faces does too, along with the mitigating actions identified to reduce those risks. There is a need for constant assessment and review.

REMEMBER THIS

1. Take risks!
2. Identify your list of risks quickly and use the premortem.
3. Apply the 3T Framework. Focus on ruin risk. If it doesn't make sense to terminate ruin risk, prioritize treating it.
4. Bow-tie your most material treat risks.
5. Develop a list of the highest priority actions to address your material treat risks.
6. Once you've done that, go back to the list and repeat with the next biggest treat risk.
7. Focus on action rather than simply keeping a risk register up to date.

Notes

1 RiskMindsTV (2018) Nassim Nicholas Taleb: 'You should study risk taking, not risk management' [online video], www.youtube.com/watch?v=4P47UTF0tZA (archived at https://perma.cc/QTU9-MJKX)

2 Kaplan, R S and Mikes, A (2012) Managing risks: A new framework, Harvard Business Review, June, https://hbr.org/2012/06/managing-risks-a-new-framework?autocomplete=true (archived at https://perma.cc/LCS4-T3PD)

3 Uhlmann, D (2020) BP paid a steep price for the Gulf oil spill but for the US a decade later, it's business as usual [blog], The Conversation, 23 April, https://theconversation.com/bp-paid-a-steep-price-for-the-gulf-oil-spill-but-for-the-us-a-decade-later-its-business-as-usual-136905 (archived at https://perma.cc/6VX7-3TM6)

4 McIntyre, G (2020) What percentage of small businesses fail? (And other need-to-know stats) [blog], Fundera, 20 November, www.fundera.com/blog/what-percentage-of-small-businesses-fail (archived at https://perma.cc/DW45-TV7L)

5 BBC Maestro (2022) Top 10 reasons why businesses fail [blog], 19 July, www.bbcmaestro.com/blog/top-10-reasons-why-businesses-fail# (archived at https://perma.cc/RBX9-7GKW)

6 Klein, G (2007) Performing a project premortem, *Harvard Business Review*, September, https://hbr.org/2007/09/performing-a-project-premortem (archived at https://perma.cc/K5NQ-R9XB)

7 Tetlock, P E and Gardner, D (2016) *Superforecasting: The art and science of prediction*, Random House Books, New York

3.4

Objectives: milestones, measures and dependencies

Achieving objectives is a team sport, not an individual one

Introduction

Objectives management is a land of missed opportunities. It has vast potential for helping businesses achieve their strategic goals, but we rarely come across organizations that do it effectively. People have been trying to get it right for years. Peter Drucker's Management by Objectives (MBO), introduced in his 1954 book *The Practice of Management*, took the top-down approach of management allocating objectives to employees.[1] The relatively recent evolution of Objectives and Key Results (OKRs) has turned this on its head, advocating that employees set their objectives (what they want to accomplish) and key results (how they will do it) in line with overarching strategic goals. While the OKRs system sounds great in theory, certain assumptions and attitudes which persist in organizations get in the way of the process working as it should.

We believe the main problem stems from the ownership of the objectives management process. There is an enduring and misguided view that it should sit with the HR function. Naturally, given the purpose of HR, it then becomes about the individual rather than the business as a whole. It's seen predominantly as a process that tracks individual performance development rather than overall business performance. If objectives are linked to short-term incentives such as pay and bonuses, it encourages people to game the system. Practices such as 'sandbagging' become commonplace, where people under-promise and over-deliver to maximize their reward.

There are other problems too. While high-level objectives tend to be tracked quantitively through financial results, cascaded objectives assigned to teams and individuals are rarely viewed through a data-driven lens. As an individual in the organization, there is no way of knowing if you are on track with your objectives from one month to the next and they are discussed qualitatively only in annual or bi-annual performance reviews.

Although OKRs has gone a long way to address how strategic goals are communicated, it is not commonly adopted in organizations and there is still frequently a lack of understanding about how goals link to both high-level and individual objectives. As Peter Drucker is thought to have said, 'Management by Objectives works, if you know the objectives. 90 per cent of the time you don't.' This lack of visibility can be demotivating for employees who have no way of knowing how their objectives relate to the organization as a whole. The practice of punishing failure can lead employees to disengage further and lead to risk aversion (for the dangers of this, see Chapter 3.3). The culture of punishment can backfire. An individual's ability to meet their objectives is reliant on many factors. A sales rep's ability to sell, for example, is affected by the quality of the product (R&D) and the number of leads (marketing). Organizations are systems, and none of us is an island.

It doesn't need to be this way. This chapter explains how objectives management can be flipped on its head to become a team-based process focused on strategy execution. To achieve this, decisions need to be made. Is objectives management about pay or realizing strategic goals? It can't be both. How will you respond if someone fails to obtain an objective? In sport, we succeed or fail as a team. Think of objectives management as a team sport, not an individual one. We all have a role to play and giving accountability is key for focus and clarity. It comes down to the team, plus the process and systems. We will demonstrate how to link objectives management to the value creation plan and long-term planning arc of the business and show how to turn it into a process focused on which measures you want to achieve, by when, and measure progress at organizational, team and individual levels. We will also explain how to make it visual and easy to communicate through multiple communication channels.

Like any process, our approach to objectives management requires clear communication and in all likelihood a shift in attitude across the organization. But done right, objectives management unites organizations and increases employee engagement. It genuinely improves business performance.

The struggle with objectives management is perhaps not surprising given the confusion that surrounds it. Much of this confusion stems from terminology and what things mean. So, we'll start at the beginning – with the difference between goals and objectives.

Getting your terminology straight: the difference between goals and objectives

Goals

Goals are a simple statement of your ambition. They are the big-picture, aspirational and directional results you want your organization to achieve, based on your strategy. They are broad and are neither specific nor measurable. 'Be more customer-centric' is a good example. Goals are used to set the tone and focus for objectives and to help frame them. The POAP contains three types of strategic goals which differ in breadth and complexity: the BHAG, the landmarks and the stepping stones. The BHAG is broken down into landmark goals which in turn are broken down into stepping stones. It is the stepping stones that are broken down into key initiatives and projects with KPIs. Your KPIs are defined by objectives. Financial goals are articulated through the enterprise value bridge and revenue bridge. The POAP gives the top-level detail of how these goals will be achieved.

Objectives

Objectives turn an abstract goal into a measurable outcome. They are time-specific. For example, an objective linked to the goal 'Be more customer-centric' could be 'Increase NPS to 50 per cent from 10 per cent by March 2024'. This objective identifies the Net Promoter Score as a way to measure customer health and provides a clear target which needs to be achieved by a specific date.

The red line from goals, through objectives and to actions

Figure 3.4.1 shows the red line running from goals, through to the top-level objectives which relate to the key initiatives and projects in the POAP. Top-level objectives are then cascaded through the organization to roles and

FIGURE 3.4.1 Goals link to landmarks, landmarks link to objectives, objectives link to roles

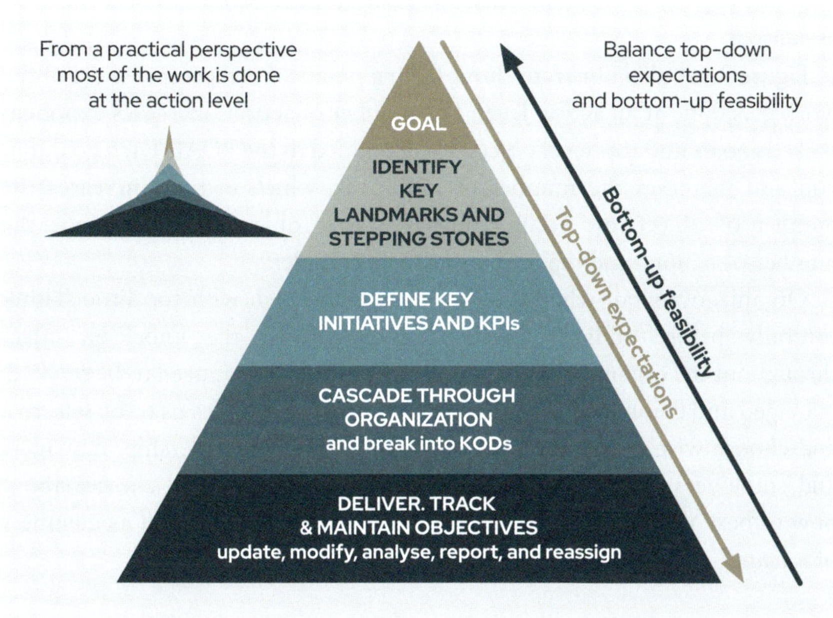

become individuals' objectives. At this point, they are broken down by Key Organizational Dimensions (KODs).

We described KODs in Chapter 1.3. They are the key lenses used to view the organization and measure performance. As a reminder, there are five common KODs: function, geography, business unit or product, segment and channel.

To cascade the objective 'Increase NPS to 50 per cent from 10 per cent by March 2024' through the organization, you could break it down by customer segment and region: Small = 33%; Medium = 50%; Large = 60%. EMEA = 40%; NA = 55%; APAC = 50%.

THE DANGERS OF TRYING TO DO TOO MUCH

In Chapter 1.3 we talked about the dangers of having too many KODs. In their book *The Founder's Mentality*, Chris Zook and James Allen discuss how growth creates complexity and complexity stifles growth.[2] So much of objectives management is about making the right choices and being aware of the dangers of doing too much. The number of KODs in an organization is a measure of complexity. Try to keep the number of KODs to a minimum and resist adding too many as the business scales. Each time a new KOD is added, you reach a new order of magnitude in complexity. Every time you add one, you are likely to increase the amount of complexity in the business by tenfold.

Figure 3.4.1 also illustrates how, from a practical perspective, most of the work gets done at an action level. The number of actions increases exponentially as goals and top-level objectives are added to the POAP. Each goal that you add increases the number of initiatives, which in turn increases the number of objectives. Adding objective after objective can explode the number of actions and make things overly complex.

Organizations fail when they try to do too much with too little. Think carefully before adding objectives and consider the knock-on effect throughout the organization of the number of things that need to be tracked, managed and completed. The POAP helps because it forces us to be selective and choose wisely. You can't do everything at once. Leadership, managers and employees must make conscious, careful and informed choices about how to best allocate time and energy – both as individuals and as members of a team.

Balancing top-down expectations with bottom-up feasibility

Objectives and Key Results is a bottom-up goal-setting framework where employees set their objectives as well as the results they hope to achieve and that they will use to measure their progress. Employees do this before discussing and approving the objectives with their manager, which increases a sense of ownership and, in theory, helps people to feel more engaged in their work. (This is necessary, as Gallup's 'State of the Global Workplace' 2023 report concluded that only 23 per cent of employees feel engaged at work. While this is the highest figure since Gallup started to measure employee engagement in 2009, it still only relates to one in four workers).[3]

OKRs was created by the CEO of Intel, Andy Grove, and later refined by John Doerr, the founder of Kleiner Perkins, a notable venture capital fund which backed Google, Amazon and many others. Google is often given as an example of a company that has mastered OKRs after John Doerr introduced the practice there. The OKRs framework takes an opposite approach to Peter Drucker's Management by Objectives, which advocates that managers should allocate objectives to employees through a top-down approach. One of the good things about OKRs is an expectation that people will hit their targets only 70 per cent of the time. If you expect people to hit their targets 100 per cent of the time, you will encourage a risk-averse culture and you won't achieve as much (see Chapter 3.3). This implies that 20 to 30 per cent of your objectives should be red or amber according to the BRAG framework. Having said that, you are required to hit or overachieve objectives such as cash targets. These should be set conservatively, particularly where banking covenant requirements come into play.

We believe in balancing these two approaches. Linking objectives to strategic goals necessitates a top-down approach, but the enormous benefit of OKRs is the involvement of the people on the ground, doing the job, who need to achieve the objectives. With OKRs, instead of being dictated to, employees feel a sense of agency and belonging.

There's no doubt that organizations are most effective when everyone within them understands the overall goals and stays laser-focused on achieving them. Organizations use OKRs to plan what people are going to produce, track their progress against the plan, and coordinate priorities and milestones between people and teams. They are also used to help people stay focused on the most important goals and avoid being distracted by urgent but less important ones.

Competencies versus objectives

Performance pay sounds great on the surface, but how do you judge performance? People are often judged solely by hard outcomes and whether or not they manage to meet their objectives. But there is often a range of reasons why someone might miss an objective. Do they have the right skills and competencies? If they do, do they have the right behaviours? Do they work well with other people? Are they determined? Are they action-focused? If the answer is an emphatic 'yes' to all of the above, perhaps there is a system and/or process failure. Perhaps the required competencies were misunderstood. Or perhaps, given the time and resources dedicated to the objective in question, it just wasn't a realistic ask.

Simplifying objectives management down to an HR process linked to pay is dangerous. It can be unfair, drive unhelpful behaviour and take attention away from strategy execution. In our view, objectives management needs to be focused on achieving certain metrics so that you know the strategy is being executed effectively. There is a caveat to this point. If someone consistently fails to meet their objectives, ask three questions: 1) Do they have the required competencies and/or behaviours? 2) Could training, coaching and support rectify the situation? 3) If the answer to both of these questions is 'no', do you need to think about parting ways? This should be a last resort. It is the hard part of management.

Objectives measures and milestones

Objectives provide a lens to view the progress towards organizational goals at a point in time. They express measurable milestones which, if achieved, will advance objective(s) towards the target. Not all objectives are the same and they have different types of targets. Some targets are milestones and others are measures. There are three different types:

1. **Static measure objectives.**
2. **Moving measure objectives.**
3. **Milestone objectives.**

With static measure objectives, the target remains the same over time. Static targets do not have a 'by when' date – the target is that the measure permanently stays at a certain level, as shown in the top-left of Figure 3.4.2. Examples of static measures are:

- Net Promoter Score of +45
- employee churn less than 17 per cent
- customer concentration 30 per cent
- usability score of more than 4.2

But with a moving measure, the target changes over time. For example:

- $ of revenue, or gross contribution
- sales targets by quarter
- EBITDA levels by month, or cash in the bank

With these measures, actuals are measured against moving targets. Moving measures can be converted into milestones by setting a specific point in time to signify when an objective needs to be completed, e.g. Q1 2025. This becomes your forecast date, as shown in the top right of Figure 3.4.2.

Milestone objectives are linked to the integrated planning process which we discuss in Chapter 3.5. They are time-bound. They signify a need to either complete a given key initiative or project by a specified date, e.g. 'Implement CRM by December 2024', or hit a key measure by a specified date, e.g. 'Achieve £30m of ARR sales by December 2025'. Within the 4D Framework, milestones are measured and tracked through the boulders, rocks, pebbles and sand – the key initiatives, projects and governed actions.

Milestone objectives are defined by target, actual and forecast dates. The target is fixed. It relates to a point in time or a specific number that is decided at the beginning of a piece of work. Actual and forecast dates, by definition, are not fixed. While it's helpful to continue to understand the original target, it's also helpful to understand when you think it will be completed. This is your forecast date. Unfortunately, they typically move backwards. For example, imagine you have a target of 1 May. In March, during a programme update, you discover that you expect this milestone to be achieved on 12 June, i.e. six weeks later. Then, in May, you discover that it will be delayed another five weeks, to 17 July. When the forecast date of 17 July is reached, it is changed yet again to 31 August. It is finally completed on this date, four months behind target. The target remains 1 May but the forecast shifts. The actual is when it's done. The middle graph of Figure 3.4.2 demonstrates this process.

Look back to Figure 1.3.3 where we explained TAF data in relation to revenue. This shows a very common scenario – we call it 'a target sponsored by the Nike swish'. Actuals trail behind the target and consecutive forecasts constantly predict that actuals will miraculously catch up. This is an aspirational picture, not a realistic one. Sadly, many forecasts are anything but realistic and organizations fail to see that their forecasts are unachievable. It's easy to constantly push for growth, and it's particularly hard for start-ups when you don't have historical numbers to use as a basis for target setting (often in the context of budget setting). The cone of outcomes can be huge. The more mature the organization and the more data you have, the more accurate your targets. Getting the balance right with setting targets is hard. Set them too high and you up the risk of failure. This can be demoralizing and can impact bonus pay. But set them too low and it means you might not be pushing hard enough to achieve a breakthrough. Could this be the mother of all Goldilocks problems?

Organizations often have multiple targets, especially in private equity-backed cases. In its Information Memorandum (IM), management produces a set of numbers for five years into the future. The investment firm produces a set of targets in the investment case for the investment committee (IC). These targets, which are typically not shared with management, will

FIGURE 3.4.2 Moving, static and milestone charts

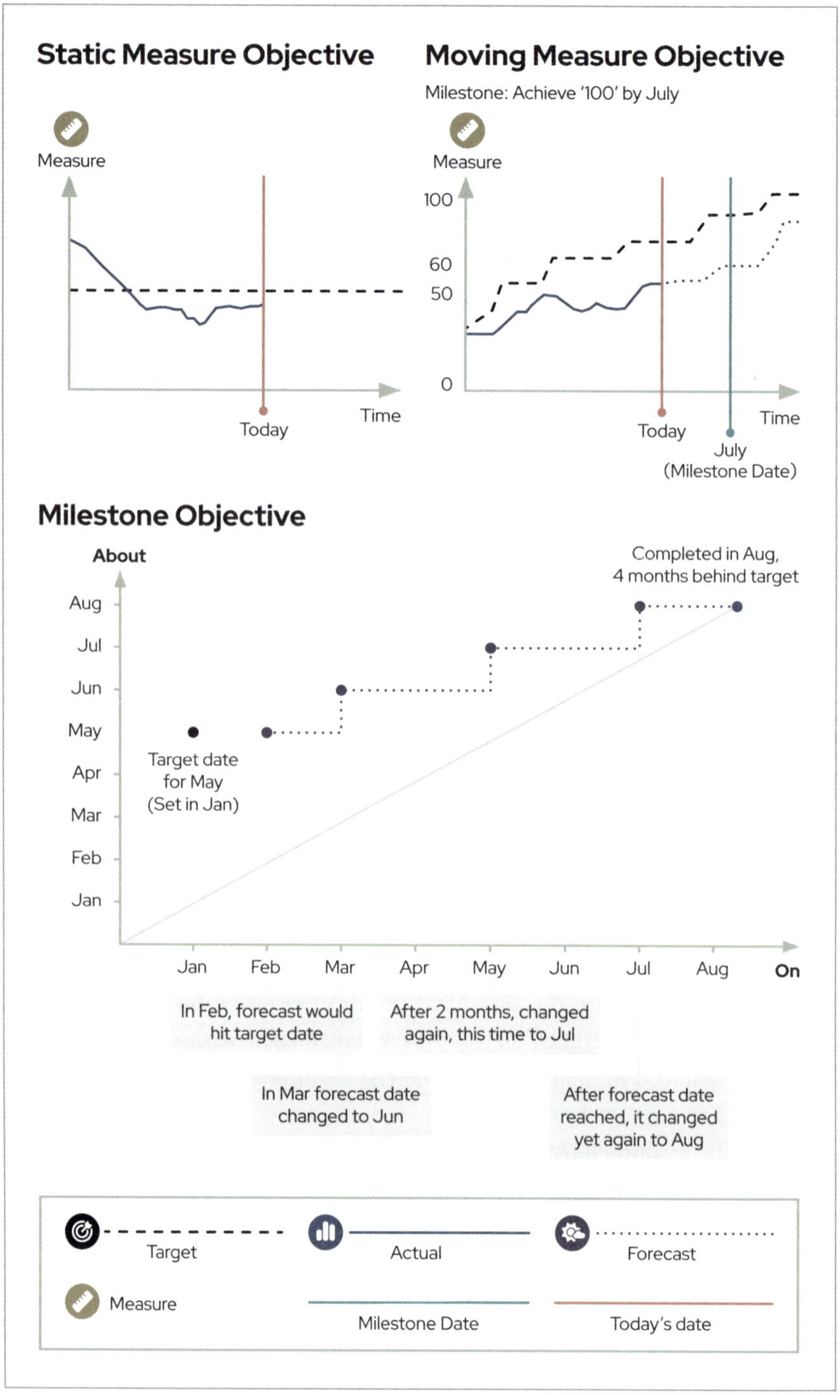

normally be lower than the targets produced by the management team. If debt is raised, a third set of targets will be set for the bank (a banking or downside case). Lastly, management suggests a budget for the board to approve each year. This approval often comes after multiple rounds of iteration, negotiation and debate. Is any of it real? It certainly has a real-world impact. Management and employee incentive plans are based on them and bank covenants are set. Also, the positive psychological impact of hitting your numbers is very real.

Setting objectives

Figure 3.4.3 describes an objectives-setting process that steps through from defining top-level objectives to cascading them throughout the organization and signing them off and then tracking them and maintaining them over time.

FIGURE 3.4.3 Objectives management can be understood in terms of a three-stage process

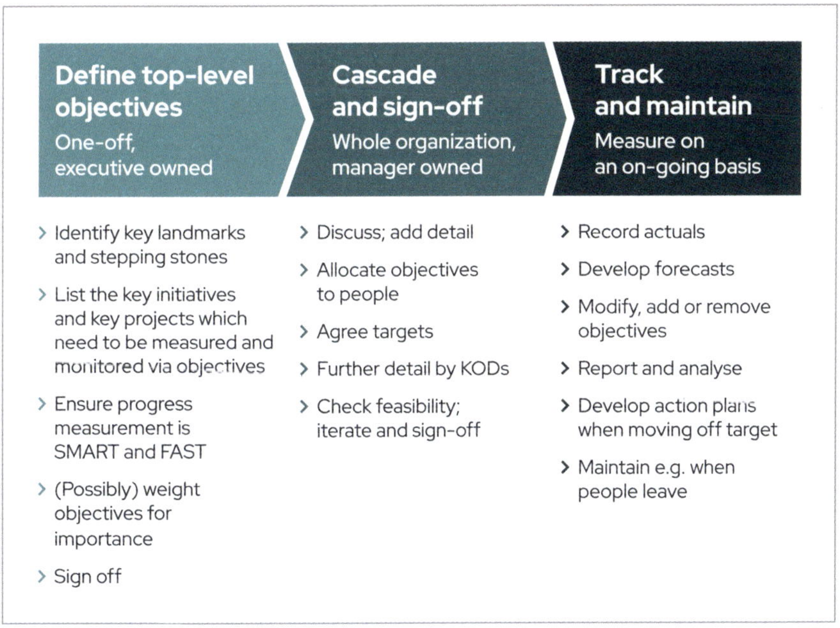

Step 1: Define top-level objectives

As we've seen, your strategic goals inform your landmarks and stepping stones which in turn inform your key initiatives and projects. Each of these key initiatives and projects gets measured via objectives. Remember that objectives are the 'what'. They describe what you are going to do to reach your goals. Here is some guidance to consider when setting them:

- Make them aggressive but realistic – be ambitious, but not overly ambitious.
- Make them tangible, objective and unambiguous. It should be obvious when an objective is achieved.
- Ensure they drive shareholder value (the achievement of an objective needs to provide clear value for the company).
- Write them clearly and prescribe to SMART and FAST rules.

SMART AND FAST OBJECTIVES

SMART and FAST are two well-established frameworks for setting objectives. Both of them enable you to manage, measure and track objectives with data. SMART stands for Specific, Measurable, Attainable, Relevant and Time-bound while FAST stands for Frequently discussed, Ambitious, Specific and Transparent. Using these two frameworks forces you to ask relevant questions and refine your objectives until they are exactly right:

- Specific – is this objective specific enough to be implemented and cascaded at the next stage of the process? Does it target a specific KOD with a clear owner?
- Measurable – how will I measure this objective? Is it a Key Performance Indicator or is it a project that needs to be delivered by a specific date?
- Attainable – is this objective sufficiently aggressive but realistic (remember the Nike swish)? Don't agree to a target, budget or investment plan that you have little hope of achieving. This might sound obvious, but it happens surprisingly often, particularly with private investors who like to push for higher budget numbers.
- Relevant – is the objective directly relevant to the strategic goal?
- Time-bound – what should the deadline be for this objective?

- Frequently discussed – which forums and meetings should include the objective in their packs?
- Ambitious – does this objective hit the sweet spot in terms of balancing ambition and realism?
- Transparent – who can track and monitor this objective? Which objectives are shared with whom? How many, and which ones are visible to the entire organization? Should any be visible externally, e.g. impact measures?

WEIGHTING OBJECTIVES

As Figure 3.4.3 shows, weighting objectives is not obligatory, nor is it common practice. It is useful only if you want to roll up all your objectives into one balanced scorecard number. If this is something you would find useful, then follow this process. It can be done if there are some objectives on your list that are more important than others. It can be a complex process, so do it only if there is a clear benefit. The swing rating method we described in Chapter 2.2. can be a good way to do it, whereby the most important objective is given a score of 100 and every other objective is given a score between 1 and 100, relative to that. The second most important objective could be given a score of 80 and the third 70. If 'x' is the most important objective and the 'y' objective is half as important as 'x', the 'y' would be given a rating of 50.

One important reason for doing this is to focus attention on whether you have sufficient resources. This, in turn, can help you to decide if you are doing too much.

Step 2: Cascade objectives throughout the organization

Cascading top-level objectives throughout the organization involves breaking them down into a hierarchical 'tree' structure. This is effectively a taxonomy. Building a good taxonomy takes time and iteration. It's a great way to structure your thinking and apply the MECE (Mutually Exclusive and Collectively Exhaustive) test. MECE was developed by Barbara Minto and is at the heart of her Pyramid Principle.[4] It's a way of checking that you have broken things down into logical groups and sub-groups, that you've included everything and that there is no overlap.

The taxonomy includes four goals taken from the POAP: 'Customer delight', 'Revenue growth', 'Product suitability' and 'People and work automation'. Taxonomy building helps you to think through what you mean by 'Customer delight'. Have you listed every objective that relates to this goal? It also includes the three types of objectives. Some are static, such as 'NPS' and 'GRR', some are moving, such as 'Consumer concentration', and some are milestones, such as 'New CRM by 2023'. It's also helpful to know which ones break down by KOD, such as 'Sales $5m' and 'ARR $13m'. These KOD objectives then cascade down through the organizational hierarchy to team objectives and finally to individual objectives. This ultimately allows objectives to be specified for roles. You can break these out to understand them in more depth as shown in Figures 3.4.5 and 3.4.6.

As you can see from Figure 3.4.4, an objectives tree is not uniform. Some goals need to be broken down into projects before breaking them down further into sub-objectives. For example, 'Build lead gen engine by June 2024' is a project linked to the 'Revenue growth' goal. It's broken down into five milestone objectives, including 'Recruit team leader' and 'Design lead generation marketing strategy'. In Chapter 3.5, we show how this project is tracked through a charter, which, among other things, lists the objectives and gives start and end dates. The box describes how OKRs fit within our objectives framework.

OKRS AND OUR OBJECTIVES FRAMEWORK

The 'key results' of OKRs are the equivalent of the sub-objectives in the objectives tree. They are the further details which break objectives down. They largely relate to who owns what. In *Measure What Matters*, John Doerr gives his classic example of an objective for the General Manager of an NFL franchise: 'Make $ for the owners.' The key results for this objective are 'Win Super Bowl' and 'Fill home stands to 90 per cent capacity'. These two key results become other's objectives – the Head Coach gets 'Win Super Bowl' and they have a more detailed set of key results, including 'Passing attack amasses 300+ yards per game' and 'Defense allows fewer than 17 points per game'. In our language, these are static measures. The first, given to the Offensive Coach, is a static measure where higher is better, and the second, given to the Defensive Coach, is a static measure where lower is better. The SVP of Marketing gets 'Fill home stands to 90 per cent capacity' with three linked key results. One of these is 'Upgrade team branding'.[5] We would call this a milestone and it would likely be a key initiative on the POAP.

FIGURE 3.4.4 An objectives tree for SaaSurve

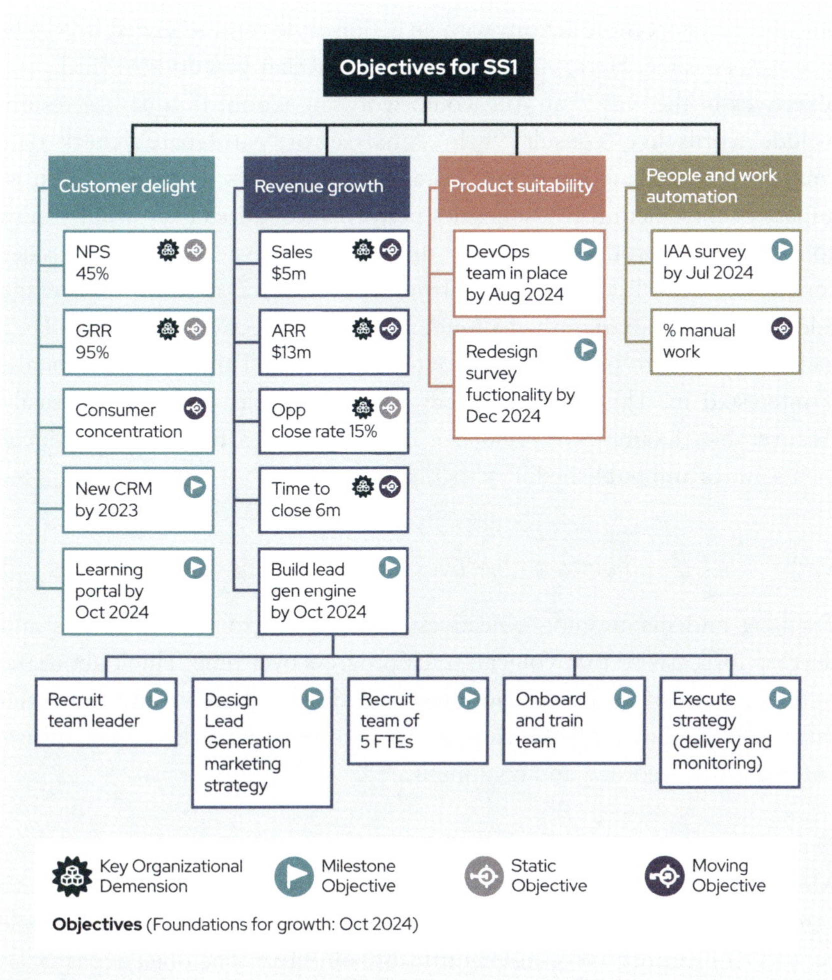

DEFINING OBJECTIVES

A large part of the cascading process involves working with employees who set and define their objectives, as well as the results they hope to achieve. When doing this, it's important to pay attention to how objectives are worded. Sentences should begin with:

> We/I will [insert objective]
>
> This will be measured by [set of Key Results]

Objectives describe outcomes rather than actions. In Chapter 4.4 we give guidance on how to word actions, particularly actions that can be completed quickly. You start these actions with an action-style verb, followed by as few words as possible. Here, you need to be careful that you do not word your objectives in the way that you would word an action. If your key results include words like 'consult', 'help', 'analyse' or 'participate', check that you're not describing an action. Instead, focus on describing the end-user impact of these actions. 'Assess sales performance' doesn't say what you're going to do or produce. Compare that with 'Achieve a 25 per cent sales conversion rate', 'Reduce the CAC from $1.50 to $1.2' or 'Improve average sales cycle from six months to four'. These are objective-style verbs. They include a means to provide evidence of completion. This is what the board is interested in. This evidence needs to be available, credible and easily discoverable. Examples of evidence include changes lists, links to documents, notes and published metrics reports.

Step 3: Track and maintain objectives using milestones and measures

Tracking and maintaining objectives requires you to record actuals and develop forecasts so that you can track progress over time. Think about the different types of measures and milestones discussed above and how each one should be quantified. Each provides data points which can be consistently applied, recorded and communicated.

REPORTING ON MOVING MEASURE OBJECTIVES

Moving measure objectives can be broken out by a range of KODs, but it's rarely practical to do it for more than two. Figure 3.4.5 shows an example of a KOD breakout for a moving measure objective. The objective is 'Sales of $10.8 million for FY24'. This example links to the high-level sales (or revenue) bridge described in Chapter 3.2. How are you going to achieve the $10.8 million? You can break it down in various ways. Because it's a moving target, you can break it down by time and you can break it down by region and segment (both of which are KODs). In the figure, the regions are EMEA, North America and APAC, and the segments are 'small', 'medium', 'large' and 'enterprise'. Eight segments are being tracked. Each region and each segment needs a different owner, team and capability as different skills are needed to manage different-sized organizations. It starts to become obvious why we say that KODs provide a measure of complexity. Look for ways to

FIGURE 3.4.5 An example of a moving target KOD breakout

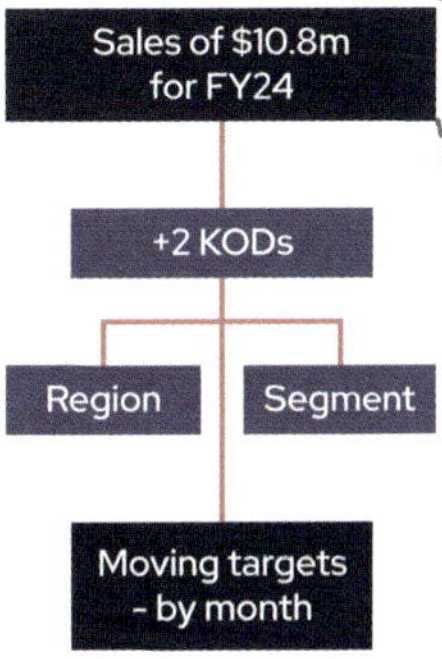

FY24 Sales		Target												
		Apr	May	Jun	Jul	Aug	Sep	Oct	Nov	Dec	Jan	Feb	Mar	
EMEA	Small	$86	$78	$95	$95	$99	$104	$108	$107	$90	$112	$115	$112	$1,201
	Medium	$76	$68	$84	$84	$87	$91	$95	$94	$97	$99	$101	$99	$1,075
	Large	$60	$54	$66	$66	$69	$72	$75	$74	$76	$78	$80	$78	$848
	Total	**$222**	**$200**	**$245**	**$245**	**$255**	**$267**	**$278**	**$275**	**$263**	**$289**	**$296**	**$289**	**$3,124**
NA	Small	$88	$79	$97	$97	$101	$106	$110	$109	$112	$114	$117	$114	$1,244
	Medium	$78	$70	$85	$85	$89	$93	$97	$96	$99	$101	$103	$101	$1,097
	Large	$79	$71	$87	$87	$91	$95	$99	$98	$101	$103	$105	$103	$1,119
	Enterprise	$59	$53	$65	$65	$68	$71	$74	$73	$75	$77	$79	$77	$836
	Total NA	**$304**	**$273**	**$334**	**$334**	**$349**	**$365**	**$380**	**$376**	**$387**	**$395**	**$404**	**$395**	**$4,296**
APAC	**Large**	**$-**	**$-**	**$-**	**$-**	**$-**	**$20**	**$20**	**$40**	**$40**	**$60**	**$60**	**$60**	**$300**
Total		$748	$673	$824	$824	$859	$919	$956	$966	$953	$1,033	$1,056	$1,033	$10,844

simplify, for example are small and medium different segments or can they be treated in the same way? Are 'large' and 'enterprise' the same? Amalgamate what you can.

REPORTING ON STATIC OBJECTIVES

Static objectives are easier to track and manage, so, practically speaking, they can be broken down by up to four KODs if necessary (more than this will be overwhelming). Take the objective 'Achieve Avg NPS of 50%'. Figure 3.4.6 shows it broken down by region (EMEA, North America and APAC), territory, segment (small, medium and large) and industry (consumer, manufacturing and retail). The figure shows forecasts for regions within different segments and industries. Those responsible for small retail businesses are forecast to hit 50 per cent, but there are issues elsewhere. Medium consumer businesses in South and Central, for example, are forecast to achieve 25 per cent.

This figure shows the matrix in action, highlighting the complexity of overlapping KODs when it comes to setting objectives and understanding accountability. There will be teams responsible for different segments, industries and territories. Where does accountability sit? This only applies to large, matrixed organizations that have gone through several phases of growth (we discuss this in detail in Chapter 4.5). Things can become complicated and conflict can arise. When I (Rupert) faced this situation at

FIGURE 3.4.6 An example of static target KOD breakdown with regional forecasts

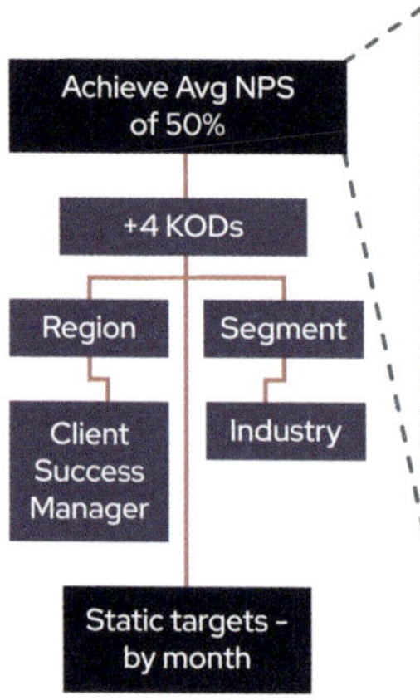

FY24 NPS		Small			Medium			Large			Avg.
		Con.	Mfg	Ret.	Con.	Mfg	Ret.	Con.	Mfg	Ret.	
EMEA	UK	25%	25%	50%	40%	40%	50%	40%	40%	50%	40%
	DACH				20%	20%	30%	30%	30%	40%	28%
	Benelux							35%	35%	45%	38%
	Sub-total	**25%**	**25%**	**50%**	**30%**	**30%**	**40%**	**35%**	**35%**	**45%**	**35%**
NA	East Coast			50%	40%	35%	45%	50%	50%	55%	46%
	West Coast			50%	40%		45%	50%	50%	55%	48%
	South and Central			50%	25%		30%	35%	35%	40%	36%
	Canada			50%			40%	45%	45%	50%	46%
	Sub-total	-	-	**50%**	**35%**	**35%**	**40%**	**45%**	**45%**	**50%**	**43%**
APAC	ANZ	25%	25%	50%							33%
	Sub-total	**25%**	**25%**	**50%**	-	-	-	-	-	-	**33%**
Total Average		25%	25%	50%	33%	33%	40%	40%	40%	48%	37%

Concentra Analytics, I removed geographical P&Ls because it got in the way of what was right for the customer. I stripped away complexity to clarify accountability.

The importance of integrated thinking

We'll end this chapter with a note on the importance of thinking about objectives as part of an integrated whole. Tensions exist between certain objectives. For example, a manufacturing manager wants high uptime and therefore long run lengths while a supply chain manager, responsible for inventory, wants short run lengths and therefore greater responsiveness from manufacturing. There is a tension between manufacturing and inventory. Many other examples exist, for example cost to serve versus customer service. It's important for these tensions to be put on the table and debated. Your strategy should provide your answers. For example, if customer service is critical, you should accept a higher cost to serve and you should be able to charge a higher price. The customers should value that service. If they don't, you have your answer.

Also, be aware of a common trap – hitting the target but missing the point. The McNamara Fallacy provides an excellent illustration of the danger of not thinking in an integrated way. History shows us how a siloed, myopic measurement drove the US to make a crucial mistake during the

Vietnam War, a war which pitted the greatest superpower against peasants running around a jungle in pyjamas (while also digging complex underground cave complexes). At the time, one of America's greatest business executives, the former Ford President, Robert McNamara, was Secretary of Defense. Google him. He was very important for a very long time. He was a Berkeley and Harvard Business School graduate. He was a Lieutenant Colonel in World War II, and one of the whizz kids who helped to reform Ford. He became President there and left five weeks later to join Kennedy's cabinet, where he stayed until 1968, after which time he went on to serve as the World Bank President.[6] McNamara had an incredible life and was one of the forces of his generation. Yet, Google him. What comes up first is a fallacy in his name: 'The McNamara Fallacy'.

This fallacy is about making decisions based solely on quantitative observations and ignoring things that, therefore, can't be quantified. During the Vietnam War, they measured success by collecting body count data. They tracked the number of people they killed against their fatalities. That measure alone was used to gain insight into how the war was progressing. It showed that America was winning. They were killing more people. Many more people.

With the benefit of hindsight, this seems like an obvious mistake. But leaders fall foul of the McNamara Fallacy all the time. Things that cannot be measured (or are comparatively difficult to measure) are assumed to be unimportant or perhaps, even, non-existent. If we manage what we measure, we also don't manage what we don't measure. By becoming fixated on one single thing, we risk overlooking things of statistical importance. Avoid the trap of measuring what is easy rather than thinking about what matters.

Final thoughts

There is an old saying, be careful what you wish for, because it might just come true. Setting goals is setting down dreams. Detailing them into specific objectives is the first step to making them real. Breaking them by KODs allocates ownership further down into the organization. Striking the right balance between ambition and realism is hard. Understanding history can help you to get it right. Focus mixed with capability and drive will always be critical (remember our point about lack of focus in Chapter 1.2). The more ambitious you are, the more critical this will be.

You won't succeed all the time and how you deal with failure can define your culture. Is failure considered a moment to learn the right lessons and improve? Or does it result in a witch hunt? If a project or key initiative fails, it's important to understand whether it was down to one person or a group. In Chapter 4.3 we look at how to build healthy, successful teams. Over-punishing failure can result in lowball targets. This is not the way to achieve breakthrough returns. Equally, if hitting targets requires a team and the right processes and systems to be in place, then why make objectives management an HR-driven process focused on pay? This is a strategy execution process. It is about learning, getting better, integrated problem solving and using all your skills to hit those greens and even, sometimes, blues.

Objectives aren't just about the upside, they also address the downside risks. One aim of objectives management is to 'catch falling knives', in other words, to understand which metrics (linked to objectives) are leading indicators of your key risks. In Chapter 4.2 we discuss board pack reporting. The board does not need to review all the metrics (this also applies to other forums – see Chapter 4.3). In Chapter 4.2 we give examples of a KPI dashboard (the Ārahi Arrow Dashboard) and two further ways to visualize key objectives: a Leaderboard and a Form Guide.

REMEMBER THIS

1. With moving targets, try to limit to two KODs. With static targets, you can go up to four KODs.
2. Do both top-down and bottom-up together to validate. If you don't do both, you'll end up in the spreadsheet strategy trap (see Chapter 1.2).
3. Objective setting should be a strategy-based process, not one based on reward. Objectives are owned by individuals, but achieving them is a team sport.
4. Don't sandbag and don't be too stretched. There is a fine balance to strike. Don't let an investor, NED or ambitious boss drive up your targets to a point where they become wildly unachievable.
5. 20 to 30 per cent of your aspirational, striving objectives should be red or amber at any one time apart from feet-on-the-ground objectives like cash which need to be set more conservatively.

Notes

1 Drucker, P (2007) *The Practice of Management* (Classic Drucker Collection), Routledge, London

2 Zook, C and Allen, J (2016) *The Founder's Mentality: How to overcome the predictable crises of growth*, Harvard Business Review Press, Boston

3 Gallup (2023) State of the Global Workplace: 2023 Report, https://www.gallup.com/workplace/349484/state-of-the-global-workplace.aspx (archived at https://perma.cc/B3GS-FQB2)

4 Minto, B (2021) *The Pyramid Principle: Logic in writing and thinking* (3e), Pearson Education, Harlow

5 Doerr, J (2018) *Measure what Matters: OKRs – The simple idea that drives 10x growth*, Portfolio, New York

6 Historical Office (2023) Robert S. McNamara, https://history.defense.gov/Multimedia/Biographies/Article-View/Article/571271/robert-s-mcnamara/ (archived at https://perma.cc/3JR5-TXL8)

3.5

The integrated plan

See the wood for the trees and understand the critical path through the forest

Introduction

In 2003, on a crisp autumn day, I (Rupert) walked into a military base that housed a multi-hundred-million-pound programme. The ambitious programme was part of Tony Blair's New Labour push to modernize the UK. We were there to conduct a review. The senior UK government sponsors (three- and two-star military servicemen) were nervous. So were the leaders of the third-party service firms doing the systems and process transformation work.

What did we find? The project management office was a cottage industry. The walls were full of Gantt charts. They'd been put there by a series of proud Prince2-certified professionals. The plan had been done in Microsoft Project. It was six files because there was too much data to fit it into one. Each file had over 1,000 lines (all pebbles and sand). It was a monster. It captured all dependencies and lags – x can finish 10 days after y or start 5 days before z. Lots of precise bottom-up detail. However, when we asked our first question, 'What milestones were everyone working towards?', no detail was there. We received a few mumbled, contradictory replies. So that was our first task. We created a one-page milestone map that stated when crucial things needed to start and when they needed to finish. We wanted to get everyone on the same page… literally.

The next question was: Is the first milestone achievable? The answer turned out to be: There was a 6 per cent chance of success. This is a precise number based on a set of calculations explained below. The 6 per cent implicitly assumed they managed to onboard all the resources required according to the 6,000-line plan. However, it wasn't close to realistic to scale the programme from a few hundred to just under a thousand in a few months, especially given that the peak resource would be needed for only a short period. They didn't have the seating capacity for starters (this was in the days before remote working became a thing). But the biggest issue was the plan. It hadn't factored in the risks. There was a risk register. There was an assumptions log (over 1,000 assumptions in Excel). Risks weren't structured into a taxonomy, or properly quantified with actions. We created another plan, driven from that milestone map and using the big meaty elements (or rocks – see Chapter 3.1). This plan had just over 100 line items.

To calculate the achievability of hitting the first milestone, we did something novel. We identified the key risks as well as the impact they would have in terms of time and the probability of them occurring. If the risk happened, we could see the delay to task x and therefore the knock-on impact on tasks y and z, which impacted many other streams of work. When you do this, you can see the **critical path** shift. The bottom-up plan was a happy path plan. The happy path rarely happens. There are hundreds of different possible routes. So we ran scenarios – a clean 1,000 to be precise – using a technique called Monte Carlo simulation (so called because of the gambling associations with that city). We then recorded the dates of all the key milestones for each scenario and plotted them to give us a probability distribution for each key milestone. The first big one had a 6 per cent chance of success. We had time to do something about it. We descoped. We mitigated risks. We delayed things that weren't needed for that first milestone and sorted the order of operation. We built a new plan, one that had a 75 per cent chance of success. It had buffer. We knew it was achievable. In the end, the programme was delivered on time.

We have debated long and hard about how much detail to include in this chapter. How much do senior leaders need to know about planning? We aim to give you enough for you to deep dive into the detail when you need to and challenge what you find. A lot of this is about understanding the critical path and identifying and removing **blockers**. After all, CEOs can be fired on the back of failed key initiatives.

Integrated planning is about connecting the dots and getting the level of detail just right so that you understand enough. As the example above shows, plans are too often so detailed that you can't see the wood for the trees. Before reading on, refamiliarize yourself with our boulders, rocks, pebbles and sand metaphor introduced in Chapter 3.1. Chapter 3.2 explained the boulders. This chapter explains how to plan at the level of the rocks – the projects and sub-projects. We structure it as a set of ten questions. Five of these can be asked during the planning process and five during the implementation of the plan. Consistently reminding yourself of these ten questions will help you to direct your focus.

During the planning process, do you…

1. take your key initiatives seriously and truly commit?
2. have good programme management disciplines?
3. have dedicated resources, including a Chief of Staff and/or a Transformation Director?
4. understand the critical path and dependencies?
5. make it visual?

During the implementation, are you…

1. communicating constantly?
2. walking the floors?
3. concentrating on removing blockers?
4. a slave to either Waterfall or Agile methodologies?
5. treating the plan as a living thing?

During the planning process

1. Do you take your key initiatives seriously and truly commit?

Richard Holmes was a Professor of Military and Security Studies at Cranfield University in Bedford, UK. Before taking this post, he had had a military career and been appointed a brigadier. He saw dysfunctional behaviours in leaders which he articulated in his 'Ten diseases of leadership'. The third of these is 'Consent and evade'.[1] Holmes believed that leaders can appear to agree with plans while secretly not supporting them. The result is misalignment and confusion. If the leaders in an organization don't own the key initiatives, no one else will. Remember that these initiatives made it onto the POAP because they are integral to the success of the value creation plan. If they fail, you fail too. If leaders aren't seen to spend time on key initiative projects, no one else will see them as important. Be interested and always show up. Be ready to dig into the details when necessary.

2. Do you have good programme management disciplines?

There's a lot to be said for a good old-fashioned programme management office (PMO). Set one up and appoint workstream leads to own each key initiative. Set up steering committees to review progress comprising the PMO, Chief of Staff (CoS) and a couple of members from ExCo. In the beginning, it might meet monthly, then move to fortnightly as the programme wraps up. As 'go-live' approaches, it might need to meet weekly or perhaps even daily. The job of the steering committee is to review the critical path, debate dependencies and remove blockers to milestone delivery. If it needs to secure more resources or capital, it seeks approval from the board.

3. Do you have dedicated resources?

You can't run a transformation programme part-time. It's a full-time job for a small group of people who have the right skills. Don't be penny-wise and pound-foolish. Depending on the scale and complexity of the key initiative, most programme offices need to comprise only two or three people. It's important to have an experienced Transformation Director (or your CoS). The programme management office reports to them. They, in turn, report to a member of ExCo, ideally the CEO. We talk about the CoS role in Chapter 4.4. We believe they are vital to the successful delivery of transformational change.

Dedicated focus with fully committed team members makes a huge difference. The cost of context switching cannot be underestimated. **Project charters** can be used to define who is 100 per cent dedicated to the project (see below for more on charters). You'll often find that people involved in projects but who aren't 100 per cent dedicated may have a lot of things on the go at once. Once you do the maths, you'll always find people who are 200 per cent allocated. They will be your best people and those who struggle to say no. These are the people who need protection.

RUPERT

For years, I failed to hit internal change project targets consistently. It was only when I made someone responsible for all key initiatives and gave them a dedicated team that things started to turn around. People often talk about business transformation not being part of their 'day job'. I made it someone's day job. There was a total of six conditions that meant we finally built the necessary momentum:

1. Make someone responsible for all the key initiatives.
2. Give them a dedicated team.
3. Produce a proper budget for external experts to help.
4. Review progress as part of the ExCo agenda.
5. Review progress in the board meeting.
6. Reduce the number of key initiatives in play at any one time to four.

It was only once we met all of these conditions that we got them done. Done and won. And we transformed the business. When we had met only four or five of them, we still failed. This list doesn't even include all the implicit conditions. We were aligned and had the drive to do it. We knew what we were doing and had the skills to do it. We also knew which skills we were missing and knew enough that we had to bring them in. We mitigated risks and celebrated successes. Lots of things came together. Was it perfect? Of course not. Every day is a learning day.

Our revenue growth in one year, after nine years, was over 100 per cent. And we were profitable. Our target became ARR in 2018 and we grew that by over 300 per cent in three years. This was the result of the transformation done years earlier. The foundations were laid at that point. The night job became someone's day job. Not all companies will have this luxury and it's harder if you don't. But it's not impossible. Nothing is impossible, it might just take more time.

4. Do you understand the critical path and dependencies?

This is the hardest technical thing to do well. There are many reasons why leaders need to understand the critical path, dependencies and how to remove blockers. The story at the beginning of this chapter highlights the importance of knowing when to take things off the critical path. John Doerr, investor, venture capitalist and driving force of Objectives and Key Results, believes that 'unacknowledged dependencies remain the number one cause of project slippage'.[2] Jeff Bezos is famous for trying to erase dependencies because they require costly coordination and slow you down. The greater the number of dependencies, the greater the number of meetings, and the more time spent communicating, capturing those dependencies or identifying the bottlenecks.

This all has a cost. So, the first thing to do is reduce them as much as you can and make teams more self-contained. It's virtually impossible to eradicate them all, so the next thing to do is understand those that remain.

THE IMPORTANCE OF ALLEN LOGIC

In 1983, James F Allen developed the calculus for temporal reasoning.[3] He specified all the ways that 'X' could be related to 'Y'. The three most common ones used in practice are shown in Figure 3.5.1:

- Start–Start: action 'Y' can begin only once action 'X' has begun, e.g. 'I can't get started because the design hasn't started.'
- Finish–Start: this is the most common. This is when someone can't get started with a task until someone else has finished another one. Action 'Y' can begin only when action 'X is finished, e.g. 'I can only start once the design is complete.'
- Finish–Finish: action 'Y' can finish only once action 'X' is finished, e.g. 'I'm waiting for the design to finish and then I can finish.' A finish–finish relationship may specify a lag, e.g. 'I can finish two days after the design has finished.'

FIGURE 3.5.1 The three most common dependency chains

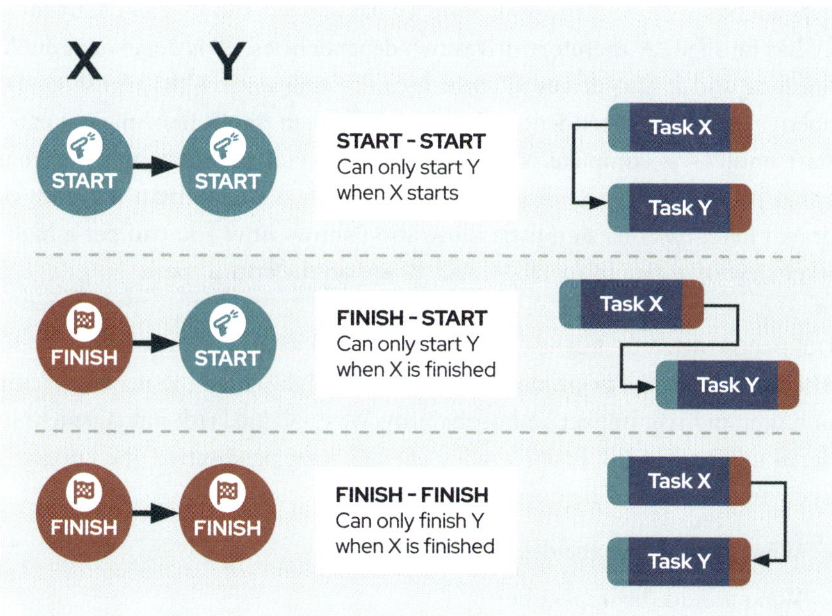

FIGURE 3.5.2 The dependency matrix

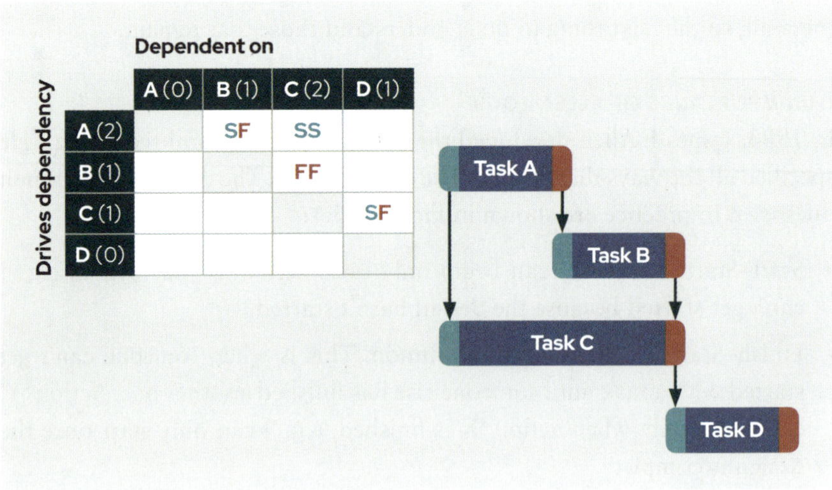

DETERMINING ORDER

Think about which projects and sub-projects (rocks) will be needed to deliver the milestone (boulder). A way to visualize this is through the dependency matrix, as shown in Figure 3.5.2. The **dependency matrix** is a form of crosstab table which enables you to focus on the number and nature of dependencies. The figure shows four dependencies. Tasks 'B' and 'C' are dependent on 'A'. 'C' can't start until 'A' has started and 'B' can't start until 'A' has finished. 'A' therefore drives two dependencies. 'B' is dependent on 'A' finishing and it also drives 'C', which can't finish until 'B' has finished. 'D' doesn't drive any dependencies but it is dependent on 'C' finishing – it can't start until 'C' is complete. Visualized like this, you can see that everything hangs on 'A' and 'B'. Reality is, of course, more complex than what we've drawn here, but this simplistic illustration shows how you can get a high-level view of where to focus. 'A' and 'B' are on the critical path.

THE IMPORTANCE OF BUFFER AND FACTORING IN RISK

The example at the beginning of this chapter highlighted the need to factor in buffer and risk impact and probability. We explained risk management in detail in Chapter 3.3. From a milestone planning perspective, the impact is likely to be a delay. The questions to ask are:

- What could cause the delay?
- What would the impact be?
- Does the impact matter enough to treat the risk?

It makes sense to treat the risks that will have the biggest impact on the critical path. If you choose not to treat a risk, think about building in buffer to allow for the likely delay. Equally, if you want to reduce the buffer, you'll need to mitigate the risk. In the example shown in Figure 3.5.2, we know that if 'B' is delayed, 'C' can't finish and 'D' will also be pushed out. It therefore makes sense to mitigate risks that could impact 'B'. It matters less if a risk has a minor impact on 'C'. As described in Chapter 3.3, we can bow-tie these risks and develop action plans for those we decide to treat.

5. Do you make it visual?

In Chapter 1.3 we discussed the importance of visualization for understanding and communicating plans. One-page updates make the steering committee's job so much easier. Below we describe various ways to visualize plans. You are unlikely to use them all and we have not gone into very much depth as there is not the space to do so. We aim to make you aware of the possibilities for visualizing things in different ways. Each gives a different perspective and might provide another insight. The methods that you pick are up to you. It's a matter of horses for courses. There are three ways of visualizing the three levels of planning.

BOULDER-LEVEL PLANNING

POAP We discussed the POAP in Chapter 3.2. It is a one-page plan that articulates the key initiatives needed to reach each landmark.

Project charter Figure 3.5.3 shows an example of a project charter. They are single-page documents which track projects linked to key initiatives. They give the following information:

- Title (name)
- Purpose (why)
- Objectives (what)
- Ownership (who)
- Timeframes (when)
- Key stages (how)

Other items that can be captured include the cost (budget, both internal and external), risks, how the project will be managed and staffed (dedicated team versus part-time) and dependencies.

A good set of questions to ask is:

- What will the impact be if we fail to deliver this? What else would be impacted and in what way?
- What if we are delayed? By one month? By six months?
- What is worse, a delay of 10 per cent or a cost overrun of 10 per cent?
- If we did a premortem and we failed, what would the likely cause be? How easy is it for us to mitigate that now and should we capture the action to do so?

Answering these questions helps with the why and the what, together with bringing the 'by when?' into clearer focus. Equally, they should help with the most important questions of all: 'Should we do this?', 'Should we do this now?' and 'Are we 100 per cent committed?'

The charter is both a marketing tool and a planning one. It helps with onboarding team members and ensuring everyone is aligned. It acts as the anchor for reporting progress and defining the success criteria for its eventual completion. It is the link between the POAP key initiatives and the inevitable detailed plan.

Milestone map We explained milestones in Chapter 3.4. They give the dates for when critical parts of the plan should start or finish. A milestone map is a simple representation of the key milestones, with a diamond and milestone name plotted on a specific point in time. Swim lanes are typically used to break things up.

ROCK-LEVEL, INTEGRATED PLANNING

Hierarchical tree Figure 3.5.4 shows a hierarchical tree diagram. It shows the parent–child relationship between key initiatives, projects and actions. The key initiative, or boulder, is on the left. This is 'Improve sales force effectiveness' and it is the parent. The projects, or rocks, are the boulder's children. There are three and Project 2, 'Build lead generation engine' also has identified sub-projects, for example 'Design lead generation marketing strategy'. The actions are the projects' children. 'Hire ABM manager' is an example of a governed action, or pebble. 'Post job spec on recruitment boards' is an example of an in-out action, or sand (for the difference between

FIGURE 3.5.3 An example of a charter for the key initiative 'Improve sales force effectiveness'

Key Initiative: Improve Sales Force Effectiveness

SaaSurve

Project name
Build lead generation engine

Purpose
Develop and grow in-house capability to generate sales leads to fuel our growth plan.

Objectives
Recruit and install team leader, recruit team of 5 FTEs, train the team to be able to generate >50 leads per month.

If don't do
Won't get leads required for ramp-up of sales force.

Costs

	Internal	External	Total (Y1)
One off	Team time, 60 hours	$25k recruitment fee	$25k
Recurring	$100k Team Lead + 5x $60k FTEs = $400k	$10k data platform licence $10k software licenses	$420k
Total (Y1)	400k	$45k	$445k

Ownership

- Responsible: Head of marketing
- Approvers: CMO, CFO
- Supporters:
  - Internal: HR Manager, HR Talent Acquisition, Head of Analytics
  - External: Recruitment agency, data vendor

Timeframes

- Start date: January 2025
- End date: December 2025

Key stages

1. Recruit team leader
2. Design Lead Generation marketing strategy
3. Recruit team of 5 FTEs
4. Onboard and train team
5. Execute strategy (delivery and monitoring)

FIGURE 3.5.4 An example of a key initiative tree for sales force effectiveness

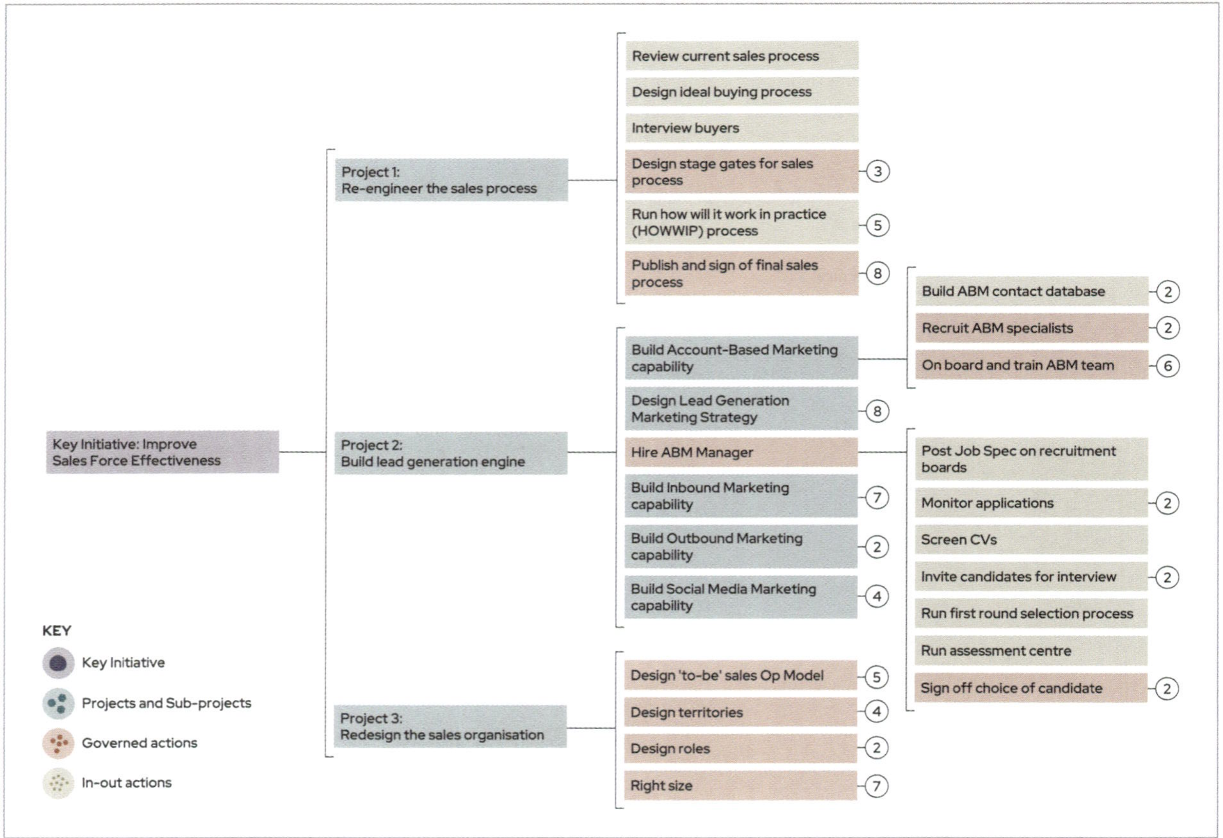

these two types of actions, see Chapter 4.4). The parents can be completed only once the children are completed. This type of planning helps you to check that you've captured everything by applying the MECE test. Are the elements Mutually Exclusive (of each other) and Collectively Exhaustive (in terms of the whole)? We discuss MECE, which was developed by Barbara Minto, in more detail in Chapter 3.4.[4]

Gantt chart Gantt charts are useful, but they can become overwhelming. They show all the dependencies and timeframes (with the x-axis being time). Our example at the beginning of this chapter explained the difficulty with Gantt charts and it can be more helpful to get an overview of dependencies by using the dependency matrix shown in Figure 3.5.2. They are designed to show the critical path, as do network maps, which we describe next.

Network map Network maps are graphs which contain **nodes** and **edges** (or links). Each node is a rock (project/sub-project), pebble or grain of sand (actions). The lines between the nodes (edges or links) either signify dependencies or a parent–child relationship. Each node can contain data, such as the label, owner, start or end date and status (done, blocked, in progress, not started – for more on this see Chapter 4.4). The power of a network map is that it allows you to see the complexity. At the same time, the issue is the complexity.

PEBBLES AND SAND-LEVEL ACTIONS PLANNING

Action table An action table is a simple table where each row is an action. Along with the action name, the columns can include owner, status, due and/or expected date and progress update.

Kanban 'Kanban', meaning billboard in Japanese, is a method developed by an industrial engineer at Toyota named Taiichi Ohno. The aim is to improve workflow and ensure tasks are completed according to urgency and demand. Kanbans allow everyone to see the priorities at any point in time: the things people are working on, how long they have had each task, the history of tasks and where they will go next. Work is prioritized according to what needs to be done 'now', 'next' and 'later'. It's a way of chunking work and checking that nothing has been overlooked. A Trello board is a Kanban.

Crosstab A crosstab is similar to a Kanban but it also has rows so you can see how things intersect. For example, each column could be a phase while each row is a person. Therefore, you can see what each person owns by phase (or whatever) of the project.

During the implementation

1. Are you communicating constantly?

We defined our five communication pillars in Chapter 1.3. Communication is key to success. It's crucial to provide regular updates on progress and celebrate hitting milestones and outcomes. A two-way dialogue is important to ensure employee and stakeholder concerns are addressed.

JON

I was involved in the integration of two businesses in the publishing industry. A major player acquired a small but successful publisher of children's books. As CoS, at the end of every day, I wrote a short email to the CFO who was the sponsor of the integration. The email summarized what had happened that day. Some days there was a lot to say. On other days, I wrote almost nothing. I included what had been achieved, what had slipped and what was planned for tomorrow. When appropriate, I included highlights, lowlights and blockers.

The CFO, who was called Charlie, loved it. He used these emails to send regular communiqués out to the wider organization. These daily emails became known as 'Dear Charlies'. Every time we ran a subsequent integration project, we referred to key communiqués as 'Dear Charlies'. Every programme needs its regular set of 'Dear Charlies', be that emails, newsletters or town hall standups.

2. Are you walking the floors?

You can't run a programme by project plan alone. We strongly believe in the importance of walking the floors. This is what Tom Peters, the business management guru, called MBWA, or Management by Walking Around, in his book *In Search of Excellence*. Programme management techniques are essential, but they can't get to the root of people issues. Leaders need to be visible. They need to interact with staff and take the temperature and pulse of various groups. The authors of *Nuts!* discuss how important this was at Southwest. They say how face-to-face communication helps employees to build 'more open and direct relationships and make decisions more quickly'.[5] Transformational change can be unnerving and understanding how people feel about it is essential.

Walking the floors is an example of how a CoS can help a CEO. As CEO, I (Rupert) spend about 50 per cent of my time travelling. I'm out in the market, with the team, with our clients or prospects. I have found my CoS to be an invaluable pair of eyes and ears on the ground, helping me to understand what's going on, especially if I'm not around. This help is practical in so many ways. We describe the role of the CoS further in Chapter 4.2.

JON

I took my first CoS role in 1999, just after my eldest daughter Ellie was born. I was working alongside John Ferrie at Smiths Aerospace, when my middle daughter Issy was born 21 months later. My last CoS role was in 2004 when Scarlett was born. A year later I joined LDC as Portfolio Director. In all these roles, I liked to walk the floors. I'd pop my head into offices to see how people were feeling. I was always surprised by how much information I – a relative stranger to most of them – managed to glean. For me, programme management wasn't about thousands of rows in the Microsoft Project document, it was about discovering which issues could stop the programme from being successful.

I remember one conversation with a director of an apparel brand that had been acquired by a much bigger retailer. It was approaching 5 pm and we were sat in her office discussing the integration challenges. She was bemoaning the fact that she hadn't seen any of the directors from the acquiring company for a fortnight. She then beckoned me to the window of her office, which overlooked the car park. 'Take a look,' she said. 'Everyone has gone home. This car park used to be full till 6.30 every night. Now no one seems to care because they think no one cares about them.' I was shocked and crestfallen that I had failed to spot this. I got straight on the phone to the CEO and we hatched a contact plan for the directors to visit the offices, starting the very next day.

3. Are you concentrating on removing blockers?

As we've said, leaders can't always get into the details of key initiatives, but steering committees can help remove roadblocks on the critical path to hitting key milestones. We know many CEOs who have suffered through not knowing the details and some who have even lost their jobs because they didn't give this enough attention.

A project might be off track or at risk because something is blocked. Figure out what would unblock it. Is it because you don't have the skills or know-how? Is it because you don't know what you need? Perhaps the scope, objectives or priorities aren't clear. This is about clear and precise communication.

The fundamental question to ask is, 'Are we on track?' Even if the answer is 'yes', you might want reassurance about budget or that you will meet quality metrics. This is the golden triangle of cost, quality and time (**CQT triangle**). Quality can also include an array of aspects such as scope or outcomes. The triangle is golden because it shows the relationship between the three primary constraints of any project or initiative.

If you are off track for controllable reasons, it can be helpful to consider which of the three CQT variables you could adjust. If time and cost are fixed and can't be moved or changed, then the quality will have to be reduced. If the quality is fixed and can't be changed, then you will have to either allow for more time given your resources or add more resources (accepting that nine pregnant women can't have a baby in a month). Or, add both more time and resources.

4. Are you a slave to either Waterfall or Agile methodologies?

People can be obsessive about certain planning methodologies. The two most common ones are Waterfall (such as Prince) and Agile. We often find that project leaders fall into one camp or the other and stick religiously to what they believe in. Both approaches have their benefits; integrated planning is about picking the best from both methods and adapting them to your context. Both methods break work down. It can be useful to use Waterfall to understand the entire period and Agile for the immediate time ahead. Agile is particularly useful for the action management stage when you're constantly reprioritizing work. Agile freezes your plan for a fixed period (which is typically two weeks). Everything outside the two-week window is fluid. And to plan how that fluidity will work, you can use the Waterfall method. Waterfall sets the direction while Agile focuses on what you need to do now.

Waterfall was used in the case study at the beginning of this chapter. It's a useful method when the order of execution matters and there are lots of dependencies and hard deadlines. As we've said, Waterfall planning helps to understand the critical path and remove blockers. The finish–start, finish–start cycle produces what looks like a set of Waterfalls – hence its name. Accurate time estimates are important for the Waterfall method to succeed. The accuracy of estimating how long something will take depends on experience. The more that you or the people planning the work have done that specific thing before, the more confident you can be in your ability to provide reasonable estimates. Unfortunately, the work required to meet an evolving scope isn't always knowable. Time estimates are still valuable so long as they don't give the illusion of certainty. Because we don't know. When you're uncertain, a range of estimates is more appropriate. For instance: a minimum, expected and maximum, or minimum to maximum with your expected being the midpoint between the two. Start with the time unit. Do you anticipate the work being completed within hours, days, weeks, months or years? Make time estimating dynamic. If your view changes, update your forecast.

Those against the Waterfall method criticize it for its lack of flexibility. They also criticize its inapplicability to many settings. They claim it's impossible to plan everything in one set of sequential steps. This is where Agile comes in.

The archetypal Agile method involves breaking work down in enough detail so that you can order it and be clear about who needs to do what and by when. This can be as simple as creating an ordered list or you can use a Kanban board as described earlier in the chapter. Work can be broken down into a set of cards. You might allocate cards to people or people might pull cards from the list.

Agile has a distinct language. The fixed periods in Agile are called sprints. Kanbans allocate tasks to sprints, with a focus on the now (the tasks you are currently working on within the current sprint), the next (the next sprint) and later (the backlog). While work for the current sprint is fixed and shouldn't change, the rest can be dynamically modified. At the smallest level, work is broken down into tasks. Together, these tasks form stories. An epic is a large body of work encompassing numerous stories. Stories come together to form themes. This language maps how we describe the three levels of planning. The themes are our boulders, epics and stories are our rocks (projects and sub-projects) and tasks are our pebbles.

In our experience, Agile can work well for action management, but it's not without its difficulties. Because in practice it often ignores dependencies and the interconnections between tasks, it's difficult to know what order things need to be done in. This can make coordination between teams tricky. Something might not appear to be a priority for you but if you're blocking someone else, it should be. Every morning I (Rupert) have a stand-up with the R&D team. We go through three agenda items per person: 1. What was achieved yesterday? 2. What's their plan for today? 3. Are they blocked? If so, where and what do they need? People are blocked on most days and the blockages are mostly easy to resolve. Our backlog has all the dependencies mapped. Blockers are shown in red. Our leaders focus on removing these.

When a developer has a long list of tasks, it can be difficult to see the wood for the trees. To get around this problem, you can arrange the work into chunks. A developer was building a key feature on the critical path. He had a list of 40 tasks. We needed to understand how to prioritize the work, so we chunked it up to seven big steps (rocks) and put the 40 things under the seven. We could then ask how long each rock would take and see the dependencies at that level. If you're at the level of pebbles and sand and with 40 pebbles on your list, it's easy to get lost. It's difficult to discuss progress and what needs to happen. I (Rupert) repeatedly see teams get stuck because they are trying to do too much. They don't understand who owns what, how long each thing will take and the dependencies. My job is to remove the blockers. It's valuable to have even just a high-level understanding of these different methodologies to help you help your team.

5. Are you treating the plan as a living thing?

Planning is fluid. You can't know everything up front. Plans are living, breathing things. As the authors wrote in *Nuts!*, 'When the plan becomes gospel, it's easy for people to become rigid in their thinking and less open to new, perhaps off-the-wall ideas.'[6]

Remember that no plan survives first contact with the enemy. A plan should be dynamic. As milestones and dependencies shift, so should the plan. It is the job of the steering committee to review the updated plan and inform the board of any material changes to the critical path and expected close dates. The board can then assess the impact and decide whether resources, capital or priorities should be changed as a result.

Final thoughts

This might sound like really basic stuff. And it is. But it continues to amaze us how often companies haven't developed this muscle. Stuff just doesn't get done. People are blocked for too long. Momentum dissipates and the sizzle turns to fizzle. The example we gave at the beginning of this chapter required a huge depth of analysis. We do not advocate going to this level of detail and analysis all of the time. Rather, we hope this chapter has helped you create a mental model for the right questions to ask. Think about the risks. Think about the resources. Think about the buffer. Take as much off the critical path as possible.

Putting a plan to paper is the easy part. Developing a plan that can suffer setbacks and constraints is another matter. Can your transformation deal with the setbacks? You can have all of the hard, physical things in place and still fail if you don't also pay attention to the soft, psychological and cultural things. Grit will get you through. Grit is a combination of resilience and stress tolerance. If you are resilient, it means you can tolerate pain without breaking. And if (or when) you do break, you can bounce back. Our stress tolerance relates to our ability to deal with emotionally demanding situations. This ability is linked to our resilience. Several things help to foster resilience and grit. Having some buffer built into the plan helps us not to feel stressed. Celebrating success is also important. This helps to build strong, trust-fuelled relationships, which also goes some way to building resilience. Rest is crucial. Ensure that members of your team have time for adequate rest. Burnout can seriously affect your ability to implement your plan.

REMEMBER THIS

1. A plan that isn't resourced and that doesn't have clear deadlines is just a dream.
2. Commit with dedicated resources and good old-fashioned programme management skills.
3. Focus on removing blockers and understand the critical path.
4. See the wood for the trees. Use visuals like the charter, milestone map or hierarchical tree.
5. Don't be a slave to a single methodology. Use a combination of Waterfall and Agile.

Notes

1 Yapp, R (2016) Professor Richard Holmes' 10 diseases of leadership [blog] Leadership forces, 16 December, https://www.leadershipforces.com/10-diseases-leadership/ (archived at https://perma.cc/E4NQ-GD5Y)

2 Doerr, J (2018) *Measure What Matters: OKRs – The simple idea that drives 10x growth*, Portfolio, New York

3 Allen, J (1983) Maintaining knowledge about temporal intervals, Communication of the ACM, 26 (11), http://cse.unl.edu/~choueiry/Documents/Allen-CACM1983.pdf (archived at https://perma.cc/9AZR-BFFS)

4 Minto, B (2021) *The Pyramid Principle: Logic in writing and thinking* (3e), Pearson Education, Harlow

5 Freiberg, K and Freiberg, J (1998) *Nuts!: Southwest Airline's crazy recipe for business and personal success*, Broadway Books, New York

6 Ibid.

PART FOUR

Deliver the plan

4.1

Introduction – the 'A' of BROP-A

This is the A for action. This is where it's at

It is now all down to execution. Can you deliver the plan? Will you get it done on time, on budget, with the outcomes you desire? We don't go into organization design or ensuring you have the right people doing the right work in the right number with the right skills, in an optimal structure. I (Rupert) covered that in detail in *Data-Driven Organization Design*. But getting the organization right is central to your ability to execute. And I strongly recommend you read that book too (but I would, wouldn't I).

This part of the book gets to action, to how we meet, align, decide and coordinate. We look at the role of the board and the information it must digest to make decisions on coherent recommendations. We start with the board because its efficiency is a major factor in how well you can deliver the plan. This efficiency is largely driven by the board pack. Our friend Sabine Dembkowski is the Managing Partner of the organization Better Boards. She uses an evidence-based process to evaluate boards and help them develop into more efficient and productive machines. Based on an analysis of 600 conversations with directors from 2018 to 2023, Sabine has identified the following as the top five critical issues in board meetings, many of which we dig into in this part of the book:

- 95 per cent of members don't listen to each other enough to build on each other's arguments.
- 92 per cent of directors do not understand how to leverage each other's strengths, experiences and expertise.
- 85 per cent of director groups are not focused on the right issues (they typically devote too much time to operational issues or, in the case of Plcs, administrative and governance issues).

- 80 per cent of boards do not talk openly about tricky, controversial issues.
- 75 per cent of directors lack mental focus. They might be physically present, but they are mentally absent. They might think of what they want to say before the meeting, say it and then check out. They typically look at their phones, answer emails or simply daydream.

Tight board packs focus on what needs to be discussed to maintain momentum towards the next stepping stone. Sabine's qualitative interview analysis has led her to conclude board papers are suboptimal. In this part, we show how board papers perpetuate the problems associated with the meetings themselves. For Sabine, the top three issues are 1) they are overly long and not enough thought is given to what is needed, 2) they lack executive summaries to help set the tone and direct focus, and 3) there is a lack of clarity about what is expected of the directors. Why is the information there? What is the director supposed to do with it? Is it there to help decide at the meeting, to enrich the discussion, or simply to provide background information? Much of this might sound familiar.

In this part, we reach the final part of BROP-A – the A for action. This is where it's at. Everything leads to this point. You've got your designed strategy. You've got your plan. But can you execute that plan with clinical precision? If you can't, what's the point? Why think through risks and objectives if it's all academic? If key initiatives aren't tracked and managed, it's unlikely they'll happen on time. If they don't get broken down into individual actions, they won't get done. As Aristotle said, 'We are what we repeatedly do.'[1]

This part of the book is about humans. It's about how we interact with each other as a group to make things happen. Humans are complicated creatures. We have different personalities and different strengths. We bring different experiences which shape the way we view the world. Coming together to get things done is not always as straightforward as it might sound. We mess things up and we waste a lot of time. We lose our focus and create inefficiencies. We get on each other's nerves, or we get on too well and forget about the task at hand. Some don't mind conflict, but others hate it. Far too often, we sidestep awkward conversations and put them off to a day that never comes, perpetuating problems.

Forums of people come together to execute the plan. These forums agree on how to do things. They determine the actions that need to be done to keep things moving along. Forums need healthy dynamics that allow for fruitful and honest discussion. The board is the most important forum in any organization. But there are many other forums aside from the board. It's crucial to understand which forums you need and for those forums to understand what meetings they need. Efficiency, productivity and action are the names of the game.

Structure and logic for Part 4

Chapter 4.2 kicks off this part with a look at the board and board packs. The board's role is to get to the nub of issues – to move things along and find solutions to problems that are affecting the organization's ability to create value. As part of this, board members need to ask good questions to understand progress and the reasons why critical metrics, projects or key initiatives are delayed. How the board asks these questions and the type of questions they choose have a huge impact on the organization's ability to maintain momentum towards the next stepping stone along the bridge. In this part, we return to QFOR-A, which we introduced in Chapter 1.3. This is our framework that provides structure to conversations to ensure they are productive and reach action. Questions lead to facts and opinions which, in turn, lead to recommendations and actions. We also look at board packs, how they can drive efficient discussion, and give some tips on writing good board pack commentary.

In Chapter 4.3 we look at the ideal make-up of a forum and the role of individual members within them. Forums hold different types of meetings with different types of objectives. You might need to hold a meeting to solve a problem, action something, share information or make a decision. As we will explain, we believe it's crucial to signpost meetings so that all participants know what they are for, why they need to attend and what is expected of them in the meeting. We all waste far too much time sitting in unnecessary meetings. Clear signposting goes some way to solve this.

Chapter 4.4 looks at action management. We are all overwhelmed by too many actions. It can lead to paralysis and an inability to get things done, especially work that requires deep thought. We look at how to manage our actions and categorize them so that we have a clearer picture of what's on our plate. This is all about reducing cognitive load. It's about getting actions out of our heads and storing them somewhere safe to be referred to when necessary. It's about tracking progress and understanding accountability.

Who captured it? In what meeting? Who's responsible for it? Who has approval rights? Who needs to support the owner and who needs to be kept informed? We are, of course, talking about CRASI, our accountability framework for action management which we introduced in Chapter 1.3.

We end the part with a concluding chapter, which looks specifically at the problems organizations can encounter as they grow.

Note

1 https://www.forbes.com/quotes/659/ (archived at https://perma.cc/GNS6-X4AQ)

4.2

The role of the board and the board pack

Introduction

It's a strange phenomenon, the board of directors. It exists to create control, governance and accountability. It sits at the very top of the corporate structure. In theory, it should embody the pinnacle of performance. It should be the most organized, economical, focused and decisive decision-making body in any organization. It should be held up as displaying the very best of everything, the bastion of the gold or even platinum standard. But more often than not, it is anything but these things. It is a Mad Hatter's tea party of chaos. Let's remind ourselves of Lewis Carroll's classic tale. In *Alice in Wonderland*, the Mad Hatter throws a tea party. All of Alice's favourite characters are there. She has just met the Caterpillar and stumbles across the Hatter and the March Hare taking tea together with Dormouse. The Caterpillar calls them mad. There is no concept of time. Rules are not adhered to. The White Rabbit arrives late, making Alice frustrated and the Queen of Hearts angry. All attendees appear to talk nonsense. Nothing is achieved. The Hatter switches places at any given time and makes short personal remarks. He recites unfathomable poetry. Chaos reigns and eventually, Alice slips away.

While most board meetings don't quite achieve this level of pandemonium, it's easy to draw comparisons. They are often disorganized, can be tumultuous and frequently don't achieve what they set out to do. Participants often turn up late or leave early and come underprepared. And yet, no one seems to do anything about it. Investors, Non-Executive Directors and management teams all seem to shrug their shoulders and accept the mediocrity of it.

In this chapter, we run through what we believe are the four key elements of effective boards:

1 The balance and composition of the board: in this section, we look at the role of boards and the various members who sit on them. Should the board set the strategy or simply approve it and ensure that it is followed? Should it ever descend into operational matters, or always stick to high-level, value creation discussion? This chapter begins by clarifying the role of the board as we see it. It's hard to discuss the role of the board without also discussing the role of the CEO, so we look at how the responsibilities of the CEO and their management team fit with those of the board.
2 The cadence of board meetings and the efficiency of board pack production: in this section, we look at the ideal frequency of board meetings and suggest a cadence of monthly trading and quarterly strategic meetings.
3 The effectiveness and quality of board pack content: this section considers board pack content. It is often poorly structured, too long and too time-consuming to read. The information is poorly presented, which makes it hard to understand and extract the key messages.
4 The effectiveness and quality of discussion and decision-making: we finish the chapter with advice on how to enable effective discussion. So much of this is about crafting the agenda and understanding how to ask pertinent questions both before and during the meeting to lead to the right recommendations and action.

This chapter does not explain how to conduct a successful board meeting. We leave this for Chapter 4.3 when we discuss how to prepare for and conduct efficient, productive and constructive meetings, whether that's the board meeting or one of the four other types of meetings that we identify. Before delving into the four key elements of effective boards, we will first look at why many people consider board meetings to be dysfunctional.

The problem with board meetings

'They're distracting. They take me away from running my business.'

'I often want to talk about strategy and all the investors want to look at is cash flow.'

'It feels like the investor is marking management's homework.'

'It's more like the Monday lesson at school – what we did at the weekend.'

'I find the board pack doesn't tell me what's going on in the business.'

'They are a real time sink. I could do without them.'

'Board packs and board meetings are overly long.'

'More often than not I tend to leave frustrated with lack of progress.'

These are just some of the comments we've had from management teams, CEOs, Chairs and investors when we've asked the question 'How do you feel about board meetings?'. They probably resonate with many of you. The quality of board meetings is an enduring problem which seems difficult to fix. We all know that these meetings are not fit for purpose. We all know that board packs can be overly long, contain unnecessary information and be sloppily put together. But we put up with it. Why? Because the problem seems huge and entrenched. The time, effort and skill required to produce a world-class board pack that enables productive and on-point discussion are considerable. The management team has a business to run. Investors have portfolios to run. No one has the time to fix it, so everyone willingly goes along to the tea party month after month or quarter after quarter.

But the problem extends far beyond wasting people's time and making them feel frustrated. Dysfunctional board packs and board meetings have a direct impact on an organization's ability to create value. Board members get bogged down trying to understand the minutiae of operational matters and the discussion can tend towards micromanagement of the detail. Added to this, and as we will discuss later in the chapter, it often takes so long to get a board pack out that the board ends up focusing on stale information.

The board cannot and should not need to know every operational detail about the company. Board members are not there to get into the minutiae. They are not there to run through the budget line by line. Instead, the board needs to trust the CEO and management team to take care of the operational details and raise issues if and when they arise (and normally at the monthly trading review rather than the quarterly strategic review – see later in the chapter). This frees up the board to focus on what is important: value creation. This leads us to our next point – the different roles in the boardroom.

The balance and composition of the board

Lack of alignment in the boardroom is often the result of a misunderstanding between different roles and different personality types. The board's role is essentially to make certain decisions. The difficulty comes when the scope of these decisions is unclear. Board members exist to represent shareholders and align their needs with those of management. They can sometimes overstep the mark and veer into decision-making territory that belongs to the CEO or management team. As we shall see later in the chapter, the board pack has a huge role to play in ensuring the scope of the board's decision-making is clear from the outset of the meeting.

We begin this chapter with a look at the role of the CEO in relation to the role of the board. As part of this, we consider two roles that form the 'executive spine' and help the CEO do their job: the Chair and the Chief of Staff. The other seats at the table are normally occupied by the management team, Non-Executive Directors (NEDs) and investors. In the simplest terms, the NEDs and investors are there to ask questions the management team is required to answer. They are there to hold management to account via appropriate challenge. How they do this has a significant impact on board and company dynamics.

The role of the CEO

The CEO is a 360 job. There's an enormous amount to think about and do. There is a huge number of different demands on your time and attention and managing the role can be extremely challenging. Figure 4.2.1 shows four different dimensions of the CEO's role as we see it. These dimensions all form part of managing yourself.

1. MANAGE IN

First you 'manage in' to the organization. This means delivering a clear and compelling strategy and setting the direction for the company – one that is distinctive, deliverable and desirable. You own the strategy. You design and deliver it. The board feeds into it, approves it and holds the CEO accountable for its delivery.

Aside from this, CEOs are also responsible for ensuring financial and operational integrity. This point is emphasized by Patrick Dunne, who is an experienced Chair who has worked with a huge number of boards. He is also the author of the book *Boards*. We return to Dunne's work later in the chapter.

2. MANAGE UP

CEOs report to the board of directors. They manage up to the board to ensure alignment between management and members. In turn, the board holds the CEO to account.

3. MANAGE OUT

Managing out is a huge part of the CEO's role. They are the most visible person in the organization. First and foremost, they manage out to customers. It's difficult to develop a great strategy if you don't know your customers inside and out. Great CEOs maintain a founder's mentality (see Chapter 4.5). They don't lose touch with their customers and they know that there's no substitute for experiencing customers' pain points first hand. As well as managing out to your customers, you manage out to the wider stakeholder group, for example your suppliers and investors. It's crucial to maintain good relations with both of these groups. You also engage with your community. Your employees are part of that community and it's important to be visible.

4. MANAGE DOWN

CEOs manage down the organization by appointing a leadership team and managing through them. You manage down to the teams that will execute the strategy. As CEO, you build the organization and, crucially, you build the culture (this is covered in a great deal of detail in *Data-Driven Organization Design*. For more on the importance of culture, see Chapter 4.5).

The role of the board in relation to the CEO

So what role, then, does the board play in relation to the CEO? The book *CEO Excellence*, written by three McKinsey partners, Carolyn Dewar, Scott Keller and Vikram Malhotra, states that the board has three primary functions:

1. Succession planning of the CEO.
2. Approve the strategy set by the CEO and executive team.
3. Monitor and manage risk.[1]

These authors are clear that the CEO sets the direction of the company and leads on strategy. The board approves that direction and strategy. We agree

FIGURE 4.2.1 The four core responsibilities of the CEO

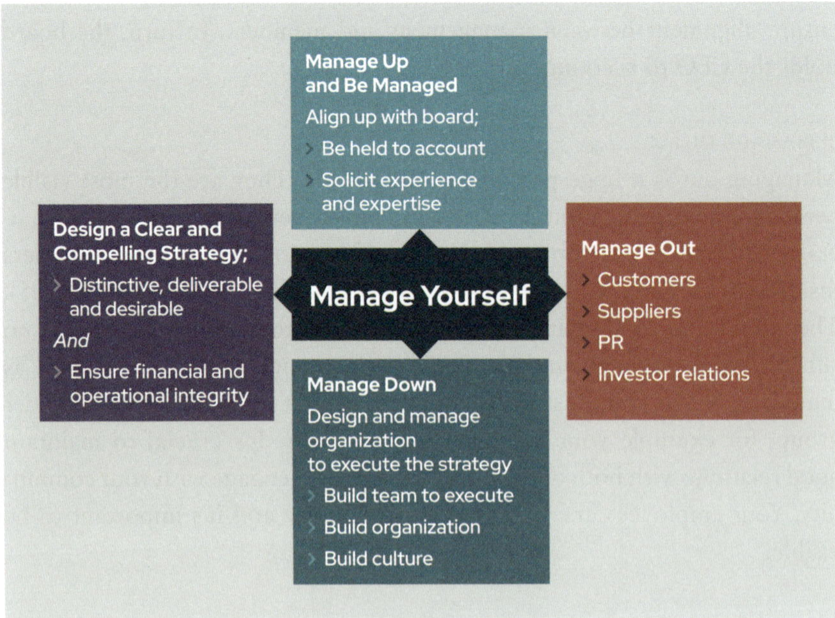

with their thinking. Board members are responsible for challenging, questioning and, ultimately, approving the strategy.

This is a contentious point and one that can cause disagreement. Sometimes, a majority investor can see the CEO as an agent appointed to maximize shareholder value for investors. This is explained very well in Lynn Stout's book *The Shareholder Value Myth*. She notes an increasing trend that sees the CEO acting as an agent for the majority investor rather than a director with a fiduciary responsibility to act in the best interest of the business. This often leads to the investor setting the strategy.[2] We agree with Stout that the agency model is flawed. Every director has a fiduciary duty to act in the best interests of the company. If a conflict of interest arises, it may be necessary for someone to recuse themselves, even if that individual is the CEO. This might be stating the obvious, but sometimes the obvious needs to be stated.

While we hate to break the Rule of Three (see Chapter 1.3 and below), when it comes to the role of the board, we need to. We would add two more functions of the board to the three listed in *CEO Excellence*:

4 Hold the CEO and the executive team accountable for the delivery of the strategy: the board needs to ensure that the right level of governance is in

place to hold the CEO to account, for example a remuneration committee or an audit committee.

5 Ensure disciplined thinking and ask the right questions: a good discussion almost always begins with a good question. Questions are powerful. They can make the difference between a productive meeting and an unproductive one. Board meetings often consist of a string of questions, fired at management to understand progress and the status of projects. But not all questions are good questions – there are such things as bad ones. As a Chair and facilitator, I (Jon) believe my role is always to ask questions that stimulate thought, debate and action. Symbolically, I look upon my role as the question mark and hardly ever the exclamation mark. We delve into this point in more detail in the fourth key element of effective boards, below.

The role of the Chair

The Chair acts as a bridge between the board and investors and the CEO and the management team. We will discuss the role of the Chair in the smooth running of meetings in more detail in Chapter 4.3, including giving some tips on meeting hygiene and how to chair the meeting itself. The Chair owns the agenda. They own the meeting and the process. They are in control of the discussion and they craft the story that they want the board to hear. Outside the meeting, the best Chairs also act as coaches to the CEO. They give the tough love and a shoulder to cry on. They also give the CEO and senior team room to breathe. Gary Flowers, former CEO of Australian Rugby whom we introduced in Chapter 3.3, believes that Chairs and NEDs should show a keen interest in the business without trying to run it – he calls it a 'noses in, fingers out' approach.

RUPERT

Richard Thompson was my Chair for eight years. He approached the role as a coach and mentor. He handwrote feedback for me using numbered bullet points. Over lunch, he would read his well-considered thoughts so that I could listen and reflect. After some discussion, he would hand me the list. Ownership was transferred. It was over to me.

We also prepared for board meetings over lunch or breakfast (feedback sessions were never at breakfast and celebrations were kept for dinner or the tennis club – Richard was a keen tennis player, playing in the junior championships at Wimbledon in his youth). The prep was always the same and focused on zooming in on the key one or two issues. Richard could zero in on what mattered and not get distracted by the noise. By this point, he had managed more than ten funds over 40 years. I got lucky. I benefited from the experience of someone who had seen it all and had had dozens of run-away successes. He was bright and competitive. When I went to Silicon Valley to raise money, he suggested that I speak to just one person, an old friend of his. That person was Don Valentine, the guy who spotted and backed Steve Jobs. Don gave me four hours of his time (the meeting was booked for one hour). Researching for this book has led us to read a lot about boards and Chairs. Richard was an exceptional Chair, perhaps, even, an exception.

Patrick Dunne is a serial Chair who has written several books. In *Boards*, he summarizes how he sees the Chair's role:

1. Lead in the determination of the organization's vision, purpose and strategy.
2. Ensure that the board has clear visibility of the results.
3. Ensure that effective relationships are maintained with all stakeholders.
4. Run the board and allow the CEO to run the company.
5. Implement investment strategy/exit.
6. Judge the executive team on operational/financial performance.
7. Manage change.[3]

Point 1 differs from our view that the CEO should determine the strategy and the board approve it. But Dunne goes on to say that the executive team is 'normally driving the creation of strategic options and must own the strategy that they will be responsible for executing'. Points 2 and 6 are related – Chairs give boards visibility of the results and judge the executive team. Point 3 is less convincing than the rest. What does this mean and why is it singled out in this way? It seems a very broad point. Point 4 makes it clear that the CEO is responsible for managing the executive team. We agree. If the Chair and board tried to do this, lines would become too blurred. The CEO needs to be responsible for hiring the management team, not the board.

We believe the following six points provide a full definition of the Chair's role. We have used *CEO Excellence*'s definition of the role of the board as a base and added further points from *Boards* and our own experience:

1. Succession planning for the CEO.
2. Approve the strategy.
3. Monitor and manage risk.
4. Ensure clear visibility of results and judge the executive team accordingly.
5. Allow the CEO to run the company.
6. Act as a coach and mentor, especially to the CEO.

Some of these points will be undertaken in collaboration with the rest of the board. If the Chair (and the board in general) is unhappy about Points 4 and 5 on this list, they should revert to Point 1. It is worth noting that Point 3 – to monitor and manage risk – is absent from so many definitions of the board's role. But the McKinsey team behind *CEO Excellence* are explicit about this point. We agree that it is necessary and that most boards (and executive teams) do a pretty poor job (see Chapter 3.3).

The role of the Chief of Staff

The Chief of Staff makes up the second half of the executive spine. It's hard to find other books that discuss this role and, to our knowledge, most CEOs (at least those of PE-backed businesses) don't have one. We believe this is a huge mistake.

Before delving into what the role entails, it's appropriate to first reflect on why CEOs need the support offered by a Chief of Staff. It's very difficult to comprehend the CEO's role unless you have sat in the seat. CEOs manage and are responsible for a huge amount (we delved a little into the realities of the role in Chapters 1.2 and 1.3). We find it baffling how often organizations don't embrace a role that is designed to support the CEO and help with the smooth running of the company. It's common for the board and investors to see it as an extra cost line. They may even remove it at the point of investment.

Jeff Bezos' first Chief of Staff was someone called Andy Jassy. At the time of writing, Jassy is the president and CEO of Amazon. He joined Amazon in 1997 as a marketing manager and progressed into a role called 'technical advisor'. Colloquially, he was known as 'Jeff's shadow'. This role was, effectively, a Chief of Staff. Bryar and Carr discuss his role in *Working Backwards*, saying it had two main responsibilities: 1) to help Jeff be as effective as possible and 2) to help them learn from each other. They quote Jassy: 'I was expected to contribute immediately, to come up with ideas… and be a sounding board for Jeff.' He went on to lead AWS from 2003 to 2021 before being appointed as Bezos' successor in the fourth quarter of 2020.[4] As Chief of Staff, you are expected to contribute as well as be the CEO's sounding board and amplifier. We both give our views of this vital role below.

RUPERT

I am far more effective when I have a Chief of Staff. I also find my job more pleasurable. Due to the demands of the CEO role, it's also easier for those I manage when I have a Chief of Staff in place. It gives me more time, as well as eyes and ears in the business. They capture my actions. They ensure good hygiene for the meetings that I chair (see Chapter 4.3). They ensure that all key initiatives are clear and are executed well.

It's important to find the right person for you. I've been lucky to find people who complement my spiky strengths. They need to be discrete, as you need to be able to trust them with highly sensitive information. They need to be able to smooth over ruffled feathers when necessary. They also need to be able to work alongside the entire executive team. Just like the CEO and the Chair, the Chief of Staff thinks about the entire business. This is different from other executives (for example, the CFO thinks about the numbers and financial performance, the CTO thinks about the product and the CHRO thinks about the people).

JON

I was a Chief of Staff several times in my early career executing transformational change. CEOs often asked me to help them out by doing some work that I felt went well beyond my skillset or the scope of my role. In Chapter 1.3, I mentioned my first transformational programme for John Ferrie in the aerospace industry. John asked me to chair a procurement meeting for the two businesses being merged. I had almost zero experience in procurement, but I did it and learned a huge amount in the process.

As a Chair, I have found the Chief of Staff to be an invaluable tool. They help prepare board papers to increase the speed of board pack production. They fill in the gaps of management with help on everything from chasing sprint reviews with the IT team to preparing pricing models with the bid team. In short, they are the glue that holds the senior team together. Because of that, they have valuable insight into team dynamics and what is going on in the business.

Balancing personalities in the boardroom

We introduced the Disney concept in Chapter 3.1 to frame the constituents of a team and different ways of thinking. The other framework we like to use is colour personality profiling. Many different versions of colour personality profiling exist, but the basic thrust of them all is that everyone's personality consists of a combination of four broad categories expressed through colours: red, blue, green and yellow. It has its roots in DISC theory: Dominance, Influence, Steadiness and Compliance.[5] We all lean more towards one colour than the others, but only 5 per cent of people can be defined by a single colour. The vast majority are a combination of at least two of the colours.

Thomas Erikson writes about colour profiling in his book *Surrounded by Idiots*. Erikson wanted to show his father that he wasn't surrounded by idiots, he was just surrounded by people who were different from him. Erikson describes reds as quick, strong, competitive types who are direct, sometimes rude and strong-willed. They are decisive and impatient. He describes blues as introverted, logical, precise perfectionists who like detail but don't like taking risks. Yellows are gregarious storytellers who like to entertain and often display a sunny, optimistic take on life. This leaves the

FIGURE 4.2.2 The composition of the board in terms of colour profiling

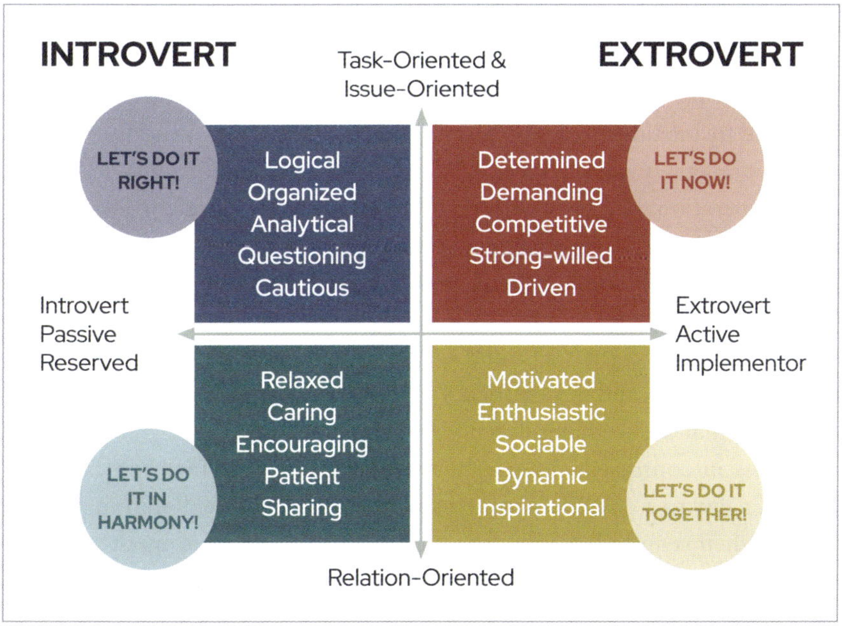

greens. They are friendly, loyal, caring, patient types who don't like change and tend to put things off.[6]

Figure 4.2.2 shows how these colours can translate to key roles in the organization. CEOs are often predominantly red, CFOs are often blue, CHROs are likely to be green and CSOs (sales leads) are likely to be yellow. The colours have their strengths and weaknesses. The point is that any team, including a board, needs a diversity of thought across all four colour types. If a board is all red types, decisions and actions would be made with little thought about risk or taking the team with them. A blue board would never get anything done, weighed down with risk assessment and analysis paralysis. Boards full of yellow would tell stories all day and believe their hype. They would probably retire to the bar very quickly. Greens would avoid any sort of criticism or decision-making for fear of upsetting anyone. But the discussions would be fun and everybody would get along famously.

Board meeting cadence and the efficiency of board pack production

The frequency of board meetings varies from business to business. It largely depends on the size and needs of the organization and these needs can change over time or for periods, for example during mergers and acquisitions. As a general rule, when it is business as usual (if there is such a thing), most boards meet either monthly or quarterly. And each time they meet, the meeting format is the same.

Many of the commonly cited problems related to board meetings could be solved by introducing a shorter monthly trading review in addition to the longer, strategic quarterly meeting. They provide an opportunity to discuss urgent operational matters without allowing them to distract from strategic discussion. This is an increasingly common approach which, in our experience, works well. Standardized and efficient, monthly trading reviews usually last for 60–90 minutes. A monthly board pack is produced, the full board attends, and the CFO and CRO lead the meeting. The focus is on core, routine KPIs and key metrics, particularly those that are red and amber and those that are trending down (see Chapter 1.3).

This is in contrast to quarterly strategic meetings which typically last for half a day to a day. Members of senior management will join the board, as and when required. While the monthly meetings are led by the CFO or

CRO, quarterly meetings are led by the Chair. We explain more about these two different board meetings in Chapter 4.3, including meeting hygiene for each.

The monthly trading review and the quarterly strategic meeting require their own board packs. A good board pack gives just enough information for the meeting it is intended for. A monthly trading review board pack should be all about automation, speed and the timeliness of the information. A quarterly board pack should highlight the key strategic issues that need to be discussed.

The board pack production process

Board papers, on the whole, miss the point. They should be a tool for enabling productive boardroom discussion by focusing attention on the key issues. Instead, in the vast majority of cases, they are overwhelming and difficult to read. They lack focus and key messages are lost in reams of unnecessary detail.

Board members are busy people. Investors, NEDs and Chairs often sit on numerous boards and might have five to six board packs to read a month. That's a lot to absorb and process, especially when you consider how long many of them are. It's not uncommon for a pack to exceed 25,000 words and be 150 pages long. Generally speaking, the larger the organization, the longer the board pack. According to research carried out by the Institute of Chartered Accountants in England and Wales (ICAEW), an average board pack for organizations with an annual turnover of less than £10 million is 125 pages. An organization with an annual turnover of £100 to £500 million is likely to produce a board pack of 195 pages. And a turnover of over £500 million? Board members will likely be asked to plough through 256 pages of content. The same research found that 64 per cent of people say that their board papers fail to enable their board to have focused conversations about key issues. 52 per cent say that the key messages are hard to find and are not clearly presented.[7]

For most companies, board pack production is a manual chore that typically starts immediately following month- or quarter-end. It consists of six steps, as shown in Figure 4.2.3. The CFO leads the production of management accounts and analysis for the board pack. This can take anywhere from seven to 21 days. Next, contributors produce an initial draft of their sections, with input from across the business. The CEO uses these

FIGURE 4.2.3 A typical board pack production process

Month End ↓	Description	Lead	Support	Timeframe
1 Management accounts	Production of management accounts plus analysis for the board pack	CFO	Finance team	7 - 21 days
2 Section contributions	Initial drafts of individual sections, input from across the business	CFO/CEO	Senior team	3 - 5 days
3 CEO summary	CEO proofs, prepares Exec Summary and 'state of the nation'	CEO	CFO/ thought partner	2 - 3 days
4 Circulate papers	Company Secretary circulates the finalized pack to board members	Company secretary		1 day
5 Pre-read and preparation	Board members pre-read the pack and prep for the board meeting	Board		3 - 7 days
6 Board meeting	The board meeting	Board	Senior team (as and when required)	1 day

contributions to write their summary and, ideally, sense checks it with a thought partner. Papers are then circulated to board members by the Company Secretary and the pre-read and preparation begins. Board members are, ideally, given a week to prepare for the meeting. The elapsed time between month- or quarter-end and the board meeting could be as little as seven days or, more likely, as many as 38 days. Introducing automated monthly trading review packs focused on key facts goes a long way to solving this issue.

Board papers don't need to be dreaded. They don't need to be stress-inducing. They don't need to suck as much time as they do. The next section looks at the third key element of an effective board: high-quality board packs.

The effectiveness and quality of board pack content

We start this section with what to include in a monthly versus a quarterly board pack. We end it with a few tips about how to write board pack commentary (commentary should primarily be reserved for the quarterly pack). This is a big topic, which ties in with communication theory and strategies for producing clear and succinct writing. We only have room to scratch the surface, but this should be enough to make your board packs more digestible, clear and enjoyable to read. There are three overarching things to address:

1. Content.
2. Commentary.
3. Presentation.

Board pack content

A clearly defined structure transforms the experience of writing and reading board packs and it can help enormously to reduce their overall length. On average, a person can read 30 pages in an hour (clearly, this varies depending on the density of information on the page and the clarity of the presentation). Most board members devote two to four hours per board pack, regardless of its length. This allows for the consumption of only 60–120 pages of content, at the most. Gary Flowers recalls his early days at the helm of Australian Rugby Union. He had not been in the post long when a NED came into the boardroom ahead of the meeting and threw the board pack of around 400 pages across the table, barking, 'If you think I'm reading that you've got another think coming. Your job is to distil that down into the key messages.' Flowers says, 'It was an important lesson learned for me: more often than not, less is definitely more.'

There is a difference between the content that goes into a monthly trading board pack and a quarterly strategic board pack. Monthly board packs should be standard and automated and predominantly consist of charts and tables. Commentary takes time to produce, so use it very sparingly in monthly packs, if at all. These packs should be pithy and well designed so that board members can scan through them easily. The aim is to get them out as close to month-end as possible so that the board can work with fresh information. Focus on facts, for example where you are against budget and key actions. Be guided by the Four Cornerstones of Corporate Health introduced in Chapter 3.4: finance, customer, people and planet, and specifically your BRAG warning system. Highlight the reds and ambers and look at the trends, particularly those going the wrong way. The board's purpose is to spot the falling knife before it has started falling. An example contents list for monthly packs is given in the box.

EXAMPLE CONTENTS FOR THE MONTHLY TRADING PACK

1. Cover

Includes the title, the period that the pack covers, the dates that the data and commentary were frozen (as pipelines and sales data change every day) and the distribution list.

2. Table of contents

3. Agenda

The agenda is not the same as the table of contents (see later in the chapter). It should include location, attendees and timings. An example agenda for a monthly meeting is given later in the chapter.

4. Minutes from the previous meeting

Board meeting minutes need to be approved as a legal requirement. Ideally, meeting minutes should be approved within five to seven days (see Chapter 4.3), so they shouldn't need to be approved in the meeting. The board should just note that the minutes were approved and the date that it happened. If they aren't approved before the meeting, then it needs to happen in the meeting and be added to the agenda. Note that approving minutes three months after the meeting they were taken in is a waste of time. It's very unlikely that anyone will be able to remember who said what or what was agreed. These minutes could go in the Appendix at the back of the pack rather than up front. If this approach is taken, a summary of key approved recommendations and actions can go here with all carried forward actions.

5. Executive summary monthly output

In the monthly trading pack, an executive summary is generated automatically. It is the same each month, so you get into the routine of reviewing the same things. It shows six charts. Most have two lines, a budget and an actual. Budget lines are coral red (a budget is signed in blood) and actual lines are blue (for true – for more on this, see later in the chapter). The output shows both charts and a data table to cater for all preferences. Some people like to see trends in a chart, while others prefer to see the numbers. Most like to see both. An example of SaaSurve's monthly output is shown in Figure 4.2.4.

6. Form Guide

The **Form Guide**, like the Executive summary, is generated automatically for the monthly pack. It contains a similar set of measures as those that are on the POAP. The Form Guide includes 13 months so you can compare performance to the same time last year. An example of SaaSurve's Form Guide is shown in Figure 4.2.5. The 'Net Promoter Score' is an example of a metric that is stable and strong. 'Time to close' is an example of a metric that was good but got worse. As of March 2025, it seems to be improving again, but you'll only know if this is true once you've had the opportunity to review more months into the future. It's still taking twice as long to close as it was at this time last year. The conversion rate is erratic. There's no clear trend so this may be cause for concern.

7. Leaderboard

An example of SaaSurve's **Leaderboard** is shown in Figure 4.2.6. The Leaderboard shows monthly figures. It shows the same metrics as the Form Guide but only for March. Note that the Form Guide and Leaderboard together consider three dimensions: time, KPIs and KODs. You can only look at two dimensions at once. The Form Guide looks at KPIs by time while the Leaderboard looks at KPIs by KOD. In this example, the KOD is region. There are three regions: EMEA, APAC and North America. The KODs are broken down into territories. The territories with the most red and amber are at the top of the list.[8] This directs focus to the area with the greatest number of issues. Most time will be spent discussing root causes and recommendations to rectify the problems. Management should note the straight blue on customer churn. A remarkable result for SaaSurve. They should celebrate this. They should also celebrate the stellar results across EMEA and APAC. These two regions are mostly green and blue. Most things are going exceptionally well in EMEA and therefore it should be easier to unpick the things that aren't going so well in North America. It should be noted that this is a region-wide issue. Four of the worst-performing territories are in North America. The last thing to note is that 'Time to close' is the worst-performing KPI, with only two of the eight territories hitting the less-than-six-month target.

8. Finance health (written by CFO)

- Limited commentary on key metrics and other highlights/lowlights if necessary
- Charts and tables on performance, including:
  - 13-week rolling cash flow forecast
  - Debt covenant forecast if applicable
  - H1: actual only; forecasts, e.g. H2 6A+xB outturn; Q4 re-forecast 9A+3RF (A = actual; B = budget; RF = re-forecast, e.g. H2 has six months of actuals and six months of budget)

9. Customer health (written by Head of Sales/CEO)

- Limited commentary on key metrics and other highlights/lowlights if necessary
- Pipeline forecast on sales
- Trend charts and tables

10. People health (written by CHRO/CEO/COO)

- Limited commentary on key metrics and other highlights/lowlights if necessary
- Trend charts and tables

11. Planet health (written by whoever is appropriate)

- Limited commentary on key metrics and other highlights/lowlights if necessary
- Trend charts and tables

12. Actions (the meeting should end with actions)

- Brought forward from the previous meeting

Appendices

Detailed finance reports
Including profit and loss account (P&L), cash flow and balance sheet. The 13 months and the variance tables. Financial ratios like S&M as per cent of revenue; debt to EBITDA, people to non-people cost by P&L line item. Many P&L line items can be seen as KODs, but not all. For example, property and infrastructure might be stable, small and not worthy of debate. So, the appendix only needs to include the spend versus the budget and if it's showing red or an alarming trend or volatility, the CFO might decide to bring this to the attention of the board with any additional comments, but especially any recommendations and actions.

Governance rules

Details of the shareholder agreement and article rules. These should outline management's authority and where explicit board or investor approval/consent is needed. It is easy to forget these and it's helpful to have them to hand.

Funding structure (if required)

JON

You'll note that we don't have a separate lens for operational health in the monthly trading pack. This is deliberate. As Chair, I constantly want to keep things out of the weeds. I find management teams don't help themselves because they include too much operational detail, which begs questions and drags the conversations into the bulrushes. Key operational KPIs should be incorporated into all four lenses. For example, a supply chain metric like OTIF (On-Time In-Full), which also reflects your ability to serve customers on time, could be included in the customer dashboard. Obsolete inventory – another supply chain metric that relates to how much inventory a company still has after it should have been sold – could go in the finance dashboard.

FIGURE 4.2.4 An executive summary from SaaSurve's monthly trading pack

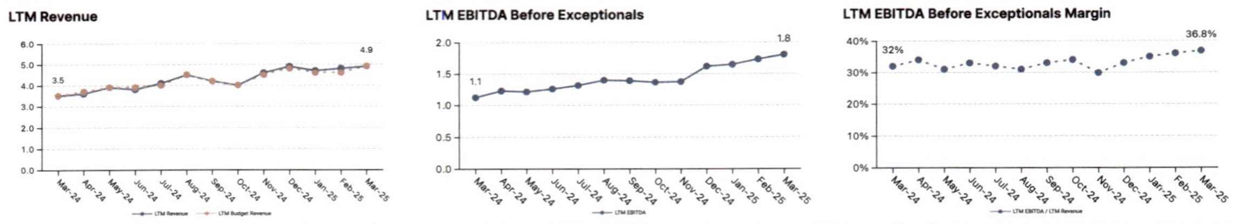

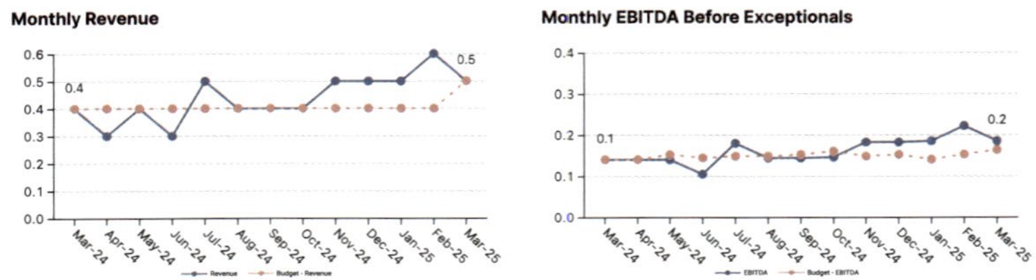

Net Debt

	Mar-23	Mar-24
Cash, £k	3,281	4,201
Third Party Debt, £k	-	-
Loan Notes, £k	-	(2,305)
Other Debt-Like Items, £k	(1,293)	(284)
Net Debt, £k	**1,988**	**1,612**
Covenants Certified by CFO as met?	-	Forecast Pass

Key Trading Metrics

	Mar-24	Apr-24	May-24	Jun-24	Jul-24	Aug-24	Sep-24	Oct-24	Nov-24	Dec-24	Jan-25	Feb-25	Mar-25	Δ	Δ%
LTM Revenue	3.5	3.6	3.9	3.8	4.1	4.5	4.2	4.0	4.6	4.9	4.7	4.8	4.9	1.4	40%
LTM EBITDA	1.1	1.2	1.2	1.3	1.3	1.4	1.4	1.4	1.4	1.6	1.6	1.7	1.8	0.7	60.7%
LTM EBITDA / LTM Revenue	32%	34%	31%	33%	32%	31%	33%	34%	29.8%	33%	35%	36%	36.8%	4.8%	15%
Revenue	0.4	0.3	0.4	0.3	0.5	0.4	0.4	0.4	0.5	0.5	0.5	0.6	0.5	0.1	25%
EBITDA	0.1	0.1	0.1	0.1	0.2	0.1	0.1	0.1	0.2	0.2	0.2	0.2	0.2	0.0	32.1%
EBITDA / Revenue	35%	35%	35%	35%	36%	36%	36%	36.5%	36.5%	36.5%	37%	37%	37%	2%	5.7%
Budget - Revenue	0.4	0.4	0.4	0.4	0.4	0.4	0.4	0.4	0.4	0.4	0.4	0.4	0.5	0.1	25%
Budget - EBITDA	0.1	0.1	0.2	0.1	0.1	0.1	0.2	0.2	0.1	0.2	0.1	0.2	0.2	0.0	16.6%
Budget EBITDA / Budget Revenue	35%	35%	35%	35%	36%	36%	36%	36.5%	36.5%	36.5%	37%	37%	37%	2%	5.7%
Inv. Case - LTM Revenue	0.4	0.4	0.4	0.3	0.5	0.4	0.4	0.4	0.5	0.5	0.5	0.6	0.5	0.1	25%
Inv. Case - LTM EBITDA	0.1	0.1	0.1	0.1	0.2	0.1	0.1	0.1	0.2	0.2	0.2	0.2	0.2	0.1	100%
Inv. Case - EBITDA / Budget Revenue	35%	35%	35%	35%	36%	36%	36%	36.5%	36.5%	36.5%	37%	37%	37%	2%	5.7%

FIGURE 4.2.5 A Form Guide from SaaSurve's monthly trading pack

Form Guide

	Mar-24	Apr-24	May-24	Jun-24	Jul-24	Aug-24	Sep-24	Oct-24	Nov-24	Dec-24	Jan-25	Feb-25	Mar-25
SALES EFFICIENCY													
# Opportunities Generated (Moving target)	18	23	18	31	19	18	21	26	32	24	45	50	59
% Conversion Rate (Static target)	18%	20%	19%	19%	14%	14%	24%	23%	26%	19%	17%	15%	20%
Time To Close (Months) (Moving target)	4	4	4	5	5	5	6	6	6	10	10	10	7
Total Sales ($k) (Moving target)	427	400	276	348	390	350	458	488	512	302	323	326	477
ACCOUNT HEALTH AND GROWTH													
Net Promoter Score (Static target)	35	37	38	37	40	37	34	37	39	40	38	36	39
Gross Revenue Retention (Static target)	85%	86%	88%	90%	90%	90%	92%	91%	89%	92%	91%	90%	86%
Net Revenue Retention	104%	105%	104%	105%	105%	107%	106%	110%	108%	109%	100%	104%	109%
SALES TEAM HEALTH AND STABILITY													
Churn (#) (Moving target)	2	0	0	1	3	0	1	0	2	1	0	0	0
% Reps above OTE (Static target)	14%	17%	23%	24%	12%	14%	18%	22%	23%	27%	21%	21%	35%
% Failing (Static target)	26%	22%	25%	20%	26%	23%	18%	20%	14%	12%	9%	8%	9%

Measure	Red	Amber	Target	Green	Blue
# Opportunities Generated, $k (HiB)	30 ≤	30 - 35	35	35 - 60	60 ≥
% Conversion Rate (HiB)	15% ≤	15% - 20%	20%	20% - 25%	25% ≥
Time To Close (Months) (LiB)	8 ≥	8 - 6	6	6 - 4	4 ≤
Total Sales, $k (HiB)	300 ≤	300 - 400	400	400 - 500	500 ≥
Net Promoter Score, $k (HiB)	10 ≤	10 - 30	30	30 - 40	40 ≥
Gross Revenue Retention (HiB)	85% ≤	85% - 90%	90%	90% - 95%	95% ≥
Net Revenue Retention (HiB)	90% ≤	90% - 100%	100%	100% - 120%	120% ≥
Churn (#) (LiB)	3 ≥	3 - 1	1	1 - 0	0 ≤
% Reps above OTE (HiB)	15% ≤	15% - 25%	25%	25% - 30%	30 ≥
% Failing (LiB)	25% ≥	25% - 15%	15%	15% - 10%	10% ≤

Key HiB: High is Better
LiB: Low is Better

FIGURE 4.2.6 A Leaderboard from SaaSurve's monthly trading pack

Leaderboard

		SALES EFFICIENCY				ACCOUNT HEALTH AND GROWTH			SALES TEAM HEALTH AND STABILITY		
GROUP LEADERBOARD AS AT MAR-25	Region	# Opportunities Generated	% Conversion Rate	Time To Close (Months)	Total Sales ($k)	Net Promoter Score	Gross Revenue Retention	Net Revenue Retention	Churn (#)	% Reps above OTE	% Failing
South & Central	N	4	11%	10.2	$29	15	82%	87%	0	15%	25%
Canada	N	4	14%	9.3	$33	-10	70%	92%	0	22%	20%
East Coast	N	5	20%	10	$76	49	75%	114%	0	23%	15%
West Coast	N	10	15%	10.6	$57	25	81%	100%	0	25%	15%
Benelux	E	6	21%	5.8	$38	41	91%	110%	0	42%	5%
ANZ	A	3	25%	6.5	$14	42	90%	100%	0	100%	0%
UK	E	12	26%	5.6	$143	52	93%	116%	0	41%	5%
DACH	E	15	22%	6.4	$86	44	92%	121%	0	36%	0%
NA		23	15%	10.2	$196	27	78%	99%	0	22%	18%
APAC		3	25%	6.5	$14	42	90%	100%	0	100%	0%
EMEA		33	23%	6.0	$267	48	92%	117%	0	39%	3%
Total		59	20%	7.7	$477	39	86%	109%	0	35%	9%

In contrast, quarterly strategic meetings need a bespoke pack, containing richer and more detailed material focused on strategy execution. They also, crucially, include risk management and an update on the key initiatives. These packs take much longer to produce than the monthly trading packs as they contain more commentary and need more thinking time.

We suggest that quarterly strategic packs contain two sections. Section A focuses on strategy execution while Section B focuses on corporate health (i.e. it's the same as the monthly pack). Ideally, Section B would be covered in an hour or less or it could even be dealt with in a separate meeting. An example contents list for the quarterly strategic meeting is shown in the box.

Note that while the strategic pack contains more detail than the monthly pack, care should be taken over the amount of detail included. Board packs tend to grow and grow because more detail is added each period – another KOD, another breakdown. Think carefully before you incorporate something and if you do add something new, see if you can take out something else to compensate for the extra material. Below we write about the importance of focusing on what the reader needs to know when writing commentary. The same is true when it comes to stats and numbers. An example is the number of line items in a summary P&L account. How many line items do you have under indirect costs (often called overheads)? Can you keep it to seven? If any line item forms less than 5 per cent of the total, can it become a subtotal of a similar line item? If any line items are never discussed, do they need to be included? The board pack gives you discipline. Disciplined thought and disciplined action.

The box shows an example contents list for a quarterly strategic meeting. Any commentary should be strategic and focus on the challenges and risks to long-term health, as well as any issues affecting the business' ability to hit its value creation plan milestones.

EXAMPLE CONTENTS FOR THE QUARTERLY STRATEGIC MEETING

Section A: Strategy section

1. Chair's opening remarks

The Chair's opening remarks include the key issues, questions, recommendations and focus for the meeting. Ideally, no more than three of each.

2. CEO View from the Bridge

The **CEO View from the Bridge** gives highlights and lowlights (preferably no more than three of each) and the key issues from the pack. It is essentially an executive summary of key strategic discussion points. While the meeting discussion will focus on lowlights and issues, it's critical to include the highlights and celebrate the successes. Achievements build on achievements. An example of a CEO View from the Bridge from SaaSurve's quarterly pack is shown in Figure 4.2.7.

3. Ārahi Arrow Dashboard

We explained the Ārahi Arrow in Chapter 1.3. The Ārahi Arrow Dashboard distils information about key metrics defined in the POAP into one icon. An example from SaaSurve's quarterly pack is shown in Figure 4.2.8. It gives a quick overview of metrics in the Form Guide and Leaderboard. If the management team wants more detail, they can refer to the monthly output.

4. Update on value creation initiatives in play

This is a summary of each live key initiative using one-page charters. Charters link to the POAP. Use a template and update it each meeting. It should include achievements since the last meeting and the plan for the coming period (i.e. what has been done and what is going to be done). It should include where you are versus plan and if you are behind, the reasons why this is the case (not the same reasons previously highlighted in the pack). It should include issues, risks and mitigating actions. The focus should be on recommendations (including any help that is needed) and actions. Recommendations require debate and board approval.

5. Customer and competitive intelligence review

Commentary on:

- Value landscape update, including competitor update
- Customer health issues, including feedback from customer interviews

6. People – strategic deep dive

Commentary on:

- Succession planning, talent acquisition, retention and development
- Culture, organization design and workforce plan updates
- Employee engagement, etc.

7. Finance – strategic deep dive

Commentary on:

- Financing related to strategic or long-term commercial finance issues, level of debt, quality of earnings
- Timings of the next landmark liquidity/investment event

CFOs often write commentary that restates numbers that are in the tables. We question whether this is necessary. The quarterly pack doesn't require commentary on the dashboards or trading numbers.

8. Planet health

Commentary on:

- Key ESG issues and challenges

9. KOD and key initiative deep dives

To be clear, this is not a review of trading by KOD. That should happen monthly. KOD deep dives are about the key initiatives in play. The deep dive is likely to be two to three pages:

- key questions with recommendations and actions, highlights and lowlights, a KPI summary for the KOD with actuals versus targets versus Same Period Last Year (SPLY). Show the absolute number and delta percentage
- progress on key initiatives for the KOD, using the same format
- specific risks with action updates

Have no more than two or three deep dives per pack – more is too cognitively demanding. They are a great way for the executive committee and other team members to get more exposure. For example, you might do a deep dive into R&D or operations (although these may also have their own sections). Anything requiring board approval needs a deep dive. For example, the launch of a new office, launching a product in a new market, an acquisition, rebrand, or a new initiative. Any initiative in the red, especially one that has been there for some time will need a deep dive.

10. Strategic risk

Commentary on overall corporate risk as well as those the board is focused on with progress of mitigating actions. The focus should be on what has been achieved and planned actions. Possible deep-dive into one to two risks, using the bow-tie framework.

11. Summary of all recommendations and actions by section and KODs

This repeats and summarizes the recommendations and actions in the pack.

Appendices

SOAP

POAP

Governance rules

Details of the shareholder agreement and article rules. These should outline management's authority and where explicit board or investor approval/consent is needed. It is easy to forget these and it's helpful to have them to hand.

Section B: Monthly pack contents and appendices

Board pack commentary

There are whole books written about how to communicate effectively in your writing. In our view, there are two that every business executive should have on their bookshelf. The first is *The Pyramid Principle* by Barbara Minto.[9] The second, written much more recently, and which draws on similar ideas as *The Pyramid Principle*, is *The Bezos Blueprint* by Carmine Gallo.[10] Bezos is a champion communicator. Gallo demonstrates how he uses a few simple tricks and rules to engage his audience and communicate in a simple yet compelling way. He draws particularly on Bezos' shareholder letters and demonstrates that 'the way to the top is paved with the fewest words'.

Words matter. The words that you choose for your board pack have a direct impact on the success or failure of the company. The board pack is a piece of journalism. Its job is to capture attention, give the reader the information that they *need* to know and inspire action. In an article for *Harvard Business Review*, Bill Birchard writes that brain scans reveal how people respond to the written word. Regardless of whether you are writing an email to a colleague or commentary for a board pack, you can write in a way that

FIGURE 4.2.7 Example of a CEO View from the Bridge from the quarterly pack

CEO View from the Bridge

✓ Solid quarter driven by customer response to KAM program

! Worrying trend with employee churn remains; significant set-back in NA

Highlights:

1. **Delighted customers:** F NPS scores continue to be strong; O Platform outperforming expectations.
2. **Improved usability:** F Usability scores are consistently improving. O Excellent work from UI/UX team together with advisory services. R Continue to increase involvement of consulting and training in UX/UI work.
3. **ARR outperformance:** O Driven by KAM and consumer industry. F Consumer industry up 50% vs Target. F Upsell in enterprise clients 75% ahead of target. O New KAM program for marque customers well received. R Increase account management resource in all large and enterprise clients.

Lowlights:

1. **Employee churn too high:** F Employee churn is further off target and worryingly high at 20% with concerning loss of key R&D talent. F Churn highest in 6–18m tenure. O Work too manual. O New joiners not buying into mission and culture. O Leaving for higher paid job. R Conduct pay benchmarking for R&D. R Review talent selection criteria. R Increase time in office for new starters.
2. **NA leadership set-back:** F As agreed, removed the NA lead. O Lost 6 months in terms of our market entry. O Won't hit FY26 opening and sales targets. R Relocate Edward Scott and his family to NA for 2 years at cost of $350k.
3. **CAC too high and not under control:** F AC off target and volatile. O Sales leads not being effectively qualified. R Review sales qualification process; R Accelerate implementation of HubSpot. Q Why are we losing deals at the negotiate stage? R Implement win/loss analysis.

Key Issues to discuss:

1. Employee churn
2. North American leadership re-boot
3. Replan NA entry and time frames

Key Recommendations to be discussed:

1. Review the hybrid working balance, especially for R&D
2. Appoint pay benchmarking firm
3. Relocate Edward and his family to NA for 2 years at cost of $350k
4. Review sales qualification process
5. Increase account management resource in all large and enterprise clients

FIGURE 4.2.8 Example of an Ārahi Arrow Dashboard from SaaSurve's quarterly pack

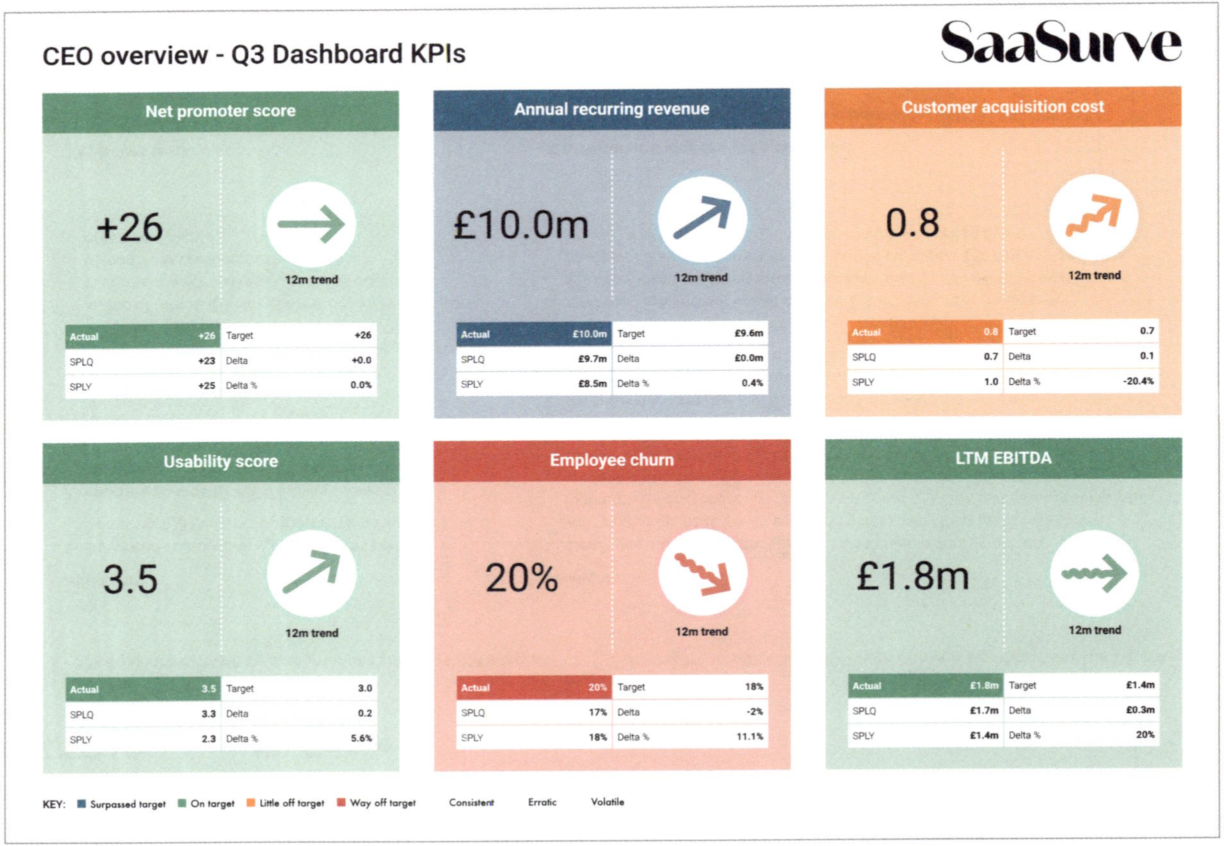

delights readers and releases pleasure chemicals in their brains.[11] This gives us all something to think about. When was the last time you felt delighted when you read a board pack?

The advice in this section applies to anyone tasked with writing content for a board pack. The efficiency and effectiveness of board meetings start with individual contributors. When everyone takes the necessary time to refine their work, it's easier for the Chair and CEO to isolate the key points to discuss at the meeting (see later in the chapter) and easier for the board to read and consume the pack. Anyone writing content for a board pack should take their time to write short, impactful sentences and paragraphs. The adage, often accredited to Churchill or Mark Twain, springs to mind: 'I didn't have time to write a short letter, so I wrote a long one instead.' This is central to our fourth communication pillar in Chapter 1.3: Refine, refine, refine.

KNOW YOUR AUDIENCE – GIVE THEM THE NEWS, NOT NOISE

Our friend, Helen Hodges, an executive coach, talks about giving news, not noise. This is so spot on. Say it, don't spray it. Board members don't sit on boards because they enjoy reading about the daily trials and tribulations of management teams. They do it because they are invested in the company and have a huge amount of experience that they want to share. They want to feel useful. As they read through board packs, they want to identify where they can help and come prepared. They want to leave the meeting feeling that it was a productive use of their time (see Chapter 4.3). Help them to be useful by being clear about what you need from them. Isolate your key messages and questions. Don't drown them in information. They won't have time to read it, let alone try to decipher what it is that you need.

Too often, board meetings can feel like the board checking up on management. This is a chicken-and-egg situation. Is it the fault of the board or is it the fault of the board pack? Perhaps the board are just doing their best with the information they have been given. No one's pulled out the key messages. No one's told them where to direct their focus, and because operational information is included in the pack, that's where the discussion goes.

This is a vicious cycle. As operational matters are too often the focus, the next time management teams write their commentary they include everything. If the board asks about the minutiae, that's what they include. They want to look like they've been busy. They want to show how much they know. They are very keen for the board to see how integral they are to the business. This is a missed opportunity for getting the most out of the board. Board pack commentary is an opportunity to put your key messages and questions in front of a bunch of very experienced and knowledgeable people.

To do this, follow one of the key rules of journalism: know your audience. Tell them what they need to know, not what you find interesting. Ask yourself:

- What are your readers' concerns? What are the key things on their minds?
- How much detail do they need? What do they *not* need to know?
- What do they already know (building on prior knowledge helps to spark interest)?

KEEP THINGS AS SIMPLE AS POSSIBLE BUT NO SIMPLER

Our third Communication Pillar is 'Make things as simple as possible but no simpler'. Imagine that you only have five minutes with the board. What's the one thing that you would want to communicate to them in that time? Make sure your commentary gets this message across loud and clear.

This links to Barbara Minto's advice that ideas in writing should start with your one key message and be followed by layers of argument in a logical order (see Chapter 1.3). Isolating this is not easy. This advice is particularly pertinent. In *The Hard Thing About Hard Things*, Horowitz talks about having to explain to the board that he thought it would be best to sell all their customers and change business: 'It was messing with my mind. In order to finalize that decision, I wrote down a detailed explanation of my logic.'[12] If Horowitz had followed Minto's advice, he would have begun with his one key message and followed this with structured arguments about why he felt this was a necessary thing to do.

Of course, discussion will need to extend beyond just one thing. In Chapter 1.3 we also write about the Rule of Three and Minto's rule, 'the magic number seven, plus or minus two'. The underlying message is to limit your ideas as far as is practicable. Ideally, this rule should be evident throughout the board pack, in all section contributions. Figure 4.2.7 shows an example of a CEO's View from the Bridge using the Rule of Three. It presents the global picture and draws out the key areas to focus on in the meeting. It is the beginning of the story, so make it compelling.

MAKE COMMENTARY READABLE

Board packs are not the place to demonstrate literary flair. Keep your language simple. No one's ever going to complain that your text is too easy to read. But there's evidence that if people can't understand what you're saying, they won't trust what you're saying.[13] Hence, by maximizing readability, you also maximize credibility.

Gallo writes about this in *The Bezos Blueprint*. He describes how communication was, and still is, at the heart of Amazon's success. Bezos recognized its importance from the beginning, writing that famous first letter to shareholders in 1997, in which he told them that 'this is Day 1 for the Internet and, if we execute well, for Amazon.com'.[14] As part of the research for his book, Gallo analysed all 24 of Bezos' shareholder letters sent between 1997 and 2020. What he found was an ability to communicate complex topics in simple writing that would be accessible to the vast majority of readers. No complicated words. No unexplained acronyms. No overly long sentences designed to convey the breadth of his knowledge. None of that. Just plain, straightforward, simple ideas communicated in a way that delighted and enthused the reader.

We suggest following three simple rules to produce readable, clear, crisp and on-point board pack writing:

1. Use simple, active language and short sentences.
2. Use the QFOR-A discipline.
3. Check and edit your work.

USE SIMPLE, ACTIVE LANGUAGE AND SHORT SENTENCES

Readability formulas can be used to assess how easy it is to read and understand a piece of text. Various readability formulas exist and on the whole they all strive to achieve the same thing – shorter words and sentences.

The **Flesch-Kincaid Readability Test** is the most widely used. It is a descendant of the Flesch Reading Ease Test, which assigns text a score between 1 and 100. The higher the score, the more readable the text. The Flesch-Kincaid Readability Test translates this score into a US grade level.

The Flesch-Kincaid Readability Test uses the number of words in a sentence, the number of syllables per word and the percentage of sentences written in the passive voice (as opposed to the active voice – see below). For example, a Flesch Reading Ease score of between 70 and 79 is equivalent to an average reading level of someone in the eighth grade in the US (for our UK readers, this is equivalent to Year 9). It relates to a mode of writing called 'plain English'.

Perhaps surprisingly, we should all be aiming for a maximum of eighth-grade level in our business communications. The aim is to make our writing easily understandable by someone aged 13–14. Importantly, the score doesn't reflect writing ability. The aim is not to write like an eighth grader. Rather, it is to write in a way that an eighth grader can easily understand.

The examples in the box show how text can transition from being classed as needing college-level education to needing seventh-grade education. The 'before' example is taken from a real board pack, albeit modified to anonymize the source.[15]

Before

On track to deliver product capabilities for the first release of ICM by early August. However, there is a dependency on the API penetration testing (SOC2 requirement), scheduled to begin in mid-July, which may delay release if material remediation tasks are found.

Average words per sentence: 21

Average syllables per word: 1.8

Passive sentences: 50%

Flesch reading ease score: 33.2

Flesch-Kincaid reading level: College

After

The first release of Interactive Conjoint Module (ICM) is due on 10 August. Testing how it links to other systems is due to start on 15 July. Any problems found during the testing could delay the release.

Average words per sentence: 12

Average syllables per word: 1.4

Passive sentences: 0%

Flesch reading ease score: 72.2

Flesch-Kincaid reading level: Seventh grade

It's all about keeping text as simple as you can to reduce cognitive load and save people time. It's about saving people the bother of looking up unusual words or acronyms. As Bill Birchard writes in his article: 'Simplicity increases what scientists call the brain's processing fluency… the reader doesn't have to exert too much brainpower to understand your meaning.' Here are some simple rules to follow:

- Cut the fat. Sentences that are longer than 25 words can be hard to follow. Break longer sentences into two and check your use of the word 'and'. Could it be replaced by a full stop?
- Avoid unnecessary words, including adjectives and adverbs. Check for tautology. For example, the word 'currently' is rarely needed – writing in the present tense is enough. 'Going forward' is usually unnecessary – writing in the future tense is enough. 'Due to the fact that' can be replaced with 'because'. 'No later than [date x]' can be replaced with 'By [date x]'. 'I am of the opinion that' can be replaced with 'I believe'. There are many, many more examples we could give…
- Give clear dates and targets. Don't be non-committal. Don't talk about 'late July' or 'mid-August'. Clear dates allow people to plan. They give teams targets to aim for, which makes it more likely that it's going to happen.
- Check your text for unusual or long words.[16] Warren Buffett famously imagines that he's writing to his sisters, Doris and Bertie: 'Though highly intelligent, they are not experts in accounting or finance. They will understand plain English, but jargon will puzzle them. My goal is simply to give them information I would wish them to supply me if our position were reversed. To succeed, I don't need to be Shakespeare.'[17]
- Write in the active voice and be direct – use the pronouns 'I', 'you', 'we'.

We'll expand briefly on this last point. The active voice can be difficult to understand, particularly as many of us are used to writing in the passive voice. It uses a subject-verb-object sentence structure (where the subject performs the action). Active sentences are punchier, shorter and easier to follow than passive sentences. Writing in the passive voice is very common, but it can make sentences unclear and hard to follow. Passive sentences take a much more roundabout route to get to the same idea.

The structure of passive sentences also allows writers to be woolly about responsibility. It puts more emphasis on the object of the sentence. But it's the subject that misses a deadline or is responsible for a project veering off track. Accountability matters in the boardroom. Responsibilities need to be clear so that appropriate action can be identified to help. Compare the following two examples. The first is written in the passive voice. The second is written in the active voice and uses the QFOR-A discipline, which we explain in the next section:

'The restructuring deadline might be missed. The scope of the project has been underestimated. A consultant is recommended to help.'

F: We are not on track to hit the restructuring deadline.

O: We underestimated the scope of the project.

R: Hire a consultant to help.

USE THE QFOR-A DISCIPLINE

The example given above illustrates more than the need to write in an active voice. It also shows how the QFOR-A discipline, introduced in Chapter 1.3, can keep your commentary succinct and on point. It gives the facts – that the team is not on track to deliver the restructure. It gives an opinion – the scope of the project is too wide for them to cope with. And it gives a recommendation – they propose getting external help.

Using the QFOR-A discipline is the quickest way to get to action. When section contributors are writing their commentary, they can think of the questions the board will most want to know. Very often, the question is simply, 'Are you on track?' Contributors can assemble their commentary in a fact–opinion–recommendation sequence to enable a discussion that will result in action. In this case, the captured action is likely to be to source an external consultant.

Too often, it's hard to tell whether something is a fact or just someone's opinion. Opinions are sometimes presented as facts and it's difficult to sift through and reach the truth. Signposting with QFOR-A goes a long way to resolving this. It also helps the board to spot tangible recommendations so you can get to action.

CHECK AND EDIT YOUR WORK

Board packs can be littered with poor punctuation and grammatical errors. At best, these slow down the reader. At worst, they irritate them. Remember that the aim is to delight. We've all produced commentary right up to the wire without leaving ourselves time to go back and check it. Try not to do this. Use the available tools to help. Grammarly's suggestions are invaluable.

It has a readability feature, as does Microsoft Word (found under its 'Spelling and Grammar' tab). These tools speed up the process considerably. Editing also helps you to double check for 'padding' that is immaterial to the board meeting.

Don't expect to write like a pro from the off. This chapter has run through a few simple rules, but it takes time to hone your skills. Even pros need to go back and check their work to improve it, tighten it, remove unnecessary words and phrases and check that the messaging is all on point. In *The Bezos Blueprint*, Gallo is at pains to point out that Bezos improved as a writer throughout his tenure as CEO at Amazon. His 1997 letter to shareholders had a Flesch-Kincaid Grade level of 10. His 2020 letter to shareholders was over twice as long but he got his average words per sentence down from 20 in 1997 to 16 in 2020. And he reduced his Flesch-Kincaid Grade level to 8.

Improving your writing skills can be an enjoyable experience. It feels great to produce writing that you know hits the mark. Often, all it takes is a little more time and a little more thought.

Board pack presentation

Reducing cognitive load isn't just about the content and commentary. It's helpful to create a consistent visual language that runs throughout the board pack and allows people to absorb information at a glance. Above we showed how statements can be presented using QFOR-A so readers can immediately sort the fact from the opinion and so on. When you see something, the meaning should be obvious. You don't need to spend time deciphering what's in front of you.

Colour and shape help enormously. The use of red, amber, green and blue on the Leaderboard made it easy to see which companies were a concern and in which areas. The use of colour in the Form Guide helps to see the trend over time (see Chapter 3.4). Figure 4.2.9 shows an example of a board pack chart legend. P&L are always shown by a circle. Balance sheet and cash are shown with a cross. A target is shown with a dashed green line, as we've seen throughout the book. An actual is a solid blue line (it's blue because it's true). A forecast is a purple dotted line and a budget is a coral dashed line. It's red coral because it's a promise signed in blood. A budget is a type of target so it has the same type of dotted line as the target. If it's a rolling number like LTM, we use thicker lines than if it's monthly.

FIGURE 4.2.9 A chart legend for a board pack

Chart Legend

P&L Item	Circle Markers	
Balance Sheet / Cash Item	Cross Markers	
Target	Dark Green Dashed	
Actual	Blue Solid	
Forecast	Purple Dotted	
Budget	Coral Dashed	
LTM	Thick Line	
Monthly	Thin Line	
Measure	Solid Line	
Ratio / Margin	Dot and Dash Line	
Positive numbers	Black	100
Negative numbers	Red and Brackets	(100)

The look of the page is also important. Reduce visual clutter as far as possible. Here are some simple rules to follow:

- Ensure key messages are at the top of the page to allow the reader to scan through the pack and find what they are looking for.
- Put the most important message in the top left of a presentation slide.
- Ensure sufficient white space. Uncluttered pages help the reader distinguish between different elements on the page and the eye can pass easily from one to the other.
- Never make lines more than 40–60 words long. Your eye gets lost trying to return to the beginning of the next line.
- Make bullet points no more than two lines long.
- Aim not to include more than one decimal place.

The effectiveness and quality of discussion and decision-making

Effective boards have productive discussions and make good decisions. We believe the board's decision-making follows a process of percolation and distillation, as shown in Figure 4.2.10. This process flows from writing board pack commentary to nailing down an agenda, facilitating the meeting and nailing down decisions and actions. We introduced the idea of percolation and distillation in Chapter 1.3.

The percolation and distillation process in the context of the board meeting

The **percolation and distillation thinking process** starts before the board pack is published. Management teams and the CEO think through the key issues. The main questions percolate in their minds before they distil them into the key ideas – the questions and recommendations that the board needs to address. This percolation involves mulling over a huge number of things and distilling them down to the key points.

The board pack represents the distillation of these ideas. Board members may have questions as they review the pack and do their percolation and distillation. Collecting and collating these before the meeting can make the meeting run more smoothly. Increasingly, tech is making this process more efficient.

The CEO and Chair take the board pack and they percolate and distil further to nail the key issues, questions and recommendations that need to be addressed in the meeting. This is when they craft the agenda. Importantly, sections in the board pack are not the same thing as agenda items. Too many board meeting agendas simply follow the board pack's table of contents, meaning that the meeting becomes nothing but a replay of the board pack. Curating the key questions and observations into a small list is fundamental to an effective meeting. Any others can either be actioned offline or parked for another day (probably the following meeting).

The box shows examples of monthly trading and strategic quarterly agendas distilled from the relevant board packs. Note that the quarterly agenda can be divided into two parts – Part A is the strategic review, which focuses on long-term value creation. Part B is the same as the monthly trading pack agenda and could be done in a separate meeting.

FIGURE 4.2.10 The percolation and distillation thinking process

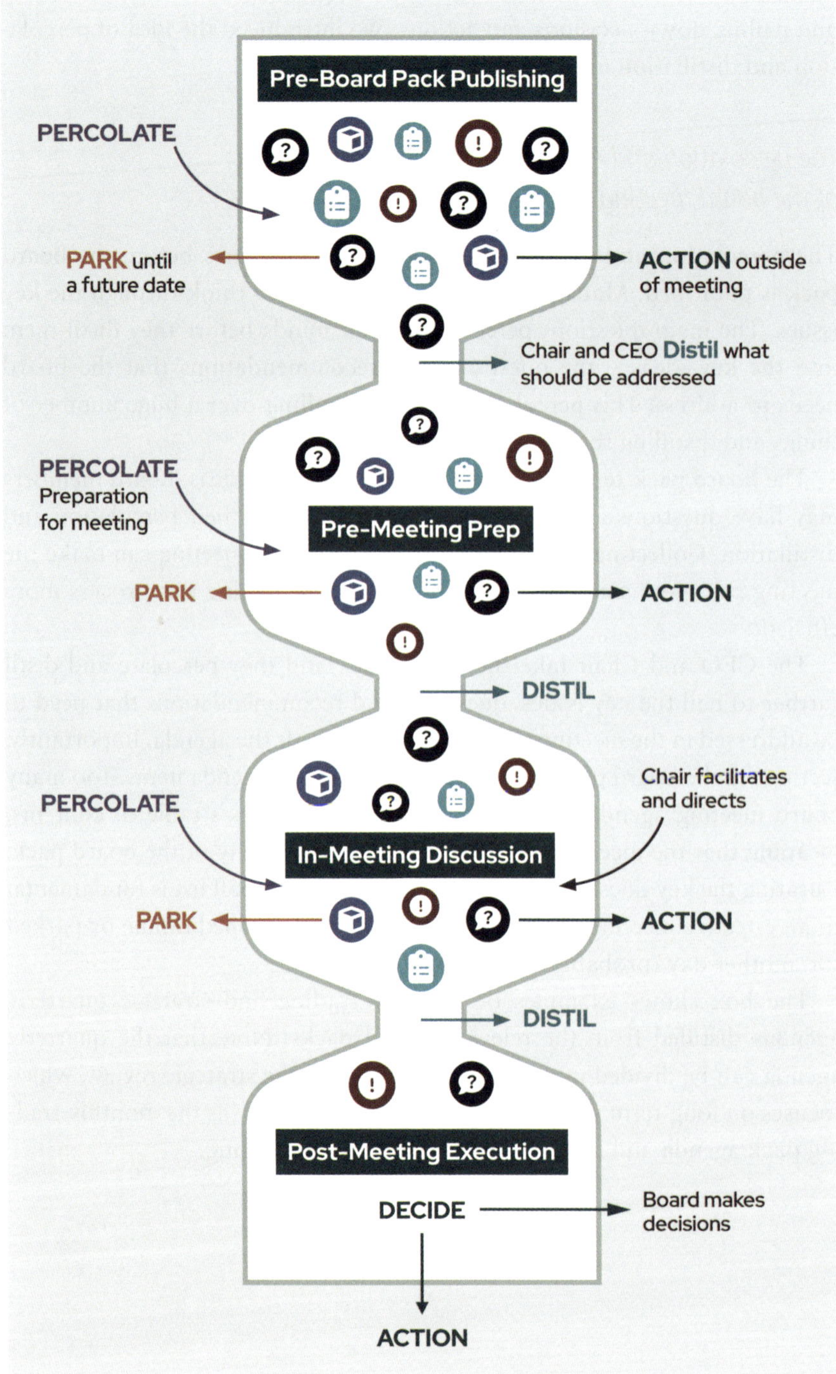

MONTHLY TRADING AGENDA

1 Matters arising and minutes from the previous meeting: this should be a record of signing off only (they should be signed off within five to seven days).

2 Review of Corporate Health, focusing particularly on reds and trends

3 Chair's opening remarks: this should include key issues, questions, recommendations and focus for the meeting. This should drive the discussion and set the scene for the main decisions.

4 CEO View from the Bridge: including the key points on overall trading and highlights/lowlights for the month

5–8 Key issues and questions to discuss (if necessary): ideally, no more than 3–4 issues relating to trading and performance

9 Items requiring board approval

10 Review of actions brought forward plus actions agreed upon at this meeting

11 Date of next meeting

Quarterly strategic agenda

Part A: Strategic review

1 Chair's opening remarks: these should include key issues, questions, recommendations and the focus for the meeting.

2 CEO View from the Bridge

3 Review of value creation initiatives in play

4 Key questions to discuss

5–7 Strategic topics to cover (ideally no more than 2–3)

8 Other strategic topics/presentations

9 Review of actions brought forward plus actions agreed upon at this meeting

10 Date of next meeting

Part B: Trading and performance (see above monthly trading agenda)

In the meeting, percolation and distillation happen again. The agenda represents the distillation of the key issues in the board pack and this provokes further questioning, ideas and discussion, which the Chair facilitates. Note that board members often request agenda items for the future. This will be recorded in the minutes as an action (see Chapter 4.2). Adding this to the agenda means that the action has been completed. The in-meeting ideas and discussion are eventually distilled into decisions and action points.

At each stage of the process – pre-board pack publication, pre-meeting preparation and in-meeting discussion – the key actors decide what to distil, what to park until a later date and what to action outside of the meeting. After the meeting, recommendations are actioned, which kicks off more percolation. These thoughts loop into the next meeting and the process starts again. It's worth noting that while this process is very applicable to board meetings, it is generic and can be applied to any of the meeting types we discuss in Chapter 4.3.

Using QFOR-A to enable effective boardroom discussion

In Chapter 1.3 we introduced the QFOR-A discipline: Questions, Facts, Opinions, Recommendation and Action. The point of every board meeting is to determine the right set of actions necessary to continue along the path to value creation. Nowhere is QFOR-A more important than in the boardroom. The emphasis should always be on ascertaining the facts and opinions that will lead to the 'so what?' – the recommendations and action. But this doesn't always happen. In their article 'The surprising power of questions', Alison Wood Brooks and Leslie K. John discuss how business leaders' lack of training in asking questions often leads to them getting it wrong.

The authors also write about how people have conversations to accomplish two major goals: information exchange (learning) and impression management (liking).[18] Great questions are driven by a genuine intent to learn. Questions asked for the sake of impression management are never worthwhile. They are motivated by selfish desires – to show off, challenge, exert power or simply say something and have a voice in the room (see Chapter 4.3 for the Chair's role in moving the discussion on). Before asking other people questions, board members would be wise to first question themselves. What's your motivation? Do you have a genuine desire to understand? Are you seeking to score points? Or is it just time you piped up?

There are many different types of questions. For boardroom discussions, we think it is helpful to be aware of nine. These fall under three broad categories: 'quick', 'seeking to understand' and 'unhelpful'.

QUICK QUESTIONS

1. Closed These questions invite a one-word answer, which is often just yes or no. They can be used to ascertain facts. Examples include 'Did you miss the target?'.

2. Execution These are closed, forward-looking questions. They are used to establish a prediction (what, when, how). For example, 'When will x be complete?'

3. Pre-meeting recall These are a category of closed questions which are backwards-looking and used to establish facts related to what, when and how much. For example, 'What was x in period y?' (Note that recall questions fall into two categories – 'quick' and 'unhelpful' – this is the seventh type of question described below.) People often need to look things up to answer these questions which is why they are best asked before a meeting. Recall questions asked during a meeting can be a different story – see below.

SEEKING TO UNDERSTAND QUESTIONS

4. Root cause These open questions are used to find out why something has happened. They are used to understand the causes and sequences of events that have resulted in something happening. These questions are sometimes called funnel-focusing questions. They begin broad and then narrow to a specific point. They are useful for discovering very specific information, for example, 'Why does Bridget consistently achieve 200 per cent of her on-target earnings? Why doesn't Adam?' Root-cause questions often lead to a testable hypothesis.

5. Opinion seeking These open questions are used to understand thoughts, feelings and beliefs. They most often begin with 'Why do you think…', for example, 'Why do you think x happened like that?' 'When should we open a US office?' These questions are sometimes called funnel-expanding questions. A series of questions is asked to encourage the respondent to gradually expand their thinking from a specific point.

6. Clarifying These open questions are a little like execution questions, but they invite a more expansive answer. They seek clarity, for example, 'How is the process going to work?' 'What steps will you take to ensure x happens?' They can be used to understand the philosophy, principles or methodology underpinning an idea. For example, establishing a set of rules to guide decision-making before signing off on a budget.

UNHELPFUL QUESTIONS

7. In-meeting recall While recall questions are okay to ask before meetings, we would advise against overusing them in meetings. There will be times when someone genuinely wants to know facts about something that happened in the past to help their thinking and decision-making. But we have observed people using them to trip respondents up and score points. These questions are too often used for impression management – people can ask them to show how on the ball they are and/or highlight how someone else has failed. Asking 'How much did you spend on x?' in relation to a project in the red might not be particularly helpful. Always stop and question yourself first – 'Why do I really want to know this?' and 'Will the answer help to resolve this issue?' Be sure that you're not simply trying to highlight someone else's mistakes in a public forum.

8. Leading These questions are used too often and often unintentionally. They are useful for revealing biases or, if left unchecked, can introduce bias. As the name implies, they are designed to lead the respondent down a particular path. Examples include: 'What problems did you encounter with the project?' (this seeks a negative response) or 'What did you enjoy most about the project?' (this invites the respondent to find the positives, even if there weren't any). This type of question could be turned into an opinion-seeking question by asking 'What did you enjoy and dislike the most about the project?'.

9. Loaded These seemingly straightforward, closed questions are sneaky. Never use them. They are loaded with an assumption about the respondent that will implicate them in some way. They are unfair and designed to trap. Lawyers and journalists famously use these types of questions. Examples include: 'Have you stopped fudging the numbers?' 'Do you think this project was less of a failure than your last one?'

AN EXAMPLE OF USING QFOR-A IN THE BOARDROOM

If a key initiative, project or set of actions is showing as red or amber (see BRAG in Chapter 1.3), the board needs to find out why. Questions should aim to uncover the root causes of problems or delays so that you can get to recommendations and actions. In our experience, delays often come down to one of three reasons. Asking the right questions helps to establish what factor or combination of factors might be to blame:

1. The project is blocked. If this is the case, find out who is blocked and how to unblock them (this comes down to dependencies – see Chapter 3.5).
2. There isn't enough time or money, or the scope is too wide/the quality is unattainable with the time and/or money available (see Chapter 3.5 for the CQT golden triangle).
3. Individual or team capabilities or knowledge gaps. This isn't always straightforward to diagnose, but it's critical to find out what's going on to reach clear action. One of three things is normally going on:
    - An individual or group knows that they lack the knowledge and are up front and honest about it. Self-diagnosis is ideal to address knowledge gaps and reach clear recommendations. Unfortunately, it's common for people to feel embarrassed or nervous about admitting to gaps in their knowledge or capability, so this scenario is also quite rare.
    - The board can see that an individual or team lacks the knowledge, skills or capabilities, but they don't realize it. In this scenario, the board can ask whether outside expertise is necessary to complete the task.
    - Individuals and teams are unsure and confused. They are wrestling with a problem and trying to figure it out. They don't know if they've got the right capability and knowledge or not, but they need help to work it out.

Final thoughts

There is no substitute for a sound business with a strong economic model operating in a growing market. There is also, as this book attests to, no substitute for good strategy design. Both of these things can be undermined if the board is ineffective. Boards exist to support organizations with their value creation objectives. More often than not, they do not function as they should. Board papers do not help to drive a productive discussion aimed at strategy execution and value creation and the collective experience in the room is wasted, meeting after meeting. According to research conducted by Board Intelligence, this problem is particularly acute in the world of private equity. They found that '86 per cent of PE investors believe board packs contain too much information, and 51 per cent of directors say they can't rely on their board packs to identify key issues early enough'. Furthermore, while 81 per cent of respondents identified value creation as the main purpose of board meetings, only 29 per cent found that to be the actual focus.[19]

We appreciate the irony of this chapter. We had a lot to say and, if you've made it to the end, you've read over 13,000 words. The good news is that we've written it at a Flesch-Kincaid grade level of 8.2. It's in plain English, so we hope you've found it an easy and enjoyable read.

REMEMBER THIS

1 Be clear about everyone's role.

2 Break board meetings into two: quarterly strategic and monthly operational.

3 Use QFOR-A and active, simple language.

4 Good preparation leads to good meetings. It is the job of the CEO and Chair to isolate the key questions and for all board members to build the discipline to ask good questions.

5 Give the board pack visual impact by using a range of tools such as BRAG and the Ārahi Arrow.

Notes

1 Dewar, C Keller, S and Malhotra, V (2022) *CEO Excellence: The six mindsets that distinguish the best leaders from the rest*, Nicholas Brealey Publishing, London

2 Stout, L (2012) *The Shareholder Value Myth: How putting shareholders first harms investors, corporations and the public*, Berrett-Koehler Publishers, Oakland, California

3 Dunne, P (2021) *Boards: A practical perspective* (2e), Governance Publishing & Information Services Ltd, London

4 Bryar, C and Carr, B (2021) *Working Backwards: Insights, stories and secrets from inside Amazon*, Macmillan, London

5 Disc Group (2022) Where do DISC profiles get their colours? 22 November, https://discassessment.co.uk/where-do-disc-profiles-get-their-colours/#:~:text=While%20there%27s%20some%20variation%20between,a%20cool%20and%20icy%20blue (archived at https://perma.cc/ZAU8-PRU8)

6 Erikson, T (2019) *Surrounded by Idiots: The four types of human behaviour (or, how to understand those who cannot be understood)*, Vermilion, London

7 ICAEW (2019) Information overload: Effective boards and committees in financial services, www.icaew.com/-/media/corporate/files/technical/financial-services/thought-leadership/information-overload-board-packs.ashx#:~:text=This%20is%20not%20the%20responsibility,what%20is%20given%20to%20them (archived at https://perma.cc/TSN7-JMKK)

8 For those interested in how we ordered the territories, blues scored 1, greens scored 0, amber scored –1 and red scored –2. The territory with the lowest score is at the top of the list

9 Minto, B (2021) *The Pyramid Principle: Logic in writing and thinking* (3e), Pearson Education, Harlow

10 Gallo, C (2022) *The Bezos Blueprint: Communication secrets that power Amazon's success*, Macmillan, London

11 Birchard, B (2021) The science of strong business writing, *Harvard Business Review*, July–August, https://hbr.org/2021/07/the-science-of-strong-business-writing (archived at https://perma.cc/5XN2-7ABK)

12 Horowitz, B (2014) *The Hard Thing About Hard Things: Building a business when there are no easy answers*, HarperBusiness, New York

13 Otago Bulletin Board (2014) Simple sentences more honest, University of Otago, 27 June, www.otago.ac.nz/otagobulletin/research/simple-sentences-more-honest (archived at https://perma.cc/4KZE-5F3D)

14 Amazon.com (archived at https://perma.cc/Q9T2-FJ78), 1997 letter to shareholders, https://venturebeat.com/wp-content/uploads/2010/09/amzn_shareholder-letter-20072.pdf (archived at https://perma.cc/79SE-63SQ)

15 We used a combination of Microsoft Word and https://goodcalculators.com/flesch-kincaid-calculator/ (archived at https://perma.cc/M5T7-EZGE) to calculate these scores

16 Note that readability formulas give us only part of the picture. They judge the word choice on length alone and do not tell us how well known words are, particularly in the context of our own organizations and boardrooms. We can use them as a guide while applying our own judgement about how our text is likely to land with our audience

17 A Plain English Handbook (1998) US Securities and Exchange Commission, August, www.sec.gov/pdf/handbook.pdf (archived at https://perma.cc/534H-2ZKV)

18 Brooks, A W and John, L K (2018) The surprising power of questions, *Harvard Business Review*, May–June, https://hbr.org/2018/05/the-surprising-power-of-questions (archived at https://perma.cc/2EJZ-UHUU)

19 Pantelides, M (2019) The role and value of board meetings in PE-backed businesses, [blog] Board Intelligence, 3 March, www.boardintelligence.com/blog/the-role-and-value-of-board-meetings-in-pe (archived at https://perma.cc/7MPG-3UED)

4.3

Forums and meetings

Meetings that don't result in action are nothing but group therapy

Introduction

Business is a team sport and teams are made up of strange creatures called humans. We are an emotional species and we are all different. We all have different drivers, personalities, experiences and pressures. A big part of executing the plan involves us coming together for a range of different reasons: to get stuff done, align, learn, decide and solve problems. We do this through meetings.

Meetings are the subject of a lot of ridicule. John Cleese and Antony Jay wrote a brilliant comedy business training video in 1976. Called *Meetings, Bloody Meetings*, it includes a scene where Cleese is sat in bed reading a board paper. His wife, sitting next to him, asks why he can't do his work while he's at work. He replies that he can't because he's in meetings all the time. He then goes on to summarize what many of us experience every day. He arrives at meetings late because his previous meeting overran. He then has to leave early to get to his next meeting while arranging to finish the meeting he's in at another time. When his wife asks if it would be easier if she came and slept at the office, he invites her to come and sleep at the meetings because that's what everyone else does.[1]

Despite the film's dated appearance, the content remains incredibly relevant in today's business world. Cleese describes a phenomenon we know only too well – being 'back-to-back'. It feels like there's only slight exaggeration for comedic effect. While people might not sleep in meetings, they are commonly disengaged. We often don't need to be in the meetings we're asked to attend and many people deal with this by being on their phones or laptops, or simply staring into space wondering what to have for dinner.

Research shows that executives spend an average of nearly 23 hours a week in meetings. This is up from less than 10 hours in the 1960s. So whatever people were feeling in 1976 at the time of Cleese's film is magnified in today's world. Perhaps this wouldn't be so bad if people felt it was a productive use of their time, but only 17 per cent report feeling this way.[2] We've complained and joked about the meeting problem for years. And we all accept it as part of working life. It got worse during the pandemic when five-minute chats at someone's desk were replaced with 30-minute or hour-long Teams or Zoom calls.

Wasting time in unnecessary or poorly executed meetings has a direct impact on value creation objectives. Meetings have to be worthwhile. They eat into the time we have available for what Professor Cal Newport describes as 'deep work'.[3] When you perform 'deep work', it means that the task at hand has your undivided attention. It enables you to achieve something challenging and worthwhile. It is directly opposed to shallow work, which includes things like answering emails, Slack messages or performing manual admin tasks. These are the types of tasks which could be categorized as 'in-out actions' (see Chapter 4.4). Everybody, without exception, should leave a meeting feeling that it was a productive use of their time.

This chapter begins by justifying meetings. We argue that they do need to exist, despite their many drawbacks. We then look at forums. Forums have members who attend one or more meetings, which can be divided into different types. The rest of the chapter is devoted to what good meetings look like. We divide the discussion into three phases: pre-meeting, in-meeting (with a heavy emphasis on 'meeting hygiene') and post-meeting.

To be clear, in this chapter we're not just talking board meetings. We're talking about executive committee meetings, sales, operations, geographical or business unit leadership meetings. We're talking about developers' daily scrums and ad hoc problem-solving meetings. The advice in this chapter can be applied across the board.

Forums

If meetings are such a waste of time and so open to ridicule from the likes of John Cleese, should we just stop having them? Do they have any point to them at all? Warren Buffett famously tries to have as few meetings as possible and it works for him. As Bill Gates wrote in an article for *Harvard Business Review* entitled 'What I learned from Warren Buffett': 'He's good at saying no to things. He knows what he likes to do – and what he does, he does unbelievably well. He likes to sit in his office and read and think.'[4]

We believe that meetings are important. Done well, they provide the opportunity to confront your brutal truth. They allow you to assess progress, solve problems, make decisions, share information and wrestle with ideas. What's important is knowing why you're meeting, having the right people in the room to ensure an efficient, productive and constructive discussion, and ensuring that every meeting results in action to drive progress.

Forums are groups of people who work together to get something done. Much of this work is done through meetings. They decide which meetings are necessary to drive action. Generally speaking, they have four types of members – a Chair, a Secretary, participants and observers. The Chair owns the forum and the meetings that it holds. They are responsible for creating the agenda and determining what to discuss. They have a pivotal role in ensuring meetings run smoothly, which we discuss later in the chapter. The Secretary is responsible for taking minutes and capturing actions. They are also responsible for circulating the minutes after the meeting in a timely fashion (see below). The Chair should never be the one taking the minutes (this happens too often).

So what about participants and observers? Our favourite way to explain this dynamic is through a fable about Chicken and Pig. Chicken and Pig are good friends. One day, Chicken says to Pig: 'Hey, I want to go into business with you.' Pig replies: 'Oh, that's amazing. What kind of business?' 'Well, it's a restaurant.' 'Even better!' says Pig. 'What shall we call it?' Chicken replies 'Bacon and eggs.' Pig goes quiet. After a few minutes, she murmurs: 'I don't think so, Chicken. That would make me committed and you an interested party.' Participants are committed to the forum and any meetings that it holds. They actively participate and are responsible for giving facts, opinions and recommendations that lead to actions. They are like Pig. Observers are like Chicken. They are interested parties.

Forums are set up for numerous reasons, particularly to oversee initiatives and ensure things happen. They can cross functions or be for one function only. Below are some scenarios when forums are helpful:

- The board.
- Key initiative forums: these are effectively project teams. As key initiatives are cross-functional, these forums are too. Forum members decide

what meetings are needed and when to keep the key initiative on track. Once the key initiative is completed, the forum is dissolved.

- Ongoing, in-function forums – sales, HR, leadership, and finance committees.
- KOD forums – in larger organizations with matrices, each KOD has its own forum. For example, if geography is important, the head of each geography and their leadership team will form a forum.

Each forum requires a Terms of Reference (reasons for meeting and objectives, frequency of meeting, constituent members). While unnecessary for forums such as an Audit Committee or Remuneration Committee, it's good practice for forums with cascaded objectives to have a POAP (see Chapter 2.2). This should be distilled from the board's POAP.

Care should be taken to design forums to include the right balance of people. The aim is for forums to benefit from diversity of thought and opinion. You need the right mix of personality types and the right mix of extroverts and introverts (and part of the role of the Chair is to ensure that everyone gets a chance to speak – see later in the chapter). For more on this see Chapter 4.2 where we wrote about colour personality profiling. Forums are, essentially, teams. Some effort may be required to work on the dynamics and relationships within the team. To do this, it's helpful to understand the five functions of a high-performing team.

Five functions of a high-performing team

Great, high-performing teams are not an easy thing to achieve. It's not just about having people with the right skills and competencies. Teams can only be great when people work and behave in a certain way as a group. Too many teams suffer from flawed thinking and a flawed attitude, at both an individual and group level. Teams that don't get these things right are highly likely to fail.

In 2002, Patrick Lencioni published the popular business fable *The Five Dysfunctions of a Team*. The basic premise is that five dysfunctions can affect a team's ability to perform. These are:

1. Absence of trust.
2. Fear of conflict.
3. Lack of commitment.

4. Avoidance of accountability.
5. Inattention to team results.

The dysfunctions are visualized as a triangle, with 'Absence of trust' at the bottom and 'Inattention to team results' at the top. A dysfunctional team can't execute strategy effectively.[5]

Our friend, John Brown, has inverted this model to make it the five functions of high-performing teams, as shown in Figure 4.3.1. He prefers to focus on the positive rather than the negative:

- 'Trust' is at the top. In a high-performing team, everything is predicated on trust – it is a force multiplier. Trust means being vulnerable – admitting weakness, asking for help and taking risks in offering feedback. Transparency and openness are the keys to building trust. The old adage is true: trust is hard to gain and easy to lose. It's commonly lost during and after mergers and acquisitions. Success often depends on a culture of trust. Without trust, team members will find it difficult to show their vulnerabilities within the group.
- 'Productive conflict' is next. Too many teams are happy to put up with false harmony. But this doesn't get difficult issues out into the open. Don't see conflict as a taboo. Get it out on the table so that you can have constructive debate and open communication. It's okay to disagree and it's liberating to be part of a team that is happy to argue productively to get to the brutal, total truth. Very often problems need to be wrestled with until a team can find a constructive way forward. Productive conflict is a huge timesaver. It means you don't get stuck in the same negative patterns, returning to the same problem time and again. Productive conflict can be challenging in companies that have a dominant CEO. The second of Professor Richard Holmes' '10 diseases of leadership', introduced in Chapter 3.5, is 'Failure to recognize that opposition can be loyal'.[6] It's up to executives to create a culture where subordinates feel free to challenge leaders. In high-performing cultures, employees feel safe and comfortable saying what they think, even if it isn't always what others want to hear.
- 'Full commitment' requires team members to consider everyone's ideas, decide and get it down. It doesn't mean that everyone needs to agree. But it does mean that you need clarity and genuine buy-in. Too often, people feign buy-in to ideas and policies and then act in a way that is contrary to their 'commitment'. This only creates confusion and can stymie

FIGURE 4.3.1 The five functions of high-performing teams

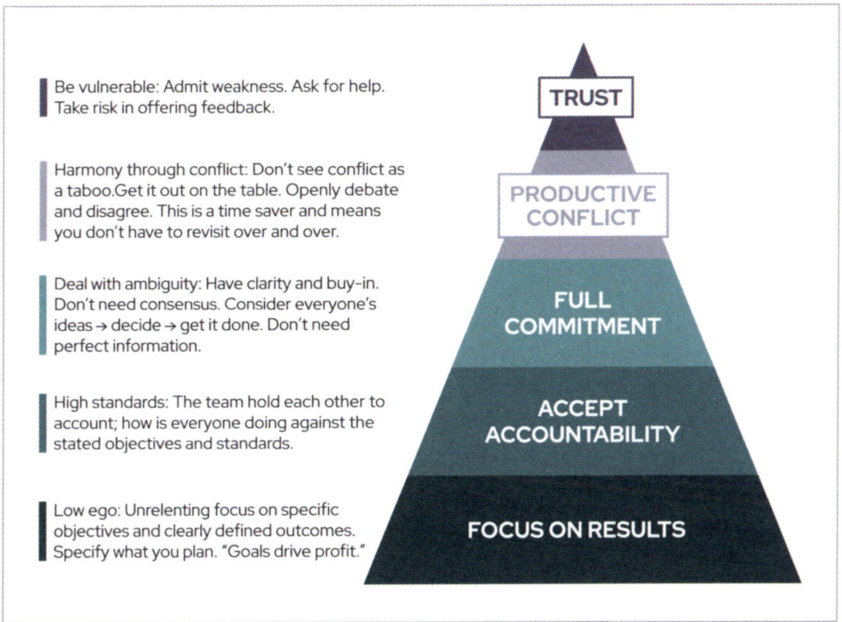

strategy execution. Everyone must unite and commit to the clinical execution of your strategy.

- 'Accept accountability' requires the entire team to hold each other to account. Everyone is accountable for their behaviour and for calling out other people's poor behaviour too, both peers and superiors. Everyone is responsible for setting and maintaining high standards and for achieving their objectives.
- 'Focus on results' – high-performing teams have an unrelenting focus on specific objectives and clearly defined outcomes. Team members keep their egos in check and put team success before their own. Dysfunctional teams contain individuals who allow their ego and their status within the organization to drive their actions.

RUPERT

The User Experience/User Interface (UX/UI) team at Ārahi has something called the 'kitchen sink'. It means that every component is created on a 'page', so that developers can use it when writing their code. It is part of the design system, it makes the platform easier to develop and easier to change (if you change something in the kitchen sink it changes everywhere). We encountered an issue during one of our routine working meetings (which we call our daily 'stand-ups'). The time and effort it would take to complete the kitchen sink was far greater than initially expected. We had done a spike and proved the assumption that this was a good idea and do-able. We had therefore committed to moving forward with it (in software development when something is technically uncertain, it helps to spend one or two days trying to solve the most complex unknown. The intention is not to produce production-ready code, but simply to prove a way to solve the problem).

However, as we moved forward, it became clear that the effort required by some of our software engineers was going to impact the schedule of one of our critical features. This was a feature that the commercial team needed to bring to market. However, not building the kitchen sink would have a long-term impact on our development productivity and the overall look and feel of the product. It was a passion project for the UX/UI lead. So immediately after our 'stand-up' (helpfully we were all in the office) four of us had another unscheduled meeting to resolve the issues. This group was made up of the two lead engineers, the Head of UX/UI and me. We printed off the backlog of component areas. There were 25 in total. Based on some criteria we developed together, and after some debate, we placed them in one of three buckets. These were 1) 'no-brainer – we all agree to do it now', 2) 'delay' and 3) 'debate – we can't agree'. Of the 25, seven went into the no-brainer bucket, ten were put into 'delay' and eight were put into 'debate'. Our debating resulted in four more going into the 'no-brainer' bucket, which now contained 11 component areas in total. The overall work was reduced by over 60 per cent and it meant we could push the workstream forward.

This was all done in less than an hour. We committed. We all felt listened to. At times, it was a bit heated. At one point, after a well-articulated argument from one of the lead engineers (let's call him Adam), the UI/UX lead said 'Ok, fine, let's just leave it.' But he wasn't fine. And no one should just cave. Everyone needs to feel listened to and we needed to hear his view. We listened and we learned. The conflict was fine. It was productive.

We got an outcome. Our recommendation was to do 11 and delay 14 (for some undefined period). We then agreed on the actions and documented the outcome to keep the team informed. Other actions were agreed. We moved on.

Categorizing meetings according to their type

Generally speaking, people meet to perform one of four activities: to solve a problem, to action something, to share information or to make a decision. These four types of meeting objectives can be understood in terms of the acronym **PAID: Problem-solving, Actioning, Information sharing and Deciding**. Meetings can be further categorized according to two factors: whether they are recurring or non-recurring and whether they have a single objective or multiple objectives. Figure 4.3.2 demonstrates the categorization of various meetings according to these factors.

A board meeting is an example of a multi-objective recurring meeting. This is the top right-hand quadrant of the figure. The board performs various activities. Members meet to share information, solve problems and make decisions. This is the 'fullest-fat' meeting, but there are others with similar levels of complexity. (We've explained our 'full-fat' concept before concerning strategy in Chapter 2.1 and the bow-tie framework in Chapter 3.3.) Take Executive Committee meetings. These meetings involve the CEO and their direct reports and they are chaired by the CEO. Similarly, each KOD leader will have a senior leadership team that needs to meet. For example,

FIGURE 4.3.2 The different meeting types

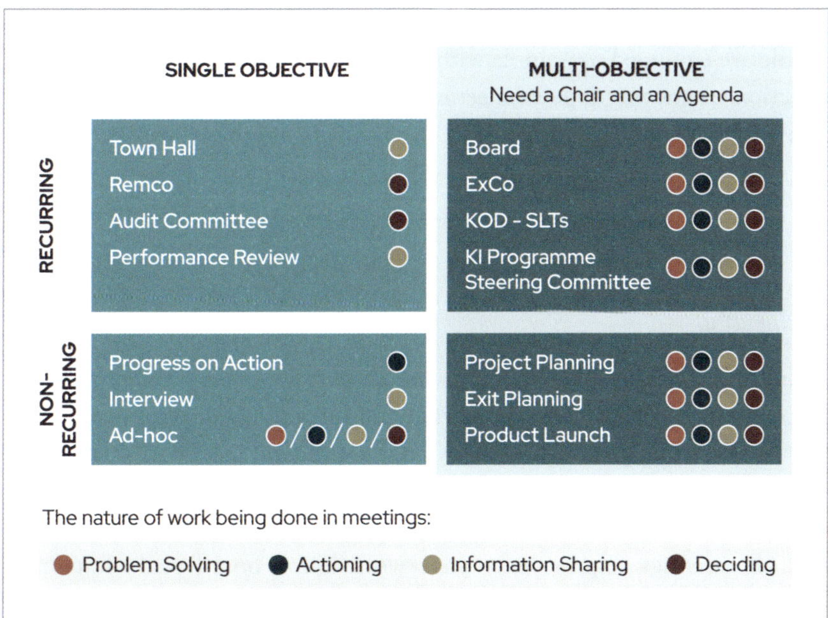

an HR leadership team or sales leadership team. These meetings have a Chair, actions brought forward from the previous meeting and Terms of Reference. Meetings in the bottom-right quadrant also have multiple objectives. These meetings also need a Chair, papers and the produce actions. But they may occur only once or on a more ad hoc basis. They are more focused on solving a problem, working something out or planning a set of activities, for example sorting pricing, launching a product or planning a campaign.

Recurring, single-objective meetings aim to do one thing regularly. Town hall meetings have lots of people and one objective – to share information, for example company news or upcoming changes. Sometimes, there is no limit to the number of people who can attend these meetings. Remuneration Committees or Audit Committees are governed meetings with the single objective of signing off a set of proposals.

Non-recurring, single-objective meetings are probably the most common type. They can be as simple as two people getting together to progress an action or solve a problem. These meetings are often held on an ad-hoc basis (see the example of healthy conflict in Rupert's box). They are often needed to wrestle with a specific issue that needs to be resolved.

It can be helpful for calendar invitations to signpost meetings according to their type. There will inevitably be some crossover, for example deciding meetings could contain elements of problem-solving, but it's important to limit this as far as possible. If you don't, you can end up with too many people in a room trying to solve a specific problem that only a handful of people are equipped to grapple with. If a meeting is veering too much in the direction of another type of meeting, park the issue and set up a separate time to discuss it.

What makes a good meeting?

Pre-meeting

A meeting can only be as good as the preparation that goes into it. This preparation is largely about preparing and reading paperwork (and percolating and distilling thoughts – see Chapter 4.2), and meeting hygiene.

PREPARING AND READING PAPERWORK

Not all meetings require hefty paperwork like a board pack. But many require some, or they require certain participants to put together information to share at the meeting, such as a PowerPoint deck. We don't have the space to delve into the ins and outs of how to create a good PowerPoint presentation, but we would like to flag that PowerPoint isn't always the answer. Jeff Bezos banned PowerPoint at Amazon in 2004. In an email to his senior executives, he told them to focus on memos instead. In his eyes, PowerPoint presentations are too passive and fail to engage audiences. He also felt that people focused too much on graphic presentation and not enough on the key messages in the slides. He favoured memos as a way to get people to think deeply about what they wanted to write and to structure their ideas logically. Attendees would sit and read the memo for 30 minutes at the beginning of each meeting, and then they would debate. Meetings at Amazon were, and still are, about active communication rather than passive listening.[7]

We're not saying that replacing PowerPoint with Word memos is necessarily the way forward for every meeting. But we do advocate thinking about the best way to get the information across. For example, it could work well to prepare a short Word document for a problem-solving meeting and have everyone read it before launching into a debate. That way, everyone starts from the same place, with the same information.

In Chapter 4.2 we looked at the different types of questions that can be asked in meetings to enable a productive discussion and get to action. As part of meeting preparation, think about any questions that can be asked before the meeting. You will remember that we gave 'recall' questions a dual categorization – when they are asked before the meeting begins, they can be helpful. People should be encouraged to ask any recall questions before the meeting begins.

MEETING HYGIENE

The way that meetings are organized, the consideration given to the comfort of meeting participants and the space in the room are known as meeting hygiene. It can have a huge impact on the efficiency of the conversation. Lots of the advice we give here might sound like grandma teaching you to suck eggs, but it's amazing how often meetings suffer because people don't think these things through.

Meeting hygiene is like housekeeping. It aims to increase meeting productivity by ensuring attendees are comfortable and not distracted. Paying attention to meeting hygiene is particularly important for long meetings, such as quarterly board meetings (see Chapter 4.2). For these types of meetings, hygiene can include providing coffee and tea and lunch, and also ensuring that an adequate number of breaks are worked into the schedule. It also means allowing time at the end to wrap up and capture and distribute actions. Meetings often overrun for this reason. Below is a list of other things to consider.

Remote or in-person? In our view, some meetings can be remote, while others very definitely need to be in-person. For example, information-sharing meetings can be online. As these meetings are mostly passive, those who run them should take care not to bore people with endless PowerPoint slides. Problem-solving and actioning meetings, on the other hand, are most effective with a small number of people and they are best done in person. It's difficult to genuinely solve problems working remotely over video-conferencing software. For these meetings, ideally aim for two to four people and don't go above eight. As discussed in Chapter 4.2, monthly trading board meetings should only take an hour. They are more about information sharing than problem-solving and as such they don't need to take place in person.

Space and set-up in the room As a general rule, not enough attention is given to room layout and fundamentals that contribute to the comfort of forum members. Rooms need to be big enough, have natural light wherever possible with comfortable seating and enough space to move around. If your meeting room is small and pokey, it will frustrate and irritate attendees.

Whiteboards support thinking through issues. They are helpful to thrash out ideas and solve problems. Standing around a whiteboard rather than sitting around a table is a great equalizer. It helps to break down hierarchical barriers. Give everyone a pen and encourage them to get stuck in. At Ārahi, our happy place is around a whiteboard. Even our tables are whiteboards.

As Chair, I (Jon) became quite particular about the room layout for board meetings, training events and workshops. It comes from my training days at PwC. I always liked to 'sleep on the room'. In other words, I liked to visit the room the night before to check the size, layout and comfort and make any necessary changes. Too often, I found the choice of room sub-optimal (they were normally selected by a course administrator who hadn't taken these factors into account). For governed meetings, it's the Chair's responsibility to curate the room and to create a constructive environment for the meeting. On many occasions, I changed the layout or even insisted on moving to a bigger room.

In-meeting

Meetings are like stories. They have a beginning, a middle and an end. Multi-objective meetings require a Chair to run them. The Chair is most often the person responsible for crafting this story. Aristotle knew a thing or two about making speeches. His advice 'tell them what you're going to tell them, tell them, then tell them what you told them' has been used by generations of business leaders and heads of state. In multi-objective meetings, the agenda, coupled with the Chair's opening remarks, is where you 'tell them what you're going to tell them'. As we saw in Chapter 4.2, the opening remarks for board meetings should include the focus of the meeting and the key issues, questions and recommendations. The main part of the meeting is where the Chair 'tells them' – this is where you run through the agenda. Crucially, 'tell them what you told them' involves summarizing and agreeing to the key points and actions at the end of the meeting.

Single-objective meetings do not require an agenda and they don't necessarily need a Chair, although it can be effective to alternate the Chair in a group of equals, such as a team progress meeting. This keeps it fresh and interesting and ensures that everyone stays invested. It also means that each meeting member can develop their chairing and facilitation skills.

There are some other dos and don'ts for the person chairing a meeting. These are mainly applicable to multi-objective meetings.

Dos:

- Start and end with socializing. Talking is an important part of relationship building. We're all humans and we need to build rapport. Don't jump straight in. Allow people to catch up with each other first. It's very important to end meetings well with relationships intact. It means that the next time you meet, you'll begin on a good footing.
- Move the discussion on. In Chapter 4.2 we discussed good and bad questions to ask in a meeting. Part of the Chair's role involves figuring out whether or not a question is a good one by applying the materiality test: Is it relevant and material to the meeting? Does it need to be answered now for us to proceed? If it's not relevant, the Chair is probably best off dismissing it or parking it and asking for a written response as part of the follow-up to the meeting.
- Keep the QFOR-A discipline at the forefront. Do you have sufficient facts and opinions to reach a recommendation and get to action?

- Manage the different personalities in the room. Find ways to get the introverts to express their views and the extroverts to listen more.
- Cut waffle and watch out for hoodwinking. Sometimes, people give an overly long explanation in response to a question that requires a one-word answer. Politicians do this all the time. In these cases, the Chair should think of themselves as the journalist. Ask the question again. Point out that they didn't answer it.
- Beware of the 'law of triviality'. The authors of *CEO Excellence* recount an excellent story first told by C. Northcote Parkinson in *The Pursuit of Progress*. A team had three investment decisions to make in a meeting. The first item on the agenda was a £10 million nuclear power plant. This was approved in two and a half minutes. The second was the colour they should paint their bike shed, which took 45 minutes. The third was a new coffee machine for the staff room. After one hour and 15 minutes of discussing this, they decided to postpone the decision until the next meeting. Groups of people can give too much attention to trivial details, especially if the entire group can relate to the issue being discussed.[8] Keep focused on important topics and watch out for how time is allocated in the meeting.
- Sometimes you might want to ask everyone's opinion in turn. If possible, try to ask the most senior person in the room last. That way, junior attendees can't just fall in line with the highest-ranking opinion.

MAKING DECISIONS

It's worth including some specific advice or making decisions in meetings. A recommendation requires a decision, but it's not always clear who that decision belongs to and how it should be made. There might just be one or two decision-makers or decisions may require consensus. Ultimately, decisions in most meetings require consensus. For those who like to watch old movies, the 1957 film *12 Angry Men* starring Henry Fonda gives a classic snapshot of American history. Nominated for three Academy Awards, it is regarded by many as one of the greatest films ever made. It is also a very good example of why consensus decision-making is a very important way of operating.

Decisions are rarely made by a show of hands. It breeds resentment and may indicate that not all issues have been raised or fully discussed. I (Rupert) have sat in hundreds of board meetings. I've only seen a decision go to a vote once. There was a difference of opinion about strategy. One of the board members wanted to discontinue the development of a product platform. He put it to a vote. I had my resignation letter ready to hand in if I lost. Thankfully, it was voted down six to one in my favour. Our difference in opinion meant that the board member left. We parted ways amicably.

However, the consensus view is not always the brave view. Paradox 4 in Chapter 1.2 is called 'Benign dictatorship versus democracy'. There are times when one person (often the founder) has the necessary insight and drive to take risks. As a general rule, the crowd is more risk averse. The crowd wants more debate. More data, more analysis. Consensus decision-making can mean that you can't move quickly. Corporate benchmarking culture leads to analysis paralysis, whereas the entrepreneurial spirit is more about experimenting, learning and making mistakes.

Decision-making isn't always a linear process of collecting facts, analysing, discussing and deciding. It's rare to be in full possession of all the facts. Facts lead to more thoughts and discussions (i.e. expressed opinions) as well as more questions. If you wait until all the possible questions have been asked, you'll likely have waited too long. Former US Secretary of State Colin Powell is credited for the 40/70 rule. This stipulates never to decide with less than 40 per cent of the information as you won't have enough but not to wait until you have 100 per cent as this will mean waiting too long – 70 per cent was enough for Powell to decide and act. Moving fast and being able to deal with ambiguity is an advantage.

There's no right or wrong answer to the benign dictatorship versus democracy problem. There are pros and cons of each approach. At Investec, Ian Kantor gave everyone approval rights. He believes very strongly in this philosophy as an effective way to get everyone to commit (remember that one of the five functions of a high-performing team is full commitment). We heard his views on reconciling differences in Chapter 1.3.

CONDITIONAL DECISIONS

The world isn't always black and white, and approval isn't always a simple binary yes or no decision. There are often buts in life. Figure 4.3.3 shows the difference between hard, unconditional approvals and conditional approvals. It's important to understand this, as illustrated in Rupert's story below. Often, recommendations are approved only if certain conditions are met – think of this as a 'yes, but' decision. Things can also be rejected for the present moment but reconsidered if certain conditions are met or if circumstances change – think of this as a 'no, but' decision. Conditional approvals and rejections are in direct contrast to unconditional approvals and decisions. An unconditional approval means you can move straight to action. An unconditional rejection means that the case is closed and you move on.

RUPERT

I had an interesting discussion with a friend about decision-making in meetings. She was telling me about a business unit lead who had taken a budget request for a critical programme to a meeting. The board had rejected the proposal but given some conditions which, if met, might result in an approval. All the business unit lead heard was the word 'rejected' and left the room with a definitive answer. Dispirited, she told my friend about her ideas to find the budget through other means. My friend said, 'Hang on. That wasn't the decision at all. Look at a, b, c and change x, y, z and you can take it back to the board.' My friend heard one thing and the business unit lead heard another. The board wasn't clear enough.

This is a common scenario. Five people can go into a room, discuss a bunch of stuff, debate and reach a decision, and then leave the room with divergent views about what was agreed. The answer is to bring clarity by documenting decisions. Align on aligning.

FIGURE 4.3.3 Conditional and unconditional decisions

	Approve	Reject
Conditional	**Approved** *But on these conditions... (x, y, z)*	**Rejected** *But if these conditions are met, we may reconsider... (x, y, z)*
Unconditional	**Approved** *Move straight to actions*	**Rejected** *This case is closed* OR **Rejected** *Because x, y, z*

Post-meeting

Meetings should end with a clear sense of required actions. And after a meeting, the actions should get done. This is when you get the reward for the time invested in the meeting.

Central to this is circulating the minutes. In our view, minutes need to be circulated 24 to 48 hours after the meeting, while it is still fresh in people's minds. Have a process to approve them within five days. The faster the better. As we say in Chapter 4.2, if, for some reason minutes don't get approved in between meetings, it may need to happen in the meeting, but this should be by exception only.

Managing your meeting time

In Chapter 4.2 we discussed the four core responsibilities of the CEO. Part of this is managing yourself, which means managing your time. Of course, this doesn't just apply to CEOs, it applies to all of us. We all need enough time to get the core components of our job done. I (Rupert) colour-code my calendar according to meeting type. Meetings are often arranged 18 months in advance, so calendars should go two years out. I also block time for deep thought, travel and conferences. This ensures that you not only have enough time on a day-to-day level but also weekly/monthly/annual level to get things done. We all need time for Newport's 'deep work', but it can be difficult to protect it. Colour coding enables you to check that you have enough deep thought time in a day, a week, a month or a year.

It's common for people to be invited to meetings that they don't need to be at. Often, the person sending the invitations may not know exactly who needs to be there so they over-invite to cover all bases. Or people may get invited so they don't feel excluded. Every time someone is invited to a meeting, it's time they won't get back. It has a cost. You can work out this cost by using salary data and the amount of time people spend in meetings. Every time someone is added to a meeting, think of the cost of that person when they are fully loaded. The people sending invitations should think carefully about who needs to be there. This can be solved by considering forum members when crafting the Terms of Reference. The people receiving invitations should think carefully about whether or not their presence is really necessary. You may need to be there for only one agenda item. You may only need to be kept informed of the recommendations and actions through the minutes. We all have agency in this and we shouldn't feel concerned about excusing ourselves from meetings that aren't a productive use of our time.

Final thoughts

Meetings that don't result in action are nothing but group therapy. Forums have a responsibility to ensure that every meeting they run ends in action and that these actions are brought forward to the next meeting with progress updates. This is particularly the responsibility of the Chair.

Meetings have to be worth our while. Too many of us simply manage our time. We're constantly treading water, too caught up in the busyness to do anything about it. We run from one meeting to the next, not stopping to question whether or not we need to be there. What we should be doing is making time – blocking out chunks in our diaries for deep, productive work. Time is fixed. There are only 168 hours in a week. What you do with those hours is crucial to your success, failure and overall happiness and well-being. As Albert Schweitzer is thought to have said: 'Success is not the key to happiness. Happiness is the key to success. If you love what you're doing, you will be successful.' No one loves sitting in endless meetings. Warren Buffett flies private to save his most precious commodity – time. In the 1999 movie *The Matrix*, Morpheus said that 'time is always against us'. If someone steals £100 from you, they can be prosecuted. And yet if someone books an hour of your time for a meeting you don't need to attend, what consequences do they face? None at all.

REMEMBER THIS

1. State the objective of the meeting.
2. Ensure the agenda allows you to achieve that objective.
3. Ensure the right people are there (and the unnecessary people aren't).
4. Capture actions, owner and completion dates.
5. Distribute actions and follow them up.

Notes

1 Meetings, bloody meetings, www.youtube.com/playlist?list=PLn8FlhZQ69X9JuWars3SReMQi0gDlj-M6 (archived at https://perma.cc/ZE87-KD5E)

2 Perlow, L A, Hadley, C N and Eun, E (2017) Stop the meeting madness: How to free up time for meaningful work, *Harvard Business Review*, July–August, https://hbr.org/2017/07/stop-the-meeting-madness (archived at https://perma.cc/RHE9-4GJC)

3 Newport, C (2016) *Deep Work: Rules for focused success in a distracted world*, Piatkus, London

4 Gates, B (1996) What I learned from Warren Buffett, *Harvard Business Review*, January–February, https://hbr.org/1996/01/what-i-learned-from-warren-buffett#:~:text=He%20doesn%27t%20invest—take,does%2C%20he%20does%20unbelievably%20well (archived at https://perma.cc/EQY4-XVCR)

5 Lencioni, P (2002) *The Five Dysfunctions of a Team: A leadership fable*, Jossey-Bass, San Francisco

6 Yapp, R (2016) Professor Richard Holmes' 10 diseases of leadership [blog] Leadership forces, 16 December, https://www.leadershipforces.com/10-diseases-leadership/ (archived at https://perma.cc/N78W-22GY)

7 Locke, Taylor (2019) Jeff Bezos: This is the 'smartest thing we ever did' at Amazon, CNBC Make It, 15 October, www.cnbc.com/2019/10/14/jeff-bezos-this-is-the-smartest-thing-we-ever-did-at-amazon.html (archived at https://perma.cc/5FMM-AZQN)

8 Dewar, C (2022) CEO Excellence: Make your team the star, StartupNation, 15 March, https://startupnation.com/books/ceo-excellence-make-your-team-the-star/ (archived at https://perma.cc/Y7NN-78RK)

4.4

Action management

Give inaction no room to hide

Introduction

Just as all roads lead to Rome, all chapters in this book lead to this point. BROP-A ends with action. QFOR-A ends with action. Action is the endpoint of the red line that flows from the high-level strategic thinking that informs the POAP and stepping stones, through to the integrated plan and the key initiatives, through to the board meeting and other forums and meetings set up to oversee projects. Everything leads to what we do day to day. Aristotle supposedly said, 'We are what we repeatedly do.' Nike's motto is 'Just do it'. Integrity is about doing what you say you're going to do. In the world of business, those who get stuff done are valued highly. Good meetings end with an alignment between participants and a determination to crack on and 'do it'.

'Just do it'... right? It's all very well to say it, but *how* do we 'just do it'? How do we make it so easy that we don't even see we are doing it? How do we manage what we do? How do we decide what to do now, later today, tomorrow, next week or next month? How do we fit in all our meetings and still get through our to-do list? What happens when life gets in the way – an urgent issue crops up, a customer complains or a stressed colleague or friend needs a chat? The real world of getting stuff done involves lots of separate actions being done by lots of different people. How do you understand the chain of actions and which actors are involved in that chain?

This chapter guides you on how to answer these questions. It naturally follows on from Chapter 3.5 (where we introduced the integrated plan), Chapter 4.2 (where we looked at the role of the board and the board pack) and Chapter 4.3 (where we discussed the role of forums and meetings). It gets to the very core of BROP-A's A by showing how to plan and manage the day-to-day actions necessary to implement your integrated plan and reach the next stepping stone along the bridge. Action management reflects the most detailed view of activity in the organization. It provides granular detail of what needs to be done, by whom and by when and enables tracking of progress towards goals and objectives. Returning to the analogy of boulders, rocks, pebbles and sand (see the chapters in Part 3), this chapter focuses on the pebbles and sand – two different types of actions which enable the rocks and boulders to happen.

Why is action management important?

So far, this book has been about strategy design and planning. But no matter how good your designs and plans look on paper, success depends on getting things done on the ground. It depends on how we manage the hundreds, if not thousands, of tasks necessary to implement the integrated plan.

Too often, great ideas and promising initiatives start with drive and enthusiasm and over time get lost in the general black hole of stuff that needs to be done day to day. Common stumbling blocks include the following:

1 People don't understand how (or believe that) a project supports the strategy of the business. This is why we believe in the power of the one-pager. It communicates strategy so that people can understand why they are doing something.

2 People do not always know what they or others are responsible for or what deadlines they are working to. One part of a project might get finished but it might not be passed on to the next person, so it falls between the gaps.

3 Leaders jump from one priority to another, giving impetus to different initiatives on a whim. This lack of consistency means that projects can get dropped and forgotten about.

4 People's days are full of overly long, unnecessary meetings (see Chapter 4.3).

5 People politics delay necessary but tricky conversations – often to a day which never comes.

The importance of action management is emphasized by so many experts. In *Good to Great*, Collins talks about disciplined action. Rumelt constantly refers to the need for action to be governed by a strategic guiding policy. Drucker talks about 'the work' before the workforce. Almost everyone we meet talks about the importance of strategy execution – about getting things done. About action.

There are so many productivity books published and many are the most popular business books around. Take Stephen Covey's *The Seven Habits of Highly Effective People*,[1] Dave Allen's *Getting Things Done*,[2] Atul Gawande's *The Checklist Manifesto*[3] or Gary Keller's *The One Thing*.[4] All are tailored towards understanding how to manage your actions effectively. That's no surprise. Actions arise everywhere we turn. Risk management leads to actions. Key initiatives get broken down, eventually, into actions.

It is a tricky thing to get right. How many of us can say we do it effectively? We all use lists to help us in our daily lives at work and home. But how systematic and consistent are you? How disciplined are you? If we are so busy, why don't we get things done? Do you understand the impact of the delay if you are behind with something? And what that delay might mean for somebody else? Do you overlook things, despite your list? Do some mammoth and daunting tasks get moved from list to list, month to month? Do you sometimes find yourself blocked because you need someone else to do something first before you can complete your action? Action management is a big issue for many people. It's a need which is evidenced by the growing market in action management software (think Monday, Asana, Trello or MS Project). It's a big reason why we built Ārahi.

In his book *State of Denial*, Bob Woodward, a renowned US journalist and author, recounts the failings of the Iraq war. Much of the story centres on Donald Rumsfeld, who was Secretary of Defense at the time and is famous, in part, for talking about known knowns, known unknowns and unknown unknowns (see Chapter 3.3). According to Woodward, Rumsfeld recorded actions on little pieces of white paper which became known as 'snowflakes'. As he explains, Rumsfeld sent these notes around the building: 'There were roughly three kinds – administrative ("Call and arrange a lunch with Fed Chairman Alan Greenspan"), simple thoughts or personal reflections, and calls for information or action.' These snowflakes were managed by one of his aides, Rear Admiral J J Quinn, who delivered them by hand if they were urgent and important: 'The snowflakes were fast and furious… Suddenly there would be a massive request and only hours to answer. Rumsfeld had his own tracking system, which led to more queries and follow-on snowflakes about what had happened to the unanswered snowflakes.'[5] Getting action management right in organizations starts at the top.

If you are a leader, you set the tone. So many people start the day with good intentions, only for them to go out of the window as snowflakes start to fall. Before they know it, they can find themselves buried under an avalanche of unplanned and overwhelming work. This isn't action management. It's action mismanagement. It's worth reflecting on how you dish out actions to your colleagues. Have you ever caused an avalanche of chaos sending them a flurry of orders? Rumsfeld gets a tick for having a system and structure and a cross for creating chaos.

The basics of action management

Not all actions are the same. They vary in complexity. Many are simple – 'call Bob'. No one needs to know that you need to do it or when you've done it. Nothing needs to be traded. It's a verb (call) followed by a noun (Bob). It might only take a minute, literally. These are 'just do it' actions, which we call 'in-out' actions. They come in and you can get them out just as fast. But of course, it's not always that simple. At the other extreme, some actions take concerted effort and negotiation with others who have strong vested interests. Approval might be needed from a broad range of unaligned actors who are difficult to pin down. Consider the action 'Appoint a headhunter to support hiring a NED'. It's a much more involved action than simply calling Bob. Even agreeing on a list of headhunters to invite can take weeks. Then you need to agree on the selection criteria, brief them, assess potential candidates and find time to decide. You need to coordinate diaries for various meetings (doing this for just three busy people can be hard). We call these more complex actions 'governed actions'. Lots of people care about them and might have a role in completing them. The impact is significant and hard to reverse. A governance process needs to be followed, the outcome is recorded and other people need to be kept informed.

It is not an individual sport. Actions have dependencies – you might not be able to start or finish your action until someone else has done something. Or someone else might be waiting for you to complete something. Just as life gets in the way for you, it will also for other people. Your constraints can have a knock-on effect on other people and their constraints can have a knock-on effect on you. A key person might leave or fall sick, or a system might go down. Someone might have a more urgent task on their list than the one you need them to do. This all means that we have to manage our actions as a group.

Most of us are working on many different things at once. CEOs wear multiple hats. In smaller organizations, many executives wear multiple hats. One moment they're the head sales rep and the next, the head of talent acquisition, and the next they might find themselves in event management. (In larger organizations executives focus on their specific area but they still work on many different things at one time.) Non-Executive Directors sit on multiple boards of numerous different businesses. The point is that for many of us, our actions can spiral out of control very quickly.

RUPERT

My lovely wife Vanessa is the most organized person I know. Her numerous to-do lists ensure that she gets stuff done and keeps hundreds of balls in the air. She also has, in my view, a pretty big job and a successful career. As a lawyer, she worked for two of the most prestigious US law firms (in London, but in New York for a while). She was, at times, our chief breadwinner while I pursued my entrepreneurial ambitions. But she became bored with pure law and hankered after a role where she would feel more like part of a team. A fateful conversation with a friend found her in a role reporting to the CFO of a major London university. In this role, she uses her legal skills while leading or supporting many of the most strategic programmes and partnerships. At the time of writing, she has 20 separate partnerships and programmes on the go. She has no direct reports. While reporting directly to the CFO, she also indirectly reports to or works alongside a large number of people and teams. This requires her to sit on lots of different boards and committees. She's a doer. She writes and negotiates contracts and advises various leaders on a large range of topics. She manages many relationships across the globe.

Part of my research for this chapter has involved looking at how Vanessa manages the many different things she needs to get done. Where does she record her actions? How does she stay on top of them? Does she drop balls? She started off recording actions in different notebooks. But 20 different notebooks? That's too many. So, she set up an elaborate tagging system in one notebook, tagging key action pages by project. She's also tried recording actions in Outlook. While helpful, none of these systems is foolproof. I sometimes see her hop off back-to-back calls and turn white as she realizes she might not have recorded all of her actions.

And then there is the family stuff. She has three boys and a fairly useless husband. Her mother is ageing. She takes control of most of our family admin. There's insurance to pay, dog walkers to sort and holidays to book, including car rentals, villas, flights and hotels. The list is truly endless.

Vanessa's life is likely to be typical of many of you reading this book. To manage this level of complexity, we need simple processes and methods. And we need to understand our actions on a deeper level than many of us attempt.

Abraham Lincoln is thought to have said 'Give me six hours to cut down a tree and I will spend the first four sharpening the axe'. It's worth investing time and effort to get action management right. The methods we give you in this chapter will help you to do just that. We hope that following the advice will help you to significantly reduce your cognitive load. As the productivity guru Dave Allen has said: 'Your mind is for having ideas, not holding them.'[6] It's about reducing overwhelm by taking things out of your brain, knowing that you understand your actions completely and putting them in a safe place that you can refer to when necessary.

COD: an action management framework

In *Getting Things Done*, Dave Allen proposes a five-step method for managing workflow, which has been adopted worldwide as the go-to method for organizing life and work. The method involves 1) capturing 'to do' items; 2) clarifying what each one means by determining what to do about them; 3) organizing them and putting them in the appropriate places; 4) reflecting on your list at regular intervals; 5) deciding what needs to get done by choosing the most important tasks to focus on.[7] As is the case with so many of the frameworks that have inspired this book, we have simplified Allen's method by taking the most useful elements of it and reframing it in the context of data. As should be evident by now, we apply the Rule of Three wherever possible. We propose a three-step framework called COD, which stands for:

1. Capture.
2. Organize.
3. Do.

Capturing actions

Capturing actions simply involves understanding what needs to be done, by whom and collecting everything together in one place. There are three steps:

1. Define what needs to be done.
2. Break it into individual actions.
3. Create a list of all your actions in one place.

1. DEFINE WHAT NEEDS TO BE DONE

Take your lead from the projects and sub-projects identified in the integrated plan. You'll remember from Chapter 3.5 that charters are created for each key initiative identified in the POAP. These charters list the projects and sub-projects that need to be planned, owned and tracked for the key initiative to happen. Projects are broken down into sub-projects. To return to the analogy of boulders, rocks, pebbles and sand, while the key initiatives are the boulders, the projects are the rocks.

2. BREAK IT INTO INDIVIDUAL ACTIONS

If you smash boulders and rocks about enough, they become pebbles. Smash them about a bit more and they eventually become sand. Projects are broken down into detailed lists of individual actions that people accept as their responsibility to make happen. It's a question of breaking the big things down bit by bit until you understand the detailed actions.

This is the structured, project management-led way of breaking down what needs to be done into individual actions. Of course, you will capture actions in many different ways. To-do lists arise from conversations, past or upcoming meetings and your personal life too. Capturing is all about just getting everything down.

Revisit Figure 3.5.4 for the structured process of breaking down key initiatives into projects and sub-projects, which are further broken down into governed actions and then smaller, in-out actions.

3. CREATE A LIST OF ALL YOUR ACTIONS IN ONE PLACE

Take a minute to think about all the different places you or your business might store actions. Every business, and every person, has islands of actions. You might have a list in a notepad, a separate one on your computer and yet another one on your phone. Some actions will almost certainly only exist in your head. You might have sticky notes stuck around your desk, or actions on text, email or in other correspondence that you haven't written down anywhere else. What about action logs at the end of meeting minutes? Can you recall them easily? Will you remember to do them? Given this is normal life for most of us, it's easy to see how we can become overwhelmed and occasionally drop the ball. It's also easy to see how actions that are recorded in one month's meeting are often incomplete (or not even started) when the next month's meeting comes around.

Effective action management is close to impossible when your actions are spread far and wide. To properly assess what you've got on your plate, get them into one place. It will free up your brain to think about the important stuff.

Imagine all of your actions, from all of the places that they are kept, being poured into a funnel, ready to be prioritized and organized (see Figure 4.4.1). Everything captured in or on checklists, documents, spreadsheets, brainstorm sessions, risk logs, sticky notes, notice boards, notebooks, emails or phones gets put in a long to-do list. This is not about categorizing, sorting or thinking about timescales and deadlines. It is just about creating a list. 'Call Bob', 'Appoint a headhunter to support hiring a NED', 'Source supplier for

FIGURE 4.4.1 The key to action capture is getting everything into one place

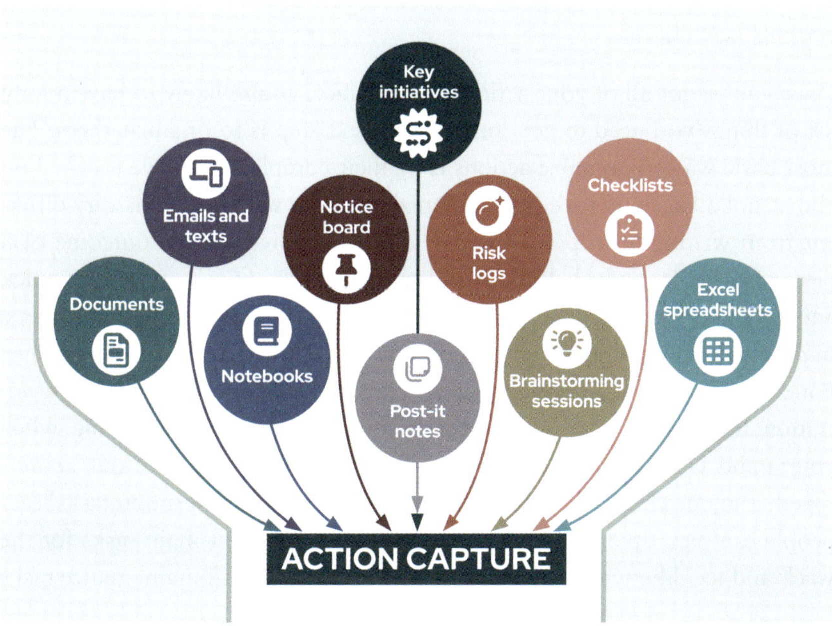

office fit-out' and 'Move infrastructure from local supplier to AWS'. All these actions sit alongside each other, despite the variation in scope and complexity of the tasks.

DOES EVERY ACTION NEED TO BE CAPTURED?

You might be wondering whether you need to capture every single thing, no matter how small. It depends on the system that you use and how quick and easy it is to capture your actions. We believe that all actions raised in a meeting should be recorded, assigned and tracked, no matter how small they are. It breeds good discipline and serves as a useful reminder of what was discussed and agreed. It could be argued that outside of meetings, there is no need to capture actions that would take longer to record than to execute. This is really down to personal preference. We may be more likely to forget those actions than our bigger, meatier tasks. Perhaps this means we should capture even the tiniest action. Another argument is the way we feel when we accomplish something on our list. It's long been known that we get a release of dopamine every time we complete a task. Maybe that's why some of us have been known to write tasks on our to-do lists even after we've completed them. We're addicted to the feeling we get when we cross them off. And as dopamine is a known motivator, this (some might argue futile) practice can spur us on to complete the next thing on our list.

Organizing actions

Once you've got all of your actions in one place, you're likely to have a long list of things you need to get done, so the next step is to organize them. The most basic way to organize actions is by their complexity. As we touched on above, not all actions are equal. Organizing dinner with a client is very different from writing a proposal for that client or delivering the outcome of a piece of work. It can be helpful to understand which of your actions are quick and easy and which need more time, thought and involvement from others. In that way, you can assign chunks of time to complete similar tasks together. For example, you might prefer to complete actions that need your full concentration, like writing or reviewing documents first thing in the morning, when your mind is fresh. You might also like to complete your in-out actions together in one chunk. At Ārahi we have a list of 'Friday afternoon tasks' that people can pick up and do when they've completed their main tasks for the week and feel like winding down before the weekend. All maintenance tasks on the list are put into the 'Friday afternoon' bucket. Developers just pick a few from the Kanban board each week and get them done.

IN-OUT ACTIONS (SAND)

In-out actions are defined by the fact that one person owns the action, it's a task that just needs to get done and the owner of the action doesn't need to tell anyone else that they've done it. Everything starts as an in-out action, and a large number of actions stay that way. They don't need to be organized any further than collecting them together and perhaps prioritizing them.

In-out actions include things like sending emails, phoning people and scheduling meetings. They can also include slightly more involved actions such as small writing tasks (e.g. blog posts), depending on the complexity of the task, whether or not there is a deadline and who needs to be involved or know about it. There are certain factors which differentiate them from governed actions, namely, they do not need:

- a timeframe
- to be monitored, tracked or reviewed by an approver
- a project plan
- a team.

The simple nature of in-out actions means that they can be described in a short sentence: one verb followed by as few words as possible to describe what needs to be done. The following could all be examples of in-out actions:

- Call Luis
- Ring the vet
- Invite Shafali to lunch
- Email the proposal to Sunil
- Introduce Diana to Edwin
- Finish writing the blog post.

The owner of the action captures it themselves. As above, the reason for capturing it is so that they don't forget to do it (and for that dopamine hit). There is no other reason. Note that if the owner wants to delegate the task to someone else, it is no longer considered an in-out action. At that point, it becomes a governed action.

GOVERNED ACTIONS (PEBBLES)

Governed actions are more complex tasks. Unlike in-out actions, they include one or more of the following:

- a timeframe
- a need to be monitored through meetings and forums
- a set of dependencies (and other people involved in the process)
- an approver and/or list of those who should be informed of the outcome.

Governed actions always involve people (individuals or groups) other than the owner of the action. This inevitably means that issues such as responsibility, approval rights, supporting roles, progress tracking and keeping people informed come into play.

There are three subtypes of governed action: 'others care' actions, 'monkey on the shoulder' actions and 'governed workflow' actions.

OTHERS CARE ACTIONS

For many actions, people other than the owner need to know about it. These actions don't have complicated workflows – there is just one person involved in them. But once they've done it, they need to let someone else know. The following are examples of 'others care' actions:

- Get tax advice on the option scheme by the end of next week and let Heidi (CHRO) know the outcome.
- Negotiate terms with Acme Inc. Ensure Ramona (CRO) and Paco (CPO) know the agreement.
- Get employee references for Maria (development candidate) and let Heidi (CHRO) know the outcome.
- Sort Christmas party and let ExCo know the outcome.

MONKEY ON THE SHOULDER ACTIONS

These actions are transferred to someone other than the person who captures them. 'Monkey on the shoulder' is learned by many management consultants during their training. When capturing actions, you ask, 'Who's got the monkey?' Of course, everyone is busy and people can be reluctant to put up their hand. But meetings can't conclude until someone has agreed to have the monkey on their shoulder. This game is helpful because it emphasizes the need for ownership to be transferred. The person who thought of or captured the action might not be the right person to own it and get it done.

Responsibility can be suggested, but it's not relinquished until someone else has accepted ownership. The following are examples of 'monkey on the shoulder' actions:

- The bank needs to be informed we might be close to breaking our covenants. Felicity (CFO) should give them a heads-up.
- Schedule an ExCo offsite. Sam to find a date and venue.
- Ekon to investigate why customer X is unhappy with their account manager.

GOVERNED WORKFLOW ACTIONS

Some critical and complex actions require approval workflows and additional support and expertise. We call these 'governed workflow' actions. Consider the following action:

- Paco (CPO) to source a supplier to do the office fit-out with support from the office manager, Marcus. Felicity (CFO) and Bridget (CEO) to approve. ExCo to be informed.

The person who captured the action assigned ownership of it to Paco. Paco will accept ownership, but he can't source a supplier on his own. He needs Marcus's help. He can't go ahead without Felicity and Bridget's approval and he also needs to keep ExCo informed. This single action has many elements with complex workflows. Getting it done is very different from getting an in-out action done, or even an 'others care' or 'monkey on the shoulder' action. There are a couple of frameworks that can help to understand how to complete these more complex actions, which we explain in the final section of this chapter: Doing actions. This is the final aspect of the COD framework.

ORGANIZING GOVERNED ACTIONS

There are several ways to organize your governed actions. Here, we explain how to do it by time, context and frequency.

Organizing by time This is the most obvious way to organize governed actions. Is there a target date the action needs to be done? If it needs to be done today, is there a target time? 12:00 or 20:00? Once you have an idea of target end dates you can sort your actions into what needs to be done now, next or later. This is about organizing them into clear timeframe buckets. Think of it in terms of sorting out a deck of cards. You have a deck of

52 cards. How could you organize them? You could put all the Aces and the picture cards (the Queens, Kings and Jacks) into one bucket, regardless of their suit (we're ignoring the Jokers). Then the remaining Spades and Clubs (consisting of 18 number cards) could go into a second and the Hearts and Diamonds (consisting of another 18 number cards) into a third. This is just breaking down the list of things to give you a clearer picture of what you need to get done and when. So now, you have the 16 cards that are Jacks or stronger in one pile – these might be the things you need to get done now. Once your most urgent tasks are in one pile, it makes it easier to sort these further if you wish. You could put the Aces together, the Kings together, the Queens and the Jacks together.

Another way to organize actions is to tag them so you can sort them and find them easily. If we continue with the playing card analogy, you could tag by colour (red or black), suit (Spades, Clubs, Hearts or Diamonds) or strength (high – picture cards, medium – numbers 7 to 10 and low – numbers 2 to 6). These tags work together, so you can search combinations, for example a search of 'high Spades' would result in all the Spades picture cards.

Organizing by context Dave Allen talks about organizing actions by context. What sort of action is it? Is it a call or an email? Is it an action you can get done on your daily commute? Or is it a cognitively demanding action that you need a period of focused time for? These actions can be tagged as 'cognitive'. Is it something that needs to be arranged (tag as diarize)? Tidying your desk could be tagged as a 'chore'. It can be incredibly helpful to tag actions that need to be done with someone else (these actions can be tagged as 'someone'). They can be tagged further to indicate who that someone is. For example – actions that you need to complete with Ekon, Felicity or Chara. When you next meet with one of these people, it would then be easy to locate the list of actions that you need to sort together.

Organizing by frequency Another context for actions is whether they are one-offs, repeat or recurring actions. We have been writing this as if we are living in a world of one-offs. In reality, most things repeat, and many actions are recurring (the difference between a repeat action and a recurring action is that recurring actions repeat on a fixed timescale). These are the types of actions you might want to set reminders for. The action 'Write CEO View from the Bridge' recurs every quarter (or month, depending on your board meeting cadence). You might need to renew your insurance once a year. Every time you start a new project you will need to perform a series of repeat actions. For example, 'List the key stakeholder contacts', 'Sort the weekly client debrief', 'Sort project codes', 'Onboard team', 'Arrange a kick-off meeting', 'Write the project plan'.

These lists of repeat actions are like standard checklists. In *The Checklist Manifesto*, Gawande talks about how checklists help us to navigate the complexities of the world around us. As a surgeon, he discusses the power of checklists in the complicated world of medicine as a tool to avoid making mistakes.[8] They are vital in life-and-death scenarios such as piloting an aircraft with hundreds of people on board or using a sharp knife to open up someone on a surgery table. The pilot or surgeon methodically progresses through each step so that they can be sure they have thought of everything. The process is set using the best and proven practices, and so long as it is followed, you can't go far wrong. Checklists are the best way to build processes for specific contexts and are proven to reduce errors. Of course, to create a checklist you first need to define what the 'best way' looks like, whether that's to onboard a new employee, perform a disciplinary process, launch a new campaign, deal with a customer complaint or organize a team offsite. In your personal life, checklists can be useful to help with packing for an annual holiday or when sending Christmas cards. The point is to make life easy and reduce or eradicate the potential for error. There's no room for error on the surgery table.

Doing actions

Doing actions require you to either simply do them and mark them as done (in the case of in-out actions) or, in the case of governed actions, provide progress updates, gain approvals or keep people informed. Getting governed actions done requires an understanding of dependency chains, as we explained in Chapter 3.5. We live in an interdependent world. Very often, some actions can't happen until something else has happened first, or some actions can't be considered complete until another action has been started or finished.

We all have blockers that prevent us from getting our work done. In *The Hard Thing About Hard Things*, Ben Horowitz describes a time when his company was in crisis and they had 60 days to live. He had a rule that if anyone was stuck on anything, for any reason, i.e. if they were 'blocked', they could not be in that state for any longer than 24 hours. He scheduled daily meetings to check that roadblocks were resolved within this timeframe: 'Whenever a large organization attempts to do anything, it always comes down to a single person who can delay the entire project. An engineer might get stuck waiting for a decision or a manager may think she doesn't have the authority to make a critical purchase. These small, seemingly minor hesitations can cause fatal delays.'[9]

THE TEN COMPONENTS OF ACTIONS

The unequal nature of actions means that some actions need larger amounts of data assigned to them than others. It depends on the context and complexity of the action. Actions can have up to ten different components, as shown in Figure 4.4.2:

1. Action – what needs to get done? This should be a short sentence with just enough detail to remember what it is.
2. Owner – who is responsible for ensuring the action is completed?
3. Status – actions are either open, closed, paused or blocked (the difference between paused and blocked is that you can choose to pause an action. You don't choose to block actions). The status is shown in BRAG colours.
4. Due date – the deadline.
5. Description – provides the context for the action to help others understand the requirements.
6. Progress update – these will be necessary for larger, more significant and more complex actions that are being tracked by specific forums and/or the board.
7. Expected close – those who need to be kept informed normally want to know when the action will be done.
8. Workflow (CRASI) – actions can require multiple actors playing a range of roles.
9. Dependencies – many actions require other actions to be done or started before they can be completed.
10. Outcome – people may need to be informed about the outcome (see CRASI, below).

In-out actions only need the three components shown at the top of the pyramid: action, owner and status. Larger and more complex governed actions – those that require other actions to be completed first, support from

FIGURE 4.4.2 The ten components of actions

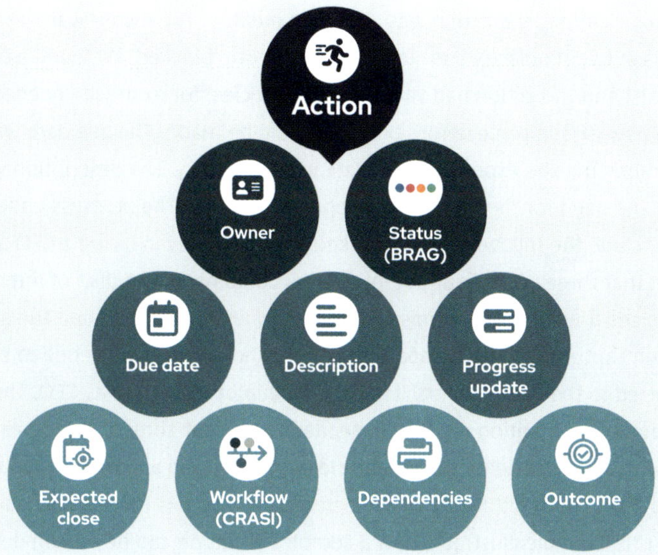

specific individuals, or that have lots of people who care about whether or not they get done – require more data components.

Note that actions can be TAF-arized, as described in Chapter 1.3. This means assigning Target, Actual and Forecast data to them. In terms of the elements above, the target is the deadline and the forecast is the expected close date. The date that the action is completed provides the actual date.

RUPERT

We had just completed a Series C investment round and one of my actions was to select an auditor. This was complex and had lots of different dependencies. According to our investors' articles, we needed to select a Big 4 auditor and check for conflicts of interest, i.e. that we didn't select a firm that was a client or channel partner. Three out of the four potential firms had a possible conflict of interest.

There would be legal and cost repercussions if we failed to hit the deadline. We were facing a delay in recruiting a new CFO, who needed to be in place before any progress could be made. We had lots of new processes, new hires to recruit, sales targets to hit and clients and employees to keep happy.

In this example, the action was 'Select an auditor'. The owner was the CFO (who wasn't yet in place). The status was therefore 'blocked'. I'd found a conflict of interest and the action had various dependencies, for example I needed to get the new CFO in place before progress could be made. The due date was 1 November, but the expected close date was 31 January. The description would include the need for the auditor to be one of the Big 4. The progress update might include the following text: 'Blocked due to a delay in hiring a CFO and the fact that three of the four potential firms could have a conflict of interest. Need to see if we can get permission from the investor to open up.' The action had been captured by the Company Secretary and ownership needed to be transferred to the CFO. For now, I had ownership of the action as CEO. The workflow would mention those who needed to be kept abreast of progress and those with approval rights. The finance leadership group and the new board wanted status updates, including expected close dates. The board had approval rights. This example illustrates how a complex situation can be broken down into simple steps.

CRASI – an accountability matrix for action management

In Chapter 1.3 we introduced CRASI, an accountability framework for action management. We'll return to Paco and his office fit-out to show how CRASI works in practice. Paco's action is described in three sentences: 'Paco (CPO) to source a supplier to do the office fit-out with support from the office manager. Felicity (CFO) and Bridget (CEO) to approve. ExCo to be informed.' There are many elements in these three sentences and a few different people are involved:

- Capture (C): Sam, the Secretary of ExCo, captures the action in a meeting. He includes the action in the minutes to give a clear audit trail.
- Responsible (R): Sam allocates Paco the action after a quick game of monkey on the shoulder. Paco accepts it and becomes responsible for getting it done.
- Approving (A): At the same time, Sam sets Felicity and Bridget as individuals who both need approval rights.

FIGURE 4.4.3 CRASI framework example

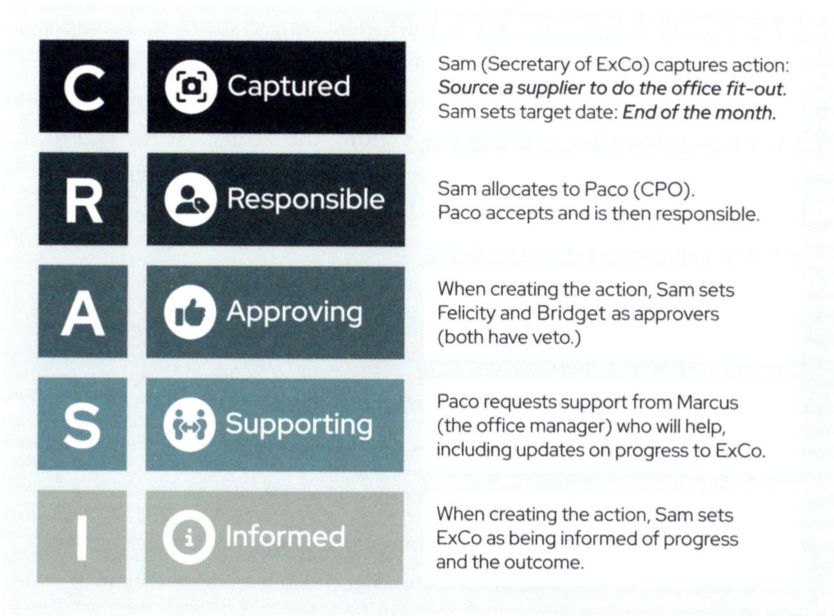

- Supporting (S): Paco requests support from Marcus (the office manager) who will help keep the progress updated for the ExCo.
- Informed (I): Sam stipulates that ExCo need to be kept informed of progress and the outcome of the action.

Final thoughts

Rumelt tells a fantastic story in *Good Strategy/Bad Strategy* about the young Frederick Taylor. Considered to be the father of management consulting, he was the first person to apply a scientific method to management. Back in 1890, when Taylor was in his early thirties, he met the wealthy steel magnate Andrew Carnegie at a cocktail party. Carnegie said to Taylor: 'Young man, if you can tell me something about management that is worth hearing, I will send you a check for ten thousand dollars.' Taylor came straight back at Carnegie and said: 'Make a list of the ten most important things you can do. And then, start doing number one.' He got that cheque.[10]

Having been through the process of researching and writing this book, we know what we would say to Carnegie. It would be similar to Taylor's response, but we would add that the one most important thing should stem from your strategy. Action management is about prioritization and focus and coming full circle back to the most important thing which, in the context of this book, is the next stepping stone along the bridge. At the end of the day, action management is about how you execute your strategic intent – it is the single most important aspect of bringing a strategy to life.

REMEMBER THIS

1. If an idea doesn't result in action, it is a meaningless idea.
2. Find a way to make disciplined action easy and habitual.
3. Capture actions all in one place, then organize and do them.
4. We are what we repeatedly do. From an organizational context, we are not only what we do as individuals, we are what we do with those around us.
5. As a leader, focus on removing blockers.

Notes

1. Covey, S (2020) *The Seven Habits of Highly Effective People* (Reissue edition) Simon & Schuster, London
2. Allen, D (2015) *Getting Things Done: The art of stress-free productivity*, Piatkus, London
3. Gawande, A (2011) *The Checklist Manifesto: How to get things right*, Profile Books, London
4. Keller, G with Papasan, J (2019) *The One Thing: The surprisingly simple truth behind extraordinary results* (Revised edition), Bard Press, Austin, Texas
5. Woodward, B (2006) *State of Denial: Bush at war, part III*, Simon & Schuster, New York
6. Allen, D (2015) *Getting Things Done: The art of stress-free productivity*, Piatkus, London
7. Ibid.
8. Gawande, A (2011) *The Checklist Manifesto: How to get things right*, Profile Books, London
9. Horowitz, B (2014) *The Hard Thing About Hard Things: Building a business when there are no easy answers*, HarperBusiness, New York
10. Rumelt, R (2011) *Good Strategy/Bad Strategy: The difference and why it matters*, Crown Currency, New York

4.5

Improving the odds of breakthrough returns

Keep the interests of the business at the heart of everything you do

Introduction

Can you walk and chew gum at the same time? Can you have your head in the clouds and your feet on the ground? Can you take advantage of the upside potential while managing the downside risk? The harsh reality is that the odds of success are stacked against you. So many try and so many fail. But enough succeed. These successes and failures provide many themes that we can all learn from. We have done our level best to build those out in this book.

You cannot do this on your own. As we have said many times throughout this book, this is a team sport. Find your mentors. Learn from them. Use them as a sounding board. Build a relationship with your Chair. Plan meeting agendas together and agree on the key things that need to be addressed. Recruit a Chief of Staff to be your eyes and ears on the ground.

We discussed our definition of breakthrough returns in Chapter 1.1. Our idea of achieving a breakthrough is tripling profits in five years, generating a 25 per cent return. The reality is that most companies don't achieve this. Most will not break through. Schumpeter's creative destruction means that those who do aren't likely to maintain their position for very long. This is our final chapter. In it, we discuss some of the softer factors to be aware of as you grow, including culture and people politics. We draw extensively on Greiner's Growth Model, an old but not forgotten framework which attempts to forecast phases of growth and crises that organizations typically experience on the journey. We start with the importance of building momentum.

The importance of building momentum

The Flywheel Effect is another concept Jim Collins developed in *Good to Great*. Collins explains that companies don't go from good to great in 'one fell swoop'. There is no 'single defining action'. No 'killer innovation'. Instead, companies build momentum. He likens it to pushing a flywheel. At first, it's heavy and extremely difficult to move. It takes a huge amount of effort to complete one turn. But you keep going and each turn becomes a little easier. The flywheel moves faster. At some point, you hit a breakthrough and the wheel starts turning by itself – 'the momentum of the thing kicks in your favor, hurling the flywheel forward, turn after turn… whoosh!.. its own heavy weight working for you'.[1] Collins' point is that companies achieve breakthroughs by building a sense of momentum. Momentum takes time to build but it is that, in the end, that generates breakthroughs. It's not possible to identify which push caused the wheel to go so fast. Rather, it is the 'accumulation of effort applied in a consistent direction'.

People use different metaphors, but a consistent message underlies them all: it's action upon action that will get you to where you want to go. Habitual action is at the root of every framework. BROP-A and QFOR-A both end with 'A' for good reason. There's no one thing, no magic pill. If there was, everyone would do it and then, boom! It would no longer be the magical one thing. Horowitz talks about how there is no silver bullet in *The Hard Thing About Hard Things*. Instead, successful companies consistently and relentlessly fire lead bullets until they achieve breakthrough success.

As we hope this book has shown, there is a set of practices that, if they become habitual, improve the odds of success. We have not said anything particularly new. Nothing we have written about wouldn't have been easily knowable from reading a dozen (or perhaps two dozen!) well-known books and articles (and numerous podcasts). Most of the wisdom in these pieces can be distilled down to a few key learnings which are very much in the general business consciousness. People talk about creating a blue ocean, Porter's Activity System (which we refined into the Value-Cap Map), or the Hedgehog Concept all the time. This book's difference lies in the fact that we have pulled it all together and translated the thinking into action that turns the dial on your ability to execute. As we said in Chapter 1.3, this requires integrated thinking. It requires you to connect the dots and then 'do the do'. It requires you to see the metrics that matter.

All the clichés are true. It requires discipline. Consistency. It requires a distinctive strategy that is hard to replicate in a big enough market where you can dominate your niche. This means excelling for customers who value a unique set of value factors that you can truly own, for your geography or industry.

The growth journey

In their book *The Founder's Mentality*, Chris Zook and James Allen talk about the pathways to sustainable growth from the perspective of two very different types of companies – a fast-growing insurgent from an emerging market and an established, incumbent multinational. Zook and Allen state that Global 2000 companies look to outgrow their markets, on a revenue basis, by an average of two times. When they analysed the number of companies that managed this ambition over a sustained ten-year period, they found that only roughly one in ten achieved it. That means that 90 per cent failed to achieve their basic growth ambitions. Of the companies that didn't make it, only around 15 per cent blamed the markets. Instead, they mainly cited internal issues, such as insufficient resources, culture (for example, risk aversion), an inability to focus or organizational complexity. The authors attribute the large degree of failure to a loss of what they call the 'founder's mentality', establishing that of the one in ten companies that achieved their growth ambitions, nearly two in three were governed by the founder's mentality. They found that founder-led companies outperformed S&P 500 companies 3.1 times in 2014.

In high-level terms, they define a founder's mentality as 'insurgency', 'front-line obsession' and 'owner mindset'. Using the Rule of Three, they define each of these three elements further:

- Insurgency is defined as having a 'bold mission', 'spikiness' and 'limitless horizon'.
- Front-line obsession is defined as 'relentless experimentation', 'front-line empowerment' and 'customer advocacy'.
- Owner mindset is defined as having a 'strong cash focus', 'bias for action' and an 'aversion to bureaucracy'.

They found that companies that started as fantastic insurgents with a high founder's mentality and no scale or scope lost their unique spark as they grew into incumbents. They describe this unique spark as a 'common set of motivating attitudes and behaviors that can usually be traced back to a bold, ambitious founder who got it right the first time around'. These companies consider themselves 'insurgents, waging war on their industry... on behalf of an underserved customer, or creating an entirely new industry altogether'.[2]

Greiner's Growth Model

To break through, your organization will inevitably increase in size and pass through various thresholds. The types of processes, management capability and activities change at each threshold. This can be viewed through the lens of Larry Greiner's growth model, which dates from 1972.[3] He analysed empirical research on organizational development in an attempt to create a model of the overall process. Greiner found that nearly all companies experience the same phases of growth (and growing pains) as they expand. Growth is characterized by periods of stability and crisis, and each phase brings a different type of crisis. For example, in Phase 1, growth is fuelled by creativity. Energetic founders create new products and find new markets. The company is small, so informal communication works fine at first. But as the company expands, more formal communication is needed. This stage ends with a leadership crisis and professional managers are hired. The firm enters Phase 2, the 'Growth through direction' phase. Greiner originally proposed five phases. He later added a sixth phase, 'Growth through collaboration', which follows a crisis of internal growth at the end of Phase 5. The phases are shown in Figure 4.5.1.

Companies reach a point where growth can only come from mergers and acquisitions activity. Greiner thought of it in terms of the age of an organization, but equally it can be thought of as organization size in terms of headcount, revenue and number of KODs. In reality, we're talking about the amount of complexity.

Every landmark that you break through means you're likely to enter a new Greiner phase. Each one brings change and presents new challenges. Each one brings inherent risks, many of them cultural, which should be factored into your risk management. At each landmark, prepare yourself for change. Think about what your POAP needs to include to help with the inevitable crises. As you change and grow, the board changes and grows with you. Every stage brings new governance with it. An insurgent company that begins life with founders making all the decisions can, eventually, transform into a Phase 6 company with multiple boards for different regions.

FIGURE 4.5.1 Greiner's growth model

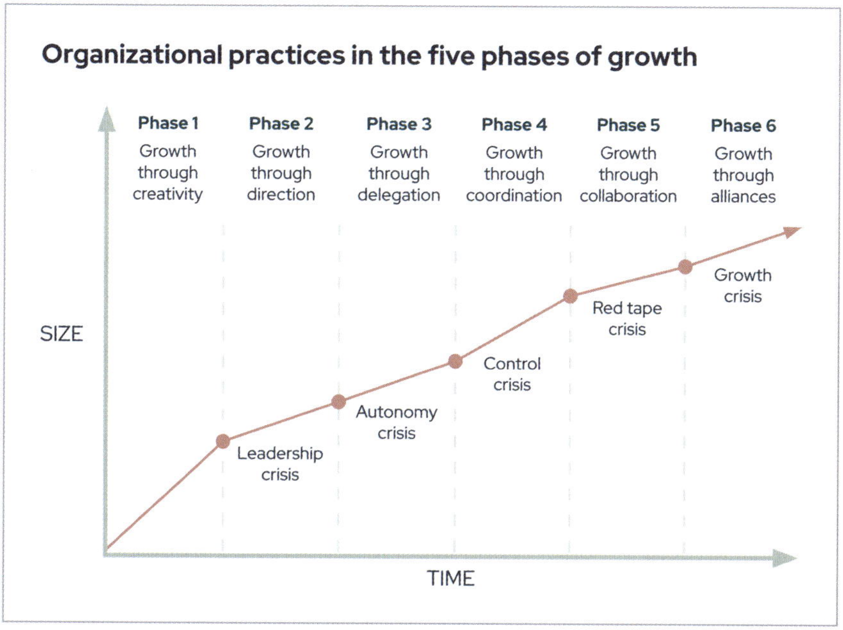

SOURCE Reprinted by permission of *Harvard Business Review* from 'Evolution and revolution as organizations grow' by Larry E Greiner, May–June 1998. Copyright © 1998 by Harvard Business Publishing; all rights reserved.

A TYPICAL TRAJECTORY

When a business is founded by a few people, everything is about the hustle. A few people might be hired, but the team is small. Everyone knows everyone else intimately. This can be an intensely wonderful experience, but it can also be stressful. It tends to go one of two ways – either you're as thick as thieves or the thing implodes before it even gets started. I (Rupert) have experienced this phase twice. They are crazy times that are the best of times. They are extremely creative. You're producing unique value from nothing. It is just cool. There is no money, or close to no money. But there's hope and unreasonable belief. With Orgvue, it took 15 months before we could show something. Most of the work was on the backend and data model. Ārahi was similar, but I had seen the movie before, so I knew the drill. I knew we had to sort the backend data layer, think hard about the brand and nail the small niche to cross the chasm on.

Crossing the chasm is a concept developed by Geoffrey Moore in his book of the same name.[4] Many companies, especially B2B tech start-ups, fall into the 'chasm' at some point. It's a metaphor for when things stop working, for when growth stalls and you don't know what to do about it. According to Moore, to cross the chasm, you should pick a beachhead. He uses the analogy of the Allied forces storming the beaches on D-Day. They focused huge resources on getting a foothold on the beaches. It took months for them to break out of Normandy, but securing their beachhead on that very first day gave them a base from which to expand. So, learn the lessons. Pick your beachhead. Find your niche. Where are you going to focus all your attention? Pick a market where people know each other to increase your chances of word-of-mouth referrals. The first phase is landing those anchor clients, delighting them, learning and improving fast through rapid iteration. This process gets you to proven market fit. In SaaS, this is widely believed to be $1 million of ARR and 10 to 20 customers. You need enough customers to show there will be repeat buyers.

There is very little structure to the organization at this point. You might have a CTO or lead developer. But by and large, titles are irrelevant. Everyone does whatever they can to pitch in and help. As CEO, I (Rupert) am the chief strategist, I pay the bills and I'm responsible for testing (QA). I also buy pizzas, coffee and office supplies. I'm a head chef and a chief bottle washer. When we first got an office, we all assembled the IKEA furniture. We held a soft launch event, my three sons and one of their friends served drinks and food, collected coats and manned the door as our welcome party (or security detail). Stories were created, memories made. A culture formed. We were entirely driven by what Zook and Allen call the founder's mentality.

Five become ten, then fifteen. At this point, it's still small enough to reap the benefits of a start-up. It's still cool. It's when you hit 20 people that, suddenly, things can get harder. In the Greiner vernacular, this would be a crisis of 'leadership'. It's when management systems and processes need to be implemented. The first phase is up and $1 million ARR or $2–3 million/20 FTE... and if you raise money, Series A (see Chapter 3.2). The next phase means you have a leadership team. You have someone responsible for finance and, at some point, HR. The 'can-do' scrappy days are over. A leadership team meets, has objectives and starts to run the business.

When you hit this point, the founders are still the driving force. They are likely to be the lead, if not only, salespeople and voice on the market. Once you hit the next threshold, be that 120–150 employees, $10 million ARR or $20 million revenue, the founder can no longer be that person, nor, indeed, can the CEO (if they are not the same). An expanded management team – managers of managers – is needed and authority is delegated. This is the Series B/C stage. You enter the realm of C-suite, executive titles. The first one to recruit is likely to be a Chief Sales or Revenue Officer. You may have four layers in your organization. You will have a proper board with board packs,

NEDs and a Chair. You will start to embed 'proper' process, be that performance management, onboarding, product release management or budgeting.

The amount of change is huge. People will constantly talk about 'professionalizing', i.e. the need to bring in functional professionals who are experts in their field. 'Grown-ups'. This is all huge. It won't feel the same and it comes with significant risk. One risk, articulated so well by Zook and Allen, is the difficulty of maintaining the culture that made you great in the first place. Beware of over-corporatizing by bringing in people from large enterprises who want the excitement of being part of a 'start-up' and 'high-growth business'. Beware of importing big company processes too early, which are designed for a Greiner Phase 5 or 6 business. It is easy to overshoot in the search for professionalism and bring in too much complexity too soon. Beware of the mercenaries.

People from big business think in terms of the size of their teams. They are professional managers, focused on building large teams. They love building fiefdoms. Their little empires. This can happen overnight. You break through a phase and the organization's structure changes. All sorts of inefficiencies start to hit.

Another risk is that you can become too internally focused. Your days involve meetings after meetings. We wrote about this in Chapter 4.3. You know you're in trouble when everyone starts talking about being 'back-to-back' and arriving five minutes late to meetings because they need a bathroom break. It means that five to ten people lose five to ten minutes of their day, waiting for Late Liam to arrive.

In Chapter 3.2 we explained Ansoff's Growth Matrix and the revenue growth bridge. At a certain point, to achieve the next step in growth, you will expand. This might mean expanding into a new geography or channel or introducing a new product. As we do this, we add KODs. We add objectives related to sales or contribution, which are broken down by KOD as described in Chapter 3.4. Each KOD has an owner – someone who is responsible for it. Who owns North America, EMEA or APAC? Who owns lead generation, sales, delivery or support? What about sales in APAC? Or credit control in EMEA? At this point, you start to need a matrix. You can hit yet another crisis. In Greiner's words, it's a crisis of red tape, and bureaucracy. Rules, approvals, submission of papers. Global meetings where different functions come together. The sales kick-off meeting for the year.

In *Data-Driven Organization Design*, I (Rupert) wrote extensively about how to design an organization for Greiner's phases. I even explained a metric to quantify bureaucracy, which is broken into the number of sub-functions needed to approve a decision and the number of levels up the organization you have to go to gain 'approval'. This is where, in my view, you need a professional group managing your organization design and the planning of your workforce, called Organizational Planning and Analysis. It's HR's twin to Finance's FP&A, and the subject of my book *Organizational Planning and Analysis*. When you reach these final stages, a whole new set of capabilities is needed. The number of roles you have will proliferate. You are running a complex beast. It risks taking on a life of its own. It becomes bloated and inefficient. The culture that made you unique is a distant memory. Your purpose, the thing that made your team fully committed, and devote an unreasonable amount of their lives to you, has disappeared. That 'special something' might be long gone. The longer you can keep it, the better. Your team are now employees. Growth may need to come from mergers and acquisitions. The innovation and creation gene has bitten the dust. Many organizations who reach this final Greiner stage hit the wall and disappear or decline back into irrelevance.

As we wrote in Chapter 1.1, the average lifespan of companies on S&P's index is likely to drop to 15 to 20 years by 2030. That's down from 30 to 35 years in the 1970s. Nokia is a great case example of what can happen. They reportedly knew what Apple was developing two and half years before the iPhone's release in 2007. But Nokia had gone too far down the Greiner curve. It was a massive set of matrices. It had 32 products across the globe with well over 50 per cent of the market. All their engineering leadership was long gone. The company was being run by accountants and organizational complexity meant that they couldn't react. As we wrote in Chapter 1.3, when Jobs returned to Apple in 1997, he removed complexity. He brought back the founder's mentality.[5]

Sustaining success: some practical advice for you and our younger selves

This could, on its own, be an entire book. As we wrap up, here are some parting thoughts and reflections. It is one thing to achieve a breakthrough. It is quite another to maintain it. In 2018, Jeff Bezos said the following about the company he had grown from the ground up: 'I predict one day Amazon will fail. Amazon will go bankrupt. If you look at large companies, their lifespans tend to be 30-plus years, not 100-plus years. We have to try to delay that day as long as possible.'[6] Andy Grove is right. Only the paranoid survive. That's why Chapter 3.3, on risk, is so crucial. Each stage in the life cycle of a business brings different risks. Way back in 1972, Greiner positioned them as certainties. So be forewarned. You know it's going to happen, so plan for it. With scale and complexity comes inevitable loss.

So, what can we learn from this? I (Rupert) am lucky. I'm having a second go at building something from nothing. In doing so, I wrote down my learnings. I have a list of 70 things I hope to repeat. Things I did well and hope I can do again. But I also have a 50-strong list of things I wish I hadn't done or could have done and didn't. I did more right than wrong, but I made a lot of 'avoidable' mistakes. Some are personal. Many relate to people. Some can't be written down and published. Many are generic. We have both witnessed many mistakes that other people have made. A simple one is: 'Revenue is vanity, profit is sanity.' It is often worse than just 'revenue'. It is headcount. When asked about a business, all too often it is easy to say, 'Oh we are now x-hundred people.' All too often, this posturing is driven by nothing but ego. Fundamentally, business growth is all about profitability and cash. It's that simple. It doesn't matter how big your team is so long as you can get this right.

Our advice is to outsource as much as possible for as long as possible. Keep the team as small as possible for as long as you can. Focus on your core. Triple down on this. How long can you keep finance, HR, infrastructure, legal and branding out? If there is a component you can buy, buy it. AWS and other cloud providers are amazing. Outsource to them. Build channel relationships – look for those who can help you sell at scale.

Another pitfall we have witnessed time and again is too much focus on exit. Exit, exit, exit. When? How much? And to whom? Our advice is to focus on building a great business, not on the endpoint. The over-focus on exit impacts investment decisions and creates myopic short-term behaviour. It also attracts mercenaries, not missionaries. After a two-to-three-year hold with an expected exit in two years, does it make sense to risk investing in a new feature, a new market, or a new acquisition? Does it make sense to invest in anything that can't pay back in a year? The 'talent' hired by senior executives is likely to be highly incentivised on LTIP (Long Term Incentive Plans), i.e. options that pay out on an event. This might represent the greatest wealth-generation moment of their lives. For many, it might be the only payout. For others, they might get another shot at it if the exit happens soon enough. Reward packages can be almost entirely focused on exit, even though the best thing for the business is likely to be to continue investing. Sadly, the best interests of the business often take a back seat to the personal motivations and drivers of managers.

At Investec, Ian Kantor's only question was often, 'What is in the best interests of the company?' Our friend Matt Lyons, an experienced private equity investor, says that the role of any board is to take care of the business in terms of all shareholders. We like this pastoral language. As a director, your fiducial duty is to the business. It isn't to any individual shareholder, it's to the interests of the business. At certain points, certain shareholders might need an exit or you might be acquired, but if that's the only focus, you lose sight of what's in the best interests of the business. Think about your incentive programmes and the risks you are creating. Everything is connected.

Because you had to 'professionalize', many of these individuals won't have been with you on the journey. They are only with you for three, perhaps five years. The principal-agent problem has been documented and researched since the 1970s.[7] Game theory has been used to try to align incentives (hence those options) and reduce moral hazard (where you have an incentive to increase exposure to risk because you don't bear the full cost of that risk). But as just described, those very incentives create new types of behaviours. LTIP makes people too risk averse. The long-term value of the business risks being damaged because a short-term event is what is most desired by those with the most information and influence. This is an internal preventable risk, as described in Chapter 3.3. If the senior executives are obsessed with exit, everyone will be. This is interesting because so much of the literature on principal-agent theory is about the agents (the managers) wanting to take huge risks so they can get big rewards (bonuses, pay increases). In *The Shareholder Value Myth*, Lynn Stout charts the rise of the principal agent whereby corporate directors and executives are hired as agents of the shareholders (principals). In this capacity, the agents' only legitimate job is to maximize wealth for the shareholders. This focus only on shareholder value all too often drives a short-term mentality and can damage shareholder value in the long term.[8]

These common traps and issues can conspire to reduce the upside. They can make the board and leaders take their eyes off the ball. They can give a more focused, better-run competitor – a competitor who may have leapfrogged you by taking a more long-term strategic approach and acting in the best interests of the business. Is this a kill-or-be-killed world? To some extent, yes. From another perspective, no. The world is a huge place. The abundance theory dictates that there is enough space for everyone. The world economy is $105 trillion. That's a crazy big number.

When things don't go to plan

You will experience failures and setbacks along the journey to breakthrough returns. You will make mistakes and you will learn. Failure can hurt. If all you can see on your board pack is red and amber, it's natural to ask yourself, what did I do wrong? Why isn't this working?

How we deal with failure is central to our long-term success. There are many soundbites that we can draw on. Former basketball player Michael Jordan famously said, 'I've failed over and over again in my life. And that is why I succeed.'[9] Churchill also embraced failure – he is thought to have said, 'Success consists of going from failure to failure without loss of enthusiasm.' Learning from our mistakes and embracing failure are part of having a growth mindset. As our organizations grow, we grow with them. We pick ourselves up, we learn, we adapt and we do better.

When things do go to plan: the importance of celebration, rest and reflection

We don't celebrate our successes enough. We don't give ourselves time to stand back and reflect on the amazing things we have achieved. We might allow ourselves a quick celebratory drink with colleagues, but then we're on to the next thing. Always pushing forward. Always chasing the next goal.

When you achieve something momentous, be sure to match it with a celebration worthy of the moment. Imagine you've just won a hundred-metre sprint, scored a penalty or smashed your final ball to victory in a tennis championship. Think how you'd celebrate then. Think how you'd drop to your knees, run to the crowd or do a victory lap of the stadium. Every stepping stone along your bridge is something to celebrate. Every landmark is even more so. You are likely to have given everything you've got to reach these moments. Intensity often builds as the endpoint draws nearer. You will have given blood, sweat and tears. Achievements like these are every bit as worthy of celebration as sporting victories.

One of the challenges we wrote about in Chapter 1.2 was trying to grow too quickly, particularly post-investment when you are exhausted and more likely to make mistakes. Growth isn't linear. Remember what we wrote about advancing and consolidating in Chapter 1.2. After a growth stage, take time to consolidate before moving on. Every time you break through a Greiner stage, give yourself time to stabilize. Invest in putting the foundations in place. In *Nuts!*, the authors write, 'At the peak of success, look for things you can do even better.'[10] We love this idea. We love its energy. But don't rush into the next thing. Take time to think about how to do things even better. The organization needs rest. And you do too.

Reflection and rest are equally important factors to incorporate on the road to success. They keep both your mental and physical health in check. Burnout is an unnervingly common problem in contemporary society. So many of us are running on empty, all the time. It can end people's careers – it's that calamitous. There are countless self-help books offering tips and advice on how to avoid it and it is well documented that rest works wonders to prevent it. Rest and *proper* sleep. Remember the 'funny' joke from Marc Andreessen at the beginning of Chapter 1.2 – how lack of sleep intensifies your emotions which, for start-up founders, tend to swing between the extremes of euphoria and terror. We know that will have resonated with many of you reading this book. So many of us do not sleep enough. We work late into the night and/or wake up in the early hours to get back to our laptops. This is not sustainable. You can't work like this indefinitely and stay healthy. When you reach a stepping stone, and even more so a landmark, allow yourself to pause. Reflect on what you've achieved and feel proud.

Our parting advice to a CEO

1. Follow the methods and adopt the philosophies described in Chapter 1.3.
2. Recruit a Chief of Staff.
3. Find a mentor, a trusted advisor who can help you navigate the paradoxes and challenges. This is someone who can be your sounding board, separate from the board, who you speak to every quarter.
4. Surround yourself with missionaries, not mercenaries. Your culture, at the end of the day, will dictate your long-term success.
5. Celebrate successes. Consolidate step changes, building in moments for celebration and organization-wide rest.

Notes

1. Collins, J (2001) *Good to Great: Why some companies make the leap… and others don't*, HarperBusiness, New York
2. Zook, C and Allen, J (2016) *The Founder's Mentality: How to overcome the predictable crises of growth*, Harvard Business Review Press, Boston

3 Greiner, L (1998) Evolution and revolution as organizations grow, Harvard Business Review, May–June, https://hbr.org/1998/05/evolution-and-revolution-as-organizations-grow (archived at https://perma.cc/Y3GG-53WW)

4 Moore, G (2014) *Crossing the Chasm: Marketing and selling disruptive products to mainstream customers* (Collins Business Essentials), HarperBusiness, New York

5 Rumelt, R (2022) *The Crux: How leaders become strategists*, Profile Books, London

6 Kim, E (2018) Jeff Bezos to employees, 'One day, Amazon will fail, but our job is to delay it as long as possible, CNBC, 27 Nov, www.cnbc.com/2018/11/15/bezos-tells-employees-one-day-amazon-will-fail-and-to-stay-hungry.html (archived at https://perma.cc/MS3D-4THB)

7 Jensen, M and Meckling, W (1976) Theory of the firm: Managerial behavior, agency costs and ownership structure, *Journal of Financial Economics*, 3(4), www.sciencedirect.com/science/article/pii/0304405X7690026X (archived at https://perma.cc/9SB8-9A3Q)

8 Stout, L (2012) *The Shareholder Value Myth: How putting shareholders first harms investors, corporations and the public*, Berrett-Koehler Publishers, Oakland, California

9 https://www.forbes.com/quotes/11194/ (archived at https://perma.cc/V4GP-FV5B)

10 Freiberg, K and Freiberg, J (1998) *Nuts!: Southwest Airline's crazy recipe for business and personal success*, Broadway Books, New York

GLOSSARY

Annual Recurring Revenue (ARR) A metric that shows the value of a business's recurring annual subscription revenue normalized for a calendar year, i.e. the money that's received every year for the life of a subscription or contract. This is different from repeat revenue which is not contractually set but is likely to repeat.

Ārahi Arrow A reporting graphic that combines three separate measures in one image: **BRAG** status of a metric, the trend of that metric and its volatility. This allows for a deeper understanding of performance and consistency over time.

Ārahi Arrow Dashboard A dashboard in the **quarterly strategic pack** that uses the **Ārahi Arrow** to distil between nine and sixteen key metrics onto one page.

arbitrage A practice where assets are purchased in one market and sold in another to take advantage of price discrepancies between the two markets. See also **multiple arbitrage**.

BHAG (Big Hairy Audacious Goal) A concept developed by Jim Collins in *Built to Last*. It is the ultimate, long-term stretch goal that you have a deep desire to achieve. This goal should feel radical in comparison to your current position.

blocker Something that is preventing progress. This is particularly relevant if the blocker is obstructing the **critical path** to hitting a key **milestone** and therefore leading to overall delays.

bow-tie framework A graphic tool used to help identify and prioritize actions to reduce the probability of a risk event occurring and the impact it could have. We use two versions of the framework: a **semi-skimmed** version and a **full-fat** version.

BRAG (Blue, Red, Amber, Green) A traffic light system used to demonstrate the status against target. Blue signifies overachievement, red signifies being significantly off-target, amber signifies being a little off-target and green signifies being on-target.

breakthrough returns A company achieves breakthrough returns if it triples its enterprise value in five years, generating a 25 per cent return.

BROP-A (Bridge, Risks, Objectives, Plan and Action) Our method for value creation planning with five specific components: Bridge, Risks, Objectives, Plan and Action.

boulders Part of our framework boulders, **rocks, pebbles** and **sand**. Boulders represent elements of **strategic planning** such as **key initiatives** on the **POAP**. Boulders get broken down into pebbles and sand.

capabilities Systems, processes and people within an organizational unit which, in combination with the competencies of those people, deliver items along the value chain.

CEO View from the Bridge A one-page summary in a reporting pack, e.g. the **quarterly strategic board pack**, summarizing highlights and lowlights and the key issues and recommendations from the pack, and ideally following the **Rule of Three**.

COD (Capture, Organize, Do) A three-step framework for action management that involves capturing, organizing and doing actions.

conjoint analysis A survey-based statistical technique used to understand the value people place on a range of variables, for example **value factors**. The technique uses multiple variable correlation analysis.

CQT triangle A visual representation of three forces in project management: cost (the money or resources available), quality (how well the project meets given requirements – scope is often incorporated in quality) and time (the time available to deliver the project). If one corner of the triangle is fixed, e.g. time, the other two corners will vary, e.g. quality is dependent on available money and/or resources.

CRASI (Capture, Responsible, Approver, Supporting, Informed) An accountability framework for action management that defines who records the action, who owns it and is responsible for getting it done, who approves it, who supports the responsible person and who needs to be kept informed of progress and/or the outcome.

critical path The longest sequence of tasks that must be done for a project to be completed.

dependency matrix A form of crosstab table that enables you to focus on the nature and number of dependencies and which is used to help calculate the **critical path**. Each row is the driver of a dependency and each column shows the tasks that are dependent on those rows.

Earnings Before Interest, Tax, Depreciation and Amortization (EBITDA) This metric is a measure of profitability focused on an organization's core performance. It is used to assess an organization's growth potential and ability to generate cash.

edge Otherwise known as 'links', edges form the connections between **nodes** in graph theory such as a network map. Like nodes, edges can contain data.

enterprise value bridge One of the bridges of **BROP-A** that shows how much you intend to grow your enterprise value over your timeframe and how.

Flesch-Kincaid Readability Test A readability formula that uses the number of words in a sentence, the number of syllables per word and the percentage of sentences written in the passive voice to score text. The score is translated into a US grade level.

Form Guide A monthly summary of a set of **BRAG**-ed measures shown over a period of 13 months. Used in documents such as the **monthly trading pack**, the Form Guide allows you to assess **KPIs** over time. This is in contrast to the **Leaderboard** which allows you to assess KPIs by **KOD** for a fixed point in time.

Four Cornerstones of Corporate Health A framework for tracking holistic value creation: customer health, people health, financial and operational health, and impact health.

full-fat, semi-skimmed and skimmed An analogy to UK milk types used to signpost different levels of detail. Full-fat represents the full method while skimmed represents a dramatically simplified version.

5S Action Framework: Stop, Shrink, Stay, Stretch, Start A method used in strategy design to determine what you should stop doing, do less of, do the same, do more of, or begin doing.

4D Framework Our value creation method: Diagnose today, Design tomorrow, Draw the plan and Deliver the plan.

Goldilocks problem The principle of not doing too much and not doing too little. This is the art of getting things 'just right'.

governed actions Comparatively complicated actions that involve one or more dependencies, governed workflows and numerous people to get them done. See also **in-out actions**.

in-out actions Simple, quick actions done by individuals without needing to involve anyone else. So-called because it takes as long to do them as it does to receive them. Only requires the title of a simple action. The status is either 'incomplete' or 'complete'.

Individual Activity Analysis (IAA) The process of collecting data to understand the work activities consuming the time and cost of the workforce (see *Data-Driven Organization Design*).

integrated plan The P of **BROP-A**. The integrated plan breaks down **key initiatives** identified in the **POAP** into projects and sub-projects and integrates risk and objectives. This is the **rocks** planning level.

Internal Rate of Return (IRR) A metric used to assess investment opportunities by using cash flow over time. It considers the rate of return (expressed as a percentage) when the **Net Present Value** of all cash flows is equal to zero. The calculation does not factor in external considerations such as inflation.

kanban A scheduling system used to improve the flow and structure of work. Work items are represented as cards on a board so that the progress of work items can be easily tracked. Work is typically structured into 'now', 'next', 'later' buckets and placed according to the urgency of the task.

key initiative An initiative that is central to the realization of an organization's strategy. At an organization-wide level, key initiatives are placed on the **POAP** and tracked by the board on a quarterly basis. Key initiatives can be understood as **boulders**.

key organizational dimensions (KODs) The key lenses through which you can view your organization and measure performance. There are five common KODs: function, geography, business unit or product, segment and channel.

key performance indicators (KPIs) A set of measurements used to assess performance. They are placed on the **POAP** and tracked by the board on a monthly and quarterly basis.

lagging indicator A measure or outcome that has already occurred, for example a previous year's profit or revenue.

landmarks Points in time that break down your **BHAG** into manageable chunks, allowing value creation goals to be understood and tracked over shorter time periods. They mark the beginning and end points of the **POAP**.

Leaderboard A summary of a set of **BRAG**-ed measures produced for reporting packs, e.g. the **monthly trading pack**, for a fixed point in time. The Leaderboard allows you to assess **KPIs** by **KOD** for the month relevant to the meeting. This is in contrast to the **Form Guide** which allows you to assess KPIs over time.

leading indicator A measure that can be used to predict future outcomes, e.g. sales conversion rates or lead sources that have the greatest impact on sales and therefore future revenue.

market segment A set of customers that places the same importance weighting on the same value factors.

milestone objective A time-bound objective that signifies a need to complete a project or initiative by a given date or hit a key measure by a specific date.

Money Multiple (MM) The final value of return divided by the investment amount. For example, if you invested 100 and got 350 back post-investment, the MM would be 3.5×. The MM is used interchangeably with the **MOIC**. MM is typically used when referring to investments in the PE world whereas MOIC is a more generalized financial term.

monthly trading meeting and board pack A monthly trading review meeting lasting 60–90 minutes and attended by the full board. These meetings have a bespoke monthly trading board pack that focuses on core, routine **KPIs** and metrics.

moving measure objective An objective where the target changes over time, for example sales by quarter.

multiple A ratio used to value a company. Enterprise value to **EBITDA** is commonly used. In the SaaS world, the ratio is more often enterprise value to **ARR**.

multiple arbitrage A buy-and-build strategy used by private equity firms to increase the value of an investment without making operational improvements to it. See also **arbitrage**.

Multiple on Invested Capital (MOIC) A metric that measures the value of an investment relative to the initial outlay. See also **Money Multiple**.

Net Present Value (NPV) A way of calculating the time value of money and therefore the present-day value of an investment. It looks at all future cash outflows and inflows. The calculation uses the Weighted Average Cost of Capital (WACC) as the discount rate.

network effects The idea that the value of a product or service increases as the number of users increases.

node In graph theory, nodes describe the fundamental unit. Nodes are connected through **edges** (or links). Nodes, like edges, can contain data.

operational planning The mid level of planning that focuses on the quarter and year ahead and is understood through the **integrated plan**. This is the **rocks** level of planning, which incorporates risk and objectives management.

PACCTACC Ārahi's process for strategy design, standing for Purpose, Ambition, Challenge, Critical value factors, Target segments, Arranged capabilities, Competition and Cash generation.

PAID (Problem-solving, Actioning, Information sharing and Deciding) A method for categorizing meetings according to their type and the objectives they aim to fulfil.

pebbles Part of our framework **boulders, rocks,** pebbles and **sand.** Pebbles represent **governed actions. Tactical planning** is done at the level of pebbles and sand.

percolation and distillation thinking process A thinking process where you intentionally allow thoughts to percolate before distilling them to nail down the key matters that need attention or the key questions that need to be asked.

Plan on a Page (POAP) A visual representation of the top-level, strategic plan on one page. The POAP contains the **stepping stones** between two **landmarks.** It includes the **KPIs** and the **key initiatives** broken into **swim lanes.**

project charter Single-page documents used to track projects linked to **key initiatives.**

QFOR-A (Questions, Facts, Opinions, Recommendations and Actions) A framework for understanding how to use four different types of statements to reach better answers and the right action.

Quality of Earnings (QoE) An assessment of how a business generates revenue, e.g. recurring versus non-recurring or high versus low margin.

quarterly strategic meeting and board pack A quarterly strategic board meeting lasting half a day to a day and attended by the full board and members of the management team, as required. These meetings have a bespoke quarterly strategic board pack, which has a different focus from the **monthly trading pack** and contains more commentary.

revenue bridge One of the bridges of **BROP-A** that shows where you expect revenue, or sales, to come from over your timeframe.

rocks Part of our framework **boulders,** rocks, **pebbles** and **sand.** Rocks represent projects and sub-projects that, together, ensure key initiatives get done. **Operational planning** is done at the level of the rocks.

Rule of Three A well-known communication tool for writing and speaking that taps into the idea that humans absorb information best when presented in groups of three.

sand Part of our framework **boulders, rocks, pebbles** and sand. Sand represents **in-out actions. Tactical planning** is done at the level of pebbles and sand.

series A, B, C funding Separate events when businesses raise funds from investors in exchange for equity or ownership.

Serviceable Available Market (SAM) The proportion of the **Total Addressable Market** that a company can reach with its products or services.

static measure objectives An objective where the aim is to keep a target the same over time, for example to keep employee churn less than 15 per cent.

stepping stone A way of breaking down time between two **landmarks**.

strategic planning The top level of planning with a multi-year timeframe from which **operational** and **tactical planning** follow. The **POAP** provides a distillation of your strategic plan. This is the **boulders** level of planning.

strategy The way you design a unique set of capabilities to deliver differentiating value factors, overcome your key challenge and economically fulfil your purpose and ambition.

Strategy on a Page (SOAP) A visual representation of the elements of **PACCTACC** on one page.

sub-objectives A way to break down objectives into further detail to show the steps necessary to achieve the overall objective.

Swim lanes A key element of the **POAP**, these are the critical lenses through which you view your business. They represent the key value-driving strategic themes that need to be tracked and managed over time to reach your **landmarks**.

swing rating scale A weighting method used to prioritize such things as **value factors**, where the most important value factor is given a score of 100 and other value factors are rated relative to this top score.

tactical planning Detailed planning that focuses on the days and weeks ahead and is performed at the actions (or **pebbles** and **sand**) level.

TAF (Target, Actual, Forecast) data Three data points that are central to executing strategy. Targets show what we aim to achieve by a point in time; Actuals show what we have achieved; Forecasts are our opinions about what we believe we will achieve.

TAF-arize The process of applying **TAF data** to different elements of value creation, for example risks or objectives.

Terms of reference A document that defines the purpose and structure of a forum.

3T Framework A risk management framework comprising three elements: Treat, Tolerate and Terminate. It is used to determine how to respond to different risks. The risks that you decide to treat can be put into a **bow-tie framework**.

Total Addressable Market (TAM) A way of assessing market opportunity that assumes 100 per cent market share.

Value-Cap Map A graph used to visualize the connections between critical **value factors**, core **capabilities**, 'how to' choices, objectives and policies.

value chain The definition of the top-level, end-to-end steps through which the company creates value. The value chain starts with the inputs and goes through the key processes that transform the inputs into more valuable outputs.

value creation The process of delivering value for three specific groups: customers, people (employees, contractors and suppliers) and shareholders (or investors), and for having a positive impact on the planet and society.

value factors The specific things that people value that determine their buying decisions.

value landscape A method used to determine the **value factors** that your industry competes on so that you can find your own market space. It includes your own and your competitors' importance weightings and scores for a set of value factors.

Weighted Average Value Score (WAVS) The distillation of your value proposition into a single number. Your score for each value factor is weighted by the level of importance that buyers assign to it. The resulting number allows a direct comparison to your competitors.

win-loss analysis A process used to understand why you won or lost new business by seeking insight from customers.

BIBLIOGRAPHY

More than 40 books have informed the thinking of this one. We have listed them below and done our best to categorize them according to type. We encourage you to read as many of these as you can. We have also listed the articles, reports and a podcast that we have found useful.

Strategy

Barthêlemy, J (2022) *Myths of Strategy: Dispel the misconceptions and deliver a winning strategy*, Kogan Page, London

Collins, J (2001) *Good to Great: Why some companies make the leap… and others don't*, HarperBusiness, New York

Collins, J (2002) *Built to Last: Successful habits of visionary companies* (3e), HarperBusiness, New York

Drucker, P (2007) *The Practice of Management* (Classic Drucker Collection), Routledge, London

Kim, W C and Mauborgne, R A (2015) *Blue Ocean Strategy: How to create uncontested marketspace and make the competition irrelevant* (Expanded edition), Harvard Business Review Press, Boston

Lafley, A G and Martin, R L (2013) *Playing to Win: How strategy really works*, Harvard Business Review Press, Boston

Lencioni, P (2002) *The Five Dysfunctions of a Team: A leadership fable*, Jossey-Bass, San Francisco

Moore, G (2014) *Crossing the Chasm: Marketing and selling disruptive products to mainstream customers* (Collins Business Essentials), HarperBusiness, New York

Peters, T and Waterman, R (2015) *In Search of Excellence: Lessons from America's best-run companies* (Profile Business Classics), Profile Books, London

Porter, M (2004) *Competitive Advantage: Creating and sustaining superior performance*, Free Press, New York

Porter, M (2004) *Competitive Strategy: Techniques for analyzing industries and competitors*, Free Press, New York

Porter, M (2008) *On Competition: Updated and expanded edition*, Harvard Business Review Press, Boston

Reichheld, F (2001) *The Loyalty Effect: The hidden force behind growth, profits, and lasting value*, Harvard Business Review Press, Boston

Rumelt, R (2011) *Good Strategy/Bad Strategy: The difference and why it matters*, Crown Currency, New York

Rumelt, R (2022) *The Crux: How leaders become strategists*, Profile Books, London

Sinek, S (2011) *Start with Why: How great leaders inspire everyone to take action*, Penguin Books, New York

Watkins, M (2013) *The First 90 Days: Proven strategies for getting up to speed faster and smarter*, Harvard Business Review Press, Boston

Zook, C and Allen, J (2016) *The Founder's Mentality: How to overcome the predictable crises of growth*, Harvard Business Review Press, Boston

Boards and CEO best practices

Dewar, C, Keller, S and Malhotra, V (2022) *CEO Excellence: The six mindsets that distinguish the best leaders from the rest*, Nicholas Brealey Publishing, London

Dunne, P (2021) *Boards: A practical perspective* (2e), Governance Publishing & Information Services Ltd, London

Stout, L (2012) *The Shareholder Value Myth: How putting shareholders first harms investors, corporations and the public*, Berrett-Koehler Publishers, Oakland

Action management

Allen, D (2015) *Getting Things Done: The art of stress-free productivity*, Piatkus, London

Covey, S (2020) *The Seven Habits of Highly Effective People* (Reissue edition), Simon & Schuster, London

Gawande, A (2011) *The Checklist Manifesto: How to get things right*, Profile Books, London

Keller, G with Papasan, J (2019) *The One Thing: The surprisingly simple truth behind extraordinary results* (Revised edition), Bard Press, Austin, Texas

Communication

Gallo, C (2022) *The Bezos Blueprint: Communication secrets that power Amazon's success*, Macmillan, London

Minto, B (2021) *The Pyramid Principle: Logic in writing and thinking* (3e), Pearson Education, Harlow

Lived experience

Bryar, C and Carr, B (2021) *Working Backwards: Insights, stories and secrets from inside Amazon*, Macmillan, London

Cohen, R (2013) *The Fish That Ate the Whale: The life and times of America's banana king*, Picador, New York

Freiberg, K and Freiberg, J (1998) *Nuts!: Southwest Airline's crazy recipe for business and personal success*, Broadway Books, New York

Grove, A (2022) *Only the Paranoid Survive: How to exploit the crisis points that challenge every company and career*, Profile Books, London

Horowitz, B (2014) *The Hard Thing About Hard Things: Building a business when there are no easy answers*, HarperBusiness, New York

Kerr, J (2013) *Legacy: What the All Blacks can teach us about the business of life*, Constable, London

Thiel, P with Masters, B (2015) *Zero to One: Notes on startups, or how to build the future*, Virgin Books, London

Professional practice

Doerr, J (2018) *Measure what Matters: OKRs – the simple idea that drives 10x growth*, Portfolio, New York

Morrison, R (2021) *Data-Driven Organization Design: Delivering perpetual performance gains through the organizational system* (2e), Kogan Page, London

Morrison, R (2022) *Organizational Planning and Analysis: Building the capability to secure business performance*, Kogan Page, London

Miscellaneous

Erikson, T (2019) *Surrounded by Idiots: The four types of human behaviour (or, how to understand those who cannot be understood)*, Vermilion, London

Hughes, D (2018) *The Barcelona Way: How to create a high-performance culture*, Macmillan, London

Maister, D, Green, C and Galford, R (2002) *The Trusted Advisor*, Simon & Schuster, London

McAllister, C (2015) *The Tin Snail*, Corgi Childrens, London

Newport, C (2016) *Deep Work: Rules for focused success in a distracted world*, Piatkus, London

Tetlock, P E and Gardner, D (2016) *Superforecasting: The art and science of prediction*, Random House Books, New York

Woodward, B (2006) *State of Denial: Bush at war, part III*, Simon & Schuster, New York

Influential articles and reports

Bain & Company (2023), *Global Private Equity Report*, https://www.bain.com/insights/topics/global-private-equity-report/ (archived at https://perma.cc/Z69E-SJT4)

Heel, J and Kehoe, C (2005) Why some private equity firms do better than others, McKinsey Quarterly, 1 February, www.mckinsey.com/capabilities/strategy-and-corporate-finance/our-insights/why-some-private-equity-firms-do-better-than-others (archived at https://perma.cc/8RMV-8AKR)

Kaplan, R S and Mikes, A (2012) Managing risks: A new framework, *Harvard Business Review*, June, https://hbr.org/2012/06/managing-risks-a-new-framework?autocomplete=true (archived at https://perma.cc/4LKT-NDM2)

Porter, M E (1996) What is strategy? For starters, it's not the same as operational effectiveness, *Harvard Business Review*, November–December, https://hbr.org/1996/11/what-is-strategy (archived at https://perma.cc/5PYL-2Q5U)

Watkins, M D (2007) Demystifying strategy: The what, who, how and why, *Harvard Business Review*, 10 September, https://hbr.org/2007/09/demystifying-strategy-the-what (archived at https://perma.cc/G3R5-KTAL)

Podcast

David Senra, *Founders*, www.founderspodcast.com (archived at https://perma.cc/QP4Q-EAD7)

INDEX

NB: page numbers in *italic* indicate figures or tables

Also from Kogan Page

ISBN: 9781398603264

ISBN: 9781398605817

ISBN: 9781398606050

ISBN: 9781398612242

www.koganpage.com

KoganPage